Beyond
Capitalism vs. Socialism
in Kenya and Tanzania

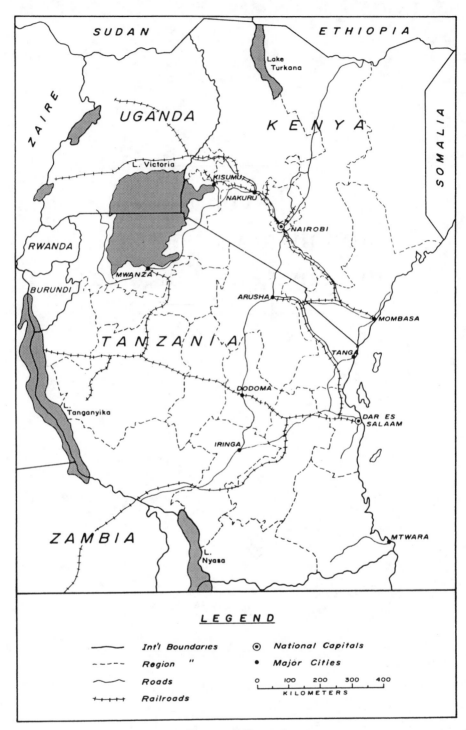

Kenya and Tanzania

Beyond Capitalism vs. Socialism in Kenya and Tanzania

edited by

Joel D. Barkan

LYNNE
RIENNER
PUBLISHERS

BOULDER
LONDON

Published in the United States of America in 1994 by
Lynne Rienner Publishers, Inc.
1800 30th Street, Boulder, Colorado 80301

and in the United Kingdom by
Lynne Rienner Publishers, Inc.
3 Henrietta Street, Covent Garden, London WC2E 8LU

Library of Congress Cataloging-in-Publication Data
Beyond capitalism vs. socialism in Kenya and Tanzania / edited by
   Joel D. Barkan.
      p. cm.
     Includes bibliographical references and index.
     ISBN 1-55587-228-X. (alk. paper)
     ISBN 1-55587-530-0 (pbk.) (alk. paper)
     1. Kenya—Economic policy. 2. Tanzania—Economic policy.
   3. Kenya—Politics and government—1978– 4. Tanzania—Politics and
   government—1964– I. Barkan, Joel D.
   HC865.B5 1994
   338.96762—dc20   94-18825
                                                      CIP

British Cataloguing in Publication Data
A Cataloguing in Publication record for this book
is available from the British Library.

Printed and bound in the United States of America

The paper used in this publication meets the requirements
of the American National Standard for Permanence of
Paper for Printed Library Materials Z39.48-1984.

Contents

Map of Kenya and Tanzania   ii
List of Tables and Figures   vii
About the Editor and Contributors   ix
Preface   xiii

1 Divergence and Convergence in Kenya and Tanzania:
   Pressures for Reform
      Joel D. Barkan   1
         A Continent in Reform? 1
         Background to Reform in Kenya and Tanzania, 4
         Four Eras of Political Economy, 8
         Beyond Capitalism Versus Socialism, 40

2 The Return of Multiparty Politics
      Michael Chege   47
         Multiparty Politics in Africa and Its Critics, 49
         A New Beginning in Multiparty Politics, 51
         Social Forces Behind Opposition Politics, 56
         State Response to Opposition, 67
         Conclusion, 71

3 Party, State, and Civil Society: Control Versus Openness
      Goran Hyden   75
         Economic Growth and Political Democracy, 75
         Conditions of Governance in Africa, 78
         Governance in Kenya and Tanzania, 79
         External Influences, 95
         Conclusions, 98

4 Economic Adjustment Policies
      Benno J. Ndulu and Francis W. Mwega   101
         Comparative Structural Features, 102
         The Political Economy of Economic Reform, 106
         Conclusions, 125

5 The Politics of Agricultural Policy
   Michael F. Lofchie   129
      The Policy Framework, 132
      Explaining Policy Variance, 149
      Policy Changes in the 1980s, 157
      Conclusions, 170

6 Coping with Urbanization and Urban Policy
   Richard Stren, Mohamed Halfani, and Joyce Malombe   175
      Kenya, 178
      Tanzania, 187
      Conclusions, 199

7 Education for Self-Reliance and Harambee
   Brian Cooksey, David Court, and Ben Makau   201
      Kenya: From *Harambee* to *Nyayo* and Beyond, 205
      Tanzania: Education for Self-Reliance, 215
      Lessons and Directions, 228
      Conclusions, 231

8 International Economic Relations, Regional Cooperation,
   and Foreign Policy
   David F. Gordon   235
      The Marginalization of Africa, 237
      Regional Relations and Diplomacy, 242
      The International Relations of Economic Restructuring, 253
      Conclusion: Responding to Global Realities, 258

Bibliography   263
Index   281
About the Book and the Editor   293

Tables and Figures

TABLES

1.1	Average Annual Rates of Real Economic Growth	22
4.1	Indicators of Economic Structure and Performance	103
4.2	Distortions of the Macroeconomic Incentive Structure	105
4.3	Ratios of Producer Prices to International Prices	106
4.4	Basic Indicators of Macroeconomic Resource Gaps in Kenya	108
4.5	Basic Indicators of Macroeconomic Resource Gaps in Tanzania	119
5.1	Tanzanian Export Crop Production	130
5.2	Prices Paid to Producers for Coffee	139
5.3	Prices Paid to Producers for Tea	140
5.4	Prices Paid to Producers for Maize	144
5.5	Prices Paid to Producers for Wheat	145
5.6	Prices Paid to Producers for Rice	145
5.7	Coffee-Maize Price Ratios	146
5.8	Grain Imports by Kenya and Tanzania	147
6.1	Population Growth of Selected Urban Centers in Kenya, 1969–1989	176
6.2	Population Growth of Selected Urban Centers in Tanzania, 1957–1988	176
7.1	Comparative Education Statistics	204
7.2	School Enrollments in Kenya	209
7.3	Parental Characteristics of Form 4 Students	225

FIGURES

5.1	Coffee Production in Kenya and Tanzania (1967–1989)	131
5.2	Tea Production in Kenya and Tanzania (1967–1989)	131
5.3	Currency Overvaluation in Kenya and Tanzania (1967–1991)	135
5.4	Maize Production in Kenya and Tanzania (1966–1988)	142
5.5	Wheat Production in Kenya and Tanzania (1966–1988)	143
5.6	Rice Production in Kenya and Tanzania (1966–1988)	143

About the Editor
and Contributors

Joel D. Barkan is professor of political science at the University of Iowa. In 1992 and 1993 he served as the first regional governance adviser for East and Southern Africa for the United States Agency for International Development. Prior to that he taught or was a visiting research fellow at the University of Dar es Salaam and the University of Nairobi. He is the author of *University Students, Politics and Development in Ghana, Tanzania, and Uganda* (1975); the coauthor of *The Legislative Connection: The Politics of Representation in Kenya, Korea and Turkey* (1984); and the editor of *Politics and Public Policy in Kenya and Tanzania* (1984). A frequent contributor to journals and anthologies on African politics, his most recent articles have appeared in *World Politics,* the *Journal of Democracy,* and the *Journal of Modern African Studies.*

Michael Chege is currently visiting research fellow at the Center for International Affairs, Harvard University. From 1988 to 1994, Dr. Chege was a program officer at the Ford Foundation where he was responsible for the foundation's programs on governance and international affairs in East and Southern Africa. Between 1977 and 1988 Dr. Chege served as senior lecturer of government, and director of the Institute of International Studies at the University of Nairobi. His primary field of research is the political economy of African development. His articles have appeared in *Foreign Affairs,* the *Journal of Modern African Studies,* the *Review of African Political Economy,* and numerous anthologies on African politics.

Brian Cooksey has taught in secondary schools in Côte d'Ivoire and Cameroon, and spent a number of years teaching sociology in the Universities of Jos, Nigeria, and Dar es Salaam, Tanzania. For the last ten years he has worked as a freelance consultant, researcher, and journalist, based in Dar es Salaam. He is a founding member of the Tanzania Development Research Group (TADREG). Brian Cooksey is coauthor of *A Sociology of Education for Africa* (1981) and has published a number of articles on education in Cameroon and Tanzania.

David Court has spent virtually all his professional life in East Africa and was for several years a senior research fellow at the Institute for Development Studies at the University of Nairobi. The coeditor of *Education, Society and Development: New Perspectives from Kenya* (1975) and the coauthor with James S. Coleman of *University Development in the Third World* (1993), he has written widely on educational issues, including articles in *Minerva, The Comparative Education Review, Higher Education,* and the *Journal of Modern African Studies.* He is currently the regional representative of the Rockefeller Foundation and based in Nairobi, Kenya.

David F. Gordon is currently senior legislative specialist for Africa to the Foreign Affairs Committee of the United States House of Representatives. Prior to joining the committee, Dr. Gordon was the regional policy adviser for economic reform for East and Southern Africa to the United States Agency for International Development and associate professor of international relations at Michigan State University. He is the author of *Decolonialization and the State in Kenya* (1986) and the coeditor of *Cooperation for International Development: The U.S. and the Third World in the 1990s* (1989) as well as articles on the politics of economic reform in Africa.

Mohamed Halfani is senior lecturer and associate director of the Institute for Development Studies at the University of Dar es Salaam. A political scientist, his work has focused on problems of urban politics and the political economy of development. With Richard Sandbrook, he recently coedited *Empowering People: Building Community, Civic Associations, and Legality in Africa* (1993).

Goran Hyden is professor of political science at the University of Florida, and formerly regional representative of the Ford Foundation for East and Southern Africa. He is the author of several acclaimed books including *Beyond Ujama in Tanzania: Underdevelopment and an Uncaptured Peasantry* (1979) and *No Shortcuts to Progress: African Development Management in Perspective* (1983), and the coeditor of *Governance and Politics in Africa* (1991). His most recent book is *The Political Factor in Development: Tanzania in Comparative Perspective* (forthcoming, 1995). He serves as president of the African Studies Association in 1994–1995.

Michael F. Lofchie is professor of political science at the University of California, Los Angeles, where he was director of the James S. Coleman African Studies Center from 1978 to 1989. He is the author of *Zanzibar: Background to Revolution* (1965), the editor of *The State of Nations: Constraints on Development in Independent Africa* (1971), and the coeditor of *Africa's Agrarian Crisis: The Roots of Famine* (1986). A specialist on agricultural policy and politics in East Africa, he is the author of *The Policy Factor: Agricultural Performance in Kenya and Tanzania* (1989).

Ben Makau has devoted his career to education. He taught at and was then headmaster of one of Kenya's major secondary schools, and was for some time director of the National Examinations Council of Kenya. More recently he has concentrated upon research and writing, most notably on the subject of examinations, computer technology in schools, the financing and administration of education, and the role of the teaching profession. He has been a consultant for a variety of organizations including the Aga Khan Foundation, the Commonwealth Secretariat, and the World Bank.

Joyce Malombe is a sociologist and a fellow of the Housing Research and Development Unit of the University of Nairobi. She has carried out extensive research in Kenya in the fields of housing and urban social problems. Her current research focuses on the problems of the disabled in urban environments.

Francis W. Mwega is senior lecturer at the Department of Economics at the University of Nairobi. A specialist on macroeconomic adjustment and public finance, Dr. Mwega has contributed to anthologies and journals in this area.

Benno J. Ndulu is director of the African Economic Research Consortium (AERC) in Nairobi, Kenya, and professor of economics at the University of Dar es Salaam where he joined the faculty in 1974. Professor Ndulu is a specialist on problems of macro-economic adjustment, trade, and industry. He is a frequent contributor to books and journals on these subjects, including *Strategies for Economic Development in Africa* (Berg and Whitaker eds., 1986), and *The Rocky Road to Reform: Adjustment, Income Distribution, and Growth in the Developing World* (Lance ed., 1993).

Richard Stren is professor of political science and director of the Centre for Urban and Community Studies at the University of Toronto. He has been carrying out research on African urbanization since the 1960s, having done his first major study in Mombasa, Kenya. He has published extensively on African urban problems and is currently directing the Global Urban Research Initiative, a twenty-five-country research project involving Africa, Asia, and Latin America. He is the coeditor of *African Cities in Crisis: Managing Rapid Urban Growth* (1989) and *Sustainable Cities: Urbanization and the Environment in International Perspective* (1991), as well as the author of *An Urban Problematique* (1992).

Preface

From the early 1960s until the late 1980s, Africa, and indeed the entire developing world, was pulled between variations of two contrasting models of development: *patron-client capitalism* and *one-party socialism.* The experiences of Kenya and Tanzania figured prominently in the debate over which model was most appropriate for Africa. Kenya, an example of the former, seemed to have successfully realized capitalist development on a continent marked by economic stagnation. Tanzania, an example of the latter, appeared to have achieved a measure of equity unmatched by other countries pursuing similar goals. From academics to the representatives of international aid agencies, observers paid more attention to these countries than to any other on the continent save South Africa and, perhaps, Nigeria.

Today the debate over capitalism versus socialism is all but dead, swept aside by a combination of economic decline and political decay in Africa and the end of the Cold War abroad. Kenya and Tanzania no longer manifest contrasting visions of the future but rather exemplify the hard choices developing countries face as they seek to revive their systems through a tortuous process of economic and political reform. Faced by a common set of problems—a declining economy, rapid population growth, a bloated and at times repressive state, mounting corruption, and the loss of political authority on the part of their leaders—Kenya and Tanzania now pursue a common set of solutions that transcend their previous differences in developmental perspective. Once noted for their divergence, the two countries are now examples of convergence as each has been forced to adopt similar reforms to overcome similar problems.

This volume traces the process of convergence by examining the politics of reform in the two countries from the early 1980s to early 1994. In the course of a turbulent decade lasting from the early 1980s through the early 1990s, the leaders of both Kenya and Tanzania were slowly forced to acknowledge that their respective approaches to economic and political development were not yielding the intended results and that it was time to chart a new course. As is normal in such situations, recognition of the need for reform was not acknowledged simultaneously by all leaders in the two countries but was itself the subject of intense debate. Some were persuaded relatively early in the process; others resisted until the late 1980s or early 1990s; a number remain unconvinced today. These calls for reform from the political leaderships of the two countries were paralleled by similar expressions among key elements in society. Members of the professions, and in Kenya of the clergy, were initially the most vocal in demanding fundamental changes in economic policy and the political system. Elements of the business sector followed, partly because they were hesitant to put themselves at risk and partly because many had adapted to the prevailing order. In both countries, peasant farmers became increasingly dissatisfied with the status quo but were powerless to do anything about it other than to adopt coping strategies. These included a retreat to the informal sector or subsistence, smuggling, self-help, and passive resistance.

Dissatisfaction and demands for reform at home were complemented by pressures for change from the international community, specifically the principal multilateral and bilateral sources of financial assistance. Beginning in the late 1970s and early 1980s, the International Monetary Fund and the World Bank began to condition aid on structural adjustment. This approach was followed at the end of a decade by conditions of political adjustment—specifically, the end to human rights abuses, political liberalization, and progress toward the establishment of multiparty democracy. These pressures for reform, which were accelerated after 1990 by the end of the Cold War and political reform in Southern Africa, have proved irresistible.

The issue today is therefore not whether political and economic reform will occur in Africa but at what pace, sequence, and configuration. The experience of the early 1990s suggests that the process will be neither smooth nor identical in all countries. In his prescient article, "Beyond Capitalism and Socialism in Africa" (from which the title of this volume is directly borrowed), Richard Sklar (1988) argues that although the debate between capitalism and socialism in Africa is over, the trade-offs between the acknowledged efficiency of capitalism and the extent to which it can provide for the basic human needs of Africans remain. Such is the challenge to policymakers charged with charting not only the overall process of reform but also the specific sequence of initiatives to achieve it. African policymakers are likewise challenged by the question of how to pursue reform on both its economic and political dimensions simultaneously, given that progress in one dimension might, at least in the short term, slow or preclude progress on the other.

In the chapters that follow, thirteen authors address these and other trade-off issues that constitute the nitty-gritty of current policy debates in the post–capitalism-versus-socialism era. The convergent experience of the two countries is most significant when studied in this context. By examining the necessity and process of reform at the macrosystemic level and in a series of specific policy areas, we hope to clarify the choices and complexities that characterize the process of renewal now occurring across the African continent.

J.D.B.

Beyond
Capitalism vs. Socialism
in Kenya and Tanzania

1

Divergence and Convergence in Kenya and Tanzania: Pressures for Reform

Joel D. Barkan

A CONTINENT IN REFORM?

The pressures for fundamental reform in the way Africans are governed are greater today than at any time since the decade preceding the end of colonialism forty years ago. Political decay and declining standards of living, coinciding with the dismantling of apartheid and the end of the Cold War, have given rise to a new politics and new economic policies. From Benin to Zambia, from Kenya to Zaire, demands for democratic governance and economic liberalization from within supported by a watchful international community are forcing a sea change in the existing order. One era of African political economy is ending, but whether this will be succeeded by what Larry Diamond and others have termed "the second liberation of Africa" (Diamond 1992) is unclear.

The twin pillars of the second liberation are the policies of economic reform—or *structural adjustment*, as they are more commonly known—and the drive to establish multiparty democracy. During the late 1980s and early 1990s a consensus emerged—among Africa's own reformers and its principal foreign providers of economic assistance—that economic reform could not succeed without concomitant reform of the political system and vice versa. Although programs of economic adjustment had been pursued in Africa since the early 1980s,[1] it was apparent by the end of the decade that such programs were falling short of their objectives without complementary changes in the political realm. Economic stabilization and adjustment measures—the reduction of budget deficits, restraint of growth of the money supply, regulation of markets, liberalization of trade, and especially privatization of state-owned enterprises—could be pursued only so far before they invariably ran up against the vested interests of those who run the state. Put differently, macroeconomic policies designed to "get the prices right" through the establishment of a market-based economy were not sufficient to bring about economic renewal because prices are unlikely to be set "right" without changes in the way African countries are governed. As long as those associated with authoritarian regimes—be they those who rule or the members of a bloated civil service or state-owned corporations—profit from corrupt practices and inefficiency, resistance to economic reform will remain endemic to the system. Only by establishing mechanisms of accountability and subjecting governmental operations to public scrutiny might economic reform be pushed through to actual implementation.

Once this requirement was recognized, *political adjustment* became the corollary of economic adjustment. And, like economic adjustment, political adjustment became a condition for continued donor assistance. Whereas in the early 1980s major international donors (including the International Monetary Fund [IMF], the World Bank, and providers of bilateral assistance) began to condition aid on the adoption of programs for economic adjustment, by the end of the decade and the early 1990s political adjustment became an added prerequisite. In its least threatening form, political adjustment entails an improvement in governmental accountability and performance, particularly in the responsiveness of state administrative agencies and parastatal bodies to the public they purport to serve (World Bank 1989a: 55–61). In its most articulated form, political adjustment requires respect for human rights, guarantees of basic political freedoms (including freedom of assembly and a free press), and ultimately a transition to multiparty democracy so that the citizens of African societies can scrutinize the performance of their rulers and change them if necessary. Generally speaking, the international financial institutions (IFIs) such as the IMF and World Bank have limited their concerns to improvement in the quality of governmental performance, or "governance," whereas the principal bilateral donors—the United States, Germany, Japan, the Scandinavian countries, and Britain—have demanded more extensive reforms to establish or reestablish democratic rule.[2]

Kenya and Tanzania have not been immune to these pressures, which have been generated by a confluence of events occurring both inside and outside Africa. Most significant has been the recognition by Africans themselves—especially members of the professions, the clergy, and in some instances the business community—that reform is necessary to prevent the collapse of the economic and political systems within which they live. By the early 1980s there was an increasing awareness that things did not work—that the standard of living in most African states was declining and that the tendency towards political repression leading to political instability, and in some cases anarchy (e.g., Zaire and later Somalia) had increased. Although their voices were initially weak, it is important to remember that the first cries for reform came from *within* the continent (Chege 1992).

A second impetus for reform from within Africa has been the progress, albeit halting, toward dismantling apartheid in South Africa. Prior to the release of Nelson Mandela from prison in February 1990 and the beginning of negotiations to achieve majority rule, leaders of authoritarian regimes north of the Limpopo River could point a finger south and rightly claim that the need for political reform was greater there than at home. Since 1990, especially since Mandela's victory in nonracial elections in April 1994, they have been unable to do so.

A third pressure for reform, and the one often (and wrongly) cited as the single most important source of change, is the end of the Cold War and its effect on the African continent. Prior to 1989 and the subsequent breakup of the former Soviet Union, individual African states could resist demands for economic and political reform by playing one superpower off against the other or by becoming a client of one superpower provided the patron accepted the status quo in the client state. With the end of the Cold War, these options no longer exist. It is important to remember, however, that resistance to economic reform in Africa, including Tanzania, began to weaken in the early 1980s, well before the end of the Cold War (though perhaps in recognition of the failure of socialism in the former Soviet Union and the adoption of economic reforms in China in the late 1970s).

A fourth and related factor is the declining importance of Africa to the West combined with Africa's increasing dependence on Western assistance. With the end of the Cold War, the West and especially the United States has no vital commercial or strategic interests in Africa. Rather Africa is viewed as a responsibility, albeit one that will be provided for on Western terms. This is particularly true during a period of economic stagnation in the Western industrialized countries as taxpayers in these societies are unwilling to finance assistance to countries that do not embrace reform.[3] The capacity of Western donors and Japan to leverage reform in Africa, and especially their inclination to exercise such leverage is greater now than any time since independence. Both Tanzania and Kenya have experienced the full brunt of donor exasperation and a willingness to force reform—on Tanzania to change its economic policies; on Kenya to move forward on both economic and political adjustment.

In this context, a unique alliance has emerged between African reformers and the international donor community to challenge those seeking to maintain the status quo. This alliance is unique because historically African reformers (especially those on the left) have regarded the West as part of the problem rather than the solution. Today the perspective is reversed. Rather than viewing the West as the center of international capitalism, bent on propping up corrupt regimes, reformers now consider the donor community an essential ally in achieving change. Indeed, one danger to the reform movement is that it has become too dependent on external support, both political and financial, instead of building its strength from within by relying on its own resources.

Donor willingness to press for political as well as economic reforms—

which necessarily involves the donors in the internal political affairs of African states—is also unique. Whatever reservations Western countries may have about engaging in a new form of neocolonialism or "trusteeship" in Africa—an accusation periodically voiced by those who resist reform— such inhibitions are seldom voiced. Indeed, it has become fashionable in some circles to argue that such interventions, as in the case of the Western intervention in Somalia, are necessary if several African states are to survive (Johnson 1993).

However, pursuit of the "twin pillars" of reform is undertaken in the absence of sufficient evidence that the two are mutually supporting in the near term as distinguished from the long. Though many studies, beginning with Seymour Martin Lipset's *Political Man* (1960), and Barrington Moore's *Social Origins of Dictatorship and Democracy* (1966),[4] have demonstrated that liberal democracy and economic development are mutually reinforcing after both have been achieved, the relationship between them with respect to the sequence of change is less clearly understood. The pressures for reform in Africa have again raised questions that have perplexed social scientists and policymakers since the end of World War II. Is economic development and the emergence of a middle class a precondition for political democracy, or does the process occur in reverse order? Are authoritarian regimes, as the experiences of China, Korea, and Southeast Asia suggest, a necessary first stage in the process of economic development and subsequent political liberalization? Will political liberalization improve governmental performance by holding those who rule accountable to the governed, or will liberalization merely unleash demands that divide and destabilize the polity (Huntington 1968: 3–56)?

In the wake of the initial chorus of pronouncements of Africa's "second liberation" in the late 1980s and early 1990s, there is a growing realization that political reform, like economic reform, is a long and difficult endeavor with many ups and downs (Diamond 1993). Both require the restructuring and rebuilding of African institutions, a process that is necessarily slow and must overcome entrenched resistance. As discussed later in this volume, the experiences of Kenya and Tanzania also illustrate these difficulties.

BACKGROUND TO REFORM IN KENYA AND TANZANIA

From the mid-1960s until the mid-1980s, Kenya and Tanzania were viewed as something approaching ideal types of political and economic development. In an earlier book, I labeled Kenya as the epitome of *patron-client capitalism* and Tanzania as a near pure example of *one-party socialism* (Barkan 1984b: 3–42). These labels were intended to capture the configurations of public policy and political institutions that distinguished the two countries from each other and that served as developmental models for the rest of Africa and students of political economy in other developing countries.

Kenya pursued a strategy that emphasized economic growth over equity and that built upon the institutions and policies inherited from the colonial era. These included an emphasis on the private sector; expanded production of Kenya's two principal export crops—coffee and tea—for which Kenya enjoyed a comparative advantage in world markets and which could be grown by small farmers; and receptivity to foreign private investment. Kenya also sought to maintain a viable system of governance by preserving, and in some cases extending, colonial institutions such as the civil service (especially the Provincial Administration), the judiciary, and the security forces. Standards of recruitment and basic procedures for these institutions remained largely unchanged. Although Kenya became a de facto one-party state barely a year after independence in 1964, representative bodies, particularly the National Assembly, remained active forums for policy debate whose members were regularly chosen through open and competitive elections. Though the regime did not change, it maintained a significant measure of legitimacy in the eyes of the public by using the electoral process to purge its least effective members. Kenya also maintained close ties with Britain, the former colonial overlord, and built upon them to establish a firm relationship with the West, including the United States. In the context of the Cold War, Kenya chose sides.

By contrast, Tanzania embarked on a bold experiment to break with the colonial legacy. In 1967, following the adoption of the *Arusha Declaration* as its blueprint for development, Tanzania turned sharply left by embracing a policy of socialism and self-reliance (Nyerere 1967b). This conception of development stressed a more equitable distribution of the country's wealth at the explicit expense of high rates of economic growth; state ownership of the "commanding heights" of the Tanzanian economy; the diminution and regulation of the private sector; deemphasis of Tanzania's principal agricultural exports—coffee, cotton, and sisal—in favor of the creation of more than 300 import substitution industries owned by the state; state intervention in the marketing of the country's food supply; and the forced villagization of the rural population. Tanzania also discouraged foreign private investment on the grounds that the interests of foreign investors, especially multinational corporations, were inimical to the country's goal of establishing an independent and self-sufficient economy.

In the political realm, Tanzania also sought to break with the colonial legacy by elevating the ruling party, the Tanganyika African National Union (TANU), to supremacy at the expense of the National Assembly, the civil service, the judiciary, the security forces, the educational system—indeed, all other institutions both public and private. Although Marxism-

Leninism never became the official ideology of Tanzania, the country imitated the governance model of Marxist parties in China, Eastern Europe, and the former Soviet Union by establishing a structure of party institutions paralleling those of the state. The state apparatus, particularly the regional and district administration, was subordinated to TANU. Private entities such as the press, labor unions, and farmers' cooperative societies were also brought under party control. In the process, professional standards of recruitment and performance were sacrificed to political ends. Representative institutions elected directly by the people, particularly the National Assembly, were subordinated to the party and reduced in importance. Although Tanzania continued to hold parliamentary elections every five years, the National Assembly ceased to be an independent forum for the deliberation of public policy.

Kenya and Tanzania also diverged in their approaches to foreign relations. Whereas Kenya maintained and expanded close ties with the West, Tanzania turned East and became active in both the Non-Aligned Movement and the liberation of Southern Africa from white rule. At the same time, Tanzania maintained healthy ties with selected Western countries sympathetic to its socialist experiment. As discussed by David Gordon in Chapter 8, Kenya and Tanzania approached the Cold War differently, each to its own advantage.

Both countries were able to attract substantial support from international assistance agencies. Until the late 1980s when its developmental performance began to flag, Kenya enjoyed a quarter-century honeymoon with the donors, principally because of its higher-than-average annual rates of economic growth and its strong ties to the West. Tanzania also enjoyed a honeymoon, albeit of shorter duration and of a different sort. Though Tanzania's rate of economic growth consistently lagged behind Kenya's from the late 1960s onward, its socialist experiment appealed to the donor community at a time when international assistance agencies stressed the provision of basic needs such as water, health, and education to rural populations. This was particularly true of the Scandinavian countries, which were themselves governed by social democratic parties until the mid-1980s and which regarded Tanzania as a noble alternative to conventional development strategy. Kenya and Tanzania were also attractive because of their success at maintaining civilian rule after independence on an uninterrupted basis. They were regarded as islands of stability in a turbulent region marked by military takeovers and civil war.

Although the divergent models of development pursued by Kenya and Tanzania attracted donors and students of development to East Africa, they engendered a measure of suspicion and at times hostility between the two states. So divergent were these strategies that until the mid-1980s, one country's model for development was invariably regarded by the leadership of the other as a recipe for *under*development. Comparisons of their developmental records were very difficult to make because no single set of indices for measuring their records was regarded as equally applicable to both. If Tanzania consciously sacrificed a measure of economic growth but achieved a corresponding measure of equity, it could not be deemed to be developing more slowly than Kenya. The relevant issues during this period were the extent to which each country reached its respective goals and the lessons each country's experience suggested for the other. It was not so much a question of which country's model was "better" as of the degree to which each was realized on its own terms.

Comparison between Kenya and Tanzania was also appealing because of their resemblances with respect to a number of variables that impinge upon the developmental process and that could be held constant or nearly constant in an examination of the countries. Both are populated mainly by small peasant households of similar cultures whose members speak Kiswahili, the lingua franca of East Africa. Both experienced British colonial rule and inherited a common set of political, administrative, and economic institutions, as well as a common market with a single currency and a common infrastructure of rail, port, and telecommunications facilities. As adjacent countries, they share a common climate and have similar natural resource endowments. Because Kenya and Tanzania lent themselves so readily to comparison, it is not surprising that until the mid-1980s more articles and books were published about these two countries than about any other on the African continent except South Africa and possibly Nigeria.

In the post–Cold War era of the 1990s and with the collapse of socialism across Africa, comparison between Kenya and Tanzania may seem less relevant, as they no longer offer contrasting models of development for examination. However, the experience of the two countries during the second half of the 1980s and early 1990s is no less profound because each has approached reform from different points of departure. Taken together, Kenya and Tanzania capture the full range of adjustments that African states are being forced to make to remain viable political economies.

Moreover, by the late 1980s, Kenya and Tanzania were no longer pure examples of parton-client capitalism and one-party socialism—if indeed they ever were. As socialism began to fail in Tanzania and the economy faltered, members of the regime including the civil service began to engage in corrupt practices to a degree that violated any pretense of a commitment to socialist values. A parallel market economy also emerged to meet demands for goods and services that the state-run economy could not fulfill (Maliyamkono and Bagachwa 1990). In Kenya, patron-client capitalism was also corrupted—literally and figuratively, and in respect to both politics and economics. The country's experience is no longer a model for stable capitalist development in Africa but rather an example of how a success story can turn sour when policies that work are undermined or reversed. A comparison of the political economies of both countries at this juncture therefore tells us much about the varying conditions that give rise to reform and about the factors that bear on the implementation of reform, not only in Kenya and Tanzania but throughout Africa.

In the chapters to follow, the contributors trace the political and economic evolution of Kenya and Tanzania in respect to a specific set of institutions or policy area. Each begins with a short review of the experience of the two countries from the late 1960s until the mid-1980s, when divergence was the norm, and then moves to a discussion of the pressures for change and the response to date. By focusing on developments since the mid-1980s, our discussion considers the process of economic and political development *beyond* capitalism versus socialism, as the two countries' developmental strategies evolve toward the twenty-first century. Though the parameters of these strategies are already clear, it remains uncertain whether the leadership in either country has the political will to see them through to implementation. Thus, in addition to examining the divergent and common pressures for reform, this study also considers the barriers that impede the process.

FOUR ERAS OF POLITICAL ECONOMY

The current period of reform in Kenya and Tanzania is the fourth era of political economy since independence. Although the years marking the beginning and end of each era vary in the two countries and are somewhat arbitrarily drawn, the four eras can be distinguished as follows. In the first, lasting from 1961 through 1966, nationalist leaders—led by Julius Nyerere in Tanzania and Jomo Kenyatta in Kenya—took control of the state apparatus bequeathed by the British and consolidated their authority to rule. The second, lasting from 1967 until roughly 1982, was the era of divergent development. It was during this period that Tanzania's experiment with one-party socialism rose and began to fall and that Kenya achieved its greatest successes through the pursuit of patron-client capitalism. The third era, one of political and economic decay, began in the early 1980s and continued through the mid- to late 1980s. The fourth and present era began in Tanzania in 1986 but not in Kenya until 1990. In this period issues of economic and political reform have dominated public debate as well as discussions within the donor community on whose assistance Kenya and Tanzania increasingly depend.

Consolidating Independent Rule (1961–1966)

In the years immediately after independence, little attention was given to the formulation of broad developmental strategies.[5] Rather, the initial challenge to the leadership in both countries was to demonstrate to their citizens and to the outside world that they could govern.[6] Their first order of business was to consolidate political authority, Africanize the civil service they inherited at independence, prudently manage the economy, and establish foreign relations with the world's major powers and potential providers of development assistance and investment. As the first African heads of state of Kenya and Tanzania, respectively, Kenyatta and Nyerere sought to come to grips with several structural realities that have proved to be enduring constraints on their nations' development. The most significant of these structural realities were, and to a great extent remain, the geographical distribution of ethnic, religious, and linguistic affiliations within each country and the geographical pattern of development and regional trade established during the colonial era.

Julius Nyerere became the first prime minister of what had been the British trusteeship of Tanganyika[7] in 1961 following an election in which his party, the Tanganyika African National Union, (TANU) won all but one seat in the national legislature. So great was TANU's electoral victory that within two years Nyerere announced the country would become a one-party state (Nyerere 1963). A commission of inquiry was established to explore the matter, and in 1965 Tanzania's constitution was amended to formalize one-party rule—a condition that was a distinctive feature of the country's political system for the next twenty-seven years.

The second important political development during this early period was the merger in 1964 of Tanganyika and the independent island state of Zanzibar. To consummate the merger, Nyerere agreed to a complicated semifederal arrangement under which the new country, henceforth known as the United Republic of Tanzania, would be governed by a president and two vice presidents. The president of the United Republic would be directly elected by the combined electorates of the mainland and Zanzibar, whereas the president of Zanzibar would automatically serve as one of the vice presidents of the union.[8] Each territory, however, continued to govern itself: TANU ran the mainland government, and the Afro-Shirazi Party (ASP) continued as the sole party on Zanzibar. On matters of foreign policy, the president of the union more or less called the tune.[9]

Although Nyerere pushed the merger in the spirit of pan-Africanism, neither partner has ever been entirely comfortable with the union. Throughout the nearly thirty years of its existence, leaders on both sides have believed that they have given more than they have received. Tensions between Zanzibar and the mainland are exacerbated by the fact that the population of the former is almost exclusively Muslim, as are the coastal areas of the mainland opposite the islands, whereas the mainland (except the coast) is predominantly Christian.

The discussion in this volume is concerned almost exclusively with the political economy on the mainland, the former Tanganyika. However, as discussed later in this chapter, the pressures for political reform in the 1990s—both on the mainland and on Zanzibar—have thrown the future of the union into question and in the process laid bare the potential for religious conflict. This potential was not appreciated in the early 1960s. Nyerere ruled a mainland that was culturally diverse but politically homogeneous; considerations of ethnicity and religion were not factors in Tanzania's political life, and TANU enjoyed near universal support.

By contrast, Kenyatta became Kenya's first African head of government in 1963 as the leader of a majority coalition, the Kenya African National Union (KANU), that was vigorously challenged by a minority coalition, the Kenya African Democratic Union (KADU). Neither KANU nor KADU was a party in the conventional sense of offering ideological or programmatic alternatives to the Kenyan electorate. Rather, the two organizations were loose alliances created in the run-up to independence through the merger of more than a dozen district-level political organizations that had been established in the late 1950s[10] and that invariably drew their membership from a single ethnic group.

A distinguishing and enduring factor in the politics of Kenya and Tanzania since before independence has been the role of ethnicity. Whereas ethnic identification has formed the basis of politics and political organizations in Kenya for more than thirty years, in Tanzania it has not. Because Tanzania is populated by more than 120 ethnic groups, of which none is sufficiently large or resource-endowed to exert undue influence on the others, ethnic and religious conflict have not—until the recent tension between the mainland and Zanzibar—been factors in Tanzanian political life. The potential for such conflict in Tanzania has also been muted by the near universal use of Kiswahili, which replaced English as the country's official language in the mid-1960s and has evolved its own political idiom, nurturing the development of a national political culture. Thus, although district-level organizations such as farmers' cooperatives emerged in parts of Tanzania prior to independence, these were not primarily political in purpose and moved quickly to support TANU.

By contrast, Kenya has less than forty ethnic groups, of which five account for 70 percent of the population. Thus, Kenyan politics have long been shaped by ethnic distinctions and continue to be so. Not only do Kenya's principal ethnic groups account for a greater proportion of the overall population than do Tanzania's, they also vary greatly in their levels of political mobilization and resource base. In the run-up to independence, KANU emerged as the alliance of the larger, more educated, more urbanized, and more politically mobilized tribes. In contrast, KADU was composed of smaller or internally divided groups that had been largely bypassed by the colonial economy, and whose members therefore tended to be less educated, less urbanized, and less mobilized. KANU's ethnic base consisted of the Kikuyu people, who reside in Central Province (the area immediately north and west of Nairobi) and parts of Rift Valley Province, and their cultural cousins, the Embu and Meru of Eastern Province. Together, these groups constitute 28 percent of Kenya's population. Support for KANU also came from the Luo, who reside in Nyanza Province along the shores of Lake Victoria and make up 13 percent of the population, and from the Kamba of Eastern Province (11 percent) and the Kisii of Nyanza Province (7 percent). KADU included the Luhya peoples of Western Province, who are Kenya's second largest group at 14 percent of the population; the Kalenjin and related peoples of the Rift Valley (12 percent); the Mijikenda peoples of Coast Province (5 percent); and several highly dispersed and nomadic groups that inhabit the vast arid and semiarid areas of the Rift Valley and remote Northeastern Province (7 percent).

With a three-to-two advantage in the combined population of its ethnic base, KANU beat KADU soundly in the parliamentary elections of 1961 and 1963, held prior to independence. Kenyatta thus presided over a very different type of regime than did Nyerere. Although both were the preeminent leaders in their respective countries, Kenyatta was forced to bargain to a much greater extent than Nyerere with an array of established regional and ethnic leaders who commanded significant followings in their home areas. The result was that from the beginning of the postcolonial period, KANU was a more overtly patron-client party than TANU. Kenyatta was also intent on wooing KADU into his fold. Using a combination of carrots and sticks—most notably the promise of cabinet and subcabinet appointments to KADU leaders who would defect to KANU and the denial of government services to the constituents of those who remained in opposition—Kenyatta persuaded KADU to merge itself into KANU in 1964. As part of this bargain, the deputy chairman of KADU, Daniel arap Moi, became the vice president of KANU and Kenya in 1966.[11] Moi served in this capacity for twelve years, succeeding Kenyatta as president upon the latter's death in August 1978 as specified by Kenya's constitution.

The presence of a powerful European community in Kenya throughout the colonial period also had a great impact on the evolution of Kenya's political economy after independence and on Kenya's economic relations with its East African neighbors. Numbering close to 60,000 at independence, the European community had dominated Kenya's politics and economy for the previous fifty years.[12] In a system of racial domination similar to South Africa's, Kenya's whites dispossessed the African population of much of the country's best farmland and denied Africans access to meaningful employment and political representation within the colonial order. The brunt of colonial rule fell on the Kikuyu, Kenya's largest tribe, which resides in Kenya's fertile highland areas north and northwest of Nairobi. Not surprisingly, the Kikuyu were the first to mobilize against the system and ultimately formed the base of the nationalist movement to end white rule. Dispossessed of their lands, Kikuyu dominated the country's principal nationalist organization of the post–World War II era, the Kenya African Union. In the early 1950s, they also organized a guerrilla force known as the Land Freedom Army whose main objective was to gain back the lands taken by the whites (Rosberg and Nottingham 1966, Throup 1987a). More than 15,000 British troops were required to quell the ensuing insurgency, known as Mau Mau, which lasted from 1952 through 1954, but which put Kenya firmly on the road to independence.

During the first years of independence, Kenyatta and his government sought to defuse the land issue by settling thousands of Kikuyu on farms purchased from the whites. Though some of these farms were in areas previously occupied by Kikuyu, most, especially those on the western side of the Rift Valley, were in areas historically inhabited by the Maasai. Through this process of resettlement, large numbers of Kikuyu migrated into portions of the Rift Valley Province. This influx threatened non-Kikuyu in these areas, most of whom had supported KADU in the elections before independence. In seeking to resolve the land issue, Kenyatta's government sowed the seeds of later enmity between the Kikuyu, of which he was the leading member, and Kenya's other groups.[13]

Moreover, Kenyatta's government appeared to favor Kikuyu in the course of Africanizing the civil service. Though the Kikuyu suffered most under the colonial system, they also benefited disproportionately from the limited opportunities it offered the African population. Marginalized by the colonial economy, Kikuyu were more aggressive than the members of other groups in seeking educational qualifications to secure employment. One result is that large numbers of Kikuyu received secondary and university educations and then, on the basis of their educational qualifications, were recruited into the civil service in proportions that exceeded their percentage of Kenya's population. In sum, the presence of a European community in Kenya prior to independence, combined with the geographic homeland of the country's largest tribe, shaped the politics of the immediate postindependence era and gave rise to cleavages based on ethnicity that have structured Kenya's politics ever since.

A second enduring legacy of the European presence prior to independence was Britain's policy of making Kenya and its capital city, Nairobi, the focus of East African regional development at the expense of Tanganyika and Uganda. Throughout the period after World War II and continuing after independence, Kenya ran large balance-of-trade surpluses with its two neighbors while incurring trade deficits with the rest of the world. Conversely, Tanganyika and Uganda ran trade surpluses with the rest of the world.[14] The net result of this system of regional trade was that Kenya's trade deficits with the world were financed by trade surpluses with her East African neighbors. Kenya was able to purchase manufactured goods and machinery from abroad to establish its industries and satisfy consumer demand (e.g., by Kenya's Europeans) because Tanganyika and

Uganda financed these imports through a combination of their exports to destinations outside of East Africa and their imports of Kenyan goods and services. British policy thus relegated Tanganyika and Uganda to be exporters of a small number of agricultural commodities—coffee, cotton, and sisal in the case of Tanganyika, coffee and cotton in the case of Uganda. Kenya became the hub of East African development, Tanganyika and Uganda the periphery.

In the years after independence, Kenya tried to preserve this asymmetrical pattern of trade, whereas Tanzania and Uganda sought to redress the imbalance. This trade system and the emergence of Nairobi as the commercial capital of East Africa also helped Kenya attract most of the private foreign investment that flowed into the region, which explains why Kenya continued to welcome such investment after independence. Not surprisingly, these developments frustrated the leaderships of Tanzania and Uganda, which by 1966 demanded concessions from Kenya in the form of managed trade and investment to achieve a more balanced process of regional growth.[15]

By the mid-1960s, Kenya and Tanzania had become economic competitors and began to define their interests and their future courses of development in different terms. Kenya, whose average annual rate of real economic growth during this period was nearly 7 percent, sought to perpetuate the capitalist system inherited at independence.[16] Tanzania, whose average rate of growth exceeded 6 percent but whose baseline level of development and ability to attract foreign investment were much lower than Kenya's, began to search for an alternative strategy.

Differences also emerged in the political realm. Though KADU had merged into KANU, Kenya remained a de facto rather than a de jure one-party state, whereas Tanzania mandated the one-party system into law. Moreover, in 1966 a new opposition party, the Kenya People's Union (KPU), challenged KANU, though it was soundly defeated in a round of by-elections known as the Little General Election (Gertzel 1970: 73–94). Perhaps most important, a significant measure of pluralism continued in Kenya in respect to the country's associational life, whereas in Tanzania independent associations—labor unions, the national women's association, the press, and so forth—were taken over by the ruling party.

These differences in approach were repeated with respect to the role and operation of the civil service, particularly in the rural areas. Both countries inherited a civil service established by the British that had operated under the direction of the colonial governor. At independence, these bureaucracies became responsible to the prime minister (later to the president) and his cabinet, and each ministry was directed independently. Under this system, political control was to be exercised solely by the relevant minister and communicated to the senior civil servant in each ministry. In the rural areas, the district, headed by a district commissioner, was the most important unit of administration. Districts in Kenya were grouped into eight provinces headed by provincial commissioners, whereas in Tanzania they were initially clustered into nine and then seventeen regions headed by regional commissioners. Districts were themselves broken down into divisions, locations, and sublocations in Kenya and into divisions and wards in Tanzania.

During the first five years of independence, these administrative institutions remained relatively intact, as the principal aim in both countries was to Africanize their ranks. The process of Africanization, however, was more rapid and politicized in Tanzania than in Kenya. At the time of independence, most senior positions within government ministries and the rural administration down through the position of district commissioner were held by expatriate holdovers from the colonial period. In Tanzania, most were replaced within a year by TANU officials. By contrast, Africanization not only took longer in Kenya, but most senior positions were filled through the promotion of Kenyans who had been groomed for these positions by the British. From the start, Tanzania's civil service took on a different ethos from its counterpart in Kenya where a commitment to the British practice of a politically neutral and technocratic service was maintained.

The Era of Divergent Development (1967–1982)

The basic features of the era of divergent development have been described above and discussed extensively in the literature.[17] Some elaboration, however, is required for readers unfamiliar with the period and to provide context for the chapters that follow. Looking back on this period, it is possible to consider the contrasting developmental strategies pursued by Kenya and Tanzania in a more nuanced manner than was done at the time. Although it was and remains appropriate to describe Kenya and Tanzania as examples of patron-client capitalism and one-party socialism, respectively, it is also clear that more than differences over ideology drove the two countries apart. The contrasting ideological perspectives of the leaderships of the two countries were the single most important variable that shaped developmental policy in this era, but other considerations also fed the policymaking process, and the significance of these variables is more apparent today than during the era of divergence. The ideological sensitivities that typified the era—of senior policymakers within the two countries, of local and expatriate academics who wrote about what was occurring, of policy analysts charged with designing foreign assistance programs, and of those responsible for charting the foreign policies of the major powers toward Africa during the height of the Cold War—so dominated the thinking of the period that they tended to obscure other explanations of what was occurring in the two countries.

As discussed in the previous section, several structural variables—ethnicity, the impact of white domination in Kenya before independence, and Kenya's position in the regional economy—contributed to the differences in the developmental strategies of Kenya and Tanzania. So, too, did individual leaders. Kenya's course of patron-client capitalism was largely the policy of Jomo Kenyatta; Tanzania's pursuit of one-party socialism was even more the product and vision of Julius Nyerere. A political theorist and gifted writer, Nyerere articulated the ideological rationale for breaking with the colonial legacy in a 1967 speech and essay known as the *Arusha Declaration* (Nyerere 1967b).[18] In what is probably the single most important contribution by an African writer to the literature on normative political theory, Nyerere first argued why capitalism was not an appropriate model for poor countries like Tanzania and then outlined the policies his country would henceforth pursue to achieve a socialist alternative. Economic growth for its own sake—which Nyerere regarded as the mindless pursuit of money, resulting in "the exploitation of man by man"—would be subordinated to the quest for a more equitable and socially just society. Such a society would be achieved through the combination of a benevolent state, which would take over and run "the commanding heights" of Tanzania's economy, and self-reliance (i.e., sacrifice) on the part of the Tanzanian people. State and society would in turn be led by a benevolent party, TANU, which would be the guardian of socialist values and the supreme institution in the land. Though Nyerere argued that Tanzania's approach to socialism was uniquely African, describing its content in terms of *ujamaa* (Kiswahili for the practice of reciprocity by members of the same family), the mechanics of the approach were remarkably similar to those set forth by Lenin in *State and Revolution* (1917) half a century before.

In contrast to Nyerere, Kenyatta did not articulate Kenya's developmental strategy within an explicitly ideological framework. He did not have to. Whereas Nyerere faced the challenge of redefining the meaning of "the good society" to justify radical changes in Tanzania's economic and social policy, Kenyatta did not. Nyerere's agenda was sweeping and holistic in scope. Its pursuit required the restructuring of many of his country's institutions, including the rural household. Kenyatta's agenda was far more limited.

Because he presided over a robust economy, Kenyatta could accommodate key interest groups, especially his fellow Kikuyu and other members of the original KANU alliance. Therefore, he was not particularly concerned with issues of inequality in resource distribution—whether between socioeconomic classes, between urban and rural dwellers, or between members of ethnic groups that had reaped advantages from Kenya's uneven development during the colonial period and members of groups that had not. Nor did Kenyatta share Nyerere's concern with the colonial legacy of unequal development at the regional level. For Kenyatta and his government, the developmental challenge was to continue, modify, and augment the institutions inherited from the colonial period, not replace them. A brief review of three key institutional arenas—party, state, and civil society— illustrates the divergent approaches taken by the two countries.

The Role of the Ruling Political Party

Nyerere sought to establish TANU as the supreme institution in Tanzanian society so that it would play a vanguard role in the country's development. The party would be the guardian and propagator of socialist values. Its leadership would determine how Tanzania would achieve socialism and self-reliance and would direct all other institutions, both public and private, toward this goal. To accomplish these objectives TANU established an extensive apparatus that paralleled all state institutions down to the village level. Basic political representation in Tanzania was via party organs, the lowest of which is the neighborhood cell of ten households and the highest the National Executive Committee (NEC). All Tanzanians would belong to a party cell or village organization. Election to each organ above the cell was and continues to be indirect—by the membership of the organ immediately below—thus guaranteeing that the outcomes of elections at each level are consistent with the views of the leadership and NEC. Party officers, including the chairman, are elected every five years. Party organs from the cell up through the ward, division, district, region, and NEC meet regularly to determine and implement policy. Organs from the ward on up maintain thousands of offices in the countryside from which to organize their activities. A nationwide delegates' conference is convened every two years.

By contrast, KANU under Kenyatta existed only in name. The party played no role in the policymaking process, let alone in defining the nation's values. Its apparatus was minimal, consisting of a network of branches at the sublocation, location, and district levels and a small party headquarters in Nairobi. Branch committees rarely met, and no party organs were created to shadow those of the state. Few branches maintained offices in the countryside. The party's national delegates' conference did not meet between 1966 and 1979. Basic political representation in Kenya was and remains via direct election to the National Assembly and to district and town councils. Although only members of KANU could stand for election and the party retained the authority to screen all would-be candidates, few were barred from running. Unlike TANU, with its elaborate organization, KANU was a patron-client network of local and regional bosses held together by Kenyatta. He dispensed patronage to subordinate leaders, who in turn provided patronage to their clients below.

The Role of the State

The postcolonial state in Kenya was mainly an autonomous administrative apparatus that Kenyatta directed in much the same manner as colonial governors before him. Policy was made by the president assisted by a relatively small circle of advisers that included trusted regional leaders and senior civil servants in key ministries; it was implemented via the ministries and the Provincial Administration. Although nominally answerable to the National Assembly, Kenyatta instructed its members to concentrate their efforts on developing their home areas and to leave the making of basic policy to him. Parliamentary debates were lively and given extensive coverage by the press, but the role of the National Assembly vis-à-vis the executive was mainly that of the friendly critic whose job was to fine tune, not challenge, legislation proposed by the president and his cabinet.

By law, elections to the Kenya National Assembly are to be held at regular intervals not exceeding five years—they have taken place in 1969, 1974, 1979, 1983, 1988, and 1992. Under Kenyatta, elections evolved into referenda on the ability of incumbents to assist the development of their constituencies (Barkan 1976 and 1978). Backbenchers who won reelection were normally promoted to become assistant ministers in reward for following the role envisioned by the president while assistant ministers were promoted to become full members of the cabinet. Rewards were thus passed out to those who not only cooperated with Kenyatta but who also demonstrated that they had a popular following in their home areas. Incompetent and unpopular MPs were pruned away.[19] Through this process, a coterie of regional leaders emerged with whom Kenyatta shared the spotlight and who contributed to the legitimacy of his regime. This system of representation, however, did not endure beyond his presidency.

During the era of divergent development, Kenya's civil service functioned in more or less the same manner it had during the colonial period. The role, structure, and procedures of the civil service, including recruitment, remained unchanged. Because of their greater accesses to secondary and university education, Kikuyus and (to a much lesser extent) Luos were recruited into the civil service in numbers that substantially exceeded their proportions of the total population. The presence of the former no doubt enabled Kenyatta to exert a measure of political influence over the civil service, particularly the day-to-day operation of the Provincial Administration.[20] Though he appointed the members of both the Public Services Commission and the Judicial Services Commission, the president could not remove commissioners once they had assumed their posts. Despite periodic pressure from the office of the president, the civil service and judiciary were able to maintain a significant measure of professionalism and autonomy.

By contrast, the principal institutions of the Tanzanian state lost their autonomy to the ruling party and departed from colonial practice. Throughout this period, the National Assembly, or *Bunge* (Kiswahili for "legisla-ture"), was emasculated by TANU, particularly by the NEC. Although elections to the National Assembly occurred at regular five-year intervals—in 1965, 1970, 1975, 1980, 1985, and 1990—would-be candidates were screened by a series of party committees at the district, regional, and national levels, which selected two candidates to stand for each seat. Up to 25 percent of the seats were filled by presidential nominees or nominees of associations affiliated with TANU, such as the national women's organiza-tion or the Tanzania Parents Association. Whereas in Kenya virtually any-one could become a candidate and only 6 percent of all legislators were nominated by the president, recruitment to the Bunge was a closed process controlled by the party. Moreover, the first duty of Bunge members was to propagate TANU policy rather than to address the problems of their dis-tricts. The result was a rubber-stamp legislature that promulgated laws fol-lowing little public debate. Press coverage of the National Assembly was minimal, as most attention was given to policy discussions within the NEC. Most important, this system of representation did not contribute to the legitimacy of the state, because it did not link Tanzania's vast and geo-graphically dispersed rural population to the central government.

The civil service was likewise placed under tight party control. Civil servants were expected to be members of TANU and adhere to a strict lead-ership code and party guidelines (Nyerere 1967b: Part V; TANU 1971). Party institutions were established to watch over all state and parastatal agencies. Particularly significant was the party's control over the rural regional and district administrations. Over the years, regional and district commissioners were either shadowed by regional and district party secre-taries, or the party appointed a single individual to occupy both posts. This systematic politicization of the civil service had predictable and deleterious results, as professional standards of administration were subordinated to criteria of party loyalty.

Civil Society

The evolution of civil society in Kenya and Tanzania also reflected and continues to reflect the divergent developmental models pursued by the two states. In Kenya, autonomous associational life was allowed to develop, indeed flourish, provided it did not directly challenge the Kenyatta regime. Rural associational life was actively encouraged. Throughout the 1970s ethnic associations such as the Kikuyu Embu Meru Association (GEMA) and the Luo Union functioned openly and without state interference, though many regarded the activities of such associations as divisive. The powerful Kenya Farmers Association (KFA), a holdover from the colonial era, Africanized its leadership, extended its membership to small farmers, and continued to represent the interests of large farmers. Primary cooperative societies expanded their activities on behalf of smallholders, particularly Kikuyu farmers in Central Province, who became major producers of coffee and tea. Churches also functioned without constraint, leading to the emergence of the National Council of Churches of Kenya (NCCK) as the country's largest and most influential nongovernmental organization (NGO). In the urban areas, the Central Organisation of Trades Unions (COTU) functioned as an independent albeit weak umbrella for Kenya's individual unions. An array of independent business and professional associations also developed, as well as a national women's organization, Maendeleo wa Wanawake. By the mid-1980s Kenya had also developed an impressive array of more than a hundred indigenous NGOs. Some, such as AMREF and CARE, were highly dependent on external funding and/or support from northern NGOs. Many others were not or had weaned themselves from their northern benefactors.

The most significant manifestation of civil society, however, was the *Harambee* self-help movement that took root in Kenya's rural areas. Encouraged by Kenyatta, Harambee (Kiswahili for "let us pull together" and Kenya's official national motto) entailed the formation of community-based organizations for the purpose of implementing small-scale self-help development projects. Typical schemes included the construction and management of primary and secondary school buildings, health clinics, local water systems, cattle dips, and so forth. The significance of Harambee is manifold and discussed extensively in the literature (Mbithi and Rasmusson 1977; Holmquist 1984; Thomas 1985; Barkan and Holmquist 1989). By the early 1980s, more than 20,000 such associations were estimated to have registered with the government, and they existed in virtually every rural community. In addition to providing communities with basic services that individuals could not get on their own, Harambee became the principal vehicle through which local communities exerted claims on the state. For example, communities that constructed appropriate-sized buildings for secondary schools and initially staffed their schools with uncertified teachers were eventually able to secure the services of certified teachers from the Ministry of Education. Because these activities were largely self-financed, Harambee also served as an informal mechanism to tax the rural rich and to secure contributions from members of the local community who had migrated to urban areas (Barkan and Holmquist 1989).

Most significant, however, was the measure of "political space" and accountability Harambee provided for rural dwellers. In a sharp break with the normal practice of resisting or avoiding the payment of taxes to the state, members of Harambee organizations willingly taxed themselves because they were confident that the funds would be put to proper use within their own community. As permanent local residents, the leaders of these organizations were likewise accountable to fellow residents to a degree state officials were not. Harambee thus became the most important arena of

rural political life. As a result of Kenyatta's exhortations that members of
the national Assembly should concentrate their efforts on constituency service, parliamentary elections became referenda on the ability of incumbents to support Harambee (Barkan 1976). Over time, the emergence of
Harambee, combined with the regular holding of elections, established a
measure of national political accountability by linking state and society
together. As long as elections were relatively open, free, and fair, the legitimacy of the state was enhanced.

By contrast, civil society institutions in Tanzania, with the sole exception of the church, were effectively crushed—and with them a measure of
the legitimacy of the regime (Tripp 1992). From the mid-1960s onward, all
independent associations were either banned or brought under the control
of the ruling party. Although a number of ethnic associations had supported
TANU in the drive for independence, such organizations were outlawed as
early as 1962. The Tanzanian labor movement was also forced into the
party in the mid-1960s, as were the national women's organization and the
Tanzania Parents Association. The most significant encroachment on rural
civil society was the abolition in 1976 of independent cooperative societies
and their replacement by the Cooperative Union of Tanzania (CUT). In a
move Nyerere later described as "my greatest mistake," associations with
long historical roots, such as the Bukoba Native Cooperative Union and the
Kilimanjaro Native Cooperative Union, were swept aside by TANU.
Rather than enhancing party control over the countryside, the move generated deep resentment and marked the beginning of a long decline of the
party's authority.

TANU's loss of authority corresponds almost perfectly with the vigor
with which the party sought to replace rural civil society with its own organization and ideology. After private organizations were abolished or
absorbed into the party, TANU proved unable to provide credible substi-
tutes. Between 1973 and 1976, 80 percent of Tanzania's rural population
was forcibly moved by the party and rural administration into ujamaa villages in the belief that villagization would simultaneously advance socialist
production and provide rural communities with basic services such as education, water, and health. Directed entirely by the party, villagization
achieved neither (Ergus 1980; McHenry 1981; von Freyhold 1979). As discussed in the next section and by Michael Lofchie in Chapter 5, agricultural
production dropped precipitously, and rural services improved only slightly. In the absence of other forms of associational life, the party could not
avoid blame. Similar problems arose in the marketing of agricultural products, especially export commodities such as coffee. Following the abolition
of the cooperative unions in 1976 and the centralization of agricultural marketing under the National Milling Corporation and the National Coffee
Board, inefficiencies became endemic to the system. Farmers eventually

retaliated by cutting back on production, selling or bartering their produce via informal markets, or smuggling.

TANU's monopolization over rural associational life also inhibited, indeed actively discouraged, the emergence of self-help community development organizations of the type that flourished in Kenya. Such organizations had long functioned in Tanzania but were now suppressed. When coupled with the fact that members of the Tanzanian National Assembly were kept on a short leash by TANU and that nominations of candidates for parliamentary elections were also under party control, rural residents had no avenues for effective representation nor means to hold the party accountable for its failures. As an expression of their declining confidence in the formal system of governance, citizens began to withdraw from economic and political life (Hyden 1980). Although TANU merged with the Afro-Shirazi Party in 1977 to form Chama cha Mapinduzi (CCM, or the Party of the Revolution) and although the supremacy of the merger was reaffirmed in a new constitution for the union, the period marked the apex of the party's authority. By tampering with civil society, Nyerere turned previous allies into adversaries and distinguished himself from Kenyatta, whose accommodating management of civil society was more pragmatic.

As discussed in Chapter 2 by Michael Chege and in Chapter 3 by Goran Hyden, the legacy of this period is still evident and affects the pace and process of political reform, including the emergence of opposition parties, in both countries. Civil society is today far more developed in Kenya than in Tanzania and has been able to exert sustained pressure for reform in a manner not yet possible in Tanzania. Civil society is nevertheless beginning to reemerge and flourish in Tanzania to fill the vacuum created by the decline of CCM (Baregu 1992; Tripp 1992).[21]

The Era of Political and Economic Decay
(1979–1985 and 1982–1992)

The early 1980s were characterized by a dual process of political and economic decay in both countries that has persisted in Kenya ever since. Signs of decay were first apparent in Tanzania. In both countries politics took precedence over economics, though for different reasons. In both countries the state pursued redistributive policies and interfered with the operation of markets, resulting in a dramatic slowdown of economic growth. In both countries the ruling elite sought to monopolize political power and shackle civil society. In both countries budget deficits soared as the state spent more than it could afford on social welfare services with a consequent rise in inflation. Corruption also rose sharply as a bloated civil service and senior elected officials became increasingly prone to rent-seeking behavior. In both countries economic decline, precipitated by the state's mismanagement of the economy, accelerated the process of political decay, as key elements in society withdrew from the system or began to challenge the authority of the regime.

As indicated in Table 1.1, economic growth slowed markedly in both Kenya and Tanzania in the early 1980s. More significant, the rate of economic growth did not keep pace with the rate of population growth, resulting in a decline in per capita income.[22] This was particularly true in Tanzania, where agricultural exports and cereal production fell and inefficient state-owned industries experienced sharp drops in production. In 1981 and 1982 alone, manufacturing declined by 56 percent and agriculture fell 14 percent (USDA 1983: 1). During the first five years of the decade, per capita income in Tanzania fell 12 percent. Although the decline in per capita income was less pronounced in Kenya, it followed fifteen years of modest yet continuous increases in the standard of living for most Kenyans, including rural dwellers.

Table 1.1 Average Annual Rates of Real Economic Growth[a]

	1965–1980	1981–1985	1986–1990	1991–1992
Gross Domestic Product				
Kenya	6.8	3.2	4.9	1.3
Tanzania	3.9	.4	4.2	3.6[b]
Agriculture				
Kenya	5.0	3.0	4.1	–2.7
Tanzania	1.6	2.2	3.7	4.6[b]
Manufacturing				
Kenya	10.5	4.1	5.7	2.5
Tanzania	5.6	–4.8	4.6	4.3[b]
Population Growth				
Kenya	3.7	3.6	3.5	3.3
Tanzania	2.8	2.8	2.8	2.8
GDP per Capita				
Kenya	3.1	–0.4	1.4	–2.0
Tanzania	1.1	–2.4	1.4	1.0[b]

Sources: Republic of Kenya, *Kenya Economic Survey* (Nairobi: Government Printer, 1986, 1989, 1993); World Bank, *Tanzania Economic Country Review* (Washington: World Bank, 1991); Economic Research Bureau, *Tanzania Economic Trends: A Quarterly Review of the Economy* (Dar es Salaam, April and July 1992).

Notes: a. Percent
b. 1991 only

This downturn in economic performance can be partly explained by external factors, including the end of the coffee boom and the second oil shock of 1979. However, the principal cause was excessive state intervention in the management of the economy to achieve political goals. As noted above, Tanzania's pursuit of socialism entailed a conscious decision by the country's leadership to sacrifice a measure of economic growth to achieve a measure of equity. This decision in turn led to a combination of state ownership of all significant manufacturing enterprises and state marketing of all principal agricultural commodities, including Tanzania's principal export, coffee. The results were predictable. From 1965 through 1980, Tanzania's overall annual rate of economic growth, as well as the annual rates of growth in agriculture and manufacturing, were roughly half those of Kenya. Though Kenya established its own parastatal enterprises in pursuit of import substitution, these state-owned industries never dominated the country's manufacturing sector as in Tanzania.

Kenya also experienced less interference and regulation of the agricultural sector. Whereas Nyerere's government disrupted smallholder agriculture by forcing rural dwellers to move into ujamaa villages and by closing producer cooperative societies, Kenyatta's government supported the growth of smallholder production by giving free rein to a variety of farmer-controlled organizations including the Kenya Farmers Association (KFA) and the Kenya Planters Cooperative Union (KPCU). Kenyan producers of agricultural exports also received a much higher percentage of the world market price than their counterparts in Tanzania. Whereas Kenyatta wanted to encourage the growth of exports and was not concerned that the benefits flowed mainly to the members of one ethnic group (i.e., his fellow Kikuyu), Nyerere was intent on equalizing incomes among all rural dwellers. Producers of coffee and other exports residing mainly in the area around Mount Kilimanjaro, in the West Lake region, and in Iringa were systematically taxed to subsidize farmers in regions where export crops could not be grown. This discrimination against producers of exports eventually resulted in a decline of foreign exchange earnings, which in turn limited Tanzania's ability to purchase the necessary inputs (e.g., fertilizer) to sustain the production of cereals. The result was that by the early 1980s, Tanzania's agricultural sector and entire economy were on the verge of collapse, whereas Kenya's agricultural sector and economy were relatively robust. Details of these policies and their relationship to macroeconomic policy, particularly with regard to exchange rates, are discussed in Chapter 4 by Benno Ndulu and Francis Mwega and in Chapter 5 by Michael Lofchie.

As indicated by its economic performance in the early 1980s and again in the early 1990s, Kenya's economy has not been immune to mismanagement. Although the Tanzanian economy lagged substantially behind Kenya's from 1965 through 1985, the differential narrowed during the latter half of the 1980s and by the early 1990s was reversed. In a development most observers would have deemed inconceivable a decade earlier, Tanzania's average annual rate of economic growth surpassed Kenya's. What explains this reversal in performance? Stated simply, Kenya replicated most of the errors made by Tanzania during the era of divergent development. On the one hand Kenya began to pursue a series of redistributive policies, which had the net effect of taxing producers of agricultural exports to subsidize social welfare services and infrastructure for rural dwellers residing in other areas. On the other, the state and ruling political party became instruments of control that undermined the electoral process and reined in Kenya's well-developed and vibrant civil society. During the late 1980s and early 1990s, corruption on the part of Kenya's top political leaders also reached kleptocratic proportions that exacerbated government deficits and increased the money supply, which in turn contributed to very high levels of inflation.

The underlying motivation for these changes has been a drive for equity and power. These concerns did not entail a newfound commitment to socialism but rather the determination of Kenyatta's successor, Daniel arap Moi, to redistribute resources away from the ethnic groups that provided the social base of the Kenyatta regime to the groups that constituted his own. Moi succeeded Kenyatta upon the latter's death in August 1978. As the deputy leader of the old KADU alliance—the alliance of the smaller, less educated, less urbanized, and less mobilized ethnic groups—Moi immediately set about to redress what he regarded as the inequities of fifteen years of Kikuyu rule.

Moi's first move was to establish control over the civil service, particularly the Provincial Administration. By 1980 all but one of Kenyatta's eight provincial commissioners had been removed, including all four Kikuyu commissioners. Roughly half the district commissioners, a disproportionate number of them Kikuyu, were also transferred out of the Provincial Administration to other departments. Prominent Kikuyu civil servants such as permanent secretaries and deputy permanent secretaries were likewise transferred or retired. Most were replaced by members of ethnic groups from the old KADU alliance, especially Moi's own Kalenjin tribe. Similar appointments were made to state-owned enterprises, marketing boards, and regulatory agencies. Tenure in these positions was also reduced. Whereas under Kenyatta senior members of the civil service would remain in their posts for five years or more, Moi rotated personnel every two to three years, often less.

Using a populist rhetoric known as *Nyayo,*[23] Moi pursued a series of other initiatives to redistribute resources away from the ethnic groups and regions which had formed the core of the original KANU alliance. These included substantial shifts in the levels of public expenditures for roads, health, water, and education away from Central Province to other regions, especially the areas of Rift Valley Province inhabited by his fellow Kalenjin. Government agricultural policy also shifted from its traditional support of small-scale growers of coffee and tea in Central Province to tea growers in Western Kenya and growers of cereals in the Rift Valley. Criteria for entrance to Kenya's secondary schools and universities were changed to provide additional spaces for students from areas previously underrepresented at the country's institutions of higher learning. Not surprisingly, these policies evoked criticism from those whose opportunities were being systematically reduced.

Moi also sought to transform KANU into an instrument of control by strengthening party headquarters and revitalizing the party apparatus in the countryside. Elections for national officers were held in 1979 for the first time in thirteen years, but elections for branch officers were not held until 1985. Notwithstanding these moves, KANU never assumed the role of TANU or CCM in Tanzania. It never became the official custodian of a national ideology or the central arena for the making of public policy. Nor did the party become an important factor in the implementation of policy by establishing a parallel organization to monitor the operations of the state. As a result, Kenya never evolved into a "party state" in the pattern of Tanzania, despite much rhetoric by Moi and his closest associates which some observers have interpreted as evidence for such (Widner 1992). Rather, through patronage and guile, Moi turned KANU into a well-financed machine of personal rule (Rosberg and Jackson 1982). By revitalizing party branches and sub-branches at the district level, Moi established a counterweight to the regional leaders that had emerged under Kenyatta and undercut their authority in their home areas. Rather than regarding regional leaders as assets who helped the regime renew its mandate, Moi regarded them as threats, especially Kikuyu ministers of long standing.

Moi's use of the party as an instrument of personal control was extended in June 1982, when Kenya's constitution was amended to make the country a de jure one-party state. Although KANU had been Kenya's only political party since the demise of the Kenya People's Union, which functioned briefly from 1966 to 1969, Moi feared a new opposition party would emerge as disaffection spread among the Kikuyu, Luo, and other principal groups of the original KANU alliance who bore the impact of his efforts to restructure the system. Critics of the move to amend the constitution were promptly detained; in August 1982 Moi was challenged by an attempted coup led by Kikuyu air force officers, but it was crushed by the army.[24]

In the wake of the failed coup, the Moi regime turned progressively inward and became more repressive, though parliamentary elections proceeded in 1983 on a more or less normal basis. Critics and suspected critics of the regime were branded as "disloyal." "Loyalty" to the president and "warnings" to opponents became the rhetoric of the regime. Beginning in 1983 and continuing through early 1991, Moi periodically questioned the loyalty of selected leaders, bringing about their expulsion from KANU and ending their political careers. This practice narrowed the circle of advisers surrounding the president to "loyalists" drawn mainly from former KADU strongholds in the Rift Valley. The result was an increasingly capricious inner circle with little understanding of the macroeconomic issues facing Kenya and a proclivity to use the financial instruments of the state for patronage needs.

Moi also took steps to curtail the autonomy of all independent centers of power, both public and private. In the public realm, the Kenya National Assembly was reduced to a rubber-stamp body comparable to the legislature in Tanzania. In 1986 the president ended whatever pretense remained of an independent civil service and judiciary by assuming the chairships of the Public Service and Judicial Service commissions, which vetted all senior appointments for these institutions. In 1988 a constitutional amendment was passed removing security of tenure for judges.

Like Nyerere before him, Moi also moved to rein in civil society. Ethnic welfare associations were banned, ostensibly to reduce tribal conflict but in fact to eliminate the countervailing social and economic power they represented, especially among the Kikuyu and related groups. In the rural areas, the independence of the Harambee self-help development organizations was curbed by using the Provincial Administration to regulate their activities. These regulations also reduced the opportunities for members of parliament to perform acts of constituency service and thus maintain their political base. Even more significant, organizations that historically championed the interests of Kenya's most productive commercial farmers had their activities curtailed or were banned altogether. In 1985 the Kenya Farmers Association was shut down and replaced by the Kenya Grain Growers Cooperative Union. The sole objective of this move was to reduce the power of wealthy Kikuyu farmers, but it dramatically reduced the level of technical support available to producers of Kenya's principal export crops, coffee and tea. In a parallel move, the Ministry of Agriculture began to interfere with the operations of the Kenya Planters Cooperative Union and the Coffee Board of Kenya. In many cases, Kalenjins were appointed to head these organizations in place of Kikuyu. In 1990 the president moved on the independent Central Organisation of Trade Unions COTU and the national women's organization, Maendeleo wa Wanawake, decreeing that henceforth they would be auxiliary associations of KANU. Only the churches, particularly the NCCK and the Catholic hierarchy, and some professional organizations such as the Law Society of Kenya were able to resist these moves.

The expansion of Moi's power was accompanied by a growing culture of sycophancy and fear. On the one hand, KANU stalwarts and parliamentarians seeking to demonstrate their loyalty loudly celebrated the president's every deed. At the same time, suspected enemies, both real and imagined, were detained, tortured, and forced to confess to trumped-up charges of sedition. Many were never charged. Toward the end of the decade, upwards of 160 political prisoners languished in jail.

As in Tanzania, the pursuit of equity, coupled with the drive for political control (particularly over the groups that had been the most productive), led to a downturn in the economy. Although Kenya's rates of economic growth picked up slightly during the second half of the 1980s, the country's economic performance dropped sharply after 1989 as the impact of Moi's efforts mounted. Not surprisingly, the quality of life and provision of social welfare services suffered. As discussed by Richard Stren et al. in Chapter 6, conditions in Kenya's urban areas deteriorated during the 1980s, as they had previously in Tanzania. The provision of education—undoubtedly the single most important social welfare service in the eyes of most Kenyans—also declined, as discussed in Chapter 7 by Cooksey, Court, and Makau.

Economic decline and political uncertainty led to increased corruption. Though corruption has long been a fact of life in Kenya, the current magnitude of malfeasance by Moi and other senior members of his government—including Kenya's vice president, and the former head of the Central Bank of Kenya—is unprecedented. In addition to the usual scam of taking kickbacks from foreign and domestic investors, Moi and his colleagues, often in collaboration with Kenyans of Asian background, have circumvented foreign exchange regulations of the Central Bank,[25] chartered and then looted the deposits of a series of local banks,[26] imported foodstuffs through unauthorized channels to avoid customs duties, and simply "printed money" by using new banknotes for unauthorized expenditures (mostly patronage) without withdrawing the old. The amount stolen or misappropriated by these individuals in 1992 and the first half of 1993 alone is reliably estimated to be in the range of $300 to $500 million, which increased the money supply by more than 40 percent. The result was a doubling of consumer prices between January 1992 and June 1993 and the crash of the Kenyan shilling to less than half its value.[27] So great has been the level of "megacorruption" that some economists estimate that eliminating it would increase Kenya's annual rate of real economic growth by up to four percentage points.

One explanation for this megacorruption is pure greed on the part of a ruling elite that does not understand or care about the impact of its behavior on the Kenyan economy. Another, more nuanced explanation is the inflationary patronage costs of the Moi regime. As previously noted, presidential appointees enjoyed fairly long tenures under Kenyatta. Under Moi turnover in these positions has been far more rapid and unpredictable. The result is an incentive to loot: One should help oneself to the spoils of office while one has the opportunity, because there is no assurance of reward for professional performance over the long term. The rapid turnover in personnel has also increased the number of individuals who must be "bought" to keep the regime intact.

Not surprisingly, Moi's mismanagement of the economy and drive to monopolize power alienated large segments of the population. The most symbolic and catalytic point in this process came in the 1988 elections, which were rigged to guarantee victory for "loyal" candidates and to defeat those who were not. Departing from the established procedure of a single round of voting via secret ballot, Moi substituted a two-step process that used open-queue voting for the first phase. Widespread intimidation and fraud were reported for both stages. Voter turnout fell precipitously to only 24.6 percent of those eligible, the lowest in Kenya's history.

By the beginning of the 1990s, Kenya had nearly replicated the economic crisis that confronted Tanzania a decade earlier, and Moi's system of personal rule exhibited many of the downside features of Nyerere's closed and overcentralized system of political control. During the 1980s, the ideological differences that had distinguished the two countries blurred. Kenya and Tanzania converged in a shared process of decay, and both became subject to similar internal pressures for reform. Key elements within both countries began to demand fundamental changes in the way these systems were run. Both also came under external pressures from the international donor community, which insisted on change if economic assistance was to be continued.

The Era of Reform (1986 and 1992 to present)

Tanzania

Because Tanzania experienced economic crisis before Kenya, it was the first of the two to confront the necessity for reform. Tanzania was also one of the first African countries to be pressured by the international donor community to accept reform as a condition for further assistance. As early as 1979 and continuing through 1985, Tanzania struggled to put its economic house in order, engaging in protracted negotiations with the IFIs and bilateral donors over how and under what conditions it would embark on a process of stabilization and adjustment. As was typical of this period, both the Tanzanians and the IFIs tried to focus exclusively on changes in macroeconomic policy, leaving questions of political reform untouched. This was easier said than done. Nyerere himself knew that economic and political reform were linked, that the economic reforms demanded of Tanzania would reverse or partially reverse CCM's policies of socialism and self-reliance and thus alter the structure of state-society relations and the political system. He considered such demands an infringement on Tanzania's sovereignty. The IFIs required Tanzania to stimulate the rebirth of export agriculture by devaluing its currency and deregulating the marketing of agricultural commodities. Tanzania was also expected to reduce its huge budget deficits by curtailing social welfare expenditures and by eventually privatizing or liquidating money-losing state-owned corporations. Each of these demands, especially devaluation, was vigorously resisted by Nyerere and his senior colleagues in CCM. From 1981 through 1984, they sought to parry the IFI's demands with a package of partial reforms. Not surprisingly, this approach did not win support from the donors.

As the Tanzanian economy continued to fall, Nyerere and the party were challenged by a group of pragmatic economists who argued that stabilization and adjustment were the only options for recovery. Dubbed "the young Turks," this group included several Western-trained economists based at the University of Dar es Salaam, as well as key technocrats at the Bank of Tanzania and Ministry of Finance. They eventually carried the day by forcing an extended debate between those (including Nyerere) committed to the continued pursuit of socialism at any cost and a more pragmatic group within the party led by Ali Hassan Mwinyi, the CCM vice chairman and Tanzania's first vice president.

In 1985, after twenty-four years as the head of Tanzania's government, Julius Nyerere retired. He was succeeded by Mwinyi, a Zanzibari, who was more inclined than Nyerere to accept the conditions demanded by the donors. Within a year, Tanzania negotiated an agreement with the IFIs known as the Economic Recovery Program (ERP), which committed Tanzania to a comprehensive package of adjustment reforms, including the eventual devaluation of the Tanzanian shilling. Details of ERP and Tanzania's negotiations with the World Bank and the IMF are discussed by Benno Ndulu and Francis Mwega in Chapter 4 and by David Gordon in Chapter 8.

Now in its eighth year, Tanzania's structural adjustment program illustrates the potential and limitations of macroeconomic reform, as well as the fact that economic reform must be matched by reform of the political system. On the upside, per capita income in Tanzania has steadily increased for the first time since the early 1970s, and overall GDP growth is at its highest level in twenty-five years. As discussed by Michael Lofchie in Chapter 5, Tanzania's agricultural sector has bounced back after being strangulated by artificially high exchange rates, forced villagization, and excessive state intervention and mismanagement in the marketing of the country's agricultural products. The most notable sign of this turnaround is that supplies of basic foodstuffs (e.g., maize) and consumer goods are more plentiful now than in the late 1970s and early 1980s. With the recovery of its agricultural sector, Tanzania is also able to earn foreign exchange to pay for needed imports to sustain its economy.

After withholding nonproject assistance, also known as "quick-disbursing aid,"[28] for most of the first half of the 1980s, the IFIs and Tanzania's principal bilateral donors have returned to finance the recovery.

Donors now provide Tanzania with roughly $1.2 billion per year. As demonstrated in Tanzania and elsewhere in Africa (most notably in Ethiopia, Ghana, and Uganda), the international donor community will respond to Africa's needs, but only after countries needing assistance commit themselves to stabilization and adjustment reforms. The Tanzanian experience also provides a lesson, especially to its northern neighbor—the longer a country delays in accepting a comprehensive package of adjustment reforms, the longer it will wait for donor assistance.

Structural adjustment, however, has not been without cost. Public expenditures on social welfare services have declined in real terms, and the quality of these services has eroded. The failure of adjustment to provide for basic services, particularly education, has offended many Tanzanians, including members of the intelligentsia who, though highly critical of Nyerere's economic policies, applauded his commitment to providing basic social welfare services for all Tanzanians.

Economic liberalization, moreover, has clearly favored some Tanzanians over others. Just as the earlier pursuit of socialism dramatized that equity is purchased with a decrease in economic growth, so too has Tanzania's acceptance of adjustment demonstrated that growth is purchased with a decrease in equity. Although Tanzania's farmers have clearly benefited from liberalization, producers of export crops have probably benefited the most. Liberalization of exchange control has also favored those traders and private manufacturers who can best take advantage of the new rules—in this case, members of Tanzania's urban-based Asian community rather than would-be African entrepreneurs. Indeed, though a principal objective of socialism was to reduce the private sector, its net effect was to prevent the emergence of an African bourgeoisie while permitting Asian business, or at least a significant portion of it, to survive. Asians have now capitalized on the new system, or are perceived to have done so, to such an extent that they have become the targets of racial hostility by those who feel left behind.

Large-scale corruption by leading members of Tanzania's political elite—including, allegedly, President Mwinyi and his family—has also increased with economic liberalization. Though these scams have yet to reach the magnitude of those in Kenya, they are significant and have undermined public confidence in Mwinyi's leadership (Msemakweli 1993; *Family Mirror* 1993). As part of a more liberalized legal environment intended to encourage growth of the private sector, Tanzania also dropped its restrictive leadership code in 1991. The code, which had barred party leaders and civil servants from owning shares in companies, renting property, or engaging in private business, was relatively successful in limiting corruption to modest levels (and to the ranks of underpaid bureaucrats). It also achieved its primary objective of preventing senior party and government officials from using their positions to establish themselves in the private sector. These same officials now have few skills or capital to contribute to an economy where the private sector is to be the engine of development. As a result, some have used their positions to obtain collaboration with or kickbacks from bona fide entrepreneurs, most of whom are of Asian or foreign origin. In the process, CCM not only has retreated from its commitment to socialism but has lost its moral authority to govern. Once the vanguard of the Tanzanian political economy, the party has become an anachronism.

Last but not least, the resumption of quick-disbursing aid has maintained rather than reduced the country's dependency on donor assistance. Such assistance now provides roughly 29 percent of Tanzania's annual budget, up from 12 percent at the beginning of the Economic Recovery Program (ERB January 1991: 54). The resumption of nonproject assistance at such high levels may now be a disincentive rather than an incentive to pursue economic adjustment policies and reduce corruption. Indeed, at the July 1993 meeting of the Consultative Group for Tanzania, the donors warned the government that its economic performance, though improved, left much to be desired and that future assistance would depend on a renewed effort at reform (World Bank 1993b).[29]

It is in this context that demands for political accountability and multiparty democracy have arisen in Tanzania, not only by longtime critics of TANU and CCM but also by Julius Nyerere himself. After stepping down as president in 1985, Nyerere continued as chairman of CCM until August 1990, when he stepped aside, again for Ali Hassan Mwinyi. During this interregnum, Nyerere continued to oppose Mwinyi's acceptance of structural adjustment because it meant the end of socialism in Tanzania. To Nyerere, Mwinyi's retreat from socialism also meant the decline of CCM and the loss of the party's raison d'être.

Disenchanted with the course of CCM under Mwinyi and sensitive to the rapid changes occurring in Eastern Europe, Nyerere began in 1990 to publicly question the relevance of the one-party state he had designed, declaring that "one party is not Tanzania's ideology; having one party is not God's will. One party has its own limitations . . . it tends to go to sleep" (Nyerere 1990). What was important to Nyerere was not the one-party state per se but a ruling party committed to socialism. CCM had lost its ideological compass by becoming a catchall for every faction among the governing elite. It was in danger of standing for nothing. As he said two years later, "a CCM which has no ideology or understood position will simply become a *bas bazaar,* a junk market where all kinds of people who want office gather together. Who wants that kind of CCM?" (Nyerere 1992). It was better for the different factions to go their separate ways and form new parties, each with a clear alternative agenda for Tanzania's future.

Once Nyerere had uttered the unthinkable, others quickly followed in calling for multipartyism. During the balance of 1990 and the first half of

1991, several would-be leaders of an emergent opposition, most notably Chief Said Abdallah Fundikira and James Mapalala, formed the Steering Committee for a Multiparty System, which organized a series of public meetings to demand reform. Mwinyi initially resisted these demands but, given Nyerere's position, soon bowed to the inevitable. In February 1991 he appointed a presidential commission of inquiry headed by Chief Justice Francis Nyalali to determine whether Tanzania should become a multiparty democracy. The commission issued its report a year later recommending the change (Tanzania 1992c). Consistent with the existing practice of party supremacy, Nyalali's report was vetted first by the NEC and then at a special party conference held in February 1992. In a nuanced and lengthy address to the conference, Nyerere firmly endorsed the recommendation of the commission:

> The kind of democratic machinery in any country which works to the satisfaction of its people will depend upon a nation's culture, its geography, its history. . . . The most efficient system of democracy in any nation—in other words, the right machinery for that nation—will therefore vary from one country to another at any particular time. And even within one country the appropriate machinery will vary from time to time. . . . CCM is a party committed by its constitution to democracy. . . . It recognizes that in the political life of any country there is a time when the people's will is best expressed and peacefully realized through a political or nationalist movement, another time when a single party system is the most effective instrument, and yet another when a multiparty system is the most efficient. . . . The time has [now] come for democracy in our country to operate through a multiparty system (Nyerere 1992).

Nyerere then asked the party to instruct the National Assembly to amend the constitutions of both Tanzania and CCM to provide for a multiparty system. He stated further that in a multiparty system it would be inappropriate to require members of the armed forces to be members of CCM and that the armed forces and civil service would be required to serve the government of whichever party was elected by the people. In effect, state and party should be delinked (Nyerere 1992).

In May 1992 the National Assembly passed the 8th Constitutional Amendment Act, permitting a multiparty system in Tanzania, and the Political Parties Act, which defines the requirements new parties must meet to qualify for registration (McHenry 1992). In the months that followed, party flags were lowered from government buildings, and several parties began operating under the new legislation. By the end of 1993, twelve had registered, most of them based in Dar es Salaam. All of these fledgling organizations are fragile and/or underfinanced. Several are also split into factions or are the products of splits within preceding organizations (e.g., the Steering Committee for a Multiparty System). None poses a serious challenge to CCM.

By late 1993 only four of the new parties had established a viable organization and following outside of Dar es Salaam: the National Convention for Construction and Reform—Maguezi (NCCR-Maguezi), led by Maberere Marando; Chama cha Democrasia na Maendeleo (CHADEMA, the Party of Democracy and Development), headed by Edwin Mtei, a former head of the Central Bank of Tanzania; the Union for Multiparty Democracy (UMD), headed by Kassanga Tumbo; and the Civic United Front (CUF), headed by James Mapalala. Support for these parties, however, is either scattered or concentrated in a few regions of the country. The NCCR-Maguezi (Kiswahili for "change") is led by a relatively young generation of professionals and draws most of its strength from Dar es Salaam and the regions surrounding Lake Victoria in the far West. It also has some presence in the southern highlands around Iringa. CHADEMA is basically an economic reform party of the upper-middle-class establishment (to the extent that there is such a thing in Tanzania) and producers of export crops from wealthier regions who have long opposed the socialist policies of CCM. Not surprisingly, the party is strongest in the coffee-growing areas around Mount Kilimanjaro and in the southern highlands. The UMD is attempting to mobilize two of Tanzania's largest but politically inert ethnic groups, the Sukuma and Nyamwezi. The party also has strength in Dar es Salaam and in Bukoba, west of Lake Victoria. The CUF has considerable strength on Zanzibar.

The weakness of the opposition has not been lost on the leadership of the ruling party. Though initially resistant to political reform, Mwinyi and CCM leaders now embrace reform, knowing that in the short run their positions are secure. Mwinyi himself is barred by the Tanzanian constitution from seeking reelection to a third term in 1995. For these reasons, political liberalization and the emergence of opposition parties in Tanzania has been smoother and far less threatening to the incumbent elite than in Kenya and has been accompanied by a greater degree of openness and equanimity. Contributing to this environment is the fact that Tanzania's first multiparty parliamentary elections since before independence will not be held until 1995.[30] Because it is confident of retaining power, CCM now presents itself as the party of reform. Whether the party can return to its ideological roots, however, is unclear.

Another result of delinking the Tanzanian state from CCM has been the reemergence of the national legislature as a significant forum for the deliberation and making of public policy. After being emasculated for nearly three decades, the National Assembly has sprung to life and asserted its independence even though all of its members belong to CCM. Most notable in this regard has been the protracted debate throughout 1993 on the future of the United Republic following the announcement by Zanzibar in February that it was joining the Organization of Islamic Countries (OIC). The announcement, which violated Tanzania's constitution but was not criticized by Mwinyi, strengthened the case long made by many mainland politicians that the union did not serve the interests of the former Tanganyika. In August a group of fifty-five mainland legislators introduced a resolution in the National Assembly calling for the establishment of a separate Tanganyika government. Though the leadership of CCM was able to prevent what would have been a embarrassing vote in favor of the resolution, the party leadership did agree to the establishment of a commission to determine the modalities of a separate Tanganyikan government within a federal republic by 1995.[31] Such independence on the part of the National Assembly would have been unimaginable in the one-party era.

Economic and political liberalization in Tanzania have stimulated the rebirth of civil society. The reemergence of independent business and professional associations in the urban areas and the reestablishment of rural cooperative societies have demonstrated that once the heavy lid of state and party is lifted in Africa, citizens will organize to take advantage of the political space allowed for these activities. The emergence of community self-help development associations similar to Harambee organizations in Kenya during the Kenyatta era further shows that in rural Africa civil society is an important and immediate product of political reform. Though associational life in Tanzania remains less broad and deep than in Kenya, its rapid growth, coupled with the absence of ethnic cleavage, augurs well for the sustainability of reform.

The emergence of a free press is likewise leaving its mark on the political system. Since 1990 more than fifteen new publications in both English and Kiswahili have appeared, including an independent daily newspaper, the *Business Times,* a thoughtful weekly called *Express,* and a biweekly titled *Family Mirror.* For the first time since the early 1960s, Tanzanians have alternatives to the official media. These new publications have rapidly gained readers through their aggressive exposure of corruption in high places and their willingness to discuss government and party policies with a critical eye. The availability of alternative print media, however, is confined largely to Dar es Salaam; broadcasting remains a state monopoly.

In summary, political reform in Tanzania has been a relatively smooth process driven largely from within. Although donor pressure was significant in bringing about economic change, it was insignificant in opening up the political system save for the fact that political change was a logical consequence of economic adjustment in a country emerging from one-party socialism. Tanzania's move toward political reform has also been eased by the relative absence of political conflict based on ethnic and/or religious cleavage. Economic reform has been perceived as favoring some groups (e.g., Asians) over others, but political reform has not. Although politicians from both the mainland and Zanzibar have called for the dissolution of the United Republic, these calls are best viewed as demands to divide power, not as an ethnic confrontation. Whether the United Republic dissolves into its constituent parts or whether the interests of Tanganyika and Zanzibar are accommodated through a new federation or confederation, political reform will have facilitated an "amicable separation" between these competing geoethnic constituencies.

Kenya

Kenya has fallen into the pattern of economic and political decay that characterized Tanzania in the early 1980s, but its approach to reform has differed from that of its southern neighbor. Whereas Tanzania vigorously resisted economic reform but was subsequently flexible in accepting political change, Kenya initially embraced economic reform but resisted political liberalization. This resistance, however, has consistently undermined its efforts to pursue economic reform. If the Tanzanian experience demonstrates that political reform is the logical consequence of economic reform, the Kenyan experience demonstrates the converse: that without political reform, economic reform is unlikely to proceed.

As argued at the beginning of this chapter, Kenya's success during its first fifteen years of independence resulted from a combination of several structural factors, including the legacy of the colonial economy, the geographic pattern of ethnic cleavage, and the approach taken by the country's leadership, particularly Jomo Kenyatta, in dealing with these conditions. The same variables have shaped the decisions taken by President Daniel arap Moi over Kenya's second fifteen years of independence, but the results have been very different.

Kenya's economy slowed in the early 1980s but revived in the latter half of the decade following the adoption of a series of stabilization policies, most notably a slowing rise of social welfare expenditures. In contrast to Tanzania, Kenya was not required by the IFIs to undertake stabilization and adjustment as conditions for continued assistance. Rather, these policies were initiated by Kenyans from within (Kenya 1982). As a reward for its initiative, Kenya received substantial amounts of quick-disbursing aid to cover budget and balance-of-payments deficits. Despite policies that had led to the economic slowdown of the early 1980s, Kenya remained a darling in the eyes of the donor community. After fifteen years of steady growth, the slowdown was attributed largely to the world recession and second oil shock of 1979. Compared to Tanzania, Kenya had a robust economy, and the fact that Kenya *appeared* to embrace reform impressed the donors.

But, as noted by David Gordon (1992b), Kenya's pursuit of economic reform was more rhetorical than real. In negotiations with the IFIs and bilateral donors, Kenya invariably made commitments to reform, only to back down from their implementation. Budget and balance-of-payments deficits continued to mount during the second half of the 1980s and early

1990s. Public sector employment and public construction projects also grew, sustained in part by the donors. Though Kenya never suffered an economic crisis as severe as Tanzania's, its external debt rose as the country became more dependent on donor support. At the same time, agricultural production, especially of export crops (i.e., coffee), began to level off. By 1988 per capita growth in the rural areas turned negative. Kenya also resisted suggestions by the donor community to deregulate internal grain markets and privatize state-owned industries. By the end of 1990, if not before, Kenya's honeymoon with the donors had ended.

Increased political repression and the rigged elections of 1988 worsened Kenya's souring relations with the donors and led to external pressure for political reform. Once considered an island of political stability and economic success in a turbulent region, Kenya was now viewed as just another African state mired in a familiar pattern of decay. With the end of the Cold War and the collapse or decline of authoritarian regimes in Eastern Europe, Latin America, and Southeast Asia, Moi's Kenya was viewed as being out of step with the times. Kenya's strategic value, particularly to the United States, which had signed a military agreement with Kenya in 1979, was likewise discounted.[32]

Donor concern mounted in May 1990 following the detention of two former Kikuyu cabinet ministers, Kenneth Matiba and Charles Rubia, who had the temerity to publicly call for an end to the one-party state. In July riots broke out in Nairobi when the government shut down street vendors in the city. At least twenty-eight people were killed. The detentions and riots, along with the continued incarceration of other political prisoners, brought on investigations by international human rights groups, including Africa Watch and Amnesty International. Kenya's principal bilateral donors, especially the United States represented by its outspoken ambassador Smith Hempstone, Germany, and the Scandinavian countries, began to express their concerns both in public and in private.[33]

Notwithstanding these rising concerns in the donor community, the most significant demands for political reform in Kenya, as in Tanzania, came from within. Indeed, changing donor sentiment was as much a response to internal demands for reform as it was an articulation of their new post–Cold War emphasis on democratization and human rights. Internal demands for reform came initially from prominent clergy, who as early as 1986 and especially after the rigged elections of 1988 voiced their concern about human rights abuses and the decline of political freedoms. Members of the clergy, especially the NCCK, were particularly vocal. Similar demands were expressed by a contingent of young lawyers who took control of the Law Society of Kenya. Although the business community remained silent, fearing retribution by the state, a few of its members quietly helped finance several small publications that were to form the core of an independent press that critically examined the policies of the Moi regime. These publications, most notably *Finance,* the *Nairobi Law Monthly,* and later *Society* and the *Economic Review,* ultimately emboldened Kenya's major daily newspapers, particularly the *Daily Nation,* to report aggressively on declining conditions in Kenya and the need for reform.

Following the detentions of Matiba and Rubia in mid-1990, other veteran politicians, grown weary of Moi, echoed their call for the return to a multiparty system. Virtually all were Kikuyu politicians or leaders from ethnic groups that had constituted the original KANU alliance led by Kenyatta. In February 1991, Jaramogi Oginga Odinga, the political leader of the Luo and a onetime vice president under Kenyatta, launched the National Democratic Party, declaring that multiparty democracy offered the only hope for an end to corruption, economic mismanagement, and unaccountable government. In August Odinga joined with eight others, including the newly freed Matiba and Rubia, to form the Forum for the Restoration of Democracy (FORD).

Faced with a growing and vocal opposition he could no longer cow into silence, Moi appointed an internal review committee to examine KANU procedures. After public hearings, the committee recommended in June 1991 that expulsions from KANU cease and that the despised system of queue voting be abolished. Both the committee and Moi, however, made it clear that despite the legalization of opposition parties elsewhere in Africa and overseas, Kenya would remain a one-party state. Defending his rejection of multiparty politics, Moi repeatedly argued that the legalization of opposition parties would lead to tribal conflict and destroy national unity. At the same time, the president no doubt feared that a united opposition including the Kikuyu would reestablish the original KANU alliance and command a majority at the polls.

The final push for repeal of the constitutional ban on opposition parties came in the form of a warning from Kenya's bilateral donors at the November 1991 meeting in Paris of the Consultative Group (CG) for Kenya. Moi's continued resistance to economic and political reform, coupled with rising demands for both by respected Kenyans, had exhausted donor patience. Convinced that broad-based economic growth requires political reform, the donors established explicit political conditions for continued assistance, setting a precedent for the rest of Africa. The donors bluntly told Kenya's representatives that future aid levels—particularly quick-disbursing aid to cover budget and balance-of-payments deficits—would depend on the "early implementation of political reform," including "greater pluralism, the importance of the rule of law and respect for human rights, notably basic freedoms of expression and assembly, and . . . firm action to deal with issues of corruption." The donors made no further commitments of aid, stating that they would "review progress in these areas" in six months' time (World Bank 1991d). In the meantime, the donors suspended approximately $350 million in quick-disbursing assistance that had been planned for Kenya. Two weeks after the CG meeting, Moi announced that the constitutional ban on opposition parties would be repealed and that the next parliamentary elections, to be held no later than March 1993, would therefore be multiparty contests.

As discussed by Michael Chege in Chapter 2 and Goran Hyden in Chapter 3, Kenya's transition to a multiparty system has been a tortuous and confrontational process compared to Tanzania's. The greater importance of ethnicity and a more vociferous civil society has sharply divided Kenya between a coalition of ethnic and class interests that supports the continuation of the incumbent regime and a potential albeit fragmented coalition that does not.

In a cynical move to shore up his ethnic base, frighten the opposition, and lend credibility to his predictions that the legalization of opposition parties would plunge Kenya into tribal conflict, Moi and his government stood idly by as "ethnic clashes" of "mysterious origin" erupted in western Kenya in December 1991. By May 1992 these had spread to virtually all areas along the borders of the Rift Valley Province, where non-Kalenjin migrants had settled adjacent to traditional Kalenjin lands. The magnitude and breadth of these clashes, which have continued for more than two years and mainly victimized non-Kalenjins (especially Kikuyu), show that the government cares little about halting them—if in fact it is not directly promoting them, as many of the victims claim. By the end of October 1993, nearly two years after the clashes began, between 1,200 and 1,500 people had reportedly died, and between 255,000 and 300,000 had been displaced or left homeless (Africa Watch 1993: 56; UNDP 1993a: 3.6).[34] They have been intended to show the migrant communities, especially supporters of the opposition, that multiparty democracy has brought them only trouble and will continue to do so.

Ethnic tensions have also fragmented the opposition and largely explain its failure to defeat Moi in the presidential and parliamentary elections held on December 29, 1992, Kenya's first multiparty balloting in twenty-six years. The elections, in which Moi and KANU won only one-third of the vote but were nonetheless returned to power, demonstrated the extent to which Kenyan voters divided along ethnic lines. In both the presidential and parliamentary elections, support for KANU and each of the three main opposition parties—FORD-Asili, FORD-Kenya, and the Democratic Party—was highly concentrated in their respective ethnic heartlands. Most of Kenya's 47 administrative districts were won handily by one or the other of the four major parties; only 26 of the 188 parliamentary constituencies (14 percent) could be regarded as contested areas. Thus, although the 1992 elections can be termed "multiparty" from a nationwide perspective, they split the country between areas voting overwhelmingly for one party or another. Further examination of the geographic distribution

of the vote indicates that Moi and his colleagues in KANU received roughly the same percentage of the vote from the same regions that KADU had
in 1961 and 1963, whereas the opposition parties drew their support from
the same regions that had supported the original KANU alliance led by
Jomo Kenyatta (Barkan 1993: 96–97; Hornsby and Throup 1995).

Such divisive results are unlikely to promote a political culture of tol-
erance and accommodation on which a transition to democracy ultimately
depends. Indeed, the elections appear to have produced a stalemate
between a minority government that feels increasingly under siege and a
majority that has yet to establish a credible and united alternative to the
remnants of Moi's system of personal rule. This situation does not bode
well for a democratic transition; it is highly unstable, and has already
sparked outbreaks of civil unrest. Given this situation, neither economic or
political reform is likely to be sustainable over the long term. Moi and his
inner circle have been reluctant embrace either, because they correctly
believe that the main beneficiaries of both will be their opponents, particularly the Kikuyu. It is for this reason that donor pressure for reform has
been met by procrastination and halfway measures, even though a demonstrated commitment to reform will result in the resumption of quick-disbursing aid.

Despite Moi's footdragging, Kenya in 1994 is a far more open polity
than it was in 1991. The era of personal rule is over, but what will succeed
it remains unclear. Although the opposition holds 40 percent of the seats in
the National Assembly, President Moi refuses to bargain with its members
to broaden support for his programs and legitimize his rule. Kenya no
longer has any political detainees,[35] but the ethnic clashes continue and
hundreds of thousands remain homeless. The press is more vibrant than at
any time since independence, but is subject to continued harassment including the detention of editors critical of the regime, seizure of publications,
and vandalism of presses. The broadcast media remain a monopoly of the
regime.

Kenya's economic performance is also mixed as representatives from
the IMF and the World Bank shuttle in and out of the country to negotiate
the conditions under which aid will be resumed. At the end of 1993 Kenya
substantially devalued its currency by letting the value of the Kenyan
shilling be determined by the market. Virtually all remaining controls over
foreign exchange dealings pertaining to investment and overseas trade were
removed in May 1994. In the agricultural sector, the government has deregulated the marketing of both export crops and food grains, most important-
ly maize. The governor of the Central Bank was replaced, and the new
chief moved to reestablish order in the banking sector, which had been
shaken by a number of scandals involving his predecessor and other senior
members of the Moi regime. These moves have stimulated the production
of agricultural exports and renewed economic growth after three years of

stagnation and decline. However, the government's budget deficit remains unacceptably high resulting in a current inflation rate of approximately 60 percent. Corruption shows only limited signs of abatement and the privatization of parastatals has made little progress.

Kenya's progress toward political and economic reform is thus like the proverbial glass of water that is both "half empty" and "half full." This situation has posed a dilemma for international donors, who must decide whether to resume quick-disbursing assistance to Kenya or shut down their programs altogether. In an attempt to break the stalemate and persuade Moi's government to proceed with reform, the donors reconvened the CG in Paris in November 1993 after a lapse of two years.[36] After noting that significant economic and political adjustments had been made but that much remained unfinished, the donors stated that they would resume disbursement of approximately $170 million during the course of 1994 provided Kenya met a number of conditions. These included continued "progress in implementing the economic reform agenda as well as strong positive steps on human rights, governance and corruption" (World Bank 1993c)." The donors were particularly concerned about continued corruption and the ethnic clashes. They openly expressed skepticism as to whether Kenya could end both and still pursue economic adjustment, stating that "the agenda of actions yet to be taken is daunting." Although the Kenya government proclaimed the CG a success, the minister of finance acknowledged that it would be difficult for the government to follow through on its commitments.

Given the current political stalemate, it is unlikely that a breakthrough to complete reform, economic or political, will come any time soon. Rather, the stalemate will continue until the protagonists are sufficiently exhausted to compromise on new rules of the game that protect and respect the vital interests of all. For Moi and KANU must eventually accept rule by the majority; the opposition must respect the rights of the minorities in the KANU (i.e., the old KADU) alliance and refrain from witch-hunts of those responsible for the excesses of the Moi regime.[37]

BEYOND CAPITALISM VERSUS SOCIALISM

If Tanzania is an example of how, after a period of resistance, the pursuit of reform can rescue a country from an acute case of economic and political decay, Kenya is an example of how conditions can steadily deteriorate until reform is embraced. Despite its acknowledged flaws, most notably its failure to maintain adequate social welfare services for the rural poor, there is as yet no credible alternative to structural adjustment policies for reviving African economies (World Bank 1994). Put simply, one cannot repeal the laws of economics, as Tanzania attempted to do in the late 1970s and early 1980s and as Kenya has done in the early 1990s. Where the state interferes with markets to pursue redistributive policies that reduce inequality between classes, between rural and urban areas, and/or between rich and poor rural areas, economic growth is sure to slow. The question is not what will happen if such policies are pursued but to what extent they can be pursued while maintaining a consistent record of economic growth. Where the rate of economic growth falls below the rate of population growth, redistributive policies will have been pursued too far. In such cases, economic adjustment is necessary to avoid economic collapse.

The impact of political reform on economic growth is less certain, in part because it is more difficult and takes more time to implement than economic reform. Though there is as yet no hard evidence that political liberalization and democratization facilitate economic reform (Callaghy 1993), the record in Africa (if not elsewhere) clearly shows that without democratization, economic reform is unlikely to occur. Until the relationship between political and economic reform is better understood, it would be unwise to justify the former in terms of the contribution it can make to the latter. Rather, democracy is universally valued because it is the least onerous system of governance for the greatest proportion of citizens. This is particularly true in plural societies marked by ethnic diversity. Where the balance between majority rule and minority rights can be maintained, the governmental process may be slow, but the interests of all groups are most likely to be served.

The establishment of democratic rule in Africa, however, will require leaders of competing ethnic constituencies and other interests to be more tolerant and more willing to compromise than they have been during the first thirty years of independence. Until leaders recognize that they have more to gain by bargaining with their opponents than by seeking to destroy them, the prospects for a successful transition to democracy will be slim. Such recognition may be on the horizon, at least in those countries that have embarked on transitions to democratic rule. Whether exhausted by the past or simply aware that the world has changed, new leaders are emerging who realize that the modes of governance that dominated Africa for three decades do not work, and that it is time to seek new arrangements for political and economic development. To the extent that an increasing number of leaders now think about politics differently than their predecessors, the prospects for democracy in Africa have risen.

It must also be recognized that in the final analysis reform in Africa must be homegrown. Reform, particularly the establishment of new institutions to implement its various components, requires indigenous roots in local soil. The experiences of Kenya and Tanzania amply illustrate this point. Where the leadership embraces reform, even with serious doubts as in Tanzania, there is transformation. Where the leadership does not, as in

Kenya, progress is much slower. Given this reality, the role of the international donor community is limited. Donors can withhold aid until African leaders recognize the need for reform, but they should be under no illusion that conditionality, whether economic or political, will guarantee a commitment to reform. Conditionality only insures that donors do not waste their resources on regimes that are unlikely to improve economic performance or that have lost legitimacy. The principal beneficiaries of conditionality in this respect are the donors themselves. Conditionality also provides a useful pretext (and thus a measure of political cover) for those pressing for reform from within, especially if they are challengers to an incumbent regime or a minority faction within such. The donor community thus can play a facilitative role by supporting the internal debate on the need for reform. Conditionality, however, is no substitute for an indigenous commitment to reform, as the experiences of both Kenya and Tanzania attest.

The experiences of Kenya and Tanzania illustrate that there is a convergence of issues and process which comprise the development debate in sub-Saharan Africa. Although they pursued very different strategies of national development during their first two decades of independence, their experiences during the 1980s and early 1990s suggest that both countries' options for future development are fundamentally the same. This reality is the common theme of each of the chapters that follow.

NOTES

1. Programs of economic adjustment to arrest Africa's economic decline were proposed as far back as the mid-1970s and became the foundation of donor policy with the publication of the so-called "Berg Report" by the World Bank in 1979. See World Bank (1979) and subsequent publications by the Bank, especially *Sub-Saharan Africa: From Crisis to Sustainable Growth* (World Bank 1989a).

2. See statement by the bilateral donors on the "Meeting of the Consultative Group for Kenya" issued by the World Bank on November 26, 1991, and a similar statement by the Consultative Group for Malawi in May 1992, in which the donors announced the suspension of new aid for both countries. In a similar vein, the United States cut off assistance to Cameroon following fraudulent elections in September 1992 and to Nigeria following the annulment of presidential elections by the military regime of Ibrahim Babangida in June 1993.

3. For a recent example of this attitude, see the statement made by J. Brian Atwood, administrator of the United States Agency for International Development, at his confirmation hearings before the U.S. Senate Foreign Relations Committee, April 29, 1993, and repeated in a statement for the Voice of America's Africa service on May 31, 1993. In the latter, Atwood stated that U.S. assistance "is not an entitlement" nor "a welfare program to be wasted" on countries that do not accept reform. See also the remarks by George Moose, U.S. assistant secretary of state for African affairs, on the occasion of the 40th anniversary of the African-American Institute, May 19, 1993.

4. For a recent restatement of this argument see Berger (1992).

5. Nyerere wrote a conceptual essay on African socialism in 1962 and is reported to have been committed to some form of socialist development as early as the 1950s. See Nyerere (1962), Smith (1971: 59), and Pratt (1976: 63–89).

6. For the best reviews of the immediate pre- and postindependence period, readers should consult the following: For Kenya see Bienen (1974), Gertzel (1970), Leys (1974), and Rosberg and Nottingham (1966). For Tanzania see Bienen (1967), Cliffe (1967), Nyerere (1967a), Pratt (1976), and Tordoff (1967).

7. Originally colonized by Germany, Tanganyika came under British control after World War I under a League of Nations mandate. British rule continued after the formation of the United Nations. Though officially a UN trust territory, Tanganyika was ruled like any other British colony and incorporated into British East Africa.

8. If the President of the union came from the mainland, as was the case with Julius Nyerere, the president of Zanzibar would be the first vice president of Tanzania. When the president of the union comes from Zanzibar, as is the case with Ali Hassan Mwinyi, the president of Zanzibar is the second vice president of Tanzania.

9. The central government's control over Zanzibari foreign relations has never been total, as the islands have maintained their own separate accounts for foreign currency earned from tourism and international trade. From time to time, Zanzibar also made its own deals in respect to securing foreign assistance, establishing diplomatic relations, and joining international organizations.

10. In an effort to suppress the so-called Mau Mau nationalist insurgency in the early 1950s, the British colonial government banned the Kenya African Union and all nationwide political organizations until 1960. District-level organizations were permitted after 1957.

11. For a discussion of how Kenyatta wooed Moi to KANU, see Throup (1987b).

12. Europeans also settled in Tanzania beginning when the country was under German rule, but the settler community never numbered more than 30,000 and was far less influential than in Kenya.

13. Dispute over which of Kenya's ethnic groups were displaced in the former White Highlands remains an issue of Kenya's political life. See *Daily Nation* (May 26, 1993).

14. At the time of independence, Kenya accounted for 65 percent of the combined exports between the three countries. By 1978 the figure had climbed to 80 percent. Throughout the period, Kenya's balance-of-trade deficits outpaced Tanzania's.

15. See the terms of the agreement that established the East African Community in 1967.

16. Though subscribing to the rhetoric of African socialism, Kenya made an explicit commitment in 1965 to the perpetuation of a market economy (Kenya 1965).

17. For discussions of the period of divergent development in Kenya see Bienen (1974), Leys (1974), Kitching (1980), and Leonard (1991). For Tanzania see Boesen (1977), Hyden (1980), Cliffe and Saul (1972 and 1973), Coulson (1982), McHenry (1981), and Nyerere (1968). For comparative discussions of the two countries see Barkan (1984a) and Lofchie (1989).

18. The essay was named after the town in northern Tanzania where Nyerere delivered a highly publicized speech based on the essay. Nyerere subsequently supplemented the Declaration with a series of essays dealing with various aspects of socialist development, most notably "Education for Self-Reliance" and "Socialism and Rural Development." These and other essays on Tanzania's strategy for socialist development are reprinted in Nyerere (1968).

19. On average 48 percent of the incumbents seeking reelection lost.

20. At the time of Kenyatta's death in 1978, five of Kenya's eight provincial commissioners were Kikuyus.

21. One notable example is the formation of what have become known as *sungusungu* societies. These are local community organizations formed to maintain law and order because the state no longer provides basic police services. Civil society is also becoming rapidly organized in the urban areas and at the national level with the formation in 1992 and 1993 of national umbrella for NGOs, the Tanzanian Association of Non-Governmental Organizations (TANGO).

22. Kenya's rate of population growth has historically been estimated as higher than Tanzania's. In 1980, Kenya's annual rate of population growth was reported to be 3.7 percent, declining to 3.4 percent in 1990 as a result of significant increase in the practice of family planning. By contrast, Tanzania's growth rate has remained fairly steady at 2.8 percent throughout the 1980s (World Bank 1993a: 175, 325).

23. Kiswahili for "footsteps." After becoming president in 1978, Moi initially used the term to convey to Kenyans that he would follow in Kenyatta's footsteps. By the early 1980s the "footsteps" he referred to were his own.

24. Circumstantial evidence suggests that up to three groups plotted separate coups, all of them dominated by Kikuyu.

25. The most flagrant example is the Goldenberg scandal, which some have termed Kenya's "Watergate." In this scam the vice president and minister of finance, in collusion with the governor of the Central Bank of Kenya, authorized government payments of an estimated 1.2 billion shillings ($200 million at current exchange rates) to be paid as "compensation" for fictitious exports of gold and diamond jewelry—commodities Kenya produces in negligible amounts. For details, see Elderkin (1993).

26. Known as "political banks" because the principal beneficiaries have been members of the Kalenjin political elite, particularly Nicholas Biwott.

27. So great was the malfeasance on the part of the Central Bank of Kenya that the IMF insisted on an overhaul of senior bank personnel, including the supervisor of the foreign exchange department, the supervisor of the department that regulates local banks, and the head of the Bank itself. Bowing to these pressures, the head of the bank, Eric Kotut, was dismissed on July 23, 1993. As a "reward" for his service, Moi appointed Kotut to head the Kenya Tea Development Authority.

28. Nonproject assistance or quick-disbursing aid comprises financial disbursements made by the IFIs and bilateral donors to cover a country's budget and balance-of-payments deficits. Such assistance should not be confused with assistance, both financial and technical, to implement specific development projects, assistance to nongovernmental organizations, or disaster relief. Donors have increasingly withheld nonproject assistance pending economic reforms while continuing other forms of aid.

29. Since the early 1990s, the World Bank has been concerned that Tanzania has implemented "the easy" requirements of economic adjustment but has not moved far enough in respect to the privatization of parastatal organizations and other institutional changes. See World Bank (1991b).

30. Local government elections may be held a year earlier.

31. This compromise was partially brokered by Nyerere, who was outraged by Zanzibar's initial decision to join the OIC and Mwinyi's failure to block the move. Many observers believe that the compromise has sealed the fate of the union and that Tanzania will ultimately split into its original constituent states. Such a move, if enacted by 1995, will also effect the elections scheduled for that year. If a new Tanganyikan legislature is established in addition to or in lieu of the National Assembly, elections will need to be held for this body.

32. The base agreement, signed during the last year of the Carter administra-

tion, gave the United States access to Kenya's international airports in Nairobi and Mombasa for military aircraft and to the port of Mombasa for U.S. naval vessels. In return, Kenya received assistance to upgrade these facilities as well as periodic boatloads of American sailors as short-term tourists on the Kenyan coast.

33. For example, in a speech to the Rotary Club of Nairobi in May 1990, Hempstone publicly suggested that Kenya get "in front of the curve" in respect to political liberalization.

34. Documentation of the ethnic clashes has been continuous and extensive. See also the report of the parliamentary committee that investigated the first year of clashes (Kenya 1992b) and the reports by the National Council of Churches of Kenya (NCCK 1992) and the National Election Monitoring Unit (NEMU 1993b) based on observations by their field organizations in the clash areas. Extensive daily coverage of the clashes, including photographic evidence, can be found in the *Daily Nation* and the *Economic Review*.

35. Though individuals are no longer detained without charge, the state continues to temporarily jail its opponents by bringing frivolous charges of sedition that are subsequently dropped. Kenyan jails also house numerous individuals who were "convicted" for a variety of political offenses during the 1980s, when state repression was at its peak.

36. Although this was the first official meeting of the CG since November 1991 that included representatives of the Kenya government, several informal meetings of Kenya's principal donors had been held in the interim.

37. There are numerous precedents for such arrangements (e.g., the recent deals that ended repressive authoritarian regimes in Argentina, Chile, and Korea).

2

The Return of Multiparty Politics

Michael Chege

In a rare display of political unanimity, the single ruling parties in Kenya and Tanzania permitted the return to competitive multiparty politics in early 1992. This was perhaps the most significant political turning point in both countries since they opted for divergent development strategies in the mid-1960s. After three decades of self-rule, both countries arrived at nearly identical policies from radically different perspectives. In addition to pursuing different economic goals, the theory and practice of one-party rule in each country were dissimilar. This chapter compares the recent evolution in party politics in Kenya and Tanzania and attempts to explain the social and economic factors underlying the convergence in policies on political pluralism after many years of contradictory experimentation in national governance. It makes use of available empirical data as well as received theoretical insights on competitive politics and their relationship to development.

If one adds to the reintroduction of pluralistic politics the diminishing role of the state in the economies of Kenya and Tanzania and the adoption of International Monetary Fund (IMF) and World Bank–funded structural adjustment policies, it is immediately evident that ideological and policy differences between the two countries are at their lowest since the Arusha Declaration of 1967. Indeed, there has already been official discussion about reviving the East Africa Community, which collapsed in ideological acrimony and competing national ambitions in 1977. There is a growing rapport between Kenya's ruling party, the Kenya African National Union (KANU), and its Tanzania counterpart, Chama cha Mapinduzi (CCM), as well as increasing contact between the opposition movements from both countries. The widespread use of Kiswahili as the lingua franca in both Tanzania and Kenya has improved communication. In addition, an open and vigorous opposition press is now part of the political landscape in both states. A brisk trade flourishes across their common boundary.

These similarities and cross-border links, however, may be deceptive. Although political opposition in both Kenya and Tanzania is a manifest backlash against incumbent one-party government, the social interests and the political arguments informing the opposition differ substantially

47

between the two countries and are the product of the politics and economic heritage of the era of ideological divergence.

At the outset, there are differences in agenda. In Kenya the new political parties place strong emphasis on efficient economic management, respect for human rights, anticorruption policies, and the rule of law. For them, discontent with President Daniel arap Moi's leadership style of personal rule, his government's ethnic-oriented policies, and the patronage network of the regime are the top grievances. Critics portray the evident administrative incompetence and economic mismanagement associated with the KANU government in the 1980s as the result of a debauched political leadership ushered in by the president, particularly after the abortive 1982 coup. In Tanzania, by comparison, the opposition's political platform focuses on disenchantment with socialism, massive corruption and racketeering under party and bureaucratic institutions, and abuse of civil liberties, roughly in that order. Though never totally absolved of responsibility for the economic disaster in Tanzania, President Ali Hassan Mwinyi and his predecessor, Julius Nyerere, have earned less opprobrium from Tanzania's opposition than Moi has in Kenya. Corruption of political leadership in Tanzania is blamed primarily on social degeneracy resulting from a catastrophic economic experiment rather than on the destructive machinations of an individual leader. This is an inversion of the reasoning in Kenya. There has been no Tanzanian equivalent of the slogan "Moi Must Go," which has been the rallying cry of the disarticulated Kenyan opposition movement since 1991.

In addition to policy and strategy differences, each country's political opposition has distinct socioeconomic attributes. In Kenya, thanks to an earlier phase of robust capitalist development, political dissent cuts across a wider and better-endowed section of professional interest groups and has attracted more international attention than political opposition in Tanzania. Civic and professional associations behind popular agitation for multiparty democracy in Kenya display a strength and sophistication that is lacking in Tanzania. Yet these advantages of Kenya's democratic movement have been increasingly undermined by ethnic factionalism—another aspect of Kenya's ambiguous heritage—which is a problem of lesser magnitude in Tanzania, where religion is the more divisive issue.

To understand the strengths and weaknesses of the new movements of political pluralism in Kenya and Tanzania, we must extend our analysis to the political arguments and the social structure of the new opposition groups and their critics. That drama, however, is played against a background of discredited performance of one-party rule in Africa and around the world. To appreciate the relevance of East Africa to the contemporary debate on democratic pluralism and development, it is useful to review some basic notions on the social origins of liberal governance and their current application to Africa.

MULTIPARTY POLITICS IN AFRICA AND ITS CRITICS

Following Africa's disastrous economic performance in the 1980s, consensus has gradually emerged among African development specialists, donors, and academics that poor governance is the single most critical constraint to the regeneration of the continent's economies. In its landmark 1989 report, *Sub-Saharan Africa: From Crisis to Sustainable Growth,* the World Bank for the first time remarked that "Africa needs not just less but better government and . . . political renewal," which could be achieved "by strengthening accountability, encouraging public debate, and by nurturing a free press" (World Bank 1989a: 5–6). In the following year, the governments of the United States, Britain, Canada, France, the Scandinavian countries, Germany, and the European Community nations announced that good governance and respect for human rights would henceforth be criteria of eligibility for development aid in Africa.

The donors were not uniformly committed to making democratic rule a condition for assistance and thus deliberately avoided making a precise definition of what constitutes legitimate and accountable governance. That task, however, was soon taken up by the advocates of democratic rule across the continent. Most sub-Saharan countries experienced renewed popular demand for the reintroduction of multiparty politics, followed by competitive elections and strict observation of the rule of law. Quite apart from ignoring the fact that rapid economic development has been known to occur under the guidance of politically authoritarian states (e.g., in Chile, South Korea, Taiwan, and Singapore), the option of multiparty government generally skirted the age-old debate on the socioeconomic conditions that make for sustained governance based on constitutional democracy.

Reinhard Bendix has traced the secular origins of government based on the mandate of people (as opposed to the divine right of kings) to post-Renaissance European "intellectual elites [who] formulated ideas in conscious response to what they had learned from abroad" (Bendix 1978: 10). The diffusion of the concept was accelerated by the rise of new independent urban communities, the printing press, and faster modes of communication. Above all, the transition to popularly sanctioned governance owed much to new economic elites who had acquired a means of existence independent of the old autocratic order; these went hand in hand with the rise of commercial activities, the division of labor, and early industrialization.

The role of educated and propertied classes in propagating democratic rule has been discussed with varying conclusions in the developed countries and the Third World. Simplifying the causal relationship between industrial capitalism and the modern European liberal state, Karl Marx contended that the latter—that is "bourgeois democracy"—was the ideological smokescreen legitimizing both the capitalist class's stranglehold over the means of production and the exploitation of the working class. Though acknowledging the superiority of modern democracy to earlier forms of governance, Marxist thinking holds that "bourgeois democracy" will be superseded by working-class political parties that would inaugurate a millennium of socialism and conflict-free classless society. It took Barrington Moore to specify that modern democracy arose not merely from the political hegemony of industrial capitalists as such, but rather out of violent resistance by the new urban commercial classes to the autocratic inclinations of traditionalist landed classes and, most important, out of liberal capitalist triumph over conservative peasant communities. On the whole, Moore was pessimistic about the capacity and inclination of the working class to usher in a democracy on its own. In his epigrammatic pronunciation following detailed comparative discussion of the fate of democracy in Britain, France, China, Japan, India, and the United States: "No bourgeois, no democracy" (Moore 1966: 418).

The positive statistical correlation between continuously functioning multiparty democracy and high levels of economic development was established by Seymour Martin Lipset, who drew from classical sources and substantial cross-national data (Lipset 1960: 27–63). Despite subsequent empirical research confirming this relationship, there remains substantial disagreement on the nature of the causal relationship between democracy and economic development. Notwithstanding the findings of Bendix, Marx, and Moore, three scholars working in Latin American countries recently concluded that capitalism strengthened democracy not by producing a modernizing bourgeoisie but rather by empowering the working classes (and sometimes the educated middle class) to oppose conservative landed classes, who appear to be the perennial enemies of popular government (Rueschmeyer, Stephen, and Stephen 1992). The role of the peasants in this process is at best ambiguous. In a highly informed and engaging analysis of reactionary arguments against the extension of universal adult franchise and the growth of the welfare state, Albert Hirschman found many fascinating cross-cultural similarities between the ideas of conservative antidemocracy and antiwelfare intellectuals and political activists, like those traditionalist landed classes (Hirschman 1991).

Despite renewed interest in liberal democracy in Africa, no studies have been done on the social basis of support for an opposition to political pluralism. For one, it is African incumbent autocrats, rather than agrarian aristocrats, who have resisted democracy the most. Comparisons from elsewhere, however, have considerable potential for enhancing our understanding of the struggle for multiparty democracy in Kenya and Tanzania and its outcomes at the current early stages. But it will also be necessary to qualify some of them and draw on other explanations to unravel the complicated political transitions the two countries have undertaken since independence.

A NEW BEGINNING IN MULTIPARTY POLITICS

Both Tanzania and Kenya came to independence (in 1961 and 1963, respectively) under multiparty constitutions. Tanzania broke earlier with that tradition and legislated in favor of one-party participatory government in 1965. The Tanganyika African National Union (TANU), its ruling party until 1977, gradually extended its control over critical sectors of civil society—the press, trade unions, student groups, and women's organizations—and was designated by Tanzania's constitution as the supreme organ in the land. Chama cha Mapinduzi formed by the merger between TANU and the Afro-Shirazi Party of Zanzibar in 1977, intensified the policy of party supremacy. Kenya, by contrast, grudgingly tolerated an opposition party, the Kenya Peoples Union (KPU), between 1966 and 1969, then outlawed it. The Kenyan government did not formally ban organized political opposition until June 1982, though it maintained a tradition of direct and indirect intimidation of constitutional dissent. Until Daniel arap Moi came into power in 1978, therefore, party politics in the two states differed substantially.

John J. Okumu and Frank Holmquist (1984) have compared TANU under Nyerere with KANU under Kenyatta. Whereas the former was a strong governing party that paralleled virtually every institution of the state, the latter was a weak coalition of ethnic leaders. Two important changes thereafter call for comment. By the late 1980s Tanzania' ruling party (now CCM) had degenerated into lethargy because of its incapacity to resolve the country's growing economic crisis. Public cynicism against the party was fueled by increasing corruption and lack of internal accountability to a broad party membership. In Kenya, meanwhile, Moi showed an increasing determination to transform KANU into a monolithic national organization like its Tanzanian counterpart, seeking to exert control over the national trade union confederation, COTU (Central Organisation of Trades Unions), the national women's organization, Maendeleo wa Wanawake (Women for Development), university student unions, youth organizations, professional associations, and other elements of civil society. Although Jennifer Widner (1992) has referred to this phenomenon as "the rise of the party state," the fact is that, unlike TANU/CCM, Kenya's ruling party represented little in the way of ideological or organizational innovation. These efforts in restructuring KANU, and the bureaucratic incompetence and corruption they were designed to cover, provided political ammunition to the nascent Kenyan opposition movement of the 1990s. The determination of the anti-KANU forces to overturn the process before the party could exert complete control explained the ruling party's unalloyed animosity toward its opponents.

Addressing a public rally in Nairobi on October 10, 1991, a day set aside to commemorate his accession to the Kenyan presidency, Moi made a scathing attack on the growing campaign against his single-party regime and indicated that he was likely to be in power for the next twenty years (*Daily Nation,* October 11, 1991). KANU at the time was at its most belligerent, having denied the broad-based opposition coalition—the Forum for the Restoration of Democracy (FORD)—permission to hold a political rally at Nairobi's historic Kamukunji Stadium.[1] Despite repeated government directives invalidating all opposition meetings, FORD nevertheless proceeded with plans for a peaceful political rally at Kamukunji on November 16, 1991. That morning Kenyan police arrested the FORD leaders who were scheduled to address the meeting and dispersed their supporters with truncheons and tear gas.

This was nearly a repeat performance of the gruesome "Saba Saba" events of July 7, 1990, when an estimated twenty-eight prodemocracy demonstrators in Nairobi and Central Kenya were shot dead. The victims were protesting the official ban of an opposition rally and the arrest of three leading opposition figures—Kenneth Matiba, Charles Rubia, and Raila Odinga. Both propertied establishment figures and former ministers, Matiba and Rubia had carried the banner of opposition to one-party rule during the first half of 1990. The government quashed their effort and detained them without trial for nearly a year. The assassination of Kenya's popular foreign minister, Robert Ouko, earlier in the year and the attempted government cover-up of the affair also fueled the opposition to Moi.

The events of July 1990 and November 1991 provoked vocal protests from Western governments—led by the United States, Germany, and the Scandinavian countries—and thinly veiled threats that external development aid to Kenya might be withheld pending domestic political liberalization and a crackdown on official corruption. Ten days after the November 16 arrests, the Consultative Group (CG) for Kenya—comprising the World Bank, the United States, all countries of the European Community, Sweden, Switzerland, Canada, and Japan—met the Kenyan government delegation in Paris to discuss extended development funding and unanimously postponed further aid pledges to Kenya until the government improved its "social and economic record" (World Bank 1991d). These were code words for accountable and honest government with toleration for opposing views and institutions.

Within ten days of the CG meeting, KANU's supreme policy organ, the Governing Council, met and ate humble pie at Moi's urging: It unanimously decided to amend the national constitution to allow the formation of the opposition parties it had sworn never to legalize. This was a swift about-face in policy, considering that President Moi had repeatedly argued that multiparty politics would induce ethnic warfare and break the country asunder. The announcement set the stage for Kenya's first multiparty parliamentary elections since 1966 and the first-ever direct election of Kenya's president. The elections, which Moi later called for December 1992, became the focus of Kenyan politics throughout the following year.

Changes followed rapidly. On December 30, FORD was registered as Kenya's first opposition party since 1969. It looked to the Kikuyu, Luo, and Luhya communities for its primary support. The first two groups had formed the core of the original KANU alliance established by Kenyatta before its merger with the Kenya African Democratic Union (KADU) in 1964. The Luhya had supported KADU and had been shortchanged by Moi. A second major opposition party—the Democratic Party (DP), led by the former vice president and minister of finance Mwai Kibaki—was registered in February 1992. It drew its support primarily from the Kikuyu political and business establishment and from the relatively prosperous northern Kikuyu, Embu, and Meru farmers who grew coffee and tea in the districts around Mount Kenya.[2] Several smaller groups also joined the fray. Three traumatic months after Moi's pronouncements, Kenya became a multiparty state, the result of dual pressures from an increasingly assertive local opposition and the donor community. At this stage, it is important to note that public outrage at the Ouko assassination, rampant corruption, human rights abuses, and the shrinking domain of individual liberties played a much greater role in galvanizing domestic and external opposition to Moi than did economic mismanagement, serious as it was.

The return to multiparty politics in Tanzania was, and continues to be, less politically acrimonious than in Kenya. Confronted by weaker political opponents and more secure in its power, the CCM never dug in its heels in the manner that the politically emaciated KANU did. Its strategy was to play for time while rejuvenating its internal strength and using the laws and threats to prevent the opposition from acquiring substantial mass appeal.

In February 1990, Chief Said Abdallah Fundikira joined nine other Tanzanians in announcing the formation of the Steering Committee for a Multiparty System, with the aim of reintroducing multiparty politics through constitutional amendments. Fundikira was independent Tanzania's first minister of justice and had resigned from the cabinet in 1963 to protest the imminent legislation introducing a one-party state. He was the hereditary chief of Unyanyembe among the Nyamwezi of central Tanzania, who (together with the allied Sukuma) constituted the largest ethnic group in the country. In this respect he bore an uncanny resemblance to the Kenyan opposition figures of the period—the Luo leader Oginga Odinga and the Kikuyu politicians Kenneth Matiba and Mwai Kibaki, who represented the two most significant ethnic groups in Kenya. Still, ethnic identity was of less political consequence in Tanzania than it was in Kenya.

In the same month, Tanzanian opposition forces received succor from a totally unexpected quarter. On the eve of his retirement as CCM chairman, Julius Nyerere—the architect of Tanzanian socialism and the one-party state—announced that one-party rule in Africa was not divinely ordained and that CCM was no longer as popular as it once was. He even went so far as to say that a "multiparty system could be desirable if only to overcome problems related to complacency in a single-party system" (Nyerere 1990). Against the international background of collapsing socialist regimes in Eastern Europe, these developments put the government of Ali Hassan Mwinyi squarely on the defensive.

In February 1991 the Tanzanian government announcement a broad-based constitutional commission under the leadership of Chief Justice Francis Nyalali to review the one-party system. Apart from hearing local testimony, the commission was expected to study the working of competitive party politics in the United Kingdom and the United States. The Western democracies at last had something to offer Tanzania by way of political experience—something denied explicitly by Nyerere's 1965 policy paper on one-party rule. The commission issued a full report with recommendations in 1992. The document revealed that a surprising 77 percent of the Tanzanians interviewed preferred the continuation of single-party rule; only 21 percent spoke in favor of political pluralism (Tanzania 1992c). Opposition to one-party government was highest in Zanzibar, at 43 percent.

Despite these findings, few experts on the country doubted that the commission would opt for political pluralism. While the country waited for the report, a shaken CCM began the process of internal renovation in anticipation of future opposition. With a membership of only 2 million among Tanzania's 27 million people, CCM began a vigorous recruitment and fund-raising campaign. The apparatchiks at party headquarters were introduced to the use of computers in a modernizing gesture. Like KANU, CCM argued that it was the only party that could hold the country together. Both parties, imitating conservatives elsewhere in the world, invoked what Hirschman (1991: 81–132) calls the jeopardy thesis—the argument that democratic reform would ruin years of accumulated national political cohesion.

This claim, however, appeared increasingly hollow against critical reporting from new independent opposition newspapers like the English periodical *Family Mirror* and the Kiwahili tabloid *Watu* (People). This press countered the perpetually one-sided reporting of the state-owned print and electronic media, exposing popular resentment of corruption and abuse of power within CCM. In cities such as Dar es Salaam and Arusha, impromptu opposition meetings were held without official permission as required by law, and unprecedented criticism of the state was expressed for the first time since the 1960s.

Despite strong official misgivings, the elbow room of the political opposition in Tanzania increased with time. In June 1991 the Steering Committee for a Multiparty System held a seminar on democratic reform in

Dar es Salaam that was attended by 3,000 delegates, with near-equal representation from the country's twenty-five regions. It issued a call for a national constituent assembly and demanded a national referendum on multiparty politics. In November 1991, to the chagrin of the government, human rights activist and committee member James Mapalala launched a new opposition party, Chama cha Wananchi (People's Party), an outgrowth of his older civil rights movement. It was promptly refused registration. There were more unlicensed opposition rallies and demonstrations in Dar es Salaam.

In January 1992, the 117-member National Executive Committee of the ruling party came out with a statement in support of political pluralism in Tanzania. The report by Justice Nyalali's commission was not yet available, but CCM thought the commission's preliminary findings sufficient to inform its epochal decision. As in Kenya, it was now up to the party national conference and National Assembly to accede to the necessary legislation—a mere formality. For all practical purposes, Tanzania had become a multiparty state once again after twenty-nine years of all-embracing one-party rule.

Although donor pressure played a less significant role in this political transition than it did in Kenya, it was nonetheless a significant factor. According to one source, "Tanzania's slow-paced movement towards political liberalization has coincided with threats of aid withdrawals by donor countries if political reforms were not implemented" (*African Analysis,* January 24, 1992). Sweden, Tanzania's principal development-aid benefactor over the years, had reduced its financial contribution to the country by $10 million in 1991 to protest the corruption and inadequate accountability of the civil service (Sorokin 1992). For his part, Chief Fundikira made a well-publicized visit in August 1991 to groups based in the United States and the United Kingdom that favored democratic movements in Africa. There he met Oscar Kambona, the onetime secretary general of TANU who had fled to exile in London in 1968.

It is vital to note that, in marked contrast to their attitude toward Kenya, the donors were more concerned with rampant corruption and mismanagement of development funds in Tanzania than they were with the country's civil liberties record or progress toward democratic rule. As one diplomat remarked: "On human and political rights, Tanzania attracts little opprobrium, but on management of the economy, it is a disaster" (*The Herald,* December 12, 1991). This observation coincided with the emphasis on economic reform by the Tanzanian opposition, as opposed to the antiauthoritarian trend of their Kenyan counterparts. This difference is attributable to the character and relative strength of the social forces behind the political opposition in the two countries, a reflection of the social undercurrents and political arguments that were in gestation in the years of the great ideological divide between Kenya and Tanzania.

SOCIAL FORCES BEHIND OPPOSITION POLITICS

The wave of popular demonstrations in favor of democratic pluralism that swept Africa from 1989 onward is now euphemistically called the "second independence." In anticipation of a liberating socialist—rather than democratic—second independence, Frantz Fanon had predicted in 1961 that the vanguard role in this movement would be played by an alliance of the peasantry and poor slum dwellers composed of the unemployed floating urban population (Fanon 1967). Fanon saw the working class and the African bourgeoisie as traitorous and reactionary. However, in both Kenya and Tanzania—more so in Kenya—the social groups that spearheaded the new opposition movements were predominantly urban and middle class, and their notions of liberal democracy were essentially Western. Such an observation is consonant with the remarks by Bendix and others on the social origins of democratic agitation in other contexts. And contrary to Rueschmeyer and his colleagues, the African working class as such played no significant role in that transition. Though African unionized labor fought as a fraternity of workers for better employment conditions and independence from party control, it tended to vote on ethnic lines outside the workplace. It is true that the middle classes, having assumed leadership of the opposition parties, subsequently drew mass support from the urban workers and the peasantry. But as in other, non-African situations, an independent, propertied, urban-based intelligentsia played a critical role in galvanizing popular support against domestic tyranny. Such a class was in turn the product of a robust and expanding market economy that provided diverse, independent economic opportunities outside the formal state sector. As comparison of Kenya and Tanzania readily shows, increased linkages with the outside intellectual, commercial, and cultural world bring notable political benefits.

Kenya

Given its economic record, Kenya stood a better chance of producing a more variegated and independent civil society—one that could draw on external connections to reinforce its domestic efforts—than did Tanzania. However, it is just as important to note that the agents of political despotism were drawn from the same urban and professional middle classes and external allies. The reason behind these cleavages is to be found in plain opportunism, misguided idealism, ethnic loyalties, and other factors that social scientists and historians have debated at length in tracing the origins of widespread support for dictatorships and totalitarianism (Moore 1978: 398–420).

The attempted coup of August 1982 in Kenya demonstrated both the extent and the limits of violent internal opposition to the authoritarian bent the Moi government had taken. So did the left-wing underground Mwakenya movement, which now claims to be Kenya's first opposition movement (*Africa Events,* February 1992: 30–31). Both were contained by the state by force of arms, which cost Kenya many innocent lives and included torture and brutal incarceration after formal show trials. In a fit of panic, the government went overboard and began systematic persecution of all dissent, no matter how well-intentioned and constitutionally grounded it was. The genesis of mass resistance to despotism, however, is actually to be traced to, among other places, the Kenyan Christian church, so often maligned by the Kenya left—once it became clear after 1982 that any forum of independent critical thought was a sitting target for a government that demanded total obedience and compliance with its policies, however unsavory they were. Nonetheless, the church spoke out as early as 1985 against the elimination of the secret ballot in primary elections and its replacement by open queue voting. For this it earned the wrath of KANU and running accusations that it was a subversive movement dancing to the tunes of its external masters. From then on, sections of the Christian church repeatedly spoke out forcefully against corruption, administrative incompetence, injustice, disregard for the rule of law, nepotism, and ethnic favoritism which were the trademarks of the Moi government. Although criticism was voiced by Catholic bishops and the Presbyterian Church of East Africa, the most vocal voices of dissent came from the local Anglican Church—the Church of the Province of Kenya (CPK). Nearly all of these criticisms were documented by *Beyond* magazine, the publicity organ of the Protestant National Council of Churches of Kenya (NCCK). In a special issue on the parliamentary elections of February 1988 (*Beyond,* March 1988), the magazine detailed widespread cases of rigging, bribery, intimidation, and coercion.[3] It provided the most damaging proof yet that the clergy had not been crying wolf.

The political attitudes of the churches were by no means monolithic. The Catholic bishops, for instance, confined themselves to general but critical and hard-hitting "pastoral letters" warning in 1991 against the emergence of a Latin American–style *caudillo* dictatorship, complete with torture and death squads. Another candid pastoral letter in April 1992 informed Moi that he was extremely unpopular and that the public had lost faith in him. There were also many outspoken and activist Catholic priests. The new fundamentalist Christian sects either backed the government or remained indifferent. In general, forthright and independent intellectual-clerics demanded the right of Kenyans to change government through electoral choice. Foremost among these were bishops Henry Okullu of the CPK Maseno Diocese, the late Alexander Muge of Eldoret, and David Gitari of

Mount Kenya East CPK Diocese. They did not, however, have the unanimous support of their church hierarchy, which actually shunned confrontation with the state.

It was the unusually independent-minded and courageous Reverend Timothy Njoya of the Presbyterian Church of East Africa who broke the ice in his New Year sermon of January 1990 by calling on African one-party regimes to beware the fate of the collapsing dictatorships of Eastern Europe and adopt multiparty democracy before it was too late. KANU condemned him roundly. In April of the same year, Bishop Okullu demanded specific constitutional changes to limit the tenure of the presidency to ten years and to permit the existence of opposition parties. The battle had by now been joined, with the ruling party hurling threats and insults rather than reasoned responses at its critics.

As Kenyans flocked to church services presided over by opposition clerics, the Law Society of Kenya (LSK)—to be precise, the critical, strict-constitutionalist wing of it—joined the fray in defense of individual liberties and political pluralism. The severely contested LSK elections of 1990 symbolized the divide between this group and a category of well-heeled progovernment lawyers who supported the status quo and argued that practicing attorneys had no business in politics. (Actually these differences were evident as early as 1986, when then LSK chairman G.B.M. Kariuki declared queue voting unconstitutional and undemocratic. He had been attacked not just by the government but also by the pro-KANU legal lobby.) The LSK activists took umbrage at new government regulations barring lawyers from litigation in land cases and requiring them to apply for commercial licenses in order to practice, and they resented consistent KANU attacks on their professional integrity.

At his inaugural dinner as the new LSK chairman in March 1991, Paul Muite frayed the feathers of the government by calling for the registration of the abortive opposition party—the National Democratic Party led by Jaramogi Oginga Odinga. In the previous year Muite had flown to the United States on behalf of Kenyan human rights attorney Gibson Kamau Kuria to collect the Robert F. Kennedy Human Rights Memorial Award, which Kuria had earned for his principled and single-minded defense of civil rights of political prisoners. The Kenya government had detained him without trial for seven months in 1987, earning itself more international notoriety in the process. From 1990 onward the prodemocracy lawyers within the LSK took up human rights cases, defended victims of political persecution, and insisted relentlessly on an independent judiciary. By the very act of defending individual rights and the rule of law, these lawyers made common cause with political leaders courageous enough to demand the right of constitutional opposition. The massed ranks of the pro-opposition urban crowd took every opportunity to show the flag in these highly visible political trials. The most dramatic of them was the year-long sedition trial (June 1990–July 1991) of George Anyona (a former legislator and prominent opposition figure since the 1970s), the academics Ngotho Kariuki and Edward Oyugi, and the politician J. Kathangu.[4]

The undercurrents of political opposition that characterized the legal profession also existed in fields such as architecture, the civil service, land use and planning, education, banking, construction, medicine, and the management of parastatals—in other words, in practically every occupation where objective performance standards and regulations had been thrown overboard in the breakneck accumulation of individual wealth by the ruling elite and the newfangled policies of "tribal balance," with its package of favors for the Kalenjin and other "neglected" ethnic groups. It became abundantly evident in the 1980s that tribal balance was a code word for extending patronage to unqualified Kalenjin in public service and state-owned corporations such as the Posts and Telecommunications, Kenya Power and Lighting, and the National Cereals and Produce Board. Tribal balance also officially sanctioned extensive rent-seeking activities through irregular imports, contracts, and illicit sale of public land.

One of the early victims of this perverse economic syndrome was the African business class, whose origins and historical trajectory were at the heart of the "Kenya Debate" on African capitalism in the 1980s.[5] The emasculation of the mainly Kikuyu African business class was an integral part of this strategy. As David W. Throup remarks, one objective of the Moi government was "to destroy Kikuyu hegemony and to dismantle the economic foundations of the Kenyatta state" by denying the ascendant capitalist class any state patronage, politically squeezing them out of business (Throup 1987b: 57–84). This policy was also applied to the export crop agricultural industry—also centered in the Central Bank of Kenya—where the Kenya (Coffee) Planters Cooperative Union (KPCU), grain marketing, the Kenya Tea Development Authority (KTDA), and the Kenya milk industry fell victim to official ethnic patronage, graft, and perennial mismanagement. The commercial, financial, and agricultural world that underpinned rapid growth in the Kenyatta days had finally been turned upside down.

As businessmen in good standing (and former Moi cabinet ministers), Kenneth Matiba and Charles Rubia were as concerned with the return to legal, pluralistic, and constitutional governance of the country as they were with the revival of efficiency, merit, and technocratic norms in national economic management.[6] From April to July 1990 they led a popular campaign on this platform and demanded the right to hold an open meeting to explain their cause on July 7, 1990. The attempt to link their efforts with Oginga Odinga (himself a businessman) and his son Raila Odinga led to official panic, and the unceremonious detention of Matiba, Raila Odinga, Rubia, and the lawyers—John Khaminwa, Gitobu Imanyara, Paul Muite, and others—who supported them. The stage was thus set for the Saba Saba[7] antiregime demonstrations in Nairobi and central Kenya, resulting in nearly thirty deaths and widespread destruction of property as police and the para-military General Services Unit quelled the uprising.

By mid-1990 political opposition in Kenya was a confluence of diverse social forces united in their opposition to personal and arbitrary state power and their strong commitment to the rule of law that would restore the integrity of public institutions in Kenya. Besides the clergy and profession-al classes discussed above, the opposition included journalists such as Gitobu Imanyara of *Nairobi Law Monthly,* Njehu Gatabaki of *Finance,* and Pius Nyamora of *Society,* principled academics such as Anyang Nyong'o, renowned environmentalists such as Wangari Mathai, gender-issues inter-est groups, and ethically committed professional opposition figures such as Oginga Odinga, George Anyona, Masinde Muliro, and Martin Shikuku. It could now also count on dejected businesspeople, dissatisfied members of the middle class save those from "neglected" groups, and the cash crop pro-ducers of central Kenya.

This broad coalition, which coalesced into FORD, required no effort to tap the groundswell of mass discontent against a regime that lacked the political wherewithal to stimulate business confidence and attract addition-al domestic or foreign investment but which nonetheless spent heavily; that practiced ethnic favoritism in schools and job allocation; that was marked by corruption and professional incompetence; and that had created an infla-tionary economy run on perpetual public sector deficits and profligate money supply, causing great economic pain. These grievances were con-flated with popular outrage against the highly patronizing authoritarian style of the Moi government and its principal supporters. An estimated 500,000 people therefore turned up at FORD's founding rally at Kamukunji on January 18, 1992. The trail had been blazed for the other opposition par-ties to follow.

It would be impossible to recount the story of the ascendancy of the opposition in Kenya without mentioning the indirect boost it received from external sources, principally because of Kenya's comparatively open inter-national economic and social posture. There were an estimated 160 foreign correspondents (including CNN) in Nairobi, and some of them provided the rest of the world with candid pictures of the cruel and sure fate that awaited opposition figures in Kenya. Indeed, the foreign press conference room at Chester House in Nairobi increasingly became the only venue available for opposition public announcements. Critical information filtered back to Europe and the United States via tourist traffic and business travel and pro-vided the political canon fodder for human rights groups and political lob-bies against U.S. and European policies toward Kenya. The U.S. ambas-sador, Smith Hempstone, himself a young correspondent in Kenya during the 1960s, took the offensive against continued abuse of human rights and repression of dissident opinion. Sections of European press and diplomatic pressure worked to the same effect in Holland, Scandinavia, Canada, Britain, and Germany. By the time the donors' Consultative Group on Kenya met in Paris in mid-November 1991, several diplomats had already hinted that extended aid to Kenya would be conditional upon political liberalization. This, as we have seen, pulled the fangs from the government's intransigence and halted its intolerance of critical opinion, if only for a while.

Having been born after a painful struggle and with so much domestic and international good will, FORD leadership soon shocked its supporters and well-wishers by engaging in fratricidal power struggles throughout most of 1992 that ultimately split the party in two. At the heart of this conflict lay strong disagreements on who was to lead the party—Oginga Odinga, the octogenarian Luo leader and former vice president of Kenya, or Kenneth Matiba, the hero of the Kikuyu since his detention in 1990. The problems of the opposition were compounded by the failure of the Democratic Party to either merge or establish an electoral alliance with FORD—a failure that was in part a function of the internal struggles within the party and its subsequent split. By dissipating their energies on internal political warfare, the opposition groups played right into the hands of KANU.

In August 1992 Odinga and Matiba consented to the registration of two FORD political parties under their respective leaderships—FORD-Kenya and FORD-Asili. This, incredibly, was a KANU government suggestion. The registration of the two FORDs and the continued independence of the Democratic Party paved the way for a KANU electoral victory in December that returned Moi firmly to power with only a 36 percent plurality of the vote. Though they outpolled KANU almost two to one, the opposition parties and their supporters split three ways. Through gerrymandering, intimidation, and one-sided electoral rules, KANU also won an absolute parliamentary majority.

Although some opposition activists found consolation in recounting the gains made in regaining civil liberties since 1990, it was impossible to deny that constitutional democracy and multiparty governance in Kenya had suffered a severe setback. Even after KANU had acceded to the demands of political pluralism, it never hid its distaste for the process. Its behavior in the run-up to the December 1992 elections involved use of the civil service to intimidate or buy opponents, unfair electoral practices, carefully calculated ballot rigging, and manipulation of ethnic loyalties. The 1993 Kenya cabinet included active supporters of these operations. With KANU commanding an overall majority in parliament, the opposition would have to fight it out in the legislature for another five years. This was to be the test of whether multiparty government would be a viable system for Kenya.

Tanzania

As in Kenya, the leading lights of the opposition to single-party rule in Tanzania were a combination of famous names in the immediate postindependence era who had fallen out with the government and young urban professionals who were dejected by the dismal economic and political record of the country. Within the Union of Multiparty Democracy (UMD), Chief Fundikira and Kasanga Tumbo—a militant trade unionist who was edged out of the Tanganyika Federation of Labor in the run-up to one-party rule in 1964—represented an earlier generation. So did Oscar Kambona—secretary-general of TANU during the 1960s—who received little public sympathy despite years of exile and petty harassment from CCM after his return in 1991.

Maberere Marando, a civil rights lawyer and renegade government security agent who later formed the National Convention for Construction and Reform Party (NCCR-Mageuzi), represented a new generation of Tanzanian political leaders. The leadership of NCCR-Mageuzi (Kiswahili for "change") appeared to attract an unusually high number of former state security employees as well as young urban professionals, most of them not previously known to the public. Other newcomers included Lucas Mahindo Kaoneka of the Tanzanian People's Party and Charles Mtikila, a rabble-rousing populist cleric whose Democratic Party espoused a radical nationalist position against Arabs and Asian merchants, whom he accused of exploiting the country. Although Mtikila could bring out unruly street crowds like those who ransacked Arab- and Asian-owned shops in Dar es Salaam in 1992, his party seemed to lack a firm social base, and was in any case denied registration by the government.

Although they all tended to be organizationally weak, the most credible of the new parties were the UMD, Chama cha Democrasia na Maendeleo, or CHADEMA (the Party for Democracy and Development), the Civic United Front (CUF), and NCCR-Maguezi. In 1992 the UMD split over strategy differences between Fundikira and Tumbo but continued to obtain support from the Sukuma and Nyamwezi. By contrast, CHADEMA established a strong base in the cash crop producing areas around Mount Kilimanjaro and the southern highlands. Led by former finance minister and Central Bank governor Edwin Mtei and ex-deputy agriculture minister Edward Barongo, CHADEMA appealed to the same middle-class elements and potentially prosperous farmers as the Democratic Party in Kenya. It was outspoken in favor of private enterprise and classical liberal political values. In addition, the alliance between the established ex-detainee and human rights lawyer James Mapalala and the dissident former chief minister of Zanzibar, Seif Shariff Hamad, led to the formation of the Civic United Front. The CUF attracted a massive following in Zanzibar, the home of President Mwinyi. By the end of 1993 Tanzania had twelve political parties.

On the whole, the opposition parties in Tanzania have lacked the inner vigor, material resources, and outward exuberance of their Kenyan counterparts. Part of the reason no doubt lies in the absence of an unpopular establishment figure whose removal could have been used to galvanize massive political outrage. However, with the exit of Julius Nyerere from the presidency in 1985, the ruling CCM party had embarked on reforms—widening the latitude of individual enterprise and permitting freer political debate— and this might have taken some of the wind from the sails of the putative opposition parties. More significant, whereas the clarion call of political dissent in Kenya was the end to the authoritarian ways of the Moi government, best exemplified in the regime's appalling human rights record, political opposition in Tanzania rallied around the question of economic change and reform of corruption-ridden public institutions. To be fair, the Civic Rights Movement of human rights activist James Mapalala and the crusading and courageous journalism of C. Stanley Kamana of *The Family Mirror* had emphasized respect for civil liberties in Tanzania. Put differently, Kenyan opposition leaders sought a new political realm in order to put the national economy on a sound footing once again, whereas in Tanzania priority was placed on transcending the economic dereliction that was *ujamaa*'s legacy, even though respect for civil rights was considered a vital political objective.

Thus, one of the rallying points of the Union of Multiparty Democracy (UMD) was the need for enhanced individual incentives in the market and less bureaucratic corruption in facilitating this process. The party was pledged to "full employment of youth . . . by adopting a fully-fledged market economy" (UMD 1991). As neither Fundikira nor Kasanga Tumbo was a champion of ujamaa, the argument sounded credible to a population suffering as much from socialist fatigue as from the spiraling cost of living that resulted from structural adjustment policies to correct the country's economic failures. As NCCR-Mageuzi leader Maberere Marando remarked: "People are disgusted with their experience of socialism" (*The Herald,* December 12, 1991). Kamana probably spoke for the wider opposition constituency when he said: "The problem with Tanzania is that it has always tried to practice socialism with people who secretly believed in capitalism" (*Washington Post,* September 26, 1990).

The number of closet capitalists in Tanzania, even under Nyerere, was probably larger than the CCM was willing to admit. At the historic February 1992 CCM congress that set the country on the road to multiparty politics, Julius Nyerere himself warned Tanzanians against electing "capitalists," though he conceded the need for economic reforms of the kind CCM was implementing already (*The Herald,* February 2, 1992). Such remarks illustrate the primacy of conflict over economic policy between CCM and UMD especially. CCM sought to graft economic reforms to the institutional vestiges of ujamaa. For instance, after five years of economic liberalization, the government had made little progress in privatizing about 360 loss-making state-owned corporations (parastatals), though putative steps were taken in early 1994. Legalizing competition against the state-owned commercial banking monopoly—the National Bank of Commerce—took three years. UMD and CHADEMA, for their part, wanted to complete the job of freeing the market forces and eliminating bureaucratic corruption where it was a fetter to individual enterprise, particularly in the agricultural cooperatives sector. And although the other major opposition party—James Mapalala's Civic United Front—took a populist line in favor of the rural and urban poor, its agenda merely reflected strong antipathy against the bureaucratic and party elite of the ujamaa regime rather than a concrete alternative economic program to that of CCM.

Besides the new opposition parties, other institutions in Tanzanian civil society bared their teeth after years of officially imposed timidity. An independent press surfaced in 1990 and undertook an immediate crusade against corruption in government and threats to individual rights. Like the parties, however, the opposition press was deficient in professionalism and short of resources. Emerging alongside the stridently critical *Family Mirror,* the new Swahili newspaper *Watu* (The People) provided a popular forum for independent thought in Kiswahili. One issue, for instance, railed against "a lot of dishonest people, bandits and looters in the ruling party who are upset when we expose their dirty deeds."[8] Such criticism could never have been expected from the state-owned *Daily News* or its Kiswahili counterpart, *Uhuru.* In addition to the politically inclined newspapers, Tanzania also gained its first independent business periodical in *The Business Times.* It was the most sophisticated of the new periodicals, coming out thrice weekly by early 1994.

Students also began to stir in what the government interpreted as pro-opposition political activism. In April 1991 the University of Dar es Salaam was closed after students staged a series of antigovernment demonstrations sparked by cuts in fellowships and distaste of institutional corruption. Three lecturers were thereafter banned from teaching duties and assigned to bureaucratic jobs before the government relented in the face of domestic and international pressure. When the university reopened in October 1991, students boycotted classes to protest the expulsion of eighty-three of their colleagues who had been rusticated after refusing to sign official bonds foreswearing "illegal" behavior on campus. They were emboldened by an unprecedented court suit against the state filed by several technical schools in Dar es Salaam that had succeeded in reinstating students expelled from these institutions. Following this example, the students at the University, via their student union, sought to nullify the expulsions from their campus by bringing a suit of their own. The students continued their militancy into February 1992, when they again boycotted classes to protest the manner in which the government introduced "cost sharing"— meaning tuition and boarding fees—and state encroachment on academic freedom. Relationships between the state and the university remained uneasy for the rest of the year; when President Mwinyi was invited to address the university community in November to speak on the CCM party platform, he turned down the opportunity just as promptly as the opposition parties had seized it.

By early 1993 the most perceptive administrators at the University of Dar es Salaam had resigned themselves to continued violent confrontations between the students and political authorities. Localized campus disputes frequently matured into concrete differences with the government over national politics. The Tanzanian state responded with as little ingenuity and as much force as Kenya did in its own disputes with University of Nairobi protesters.

Like the students, the labor unions took advantage of the government's reluctant political liberalization drive to attempt a breakaway from the confines of the domineering single party. In the 1960s the independent Tanganyika Federation of Labor (TFL) had been brought under the wings of the ruling party as JUWATA (the Kiswahili acronym for "Union of Tanzania Workers"). The unions were designated as major economic pillars in the building of socialism. But after being buffeted by decreasing real wages under ujamaa and more rapidly after the introduction of structural adjustment policies, labor leaders began petitioning CCM for a complete divorce from the shotgun marriage. When JUWATA held its annual conference in early 1991, delegates decided to form a new independent confederation of trade unions—the Organization of Tanzania Trade Unions (OTTU). OTTU opted for independent industrial-based unions with unfettered powers in collective bargaining. CCM, which claimed to be "a workers' and peasants' party," had not bargained for such a degree of union militancy. To play for time, the CCM government therefore decided not to register OTTU until the legal statues liquidating JUWATA had been passed and a new trade union bill had been approved by parliament. It was clear that the government, though willing to concede more autonomy to OTTU, was not ready to countenance independent trade unions with wage-bargaining rights. Thus, as with the university, parties, and the press, there was a standoff between liberalizing forces in civil society and a government committed to democratization but unsure of whether it could ever bottle the genie it had unleashed.

The constitutional position of Zanzibar was another interesting manifestation of this syndrome. In the wake of the February 1964 anti-Sultanate revolution in Zanzibar, the islands of Pemba and Zanzibar were incorporated into what became the United Republic of Tanzania. This move was in part meant to preempt a Western invasion to quash Zanzibar's radical revolutionary government. But the islands had been governed as a separate protectorate by the British, and an insular Zanzibari nationalism was an ever-present political phenomenon even in the best days of the union. With growing political liberalization, the increasing momentum toward autonomy and outright secession became more vocal. The issue of Zanzibar's autonomy set the limits on how far the Tanzanian government would go in tolerating new opposition groups. At the same time, the issue split the nascent political parties and made it difficult for them to make inroads into Zanzibar and Pemba.

It is ironic that one strand of separatism for the islands was led by a former chief minister of Zanzibar under the CCM government, Saif Shariff Hamad, who openly called for a referendum to determine the future of the union in 1989. He was detained for thirty months without trial for his pains until November 1990, when the government—facing an international outcry on human rights violations—charged him with unauthorized possession of government documents. Hamad, however, never gave up the cause, and in November 1991 he was reported to be propagating it in Friday prayers at the mosques and to groups visiting his home (*African Analysis,* November 29, 1991: 5). There was confluence between his efforts and those of the islands' informal pressure group, KAMAHURU (the Kiswahili acronym for "Committee for Free Political Parties"), which announced plans to set up the Zanzibar United Front Party or, failing to obtain registration under that title, the National United Front—a Zanzibari movement with token representation in the mainland. When that option proved unattainable, Hamad joined forces with Mapalala's CUF, as mentioned earlier.

KAMAHURU's dilemma in the choice of its name had everything to do with the CCM government's decision to disallow any new opposition based on one geographical area—thus outlawing Zanzibar-only parties—or a single race, religion, or ethnic group. Yet despite official distaste for cultural or sectarian political interests, political liberalization in Tanzania helped produce an assertive Islamic movement within and outside CCM and with allies in Saudi Arabia and the Persian Gulf. Aimed essentially at redressing the Christian dominance in government under Nyerere, this trend caused alarm in the Tanzanian National Assembly in January 1993, when Zanzibar joined the Organization of Islamic Countries and the CCM government enrolled in the Islam in Africa Organization. This was the last straw. In August 1993, fifty-five rebellious MPs from the mainland supported a motion to set up a separate mainland government on a par with that of Zanzibar. It took Nyerere's active intervention to postpone a standoff with Mwinyi and a breakup of the union. It was therefore resolved that CCM would first assess popular attitudes on the issue before bringing it back before parliament. Nyerere also warned that religious differences and mainland antipathy against Zanzibaris would eventually break up the country. Yet whereas opposition groups were prevented from operating on religious lines, the CCM had no compunction in doing so itself.

Like KANU in neighboring Kenya, CCM was unilaterally formulating the rules the opposition had to live with without the slightest interparty consultation on the regulations governing political competition. Also like KANU, CCM was prepared to break the rules when that worked in its favor. By late 1992, in fact, neither the CCM nor KANU had outgrown the tradition of a menacing paternalism toward political opposition, and both were using the state machinery they controlled to circumscribe the operational sphere of the new political parties while fortifying their respective political domains. Indeed, there was sufficient reason to believe that incumbent governments wanted just enough window-dressing opposition to meet the new external aid conditions—but not more. But government opponents had refused to be cowed. In both countries, political pluralism was an idea whose time had come.

STATE RESPONSE TO OPPOSITION

As noted at the beginning of this chapter, the Kenyan government stridently opposed the introduction of political pluralism until the donors met in late November 1991. Throughout the previous two years, the ruling KANU party had attacked the opposition as "drug addicts," "capitalists," "Marxists," and "foreign-manipulated puppets" whose leaders had "insects in their heads." Moi had vowed to crush the opposition "like rats." Autocratic regimes do not shed such belligerent postures easily. About a month after the Kenya National Assembly amended the constitution to legalize the registration of opposition parties, President Moi told a BBC interviewer that he remained an unreconstructed believer in one-party government: "I have not changed my mind about [the one-party system]. . . . It was because the Western media set against us because of the economic setting today. Therefore Kenyans have accepted this multiparty [system] . . . but because of the attack from the Western media" (*Society Magazine,* March 23, 1992: 5).

By March 1992 the Kenyan government refused to authorize public meetings by the opposition parties, though KANU remained exempt and continued its recruiting and political campaign program. Not until external pressure was brought to bear did the government relent. FORD and DP meetings in the previous three months had been drawing record crowds in the main urban centers of the country. With these developments, KANU's denunciation of its opponents became shrill, desperate, and outright menacing.

Also in March, the General Services Unit (riot police) viciously evicted hunger-striking mothers of political prisoners from Uhuru Park in downtown Nairobi and fired at antigovernment demonstrators in Nairobi, Kisumu, and Homa Bay, killing several. Kenyans and foreigners reeled with horror at the brute force visited upon unarmed political protesters. The backtracking to old authoritarian ways was clear. It was also evident in the National Assembly's unanimous endorsement in April of a backbench motion to curb press freedoms, as well as legislation designed to give KANU an electoral advantage in the forthcoming presidential and parliamentary elections. The latter included a provision requiring successful presidential candidates to win 25 percent of the vote in any five of Kenya's eight provinces, regardless of the population or number of voters. The measure was designed to minimize the chances of opposition victory, as support for FORD and DP was concentrated in populous Central Province, Nyanza, and Nairobi. By contrast, support for KANU was concentrated in the least populated regions, including Northeast Province (with only 1 percent of the electorate).

In the same vein, Moi turned a deaf ear to opposition demands to reconstitute the Electoral Commission to include persons acceptable to all parties, preferring instead to stick with the commissioners he appointed prior to legalizing the opposition. As registration for the forthcoming elections commenced in May and June 1992, electoral rolls in pro-KANU areas were padded with unqualified or nonresident voters, whereas would-be voters in opposition strongholds were subjected to inordinate delays when registering to vote. Approximately 1.2 million first-time voters were denied registration because the government failed to issue identification cards to citizens who had recently turned eighteen, the age of eligibility. Although opposition parties resumed public rallies, government harassment continued, as the issuing of permits for these meetings were often delayed or withdrawn. The Provincial Administration and police also inhibited the movement of opposition leaders. A near total blackout of opposition events and policy statements was maintained by the government-owned Kenya Broadcasting Corporation.

The formal split of Kenya's leading opposition party, FORD, in August 1992 therefore worked to the benefit of the ruling party. Given the difficulties the KANU government placed in the way of its opponents and the country's history of ethnic bloc voting, the outcome of the elections held on December 29, 1992, appeared obvious to anyone but the leaders of FORD-Asili, FORD-Kenya, and the Democratic Party. Despite many irregularities and incompetence, polling was generally free on election day itself, though the overall electoral process and preceding campaign had rarely been fair (Barkan 1993). Fighting in a terrain of its choice, KANU won 100 of the 187 parliamentary seats, as compared to 31 for FORD-Asili, 31 for FORD-Kenya, and 23 for DP. With the additional 12 members of parliament that Moi was constitutionally entitled to nominate, KANU had a working majority in the legislature. Even so, when all was said and done Moi and KANU had lost their legitimacy to rule. The combined opposition polled 3.3 million votes in the presidential election, compared to Moi's 1.9 million. The majority of voters had decided against Moi, but the divisions among opposition leaders had assured him a victory.

Nowhere has the loss of legitimacy been greater than in the eyes of the victims of the so-called "tribal" or "ethnic" clashes that have accompanied the reintroduction of multiparty politics and that were designed to punish opposition supporters residing in President Moi's home region, Rift Valley Province. Since the onset of the agitation in favor of multipartyism, Moi and his colleagues have repeatedly argued that political pluralism would resurrect ancient "tribal animosities" that would splinter Kenya. In a series of meetings organized toward the end of 1991 by prominent leaders of Moi's Kalenjin ethnic group in the Rift Valley, his lieutenants called for the restoration of the *majimbo* (federal) constitution Kenya used briefly at the time of its independence and for the eviction of non-Kalenjin immigrants from the province (*Weekly Review,* September 27, 1991: 5–11). They also declared the province to be an opposition-free "KANU zone." These threats were ominous to the many Kikuyu, Luo, Kisii, and Luhya migrants who had settled in the Rift Valley as farm labor or farmers since the onset of colonial rule. They believed KANU and the government as creating a self-fulfilling prophecy that the introduction of multiparty democracy would inevitably lead to ethnic animosity.

In what many Kenyans regard as evidence of such a prophecy, bands of armed Kalenjins attacked Luo, Luhya, Kisii, and Kikuyu farmers within or just beyond the border of the Rift Valley between December 1991 and March 1992. The earliest victims were Luo farmers neighboring or just within Nandi District. In the second half of 1992, Kikuyu farmers in the Rift Valley's Olenguruone area, scene of anticolonial resistance in the late 1940s, suffered the worst fate. Groups of "Kalenjin warriors" descended on their homes, burning, killing, and looting. In seemingly orchestrated attacks, Luhya farmers in Trans-Nzoia District were evicted from their lands by force. Kikuyus were attacked again in December 1992 just prior to the elections, this time in the Burnt Forest south of Eldoret.

After a hiatus of several months, the clashes resumed in June and again in September and October 1993, this time around Narok, where approximately 2,000 Kikuyu farmers were subjected to systematic arson, killings, and rapes by "Maasai warriors" not long after the KANU leader in the area and cabinet minister, William ole Ntimama, called for Kikuyu residents to vacate the Enoosupkukia area. Since the beginning of the clashes, the police have seemed in no hurry to intervene or charge the perpetrators of this mayhem, and there have been open accusations of collusion between authorities and the killer bands.[9] These charges were subsequently confirmed in 1992 by independent investigations conducted by the NCCK and by a parliamentary commission of inquiry chaired by Mombasa's Kennedy Kiliku (NCCK 1992; Kenya 1992b). Similar findings were reported by Africa Watch in 1993. By October 1993 upwards of 1,500 people had died in these "tribal clashes." In addition, an estimated 6,000 farmhouses were burned and between 250,000 and 300,000 people displaced (Africa Watch 1993; UNDP 1993a).

Though not as tightfisted as KANU, CCM was hardly charitable to the Tanzanian opposition, nor was it beyond using state power to curb legitimate political activities that contradicted it. The Tanzania government thus disallowed public meetings of the new parties until they were formally registered while (like KANU) undertaking its own vigorous campaign to register new CCM members nationwide. On October 31, 1991, the police stopped opposition supporters from holding a rally at Mnazi Mmoja independence grounds to celebrate the electoral victory of the Movement for Multiparty Democracy (MMD) in Zambia. Opposition leaders were routinely harassed by police, though less often than in Kenya. For his part, and rather like Daniel arap Moi, Tanzania's prime minister, John Malacela intimated that founders of "illegal" parties "were mentally disturbed" (*Africa Analysis,* December 13, 1991: 2). In October 1991 the Tanzanian government threatened to ban the new independent papers for "flouting ethics" and "unbecoming character" (*Daily News,* October 11, 1991). There was reported intimidation of independent-minded and critical journalists even within the establishment press (*Family Mirror,* December 1991). Rather like in Kenya, where the privately owned *Nation* and *Standard* newspapers were frequently threatened with banning orders for reporting activities of the opposition faithfully, CCM saw the new independent press as no more than an arm of the opposition.

In yet another ironic parallel with its Kenyan counterpart, the CCM argued that a multiparty system would strain national unity and create instability in a country that had avoided political upheavals since independence. This is Hirschman's "jeopardy" thesis, beloved of antidemocratic conservatives elsewhere. Chief Fundikira responded with a statement that might apply to both countries: "I must dismiss any suggestion that the multiparty system would fracture stability. . . . Repression has kept the people quiet" (*Africa Events,* September 1991: 15). The CCM's fear of fissiparous politics, particularly in Zanzibar, led to the introduction of legislation requiring the new parties to have no less than 200 sponsors from every region of the country, including Zanzibar and Pemba. It was this legislation that produced the merger leading to CUF. As in Kenya, the state-owned radio station—the only one allowed in Tanzania—continued to give the ruling party glowing coverage while making derisive comments about any opposition events on which it cared to report.

For all this, CCM was not, in terms of its future electoral prospects, in an analogous position to KANU—quite the contrary. KANU became bellicose and oppressive as the elections drew near because its more thoughtful members knew all too well that in a free and fair election the combined opposition would defeat them by a landslide. CCM was more certain of victory and did not need to subject the opposition to heavy-handed harassment of the kind it was increasingly involved in. The CCM party apparatchiks and senior state and parastatal bureaucrats did not take kindly to scrutiny and accountability of the sort the opposition and the foreign aid donors were so fond of. But the primary reasons behind keeping the new parties under some control appeared to be the danger of secession in Zanzibar, which might have complicated the emerging differences between Muslims and Christian elites in the mainland, and fear of resurgent loyalty to ethnic groups and regions of origin whose official recognition was being sought by UDM. By early 1994 there was justified concern that a new mainland government would bring the union to an end, a prospect that was viewed with some delight in sections of Zanzibar. With the retreat of the CCM from government departments, parastatals, and private firms, Tanzanians were increasingly turning their loyalties to lineage and rural origins and to religion. There was always a danger that ethnic-based parties such as those in Kenya might surface, making the country centrally ungovernable in addition to hastening the exit of Zanzibar.

By 1993 CCM appeared to have reconciled itself to governing with a fragmented and weak opposition that had no representation in parliament. Unlike Kenya, Tanzania was not due to hold elections until 1995. None of the new parties appeared to be a serious threat to CCM in popularity. The CCM hierarchy was encouraged by the electoral results in Kenya, just as much as the Tanzanian opposition was disheartened by the split in the Kenyan opposition parties, which had led to their defeat. In January 1993 Chief Fundikira was reported to be calling for a unified opposition in order to avoid the fate the upstart parties had suffered in Kenya (*Daily Nation,* January 10, 1993); as in Kenya the previous year, the call went unheeded.

CONCLUSION

The reintroduction of multiparty politics in Kenya and Tanzania is primarily the consequence of reform-minded domestic social forces under educated middle-class leadership, a part of which—like the masses underneath it—has borne the brunt of repression under one-party rule. Opposition leaders in both countries have expressed popular grievances, which the ruling parties aggravated rather than ameliorated. As Bendix remarks from a different historical context, an intelligentsia that was exposed to democratic ideas from the rest of the world played a frontal role in that transition to democracy. In Tanzania, the combination of economic calamity, bureaucratic corruption, and abuse of power fueled the opposition, whereas in

Kenya political arbitrariness, human rights abuses, cavalier trampling of institutional regulations, and disregard of the rule of law served approximately the same purpose. According to the opposition, economic mismanagement in Kenya was a product of a corrupt regime whose removal was the primary objective. In Tanzania government critics—in a reverse scenario—saw underdevelopment as the primary cause of institutional decay, venality of political power, and pervasive corruption. In both countries— more so in Kenya than in Tanzania—external aid donors, international human rights groups, and the global news media had played an important role in discrediting the authoritarian character of incumbent regimes. The democratic revolutions elsewhere in Africa—in Benin, Zambia, and South Africa—and in Eastern Europe provided a catalyzing effect. On the whole, the intensity of both political repression and popular opposition to it was greater in Kenya than it was in Tanzania.

The reasons for this difference of intensity lie in the national experience under capitalist development in Kenya and ujamaa in Tanzania, a contrast that drew much attention from comparative social analysts of the region in the 1970s. The explanation lies as much in the more heavy-handed repression of KANU as it does in the changes in civil society that were set in motion by the development policies of the 1960s.

The record of economic regression in Tanzania under socialism is no longer seriously disputed.[10] The social consequences resulting from that debacle, however, are less well understood. Ujamaa in Tanzania circumscribed the latitude not just of individual economic enterprise—which, ironically, it never banished altogether—but also of vigorous independent civic associations among commercial and professional classes, including privately engaged doctors, capitalist farmers, lawyers, clergy, businesspeople, industrialists, the private press, and dissident intellectuals. In contrast, the spectacular economic growth that Kenya achieved between 1964 and 1974, and again from 1976 to about 1980, brought in its wake two contradictory results. The first was a robust independent sector of civic institutions such as the Law Society of Kenya human rights organizations, farming associations, an activist Christian clergy, professional associations, *Harambee* self-help groups, women's organizations, and the press. By 1991 dissident coastal Muslims joined in with long-repressed grievances. All these institutions had external links with like-minded organizations in the West or elsewhere. Economic expansion also generated widespread discontent about unequal distribution of gains between social classes and—more significantly—across ethnic groups.

By the time Moi came into power, the Kikuyu were depicted as malevolent beneficiaries of an undue share of economic growth during the Kenyatta years. In the heat of political mobilization, no distinction was made between what the Kikuyu had earned on merit and what they had been given through political patronage. This, ironically, was the same treatment the Asian community had received after independence by Kenyatta. This reasoning was used to galvanize political support around Moi before and after multiparty politics came onto the scene. Contrary historical evidence of Kikuyu economic and educational advance *before* independence counted for nothing (Tignor 1976); no sense of proportion was allowed by this political sales pitch. Objective analysis of ethnic inequalities in Kenya was swamped in official repression and the Nyayo rhetoric of moral piety ("love, peace and unity"). But despite bracing himself to take on the Kikuyu, Moi could not totally control the independent civic interest groups though not for want of trying. Indeed, some like Maendeleo wa Wanawake were co-opted into KANU. Under Moi, Kenya's ruling party also recruited distinguished academics, journalists, lawyers, and civic leaders to legitimize its ideological position. The inner agenda of the Moi government, in fact, consisted of undoing this perceived ethnic-regional inequality by rapid elevation (across all social sectors) of his Kalenjin community, first and foremost, and other "disadvantaged" ethnic groups such as the Turkana, Pokot, and Maasai. None of this, however, could be done as rapidly as he wanted without blatant rule-bending, extortion, repression of all dissent, and discrimination against those—such as the Kikuyu and Luo—who were already ahead in education and the professions. The economy and national institutions suffered lasting damage as a result. Not surprisingly, it was the urban professional classes, small-scale commercial farmers, and business interests who rose in protest. If as Ali Mazrui has written, Nyerere's ujamaa was a lesson in "heroic failure" of socialism, then Moi's nyayo was an even more heroic failure in stealth advancement of ethnic equality.

The backlash to this strategy came incrementally, first from left-wing and socialist intellectuals at the University of Nairobi and subsequently from clergy, lawyers, and the independent press. By the time it caught up with the business class, principled political leaders, and the world media, it had percolated down to the urban underclasses, working people, and rural smallholders who congregated in huge numbers at opposition rallies. A propertied, self-assured, educated middle class and dejected professional and business groups—bigger and more organized than those of Tanzania—played a critical role in mobilizing the opposition masses. Kenya's middle class had prospered whereas Tanzania's had been stunted, yet even there its influence could be felt in the UMD and the stridently promarket CHADEMA. Some economic security appeared to be a minimal condition for any consequential leadership and lasting popular support for the opposition. As lawyer Paul Muite of FORD told a *Los Angeles Times* reporter: "Those who one might describe as being somewhat more endowed in material things . . . ought to be in the forefront and most concerned with the direction in which this country is moving. They are the ones who have more to lose" (*Los Angeles Times,* March 26, 1991).

The Kenyan opposition was more vocal and better organized at least in part because of those 1960s development policies TANU had abominated as un-African. In 1993, CHADEMA and UMD were Tanzanian opposition parties whose agrarian program sounded much like that of KANU in the 1960s. Perhaps the ultimate distinction in the experience between the two countries is best summarized by the Barrington Moore remark cited earlier; "No bourgeois, no democracy." As Kenya and Tanzania navigate the tortuous path to multiparty government, democratic forces cannot therefore ignore the mutually reinforcing character of civil liberties and individual prosperity. That, of course, is a greater long-term challenge than the overhauling of authoritarian rule, which is their immediate preoccupation.

NOTES

1. Kamukunji, in the populous Eastlands of Nairobi, was the venue of the Kenya African Union meetings in the 1950s and of the first national general strike in 1950. For that reason it was the nationalists' favorite rallying arena in the 1960s.

2. Though not hostile to FORD, the DP doted on the tested record of competent management of public affairs by its stalwarts but it could not match FORD in popular following.

3. The issue ran into tens of thousands of reprints before the government banned it and imprisoned its editor, Bedan Mbugua, on trumped-up charges of failing to file annual returns of the magazine to the government.

4. For Anyona's moving defense statement, documenting rights violation and autocracy in Kenya see the *Nairobi Law Monthly,* April/May 1991: 16–26.

5. See (Leys 1978) and the essays by Kaplinsky, Henley, and Langdon in Fransman (1982). Also consult the most competent evaluation of this debate by Gavin Kitching (1985).

6. In one of his interviews after detention, Matiba called for a "meritocratic government."

7. Kiswahili for "seven seven" ("July 7th"), as the day of the demonstrations became known.

8. Quoted in *The Standard* (Nairobi), November 27, 1991.

9. See the accounts of these events in *The Times* (London), March 30, 1992; *The Guardian* (London), March 31, 1992; and the *Daily Telegraph* (London), March 20, 1992. In a pastoral letter read in all Catholic churches on Sunday, April 22, the Catholic bishops charged the state with complicity in these atrocities.

10. See, for instance, Lofchie (1989: 75–142), Mueller (1980), Hyden (1980), and Maliyamkono and Bagachwa (1990).

3

Party, State, and Civil Society: Control Versus Openness

Goran Hyden

Kenya has been economically successful since independence, Tanzania unsuccessful. Such is the conventional wisdom not only in development circles (Lele and Meyers 1987) but also among academics such as Michael Lofchie (1989) and Bruce Johnston (1989) who have carefully examined available records for the two countries since the 1960s. All agree that Tanzania's socialist experience has been costly and that Kenya has strengthened its economy by allowing market forces to influence the development process and by remaining open not only to foreign aid but also to foreign investment. In short, they conclude, *policy matters.*

Equally intriguing, however, especially for a political scientist, is the fact that of the two countries, Kenya has been politically more unstable, whereas Tanzania—even though its urban population has lost two-thirds of its real income since 1969—has remained remarkably stable. Moreover, in the early 1990s, as the winds of glasnost began to blow over Africa, it was poor Tanzania rather than wealthier Kenya that showed the greatest readiness to respond to demands for political reform. These facts raise a series of interesting questions: 1) What is the relationship between economic growth and political democracy? 2) Is Africa different from other continents, and if so, why? 3) To what extent is the past a lesson for the future? 4) What influence do external factors have? By addressing these questions in this chapter, I will place the issues of governance in the two countries in a comparative perspective and examine how far politics matter in development.

ECONOMIC GROWTH AND POLITICAL DEMOCRACY

The two "classical" texts on this subject are Seymour Martin Lipset's *Political Man* (1960) and Samuel P. Huntington's *Political Order in*

Changing Societies (1968). The former offers the hypothesis that "the more well-to-do a nation, the greater the chances that it will sustain democracy" (1960: 49–50). This positive correlation between economic growth and democratization has been empirically tested and confirmed by many researchers (e.g., Needler 1968, Smith 1969, and Banks 1970). The most ambitious of these, by Bollen and Jackman (1985), tried to locate the correlates of democracy for over one hundred countries using political indicators for 1960 and 1965. They found that the level of economic development has a pronounced effect on political democracy, even when other noneconomic factors are considered, not only in industrialized countries but also in non-industrialized ones. In a more recent contribution to this debate, Lipset, Seong, and Torres (1990) conclude that the relationship between economic development and democratization in the late 1980s is even more striking than in the 1950s, when the emphasis on this correlation first became part of the growing literature on development. They argue that the intervening decades encompassed dramatic increases in various social indicators as well as in indices relating to national economic capability and citizens' expectations and demands.

Whereas Lipset and his colleagues focus largely on the "brighter" side of this correlation, Huntington takes the view that economic development leads to stability and, by implication, to democracy only in societies where the rate of economic growth is not too rapid and where political institutions are capable of handling rising social expectations. Thus, even if it may be argued that economic development increases society's capacity to satisfy these aspirations and creates new opportunities for entrepreneurship and employment, rapid growth typically disrupts traditional social groupings, produces nouveaux riches, increases the gap between rich and poor, and aggravates regional and ethnic conflict, to mention only a few possible consequences. By increasing social frustration, economic growth produces instability rather than stability. As a result, political democratization becomes more difficult, not less.

Comparativists have continued to study the institutional capacity of a given society to handle growing social tensions and manage them so that political democracy is promoted and sustained (see, for example, Migdal 1988). The problem with Huntington's analysis, however, is that it does not provide any indication of how one measures the gap between social expectations and institutional capacity. Thus, in subsequent writings on the subject, he has retained an almost unbelievable pessimism about the prospects for democracy in countries that don't already have it. In an article titled, "Will More Countries Become Democratic?" he concluded that "with a few exceptions, the limits of democratic development in the world may well have been reached" (Huntington 1984: 218).

Political trends since the early 1980s seem not only to contradict

Huntington's pessimistic conclusions but also to call into question the relationships between wealth and democracy as stated by Lipset. After all, during the last decade countries in Latin America have undergone transition from authoritarianism to political democracy during a period of economic decline and turmoil. Eastern Europe and the former Soviet Union have been liberated from communist rule, again under harsh economic circumstances. Finally, even the low-income countries of sub-Saharan Africa, despite falling GNPs per capita, have introduced democratic political reforms.

One way of understanding this new situation is to account for the role not only of structural but also of conjunctural variables (Collier and Collier 1991). The latter refer to "windows of opportunity" that emerge as a result of unanticipated changes in the relations among groups and nations. The collapse of communism and the ensuing end of the Cold War constitutes one such obvious window. But politics does not only change in response to economic factors. For example, both governments and citizens learn from negative feedback; they respond to what is happening. As a result, politics (i.e., intentional public action) must be perceived as having the capacity to shape society to an extent not addressed by studies attempting to correlate economic growth with democracy. For example, only by introducing politics as an independent variable does it become possible to explain the cyclical nature of democracy in Latin America over the past fifty or so years (Johnson and Kelly 1986). In addition, there is the question of how far external factors determine politics. The types of analyses Huntington and Lipset have carried out largely ignore such factors, whether economic or political. Yet in an increasingly interdependent world, such variables as openness to outside influences and degree of economic dependence on other countries or foreign institutions are potentially important in shaping political processes.

This is not to suggest that politics are always independent of socioeconomic factors; such is the case only when unique historical opportunities arise. For this reason, it is important to question how long the changes brought about in such situations can last. Is democracy really sustainable in conditions of economic poverty like those in sub-Saharan Africa? It may be helpful to consider democratic transitions around the world in terms of their degree of firmness. In countries like Kenya and Tanzania, the process must be treated as tentative. The distance these countries must travel in order to realize democracy is both longer and harder than is the case elsewhere, for example (in Latin American countries).

Having placed the issues of democratization in a comparative perspective, I will now examine the specific conditions for democratic governance in Africa, the difference politics has made in Kenya and Tanzania, and the role external factors have played in shaping politics.

CONDITIONS OF GOVERNANCE IN AFRICA

In order to place this analysis in its proper context, it may be helpful to remind the reader of the divergent conceptualizations of pluralism in the literature. One theory of pluralism was derived from the analysis of the evolution of democracy in Western countries, and another was developed in the analysis of Third World societies.

In the political theory of Western pluralism, which originated in criticism of the theories of state sovereignty advanced by Hobbes and Austin, society comprises a large number of voluntary associations, and society and state are clearly demarcated from each other. Many writers on political theory (e.g., Barker 1961) have elaborated on this subject, arguing that society is the active realm, whereas the state is the responsible and reactive realm (Jackson 1977). The theory of Third World pluralism is sociological rather than political in origin, beginning as it does with a concept of plural society. In his study of colonial Indonesia, the "father" of this theory, J. S. Furnivall, defined such a society as one "comprising two or more (cultural) elements or social orders which live side by side, yet without mingling, in one political unit" (Furnivall 1939: 446). In such a plural assemblage, he argued, the state must integrate these communities into one political unit by the use of coercive power; only coercive minority rule can contain the centrifugal pressures generated by communal differences.

In this conceptualization of society as segmented into more or less self-contained communities, there is no institutional basis for the operation of a pan-communal system of legitimate government, as Jackson (1977: 10) emphasizes. If this theory is applied to Africa, the implication is that rule is inevitably bound to be coercive or transformed through some form of "nation building" (Kuper and Smith 1971). What neither the Western nor the non-Western theory of pluralism considers is the possibility that African countries may develop norms that encourage an alternative system of rule. In my own previous writing (Hyden 1980, 1983, and 1987), I have referred to this system of rule as one based on an "economy of affection." Thus, what Lonsdale (1981) refers to as the "high politics" of elite competition for control of policy and the "deep politics" of state-society relations are driven by the exchange of positive sentiments rather than by debate over specific policy issues. Community boundaries are transcended through means that neither of the pluralist theories described above accounts for (Lemarchand 1972). In particular, the distinctions these theories make between "state" and "society" and between "public" and "private" lose their meaning in the community model of politics that has evolved in postindependence Africa.

In this "African" mode of conducting politics, the ultimate goal is for community representatives—patrons—to have access to the government and use it for their own enjoyment, rather than for groups to influence legislation and policies to satisfy member interests. Such policymaking tends to be "private," both in the sense that government offices are treated as private property and in the sense that patronage and spoils, unlike policies, must be managed in a discreet and secret fashion. Patronage and spoils are bestowed upon individuals, not announced as a public service. In such a conception, government becomes an object of political annexation rather than a target of policy. Government in Africa, therefore, is neither wholly "public" nor wholly "private" but rather "para-public" (Jackson 1977). The "civic" public realm is overshadowed by the "primordial" public realm, to use Peter Ekeh's (1975) conceptualization of the same phenomenon.

Because of its emphasis on patronage and spoils, African policymaking, as it has evolved after independence, is overwhelmingly distributive in character. Thus, a major concern is how resources can be most expediently spread out so as to maintain the support of clients or followers. While this "pork-barrel" type of politics is not unique to Africa, it is certainly at the core of policymaking there (Barkan 1978). It blocks out attention to other considerations that are relevant to a given issue.

In short, the conditions of governance in Africa are very different from those we know in Western democracies, and the rules of the political game have been shaped accordingly. At the same time, it is important to remember that these rules are all man-made; they are not impossible to change. With these comments in mind, I will now turn to an examination of how far governance in Kenya and Tanzania has made a difference to political stability and the prospects for democratization.

GOVERNANCE IN KENYA AND TANZANIA

"Governance" here refers to the way political leaders formulate and manage the basic rules that make up a given regime. These rules may be formal or informal, written or unwritten; for example, one can assume that the more politics is based on patronage and spoils, the more likely it is that these rules will be unwritten and informal. They tend to cover both "high" and "deep" politics—i.e., they regulate both elite competition and state-society relations. Three issues are of particular interest here: 1) how political leaders have dealt with the multiethnic character of society; 2) how they have delineated the boundaries between economy and polity; and 3) how they have treated civil society. I shall examine Kenya and Tanzania in turn with reference to each of these issues.

Ethnic Accommodation

Ethnicity became a principal social force in Kenya and Tanzania in colonial days, when the European rulers brought the populations of these territories into the global economy and forced people of different cultural backgrounds to interact with each other. Africans, perceiving the need to defend and promote their interests, formed tribal associations with latent if not manifest political objectives. As the demand and prospect for independence grew stronger after 1945, nationalist organizations began to take the place of these tribal associations. Africans realized they had a common enemy and that independence would be easier to achieve if they were united. Such unity was attained in Tanzania (or Tanganyika, as it was still called then), where none of the territory's 120 ethnic groups was strong enough to dominate the others. Thus, at independence, the Tanganyika African National Union (TANU) had only a few weak rivals, none of which could prevent the party from winning all seats but one in the elections immediately preceding independence.

In Kenya, by contrast, the forty or so ethnic groups never managed to unite into one political organization. African participation in political parties had been prohibited during the 1950s because of the Mau Mau rebellion—an uprising by members of the Kikuyu tribe, the largest in the territory. Furthermore, because Kikuyus had suffered more from settler intrusion on African lands, they had become politically more active than other groups and saw themselves as having their own agenda. The result was a split between the Kenya African National Union (KANU), a Kikuyu-dominated alliance that included leading politicians from other ethnic groups (notably the second largest, the Luo), and the Kenya African Democratic Union (KADU), formed by members of smaller tribes that feared Kikuyu domination. As colonial rule came to an end, KANU formed the government, KADU the opposition.

Ethnic Politics in Kenya

Kenya's first president was Jomo Kenyatta, a Kikuyu educated in Europe and accused by the British of having instigated the Mau Mau rebellion, for which he was detained for much of the 1950s. Representing the largest ethnic group in the country and carrying the glory of a nationalist hero, he became the unquestioned leader of Kenya at an age of approximately seventy years.

The constitution negotiated at Lancaster House in London as part of the preparations for *uhuru* (independence) in 1963 gave the country's eight provinces a fair degree of political autonomy, a principle demanded by the KADU leaders. As one of its first acts, the KANU government abolished provincial autonomy and amended the constitution to place all powers in the hands of the central government. Fearing they would be left without access to state resources, KADU politicians decided to cross the floor in 1964 and join KANU. This defection led to the creation of a new splinter party, the Kenya People's Union (KPU), which proclaimed a socialist ideology and alleged that KANU was failing to share the gains of independence with the people. However, politics continued to be centered on ethnicity (Gertzel 1970). Kenyatta's strategy in dealing with this issue is instructive.

Because he was accepted by each ethnic group as the national leader, Kenyatta could promote the interests of his Kikuyu people—especially those of the Kiambu subgroup to which he belonged—while retaining a loose alliance with patrons from other ethnic groups. Through their representation in the government, these other groups received patronage and spoils, but only in the smallest amounts required to retain their loyalty (Throup 1987b). Any attempt by individual politicians to threaten this arrangement was thwarted. Thus, when the eloquent and efficient Tom Mboya, a Luo with considerable support among various groups, including the Kikuyu, emerged as a threat to the Kikuyu establishment in 1969, he was murdered. The same happened to J. M. Kariuki, a populist Kikuyu with national appeal, in 1975. On both occasions, political stability was threatened by spontaneous street riots and planned demonstrations by students. Thus, although Kenyatta pursued an inclusivist strategy, he also assumed the Kikuyu should be allowed to get away with a larger share of the patronage benefits.

Kenyatta's ambition to place his own family and closest supporters first had its limits, however. Before passing away, he made sure that an attempt by his "dynasty" to secure the succession was foiled and that the vice president—Daniel arap Moi, originally the KADU leader—would succeed him, as specified in the constitution. This attempt by Kenyatta's coterie to further parochialize political leadership led to yet another crisis that shook the country in 1976.

When Kenyatta died in his bed in 1978, the transition was remarkably calm. Many had feared what would happen when the old man died, but Moi's reassurance that he would follow in Kenyatta's footsteps must have reduced such fears. For the first few years, Moi relied extensively on the same advisers Kenyatta had, including Charles Njonjo, a Kikuyu who led the opposition to the 1976 effort to change the constitution and thus had emerged as a kingmaker. In the early 1980s, however, when Kenyans for the first time experienced shortages of some basic commodities because of careless policies and management, cracks began to appear in the political facade of unity. Some old-time politicians (e.g., Jaramogi Oginga Odinga, once the leader of KPU) wanted to form a new party opposed to KANU. Moi, possibly fearing that his control was waning, responded by detaining these politicians—and the attorneys who agreed to defend them. He went further in 1982 by pushing through the National Assembly a constitutional amendment that made KANU the only legal political party in Kenya. However, even this did not remove all the threats to Moi's leadership. On August 1 that same year, disgruntled officers and soldiers in the Kenyan air force staged a coup, which gained spontaneous support from university students in Nairobi and led to widespread looting in the commercial area of the capital before being put down. Moi realized that he had to develop a new network of followers who owed their allegiance more directly to him. In short, he had to start from scratch.

This was not easy for a person who came from one of Kenya's most insignificant ethnic groups, the Tugen. Moi lacked the personal charisma of Kenyatta, so he had to build up a following using other means. Whereas Kenyatta had relied primarily on the Provincial Administration, the arm of the state, to secure stability and loyalty to his regime, Moi decided to strengthen KANU to achieve his ends. He insisted that all political leaders and government civil servants become lifetime members of the party, letting him more easily manage political loyalties. By expelling leaders who spoke critically of the government, he demonstrated what would happen to others engaging in the same activity. His personalized rule was reinforced by a number of appointments of Kalenjins—of which the Tugen are a subgroup—to key positions in the security and other government services (*Africa Confidential,* October 23, 1990).

His most serious challenge, however, was to govern the country without alienating the Kikuyu (Throup 1987b). Charles Njonjo had become a threat by virtue of the power he had accumulated, so Moi branded him a traitor and removed him from government, finishing him off as a political figure. Thereafter Moi had to identify other Kikuyus ready to support his regime. Since 1983 he has relied on shifting coalitions among the Kikuyu and often has been forced to play one faction against the other. The uncertainty thus created became too much for one prominent Kikuyu politician, Kenneth Matiba, who voluntarily stepped down as cabinet minister in 1988 following several efforts to rig elections in his constituency in favor of his political rival. Moi retained a Kikuyu as vice president until 1989, but since then the sense of political marginalization among the Kikuyus has intensified.

This dissatisfaction became immediately apparent when Moi gave way to pressures for change and reintroduced multiparty politics in 1992. Large numbers of Kikuyu politicians defected from KANU to the opposition, foremost among them Mwai Kibaki, once the country's vice president, and Kenneth Matiba. Though Moi initially feared multiparty politics would encourage ethnic divisions and bring the country to the brink of anarchy, he realized later that the opposition, in spite of its shared antipathy toward KANU and himself, would split up into smaller parties—and that he could help promote that process by his own intrigues. This fragmentation showed up in the outcome of the December 1992 elections—the country's first nationwide open balloting since independence—in which Moi and KANU won enough support to be returned to power for another five years.

Detribalization in Tanzania

TANU's first chairman, Julius Nyerere, became the country's government leader at independence. Like Moi, he came from a very small ethnic group, the Zanaki, but he faced different circumstances. First, he was the leader of a nationalist movement that had proved its popularity in every corner of the country. Second, no ethnic group was really very dominant in the country. Third, the entire population had access to Kiswahili, a Bantu-based lingua franca that Nyerere was quick to develop into an effective instrument of national integration. Ethnicity, therefore, was somewhat easier to manage in Tanzania than in Kenya.

The principal challenge in the early postindependence years came from Nyerere's decision to create a union between Tanganyika (the mainland) and Zanzibar (the islands off the Indian Ocean coast), which had gained independence separately in 1964 but soon thereafter saw its Arab-dominated government overthrown by an African opposition (Lofchie 1965). As part of this agreement, Nyerere accepted a nonelected political representation from Zanzibar in the Tanzania National Assembly that was disproportionately large given its relatively small population size. Until 1977 the two parts of the union had separate constitutions, but after that the mainland and the islands have operated under one and the same.

In gaining the upper hand in his political battles, Nyerere has relied on his own eloquence—in both English and Kiswahili—as well as an articulate political ideology. In addition to having inherent egalitarian principles, Nyerere's version of socialism—*ujamaa*—has enabled both leaders and followers to elevate political discourse to a level where ethnicity doesn't count. As Martin (1990) notes, Tanzania has achieved a remarkable degree of national integration by emphasizing African symbols that cut across ethnic boundaries.

Nyerere has also made full use of the strong political organization he and his fellow nationalist leaders developed before independence. Tanzania was the first African country to constitutionalize one-party rule, doing so in 1965 (Bienen 1970: 198–201; Msekwa 1974). This system allowed candidates approved by higher party organs to compete for seats in the National Assembly but ensured that every leader adhered to the official party platform and did not criticize it in public. The party's strong hold over the people reduced the risk of dissension based on such factors as race and ethnicity. Ideological scrutiny of aspiring political leaders in the elections was very close, particularly after Tanzania adopted the Arusha Declaration as its blueprint for development in 1967.

Nyerere stepped down as head of state in 1985 and as party chairman five years later, making him one of a very small number of African leaders who have voluntarily relinquished power. The smoothness with which power was gradually transferred to his successor, Ali Hassan Mwinyi, as both head of state and party must be attributed to the normative foundation laid by Nyerere, notably with regard to intercommunal relations. It is true that Nyerere, like other African leaders, depended on a small circle of close advisers, many of whom came from his home area, but his ability to rely fully on members of any ethnic group in the country gave him a larger measure of political maneuverability than his counterparts. This is not to suggest that ethnicity has vanished from Tanzanian politics—it is present, but only at levels and in contexts where it does not threaten the basic premises of the country's system of governance. This pattern could change, of course, with the decision to introduce multiparty democracy.

The role of ethnicity in the politics of the two countries has been discussed by Barkan and Chege in Chapters 1 and 2, respectively. Suffice it to say here that the way political leaders in Kenya and Tanzania have decided to handle the issue of ethnicity has given rise to a political logic that differs from the one usually accepted as typical of liberal democracies. As Riker (1962) has stated it, political leaders in liberal democracies aim for the coalition minimally necessary to achieve their policy objectives. A coalition size beyond the minimum leads to waste—i.e., political resources distributed to "unnecessary" constituencies. The communitarian model of politics in Kenya and Tanzania promotes a different logic, one that stresses inclusion rather than exclusion on the assumption that inability to represent all communities is a sign of weakness. Thus, for example, when President Moi appointed his new cabinet in January 1993, he decided that his political standing would be seriously compromised without representation by both the Kikuyu and the Luo peoples in his government, even though his party had won no seats in the districts inhabited by these groups.

Economy and Politics

If the Western model of pluralism is one of efficiency in resource allocation and the Third World model of pluralism is one of coercion, the one that emerged in postindependence Africa is one of consensus. The latter is the base on which politics rests; it is a prerequisite for stability. Where consensus breaks down because of political rivalries, the very foundation of the state is at stake, as the examples of Ethiopia, Liberia, Somalia, and the Sudan have recently demonstrated. It is imperative, therefore, that African leaders have the ability to mobilize enough resources to keep their political coalitions alive. This patronage has often been considerable, making politics in Africa quite an expensive affair. In this section, I discuss how the lines between economics and politics in Kenya and Tanzania have been affected by this approach.

"Corruption" in Kenya

Where patronage politics prevails, political accountability entails more than the client's obligations to his patron. It also includes the latter's obligation to dispense resources within his power in line with his communal obligations and to do so on a more or less indefinite basis. Such politics rest on a moral foundation of reciprocity rather than on a legal one specifying rights and duties within definite frameworks. Patronage, then, is a "rightful" practice, but it often entails violating rules and principles set out in constitutional and legal documents. Therefore, many have concluded that patronage politics is corrupt. The issue has become particularly controversial in Kenya for reasons I outline below.

Kenya adopted a market-oriented approach to development. Although there were initial pressures to nationalize resources at independence, the Kenyatta government satisfied itself with a redistribution of land to Africans, which fell far short of the expectations generated in more radical circles (Wasserman 1976). Kenyatta's pragmatism, many now argue, has paid off. Unlike countries that took more drastic measures to transform their economies, Kenya has experienced satisfactory economic growth. But how did Kenyatta use the economy to support his political objectives?

His principal strategy was to create a number of parastatal bodies, notably the Industrial and Commercial Development Corporation (ICDC) and the Kenya National Trading Corporation (KNTC), to provide credit and other forms of support for budding entrepreneurs. Much of the demand for these services came spontaneously from the entrepreneurial-minded Kikuyu, but the skewed distribution of these benefits was further reinforced by the fact that these bodies were controlled by Kikuyu appointees. With the benefit of hindsight, it is easy to see that this approach led not only to rapid Africanization of certain sectors of the economy, notably the retail sector, but also to a strengthening of Kenyatta's political base. Allocation of resources through these parastatal bodies quite closely reflected political loyalties (Leys 1974: 148–169).

In more subtle moves, Kenyatta enabled his family members and loyal followers to take advantage of growing opportunities in the private sector. Members of this elite cadre became partners in joint ventures, were appointed to boards of directors or to management positions, or were allowed to receive "commissions" from newly launched enterprises. Particularly noticeable was the appointment of Udi Gecaga, Kenyatta's son-in-law, as managing director of Lonhro East Africa, the biggest foreign conglomeration operating in Kenya.

This obvious funneling of patronage to the Kikuyu, especially to the Kiambu subgroup, caused political tensions. However, the only serious threat to this form of subnationalism came, ironically, from within the ranks of the Kikuyu themselves, who were divided among those who felt they had benefited from political independence and those who felt they had not. J. M. Kariuki appealed to the latter but ultimately became a victim of his ambition to form a broader political coalition. In this effort he had latent, if not manifest, support from leaders in other ethnic communities (Throup 1987b: 51). As discussed by Barkan in Chapter 1, Kenyatta's patronage costs were relatively low compared to Moi's. The latter's strategy of playing one faction against the other required far more resources to implement than Kenyatta's.

Moi's decision to follow in Kenyatta's footsteps implied no change in economic policy; Kenya remained a market economy, but with the Kikuyu now effectively entrenched. Moi's political challenge was to redistribute patronage to groups other than the Kikuyu. After a slow start that lost him credibility among those with especially high expectations, Moi began more actively to challenge the Kenyatta establishment in the 1980s. Most beneficiaries were loyal members of the Kalenjin elite, many of whom were appointed to key positions in the public sector. Also in the private sector, Moi used his political influence to limit Kikuyu domination. Thus, for example, Udi Gecaga was replaced as the key Lonhro East Africa manager by a close confidante of the president, Mark arap Too. In short, Kikuyus were gradually removed from top positions and replaced by persons owing their loyalty to Moi (*Africa Confidential,* December 21, 1983, and October 23, 1990). These spoils have dramatically changed the face of the public sector.

In trying to build national support and consensus, Moi has also engaged in massive funding of community development projects initiated by local representatives of the political elite. Although the exact sources of Moi's own contributions to these schemes are not known, there is reason to believe that donations from the financially strong Asian minority and profits from the president's own financial empire have enabled him to engage in this political largesse. Loyalty to the president has increasingly become an essential determinant of success in the private sector, as licenses, credits, and other benefits are channeled through politically controlled institutions and may be denied. Because these loyalties to a great extent have been built up through illicit means, followers are obviously restrained from open criticism of the president or his rule.

What Moi is doing is no different in principle from what was done by his predecessor. The question that remains is whether these political practices are truly corrupt. Many Kenyans as well as outside observers believe they are, but others consider "feathering your own nest" to be perfectly all right. Much of the controversy stems from the fact that political patronage makes the patron's interests almost impossible to disentangle from the client's. If such conduct does not violate the norms of the client, it is corruption only if it violates the norms of others. In societies where the community model of politics has taken root, such a violation will be consciously noted only where some very obvious discrimination is taking place. Political leaders know this and thus prefer to hide any sectional preferences behind the curtain of national consensus. Still, as the Moi regime has increasingly come to experience, national consensus is not the only norm embraced by Kenyans. A growing number are dissatisfied with the secrecy with which public policy is made and resources are allocated. The magnitude and nakedness of corruption under Moi has also become a sticking point with the IMF because it is now a serious threat to the economy. The perception of sectional preferences as corruption has become more widespread over the years as Kenya has become more fully integrated into the global economy and Kenyans have been exposed to models of social and political behavior that define corruption as the West does. The strength of this definition will be put to special test in the current multiparty context.

Nationalization in Tanzania

Julius Nyerere never was under the same pressure as Kenyatta was to satisfy patronage expectations among his followers after independence. He made his socialist aspirations clear quite early. They took final shape in the Arusha Declaration and the various strategy documents that followed in its wake in the late 1960s and early 1970s. Much has been said about what drove him in this direction (for the most authoritative account, see Pratt 1976). Besides such factors as a Puritan strand in his personality, his exposure to Fabianism while studying in Britain, or the persuasive example of rural communes that he visited in China, Nyerere realized the political advantages of being able to control the economy. He had a firm belief that equity precedes growth, that people's social needs must be satisfied in order to make them more productive (Nyerere 1968). Thus, he saw a chance to bring the twin objectives of development and stability together in one strategy that emphasized political interventionism. The beauty of this strategy was that he could hide his patronage maneuvers behind the official rhetoric of development in a way that was far more difficult to do in a market-oriented context like Kenya's. Whereas Nyerere could make it look as if economics and politics were mutually supportive, Kenyatta and Moi found themselves making political moves that could not be justified on economic grounds.

For much of the 1970s, the rest of the world was ready to buy Nyerere's approach to development, and he could cash in on generous flows of foreign aid that further boosted his resource base. As he continued to push socialist measures further with fewer apparent successes, however, his friends in the international community began to get cold feet. In spite of declining flows of foreign aid and demands from the IMF and World Bank that he deregulate the country's economy, Nyerere never conceded defeat and did not abandon his socialist policies until almost all economic activities of any significance had been brought under political control (Ndulu 1986).

Nyerere's ability to bring the economy under direct party control through a series of decrees gave him an almost unlimited scope for dispensing patronage. It seems there is a positive correlation between the strong support Nyerere continued to enjoy, on the one hand, and his access to resources for political patronage, on the other. From a neoclassical "efficiency" viewpoint, it can be argued that he "wasted" a lot of resources—i.e., that he secured for himself greater control than was necessary to sustain political support and stability. After all, the conditions in Tanzania were not very threatening. Moreover, he had been able to achieve remarkably broad support by promoting the Kiswahili language and the African culture that goes with it. In short, his socialist policies had erased much of the cultural foundation for capitalism in the country.

Nyerere let his strategy run full course. By the time he stepped down as head of state in 1985, the country's economy was at a low ebb. There was virtually no foreign exchange left, and manufacturing and service enterprises were suffering from the shortage; agricultural production had gone down; the physical infrastructure was in poor shape; and, above all, Tanzanians had suffered a serious decline in real per capita income (Bevan, Collier, and Gunning 1989: 64). In spite of this decay, Tanzanians did not respond by demonstrating in the streets or taking any other action hostile to the state, one reason being that they had been indoctrinated to believe that the cause of their difficulties was external, not domestic. Also important was the fact that most Tanzanians could engage in private economic activities that helped them secure their livelihood. Land was not in short supply, not even in the urban centers, where home gardens and other agricultural pursuits became very popular. For those who could not live off the land, nonagricultural enterprises grew in number. A second economy was rapidly becoming the mainstay for a growing number of Tanzanians (Maliyamkono and Bagachwa 1990). The politically important aspect of this spontaneous development is that it reduced the risk of widespread political opposition. People were not resentful of the state because through bribes they could secure needed advantages (Tripp 1990). The most harmful implication of this rapid "individualization" of commercial and productive activities was that nobody really cared about the public infrastructure needed to sustain economic health in the long run.

The Mwinyi government has tried to deal with this challenge for five years, but even with foreign aid the task is far beyond the capacity of the Tanzanian government and other public bodies. The infrastructure for national development remains inadequate and poses a serious limit to sustainable progress in the years ahead.

The communitarian model of politics, with its insistence on consensus and secrecy, has been developed in the context of two different economic systems. In both, however, it has helped divert attention away from such values as efficiency, which foreign aid theories (Riddell 1988) consider a sine qua non for progress. The result is that pressures have developed in the international community as well as in Kenya and Tanzania for aid to be channeled through nongovernmental organizations and for its use to become more transparent. This pressure has raised anew the question of what the relations between state and society should be. I now turn to that topic.

State and Civil Society

At independence, Kenya and Tanzania inherited the "Westminster model" of parliamentary government from the British. Under this model, political parties were regarded as electoral organizations whose functions were limited to stimulating electoral interest in politics, selecting and campaigning for parliamentary candidates, reflecting the interests and opinions of diverse groups in society, and organizing support for the government in power or for an alternative to it. In this sense, the party, with the exception of its parliamentary representatives, was not meant to be at the center stage of policymaking. In both countries, the National Assembly was regarded as the supreme lawmaking body, although only a section of it—the cabinet—was involved in public policymaking on a day-to-day basis. Principal decisionmaking organs of the parties were extraparliamentary units and therefore able to participate in policymaking only if consulted by their leaders, the heads of state (Okumu and Holmquist 1984: 47).

The constitutions of both countries anticipated the active participation of citizens in politics through voluntary associations and political parties. In short, state organs were seen as being accountable to independent organizations representing various sectors of civil society. After independence, however, things moved in a very different direction.

State-Society Struggles in Kenya

Kenya stayed with the Westminster model longer than Tanzania. Even after the KANU-KADU merger in 1964, the cabinet and the National Assembly retained their positions of prominence in policymaking. As KANU tried to put an end to the quasifederal constitution approved before independence and to create a unitary state, it relied on the organs of government rather than its own organization. During this critical period, KANU suffered from benign neglect. In order to better understand Kenyatta's decision to rely on the state to achieve his political ends, it is important to say a few words about the political parties that emerged in Kenya on the eve of independence.

When KANU and KADU were formed in 1960, only three years before independence, they emerged as loose amalgamations of existing district political associations controlled by a small number of patrons. Almost all of these associations, which became party branches, were ethnically homogeneous in composition. Kenyatta personally played no important role in the emergence of these parties and thus had little direct interest in them. Moreover, because local patrons controlled grassroots politics, Kenyatta was effectively blocked from direct access to the population. Instead of getting embroiled in day-to-day conflicts within the party, Kenyatta decided to stay aloof and adopt the position of *mzee* (old man) or "father of the nation" (Bienen 1974: 75).

He did not, however, cease to exercise political influence. On the contrary, he developed alternative mechanisms to strengthen his own position and that of the presidency. By staying above party conflicts, he could bypass the KANU apparatus and develop his own informal patron-client hierarchies, of which he served as the head. For example, Kenyatta held no consultations with parliamentarians for most of his time in power, setting an example that his cabinet ministers followed by ignoring the backbenchers (Gertzel 1970: 150). He also made full use of the Provincial Administration, which was created as the backbone of the new unitary state. By so doing, he may also have calmed the fears of Kenya's remaining European settlers that as the country's political leader he would encourage the influence of a rambunctious party organization (Tamarkin 1978: 306).

The rise of the presidency was institutionalized through a series of constitutional amendments in the 1960s that, among other things, allowed the head of state to detain individuals without trial and to nominate twelve members of his choice to the National Assembly. The net effects of all these changes was to reduce the power of KANU and to enable an oligarchy of cabinet ministers and top state bureaucrats to become increasingly independent and defiant of the National Assembly.

The elected representatives also gave KANU only scant attention and preferred to exercise their influence directly through the National Assembly. Throughout the Kenyatta period, members of the Assembly were very active, often exercising considerable influence on public policy. There were occasions when its challenge was seen as too strong by Kenyatta and his advisers, and in these instances he did not hesitate to take action, sometimes detaining members without trial. In sum, much of this period (1963–1978) was characterized by confrontations between the state authorities and a still relatively autonomous civil society.

From 1969 to 1982, after the demise of KPU, Kenya was a de facto one-party state. Moi's succession in 1978 did not lead to any immediate reactivation of the party. Only his decision in 1982 to constitutionalize the one-party system, thus making KANU the sole legal party in the country, was accompanied by a call to activate the party organization. What happened after 1982, however, was more a tightening of Moi's grip on his followers than a mobilization of grassroots opinions. The patron-client hierarchy he had built to replace the Kenyatta legacy was retained and strengthened by such organizational measures as the introduction of KANU life membership (which, as suggested above, became de facto obligatory for all parliamentarians and top civil servants) and the formation of a party disciplinary committee to mete out punishment against any leader who did not toe the official political line as stated by the president.

The most significant change, however, was the revitalization of the KANU Parliamentary Group, which began meeting behind closed doors. Although the minutes of these meetings have not been made public, there is little doubt that their main purpose was to eliminate the need for debate of policy issues in the National Assembly. In the 1980s, therefore, the legislative arm of government lost the significance it had in the Kenyatta days. Most Kenyans agree that it became no more than a rubber-stamp of policies initiated by the President and his closest advisers and steamrolled through the KANU Parliamentary Group.

As if this measure were not enough to secure compliance, KANU also changed its own election rules in 1985: Voters would now queue behind candidates in primary elections instead of casting a secret ballot. Any candidate receiving more than 70 percent of the votes in these primaries did not need to contest the general elections. Although it was argued that this method would rule out rigging, as the winner was determined in the open, experience from the 1988 elections and subsequent by-elections indicate that election supervisors (usually government civil servants) did not hesitate to announce winners according to the wish of the KANU leadership.

This insensitivity by the party leaders came to a head in 1990. First a respected cabinet minister, Robert Ouko, was murdered under circumstances that suggested a political motivation; then two former cabinet ministers, Kenneth Matiba and Charles Rubia, drawing on the political reform measures being introduced elsewhere in Africa, proposed a public debate about whether Kenya should become a multiparty state or not. Arguing that KANU's monopolization of the political scene and its tendency to treat politics as a private rather than a public affair had preempted the rights of Kenyan citizens to participate in politics, they wanted to submit the system to public scrutiny. The notion of multipartyism received spontaneous support, particularly among the Kikuyu, and demonstrations in favor of the idea were held in Nairobi and other cities. Rather than giving in to these pressures, however, the president ordered Matiba and Rubia detained and sent security forces into the streets to quell any further public demonstrations challenging KANU's authority.

Similar sentiments had been expressed by church leaders and lawyers throughout the 1980s. Together with growing international criticism of the Kenyan government's lack of sensitivity to the demand for political reform, these internal pressures convinced the KANU leadership to reconsider its system of governance. At a special delegates' conference of the ruling party held in December 1990, the leaders agreed to what was minimally necessary: to scrap the queuing and 70 percent rule and to eliminate the party disciplinary committee. At the same time the president decided to restore the independence of key judicial positions, something he had unilaterally taken away in the 1980s.

This retreat, however, was made only grudgingly and did not satisfy the growing opposition to Moi's rule. Nor did it please Kenya's many generous donors, who increasingly made respect for human rights and the introduction of competitive party politics a condition for future aid. The relatively open economy in Kenya and the country's extensive exposure to outside influences through tourism, modern media (among others, CNN), and the fact that thousands of Kenyans are educated abroad have given added impetus to the rise of a civil society that is not easily silenced. Ever since independence, Kenya, unlike most other African countries, has allowed a strong nongovernmental sector to exist. The autocratic rule of President Moi, therefore, has increasingly become an anachronism for many Kenyans. At the same time, they wondered what would happen if multipartyism were returned. The elections in December 1992 confirmed the vitality of civil society but left many questions regarding the implications of multipartyism unanswered.

Party Supremacy in Tanzania

Tanganyika became independent in 1961 with one party—TANU—having won all seats but one in the National Assembly. Unlike Kenya, where the political movements lacked widespread grassroots support, TANU was a genuine mass party that had built its strength in the course of struggling for independence. The country's first government leader, Nyerere, was also, and perhaps foremost, a party man. It is instructive that only a few months after independence he stepped down as Prime Minister to devote himself full-time to further strengthening the party (Bienen 1970).

All the same, in the very first years of independence the country retained much of the Westminster legacy. The National Executive Committee (NEC) of TANU and the National Assembly operated under a gentlemen's agreement. The broader policy issues were to be discussed by the NEC, whereas the latter would consider such questions as when, how, and in what order policies would be approved. To be sure, there were tensions in this relationship, and it wasn't always clear where the line between the two was being drawn. For example, in discussions of constitutional amendments in 1962, then Prime Minister Rashidi Kawawa argued that the National Assembly was the "fount of authority that must remain sovereign" (Msekwa 1974: 15). There was also a distinct belief in the minds of parliamentarians that they were superior to the members of the NEC.

The possibility of turning the country into a one-party state had been broached already in 1963, but it became more urgent as the national coalition began to unravel in 1964 when an army mutiny set in motion an attempt by trade union leaders to seize state power (Miti 1980: 189–190). In 1965 a special commission was appointed to propose the adoption of a democratic one-party system that would allow citizens a choice among individual candidates. The report, which was adopted by the National Assembly the same year, provided a turning point in party-state relations. It gave not only TANU but also the NEC new constitutional status. The NEC would not only continue to lay out broad policy but also would have the right to summon witnesses and call for papers, which previously had been the exclusive prerogative of the National Assembly. Members of the NEC would enjoy the same status as parliamentarians and receive the same pay as them (Tanzania 1965: 17). TANU was in fact made a constitutional category, and the party constitution was merged with that of the state. The overall effect of this constitutional reform was to remove policymaking from the public arena to an essentially closed one. As Miti puts it: "All conflicts were from now on to be resolved in private under the party umbrella" (Miti 1980: 193).

When these proposals were first made to the National Assembly, they met with no overt resistance. Most members appear to have agreed that these were logical steps for a de facto one-party system to take. The issue came to a head in 1968, however, a year after the introduction of the Arusha Declaration, when a group of eight parliamentarians decided to test whether the NEC or the National Assembly was really supreme. They wanted to reassert the legislature's supremacy over the party because they feared the country's headlong rush toward socialism was detrimental to national interests. The issue resulted in their expulsion from TANU and the loss of their seats in the National Assembly on the ground that they were disloyal and uncommitted to TANU's principles and program.

After that incident, party supremacy was unchallenged and further strengthened in the 1977 constitution, which was the first to cover both the mainland and Zanzibar after their merger. The party, which that year changed its name to Chama cha Mapinduzi (CCM, the Party of the Revolution), continued to strengthen its central decisionmaking organs. Its Central Committee, consisting of less than twenty senior political leaders, emerged as the real powerhouse, particularly after it had established special departments to serve its policymaking needs. Many senior civil servants were picked to fill the positions in these departments. The party organization took on many of the features associated with a communist party. Nyerere summarized party-state relations in 1974:

> TANU can call the Cabinet, any Minister, or any Government official, to account for their activities and any failure in the execution of their duty. That is at the national level. The same is true at the local level. In the

localities, the Branch, District, or Regional TANU Committees are the people's representatives. It is their task to guide and supervise the actions of all government officials in their area, and to ensure that our policies are implemented in such a way that they bring maximum benefit to the people as a whole. Further, it is through TANU that the people in our villages and towns can take part in local and national planning for future development (*Daily News,* February 23, 1974).

There is evidence that the party did exercise its role as guardian of appropriate conduct in public institutions, causing civil servants and managers in parastatal institutions to be suspended or dismissed in some instances. Many breaches of such conduct, however, went unnoticed, and others were too sensitive to resolve through punishment. Thus, the overall party record gave rise to cynicism in many circles, people arguing that the party was only ready to deal with the small fry, not the big shots.

This skepticism vis-à-vis the party continued to grow in the 1980s as the failures of its socialist policies became increasingly apparent. Though TANU/CCM continued to have some form of "parental authority" (Miller 1970), its ability to guide economic policy in a credible fashion seriously declined thereafter. At the same time, the party had effectively pulverized any opposition to its rule. Those disaffected realized they were too dispersed and that the task of overthrowing the government was beyond their capacity. With the exception of a few amateurish attempts in the early 1980s, when the economic situation was at its worst, no coups were attempted in Tanzania despite the increasingly evident gap between political promise and results. The party enjoyed a definite measure of legitimacy as an agency of law and order, if not as one of development. Many Tanzanians could not visualize their country without it. Yet the effect of this monopolization was to seriously marginalize civil society. CCM had become a party associated wholly with the state.

Party monopolization of policymaking and other nondemocratic features of CCM's system of governance became the subject of much debate in the early 1990s. Ironically, it was Nyerere, the architect of the one-party system, who first raised doubts in public about the wisdom, following the collapse of communism in Eastern Europe, of treating that aspect of the political system as permanent. Eventually President Mwinyi appointed a constitutional review commission under the leadership of Chief Justice Francis Nyalali. Its report recommended the introduction of multiparty politics (although it claimed that the majority of Tanzanians still preferred the one-party model [Tanzania 1992c]). The National Assembly soon approved that recommendation without much debate. When parties were allowed to register in 1992, no less than seventeen separate organizations applied. Following scrutiny by the Attorney-General's Office as to whether they fulfilled the qualifications laid out in the law, eight were initially registered. By the end of 1993 twelve parties had been legalized. In spite of their presence, however, the dominance of CCM has continued. It still exercises its parental authority in much of rural Tanzania. The official media still favor it. For these reasons it is not surprising that in the two by-elections held in February 1994, CCM had no difficulty defeating the divided opposition. Regular parliamentary elections are scheduled for 1995. Unless the opposition unites and fields joint candidates, the prospect of CCM maintaining its power, as KANU did in Kenya 1992, is very high.

Both Kenya and Tanzania have followed the logic of its consensual approach to politics by creating a strong center that gives guidance to policy. The Kenyans took longer than the Tanzanians to turn the party organization into an instrument for sustaining such guidance. By the 1980s, however, both had allowed the ruling party to preempt independent initiatives arising from civil society. Partly because of greater effectiveness in organization and partly because of the dispersed and relatively backward nature of Tanzanian society, this objective of "choking" civil society was particularly successful there. In Kenya, greater economic and social differentiation made it more difficult to impose such tight rule. Yet by the early 1990s civil society had begun to assert itself in both countries. A major factor tipping the balance in this direction was external pressure.

EXTERNAL INFLUENCES

Two aspects of this issue are of special relevance to this chapter: 1) the extent to which events in other countries or regions of the world help shape governance in Kenya and Tanzania, and 2) the extent to which Kenya and Tanzania are obliged to adjust their regimes because of pressures from the international donor community.

In his discussion of the problems of transition to democracy, Przeworski (1986: 52–53) has stressed that "a regime does not collapse unless and until some alternative is organized in such a way as to present a real choice for isolated individuals." Such alternatives typically do not arise in the domestic arena but become available as models through communication with other countries. Not everything that happens elsewhere, however, is turned into a model event. Some developments take on more significance than others. For example, Huntington (1984) argues that some countries serve as "pacesetters" for others. This thesis has some relevance for Latin America, where democratization in one country appears to have had a "contagion" effect. The question that interests us here is how far this thesis is applicable to Kenya and Tanzania.

To date, no African country has emerged as a pacesetter. Efforts at constitutionalizing politics in the direction of federal democracy in Nigeria have had little or no effect elsewhere on the continent, with the possible exception of Ethiopia. It is rather as if other Africans have treated Nigeria, because of its great size, as exceptional. South Africa has remained an outcast for the whole postindependence period and has emerged as a possible pacesetter only in the 1990s. It is too early to make any statement as to whether the establishment of an all-parties government of national unity in South Africa will affect political trends in other African countries.

In the absence of any model close to home, where have Africans looked for a lead? For political, if not economic, models, both Tanzania and Kenya under Moi have looked more to communist nations than to the Western democracies. As suggested above, the latter were largely rejected or abandoned in the early postindependence period. The tight systems of control associated with the totalitarian regimes, however, served political leaders emerging on a weak power base. For instance, Moi was an admirer of Ceausescu's Romania. Although it is questionable whether Kenya, as Widner (1992) argues, became a party-state in the manner of the former Soviet Union or Tanzania, Moi clearly felt more comfortable with the authoritarian model of the East than with the pluralist one of the West in building what might be best described as a clientelist machine to perpetuate his personal rule. Nyerere appears to have been less impressed by the political than by the economic aspects of the communist systems, but he often made statements that implied his admiration for their achievements.

Both leaders were taken by surprise in late 1989 when communism in Eastern Europe was abandoned overnight. The responses of the two leaders in coping with the abrupt disappearance of their model are instructive. President Moi denied that the turn of events in Eastern Europe had any relevance to his country, which, he said, has always been a market economy. Nyerere, on the other hand, admitted the challenge that this set of events posed to African countries. Clearly, his decision to encourage multiparty debate in 1990 was at least in part a response to this external factor. Thus, the regime in Kenya became more repressive, and democratization elsewhere (especially in Eastern Europe) became a lever for the forces opposed to Moi's way of governance. In Tanzania, Nyerere preempted such a move by taking the initiative, engendering greater openness and the possibility of a calm transition to democracy.

Western governments have also changed their attitude toward African regimes as a result of the collapse of communism. Whereas they kept silent on the question of democracy and respect for human rights during the first three decades of independence, either for fear of interfering in the internal affairs of another country or for more selfish reasons, they have in the 1990s begun to attach political conditions to their loans and grants to African governments. The Western position is that political autocracy and instability are at the core of Africa's difficulties in making social and economic progress. Now that Eastern European countries have shown they can transform their political systems, Third World countries, particularly those in Africa, must also do so. For a long time, the international donor community, in which the Western countries play the lead role, has argued that the principal constraints to development in Africa are physical, economic, institutional, or technical (lack of skills). None of these alone has proved to be a sufficient explanation, and in the 1990s, therefore, the donors are increasingly blaming "the crisis of governance," as the World Bank labels it in its most recent report on Africa (World Bank 1989a: 60–61). Most African governments have responded with uneasiness to these new pressures for democratization by the Western governments. The implication is that the West has the answers to what African leaders consider to be very complex sets of problems. African rulers also consider this new move by the West to be a flagrant attempt to dictate matters of each sovereign state. President Moi has been among those most angered by these dictates. Because of his long insistence on the continued validity of the constitutional one-party system, he has found himself particularly far away from the Western position on this issue.

The response in Tanzania has been more measured. In spite of his political preference over the years for the communist model, Nyerere, true to the nonaligned position of his country in international affairs, retained close relations with many Western governments, particularly in Europe. Neither he nor his successor, Mwinyi, allowed himself to get on the defensive on this issue. Instead, they raised the matter in the Organization of African Unity at its annual 1990 meeting, where it led to a resolution, adopted by all heads of state, stating that African governments do take democracy seriously and want to be given the opportunity to prove their commitment to this idea without being forced to do so by external political conditionalities. It is also significant that it was Nyerere, the architect of the single-party system, who laid out the case of multipartyism at a major meeting of the ruling party in February 1992. His argument this time was based on the need for accountability, which had gotten increasingly lost in the old system. Realizing that Africa would soon have little choice but to democratize, he reiterated that democracy must be allowed to grow in response to domestic needs and pressures (Nyerere 1992).

The insistence by Western governments on conditionalities has also been met with mixed reactions among those opposed to the incumbent governments. Some have argued that the West's position is justified because it helps the democratic forces in Africa to grow stronger vis-à-vis the many oppressive regimes. Others, however, have argued that by accepting such a position, the African opposition plays into the hands of the governments, who can accuse them of serving foreign interests. Furthermore, some have felt uncomfortable that their own pressures for greater democracy are being overshadowed by similar demands from external donors, thus leaving them in a backwater position. External factors, then, have had an ambiguous influence on recent government reform in Kenya and Tanzania. If anything, it appears that the turn of events in Eastern Europe has been the most important of these factors in encouraging a move toward greater openness.

CONCLUSIONS

The study of governance encourages us to consider the extent to which politics is an independent variable in shaping the development of society. Without ignoring the fact that economic and social forces set the stage for much of politics—and if the presumed correlation between economic growth and political democracy holds in the long run—the focus adopted in this chapter allows us to consider the possibility of exceptions. Particularly intriguing in the 1990s is that democratization is being attempted in many parts of the world in a period of economic stagnation or decline.

In the specific case of East Africa, I have tried to demonstrate that Tanzania, which is one of the poorest countries of the world and which has experienced economic decline for over a decade, has found it easier to make the transition to multiparty politics than its wealthier neighbor, Kenya. Economic growth in Kenya appears to have increased the tensions between various groups in society so much that the government has feared to abandon the one-party system and has retained an extensive security apparatus to control and suppress any political opposition. The more muted response in Tanzania may largely be explained by the fact that the ruling party and state have remained quite strong and are comparatively less threatened by bourgeois and middle-class opposition than is the case in Kenya. This study suggests that, at least among low-income countries, differences in level or pace of economic development are not necessarily correlated positively with prospects for democracy.

It also suggests that we need to pay attention to process variables, notably the influence of the accumulated experience that society carries forward. In Latin America, much of the transition to democracy in the early 1980s was generated by the failures—and oppressive tendencies—of the continent's many military rulers. Neither Kenya nor Tanzania has experienced military rule, but the lessons still count. In Tanzania the accumulated experience of failure with Nyerere's socialist policies began to generate its own dynamic in the 1980s, which somehow coincided with the trends in Eastern Europe. Even though nobody in East Africa recognized the parallel before the sudden collapse in the late 1980s of the communist systems, Nyerere and his supporters could relate to the experience of Poland and Czechoslovakia more directly than their Kenyan counterparts, who viewed the Eastern European events as a threat. Thus, Tanzania, in spite of its poverty, could make better use of this historical opportunity than Kenya and progress further toward democracy than its northern *and wealthier* neighbor. The next few years will provide more evidence as to the validity of this point.

What difference will this make in the long run? Will the fact that Tanzania has found it easier than Kenya to open the door to a more open and pluralistic political system also make a difference ten or twenty years from now? We do not really have the empirical data to answer that question. Democratization under adverse economic conditions in a world with no viable communist alternative available is a new scenario. What is happening today in Kenya and Tanzania must be regarded as tentative transitions to democracy—transitions that may or may not succeed.

4

Economic Adjustment Policies

Benno J. Ndulu & Francis W. Mwega

The economic crises of the 1980s in Kenya and Tanzania exposed fundamental weaknesses in the structures and management of both economies. There were strong similarities in the nature of and responses to the crisis in each country. This resemblance was remarkable in light of the major differences in economic management between Kenya and Tanzania during the 1960s and 1970s. However, management systems now seem to be converging as both countries strive to reverse the recent economic downturn and embark on renewed growth. In both cases, structural weaknesses, external factors, and domestic policies seem to have contributed to the stagnation of the 1980s. The ongoing efforts at economic reform and structural adjustment in both countries are similar in many respects, not only because they are both spearheaded by International Monetary Fund (IMF) and World Bank programs, but more fundamentally because of the common problems they address.

Three major features characterize the crisis in each country. First are structural features, which delimit a narrow range of policy options available to weak and dependent economies. Second is the need for stabilization in view of unsustainable resource gaps characterizing these economies. Third, and partly related to the first feature, is the perceived need for the diversification of the economies in order to create a basis for a flexible response to changing conditions.

The impacts of structural weaknesses in limiting potentials for growth and development, flexible response to changing economic situations, and overall efficacy of policy have been widely discussed elsewhere (Taylor 1987; Helleiner 1990; Killick 1990). The main structural rigidities typically include dependent openness—which subjects economic performance to external volatility, immature and distorted markets, technological backwardness, and underdevelopment of human capacity—and institutional rigidities constraining management of change; in short, the essence of development. It is, however, important to distinguish between fundamental structural weaknesses of an economy, which are an objective condition, and structural maladaptation, which is a result of economic mismanagement. Whereas fundamental structural weaknesses constrain what is achievable, structural maladaptation prevents an economy from realizing what is achievable. Structural *transformation* deals with ingrained weaknesses, whereas structural *adjustment* largely focuses on getting economies back to their achievable frontiers. Both aspects of change are important and are significantly interrelated. Currently, however, the emphasis in both countries seems to be on redressing structural maladaptation and achieving macroeconomic stability.

Apart from setting traditional short-term objectives of restoring external and closely related internal financial account balances, macroeconomic stabilization is an important facet of the medium- and long-term growth process. Variability in resource gaps has tended to produce stop-and-go situations in the development process and in the 1980s threatened to wipe out the gains of the previous two decades. How have the processes of stabilization, adjustment, and transformation unfolded in Kenya and Tanzania, and what has been their impact on the economies of the two countries?

COMPARATIVE STRUCTURAL FEATURES

Both Kenya and Tanzania can largely be characterized as having weak, dependent economies; they predominantly export what they do not consume and import what they do not produce. This dependent structure of trade has two major implications for economic performance and management. Because of high import dependence in both production and investment (Table 4.1), growth and development are closely tied to the capacity to import, whether domestically generated or availed through net foreign resource inflows. Thus, export performance is of critical importance to supporting production and investment on a sustainable basis. Second, in view of the dominance in both economies of primary exports, which are subjected to the volatility of world markets, economic performance is much influenced by external shocks. Countercyclical management becomes extremely important for economic stability. Net foreign resource inflows have tended to be procyclical, increasing when economic performance is strong and decreasing when it is weak, which puts even more stress on economic management.

The dominance of the agricultural sector in material production, food supplies, source of livelihood, and generation of import capacity is evident in both countries. However, the sector's poor technological state and supportive economic/social infrastructure seriously constrain its capacity to cope with the rapidly growing demands put on it. Policy bias against farmers, whether in terms of direct resource allocation or incentive structure, only makes difficult matters worse. The centrality of agricultural policy cannot be overemphasized in this sense.

In both countries the role of state and parastatal agencies in resource

Table 4.1 Indicators of Economic Structure and Economic Performance

	Kenya			Tanzania		
	1965	1980	1990	1965	1980	1990
Gross Domestic Product (millions U.S. $)	920	6,018	7,540	790	4,565	2,060
Percent of GDP						
Agriculture	35	28	28	46	47	59
Industry	18	19	21	14	16	12
Services	47	41	51	40	37	29
Percent of total exports:						
Fuels, minerals & metals	13	34	19	1	10	5
Other primary products	77	50	70	88	74	84
Manufactures	6	15	11	13	15	11
Percent of total imports:						
Food	6	8	10	7	13	7
Fuels	10	34	32	9	21	31
Other primary products	4	3	4	2	3	2
Machinery & transport equipment	34	28	25	40	35	35
Other manufacturers	46	28	30	42	28	25

	Kenya			Tanzania		
	1970	1980	1990	1970	1980	1990
Long-term debt service						
Percent of GNP	3	6	6	2	3	13
Percent of exports	9	19	25	6	20	18
Terms of borrowing						
Average interest rate (%)	2.6	3.5	4.4	1.0	4.7	0.8
Average maturity (years)	37	31	23	40	21	37
Average grace period (years)	8	8	6	11	6	10

	Kenya		Tanzania	
	1965–1980	1980–1990	1965–1980	1980–1990
Average annual growth of trade (%)				
Merchandise exports	3.9	1.0	–4.2	–7.4
Merchandise imports	2.4	1.6	1.6	–0.5

Sources: World Bank, *World Development Report* (Oxford University Press, 1990, 1992); UNDP/World Bank, *African Economic Indicators* (Washington, D.C.: World Bank, 1990, 1992).

allocation is highly pronounced. The state has assumed the key role of pri-mary modernizing agent and uses resources it mobilizes through its fiscal powers, external resources channeled through it, and indirect controls on private resource allocation. In the absence of more open political systems in which organized interest groups can thrash out their differences, the state's involvement in resource allocation is also often a means of balancing the claims of different interest groups and maintaining patron-client networks (Ndulu 1986). Moreover, the symbiotic relationships between the state bureaucracy and the private sector, both foreign and indigenous, creates a large quasipublic sector that thrives on protective controls and preferential access to resources. A strong symmetry of interests exists between the public sector and the so-called modern private sector, insofar as price distortions and subsidized resources impede the implementation of economic reforms. Economic nationalism, largely promoted through a mixture of state participation and encouragement of indigenous quasiprivate sector growth, is an important feature in both countries. Controls have created a rich ground for rent-seeking behavior that traverses both sectors.

There are, however, some important differences between Kenya and Tanzania. Although their economic management styles are converging, the initial conditions are quite distinct. Perhaps the most important of these differences is that Tanzania, with its long-standing aspirations for socialism, has put a much greater emphasis on tackling issues of income distribution than has Kenya. It has focused not only on distribution of income per se but also on distribution of opportunities to earn income. State ownership of land, emphasis on basic needs, and enforcement of the country's Leadership Code are the cornerstones of minimizing disparities in income-earning opportunities. This feature largely explains the significant difference in degree of private sector participation (foreign and local) between the two countries. Important changes have been taking place in Tanzania over the past five years that have reduced these differences. Foreign private investment is now being encouraged and the restrictive leadership code has been relaxed, opening doors for local elites to divert the use of rental incomes from consumption to investment.

The second difference between the two countries is the extent of distortion in the macroeconomic incentive structure, which is partly linked to the difference in the extent of state control over resource allocation. This difference is best demonstrated by the disposition of key macroeconomic indicators related to the incentive structure (Table 4.2). One widely used distortion measure is the extent of deviation of the real exchange rate from some "appropriate" norm. This misalignment, which distorts both production and trading incentives, is measured in two ways in Table 4.2. First is the deviation of the real exchange rate from its appropriate levels in 1965–1966, when macroeconomic relationships were in balance and the economies were growing reasonably. Second is the extent of deviation of the official exchange rate from the black market rate, which is considered to measure more closely the scarcity of foreign exchange. In foreign exchange–constrained economies, exchange rate misalignment is of critical concern. The other measures of the incentive structure include the real interest rate, here emphasizing the resource mobilization effect, and the rate of inflation, which indicates the extent of internal macroeconomic imbalance. To a large extent these distortions are policy related. Kenya until very recently has managed to maintain a much less distorted macroeconomic incentive structure than Tanzania.

Table 4.2 Distortions of the Macroeconomic Incentive Structure

	Real Exchange Rate Index[a]		Ratio of Parallel to Official Exchange Rates		Real Interest Rate on Savings Deposits[b]		Inflation Rate	
	Kenya	Tanzania	Kenya	Tanzania	Kenya	Tanzania	Kenya	Tanzania
1966	100	100	—	1.2	−0.5	−1.6	4.0	4.7
1970	100	70	—	1.4	1.4	0.1	2.1	3.4
1974	87	78	—	1.9	−13.4	−13.1	17.7	19.7
1978	98	68	—	1.7	−11.8	−6.4	16.9	6.6
1980	94	60	1.1	2.6	−8.1	−25.3	13.8	30.3
1985	93	42	1.1	3.8	1.6	−23.3	13.1	33.3
1986	107	60	1.0	4.7	5.3	−22.4	5.6	32.4
1987	119	88	1.1	2.7	3.9	−8.5	7.1	29.9
1988	129	104	1.2	2.1	—0.7	−9.7	10.7	31.2
1989	134	131	1.1	1.8	2.0	0.2	10.5	25.8
1990	151	149	1.0	1.5	0.9	6.3	12.6	19.7

Sources: N. H. Lipumba, N. E. Osoro, and B. Nyagetera (1990); Bank of Tanzania, *Economic and Operations Report* (Dar es Salaam: Government Printer, 1991); United Republic of Tanzania, *Economic Survey* (Dar es Salaam: Government Printer, various years); Republic of Kenya, *Economic Survey* (Nairobi: Government Printer, various); UNDP/World Bank, *African Economic Indicators* (Washington: World Bank, 1990, 1992).

Notes: a. The ratio is measured as the ratio of the weighted average of foreign wholesale prices to local CPI converted to shillings at the official exchange rate. The base year is 1965–1966. A rise in index indicates real depreciation.
b. Saving deposits rate minus the rate of inflation.

The third difference relates to policy in the dominant sector, agriculture. As discussed in detail by Michael Lofchie in Chapter 5, the difference is largely due to divergences in production incentives and marketing efficiency. A summary measure of the combination of the two factors is the proportion of the world market price received by producers. Kenya in this regard has historically performed much better than Tanzania, where high marketing costs, high margins, and residual pricing have led to low producer income and hence poor incentives for production. This problem was

Table 4.3   Ratios of Producer Prices to International Prices

| | At Nominal Exchange Rate | | | | At Purchasing Power Parity | | | |
| | Kenya | | Tanzania | | Kenya | | Tanzania | |
	Coffee	Tea	Coffee	Cotton	Coffee	Tea	Coffee	Cotton
1970	.91	.60	—	.72	.85	.56	—	.68
1972	.98	.63	.57	.57	.98	.63	.57	.57
1974	.97	.55	.43	.32	.01	.57	.41	.31
1976	.85	.57	.30	.41	.89	.59	.29	.39
1978	.64	.64	.39	.55	.90	.61	.37	.52
1980	.98	.76	.41	.52	.98	.75	.37	.47
1982	.83	.56	.52	.73	.82	.56	.28	.39
1984	.80	.66	.47	.65	.77	.64	.23	.32
1986	.70	.69	.33	1.11	.96	.85	.26	.88

Source: Uma Lele (ed.), *Aid to African Agriculture: Lessons from Two Decades of Donors' Experience* (Baltimore: Johns Hopkins University Press, 1992), Tables 2.9 and 2.10, pp. 64 and 65, respectively.

made worse by two other factors that are policy related: high inflation, which further eroded the real earnings of producers, and an overvalued currency, which constitutes an implicit tax on foreign exchange earned by producers of export crops. The latter essentially constitutes a transfer of rental incomes from earners of foreign exchange to dominant users of it, including governments. As indicated in Table 4.3, significant differences in the two regimes exist on both counts.

THE POLITICAL ECONOMY OF ECONOMIC REFORM

The process of formulating and implementing economic reforms involves a careful balancing of the different, usually conflicting interests since policy changes produce winners and losers. Unless the political system is completely closed, the disposition of economic management will be decided by the interaction of these groups through the political machinery (Sandbrook 1982: 77; Ndulu 1986: 82). Distributional issues as affected by changes in policy constitute the main areas of potential conflict and largely account for political constraints on stabilization and adjustment policies. In the absence of a sudden increase in political resources, the burdens of adjustment must be balanced among different groups (Nelson 1984).

The traditional control regime created its own beneficiaries and losers, particularly in times of scarcity. Rents from the rationing of subsidized resources (financial and real) accrued to bureaucracies and to those with access to the limited state revenues. Taxation of producers through underremuneration of producers (especially agricultural producers) has supported income transfer to both the government and those with access to subsidized products and services. Measures to protect industrial enterprises have allowed the owners to earn profits above their efficiency, usually at the expense of the users of the products, who have to pay higher prices. To the extent that such protection does not lead to a rise in productivity over time, income transfers from consumers to manufacturers are sustained.

Abrogation of the traditional control model, whether de facto via parallel markets or de jure via reforms, significantly reduces rents. Realignment of exchange rates and pricing policies benefits producers, particularly those engaged in tradables. The removal of protective structures reduces the profits of those protected, engendering resistance to reform. The clout of controls is lost to those that command them.

Kenya

Kenya has consistently followed a procapitalist development path aimed mainly at the maximization of economic growth, with only secondary emphasis on equity and the alleviation of poverty. Two years after independence, the government published a sessional paper titled *African Socialism and Its Application to Planning in Kenya* (Kenya 1965) that was to chart the development strategy of the new regime. Though self-described as "African Socialism"—a "political and economic system not imported from any country or a blueprint of any imported ideology"—the adopted development strategy was in practice managed capitalism, a mixed economy whose purported objective was the achievement of social justice. Unemployment, income inequities, and poverty were to be reduced in ways that did not hamper economic growth. Economic development was thus to be achieved through the "trickle-down" process. In the words of the sessional paper: "The most important of these policies is to provide a firm basis for rapid economic growth. Other intermediate problems such as Africanization of the economy, education, unemployment, welfare service and provincial policies must be handled in ways that will not jeopardize growth. The only permanent solution to all these problems rests on rapid growth" (Kenya 1965: 18). However, this was by no means a laissez-faire system, as the inherited state ownership and control apparatus was nurtured and extended after independence in such areas as prices and wage controls, industrial protection, and agricultural marketing.

By the early 1970s there was a perceptible change in intellectual and public opinion in favor of policies to achieve a more equitable distribution of the benefits of economic growth and to alleviate poverty. In part, this change reflected disillusionment with the trickle-down development process. In response, the government invited a mission to study the country's unemployment problem, resulting in the well-known ILO report (1972) on Kenya. This report took a broader perspective of the problem, and the "redistribution with growth" strategy it recommended had an influence on the development approach pursued in the 1970s. The new policies, incorporated into the third and fourth five-year development plans (published, respectively, in 1974 and 1979), focused on rural development and poverty alleviation, respectively.

During this time there was a secular increase in macroeconomic imbalances in external, fiscal, and investment accounts (Table 4.4). The imbalances were exacerbated by various exogenous shocks, which forced the country to turn for support to conditional financing provided mainly by the IMF and World Bank. The 1980s can be characterized as a period in which the government attempted to implement stabilization and structural adjustment programs, both to alleviate macroeconomic imbalances and to enhance the domestic and external competitiveness of the economy, with varying success.

Table 4.4 Basic Indicators of Macroeconomic Resource Gaps in Kenya[a]

	1964–1973	1974–1978	1979–1983	1984–1988	1989–1990
Current Account Deficit	0.1	–3.5	–5.9	–2.5	–5.8
Gross Domestic Savings	19.5	19.8	18.5	21.0	18.5
Gross Investment	19.9	23.3	24.4	23.5	24.3
Fiscal Deficit	–5.0	–6.7	–9.2	–5.2	–4.5
Recurrent Budget Deficit	0.8	2.3	–1.3	–1.5	–1.6
Imports as Percent of Exports	102.3	111.8	122.2	111.2	123.9

Source: Republic of Kenya, *Statistical Abstract* (Nairobi: Government Printer, various years).

Note: a. Average annual percent of Gross Domestic Product.

The development strategy pursued in Kenya was fairly effective in promoting economic growth. From 1965 to 1990, for example, the country experienced a faster annual growth in GNP per capita (1.9 percent) and a lower rate of inflation (7.9 percent) than sub-Saharan Africa as a whole (0.3 percent and 14.2 percent, respectively). The country performed best in the first decade of independence. From 1964 to 1973 real GDP grew at 5.9 percent, whereas average domestic prices rose by only 3.4 percent annually. External payment balances were also in a healthy position despite a small balance-of-payments crisis in 1971. The country experienced slower growth in merchandise trade in the late 1970s and 1980s, but did not suffer as drastic a collapse as the rest of sub-Saharan Africa. Throughout, a conventional view has persisted that the benefits of economic development have not been equitably distributed and that income distribution may even have become more skewed over time.

Many factors accounted for this good macroeconomic performance. These include land reform, in which land was subdivided into smaller holdings that were utilized intensively; extension of the area cultivated in high-value cash crops; and rapid industrialization based on import substitution. Other important sources of growth were high investment, fueled mainly by domestic savings, and a prudent fiscal policy. The budget deficit was relatively modest at 5.0 percent of GDP in this period (1964–1973), reflecting the pursuit of a conservative fiscal policy stance: Revenues expanded rapidly and expenditures were kept in check. Though domestic credit and money supply did grow quickly, the effects were not too inflationary. Nor was there severe weakening of the balance of payments—the robust economic growth increased money demand, and most of the credit (more than 80 percent) accrued to the private sector, thereby facilitating production.

The economy has since performed less well, expanding at an average annual real rate of only 4.5 percent. Meanwhile, inflation increased to an average rate of 11 percent from 1974 to 1990, then accelerated sharply (Table 4.2). In 1991 it was about 20 percent, in 1992 about 30 percent. During the first half of 1993 it skyrocketed to 101 percent, though the rate came down as the year ended. This acceleration was caused by several factors. One was the deceleration in economic growth from an average of about 5.0 percent in the late 1980s to 2.3 percent in 1991 and only 0.4 percent in 1992 and 0.1 percent in 1993 (Kenya 1993:21; Kenya 1994:18). This downturn reduced the demand for money, thereby exerting upward pressure on prices. A second factor was the nearly 60 percent depreciation of the Kenya shilling (KSh) from late 1991 to mid-1993, which increased import prices dramatically. Third was an increase in money supply, with the floating of the Kenya shilling on the interbank market in February 1993 accentuating the inflationary process. The reforms in the foreign exchange market were revoked in late March in an attempt to contain the spiral but reversed again in May under pressure from the IMF and World Bank. The balance-of-payments situation has also deteriorated, as shown in Table 4.4. Except for 1974–1978, when the country experienced an unprecedented fourfold increase in the prices of beverage exports, foreign exchange reserves were much lower than the legally stipulated four months' worth of imports, and the current account deficit was large and (except in 1984–1988) could not be compensated for by long-term net capital inflows; hence, the basic balance was negative.

Deterioration in economic performance can be traced to excessive expansionary fiscal and monetary policies, especially in the early and late 1970s; adverse exogenous shocks; and structural factors, especially the failure to expand and diversify exports. Because of a relaxation of fiscal discipline, the overall budget deficit expanded substantially in the late 1970s and early 1980s. Fiscal developments in the 1980s can be divided into a number of distinct periods. The period from 1980 to 1982 was one of large deficits. In 1983 the absolute value of the deficit was cut by two-thirds over the previous year (the attempted military coup of 1982 induced a strong attempt to restore fiscal discipline). There followed an upward trend, which peaked in 1987, after which the deficit declined because of stabilization and structural adjustment policies, particularly the Budget Rationalization Programme (Kenya 1986b); the deficit was 4.4 percent of GDP in 1989–1990. However, the deficit rose again to 10.5 percent in 1992–1993 and 7.0 percent in 1993–1994.

Major influences on government spending are, first, two large recurrent expenditures—the wage bill of the civil service, and the local currency costs of servicing the public debt, which are difficult to cut—second, political reluctance by the authorities to collect sufficient tax revenues on a consistent basis; and, third, inadequate control of expenditures (and inability to target them to achieve specific policy objectives). Whereas government recurrent revenue as a proportion of GDP declined slightly in the 1980s from 25.4 to 24.4 percent, recurrent expenditures increased from 25.4 to 28.8 percent of GDP. Large budget deficits resulted in increased government borrowing, enlarging the money supply, and a crowding-out of credit to the private sector. These effects in turn had an adverse impact on domestic prices, the balance of payments, and economic growth (Mwega 1990).

Among exogenous factors that contributed substantially to the poor performance of the economy in the 1980s were the various negative shocks the economy experienced, including the two oil shocks of 1973 and 1979; the collapse of the East Africa Community in 1977 and the closure of the border with Tanzania, both of which severely curtailed exports of manufactures; the end of the coffee boom in 1977; the military coup attempt of 1982, which reduced business confidence and caused some capital flight; and droughts (the worst in the country's recorded history in 1984), which curtailed agricultural output. In general the country experienced a serious decline in the terms of trade, with the terms-of-trade index declining from 114 in the mid-1970s to 71 in 1990. As a consequence of the resulting pressures on the balance of payments, there was severe import compression, especially in the first half of the 1980s, when import volume decreased by nearly 10 percent. There was an improvement in the situation from 1986 to 1989; the volume of imports increased by 24 percent following a 40 percent increase in coffee export price in 1986. Ironically, the poor performance occurred after the government borrowed heavily and then pursued the stabilization and structural adjustment policies urged by its external creditors. By 1990 Kenya had an external debt of $6.8 billion, of which about 70 percent was long-term credit to the public sector or publicly guaranteed credit to quasipublic institutions. Debt service charges increased from 4.0 percent of export earnings in 1974 to 21.4 percent in 1980; by 1992 they constituted about a third of export earnings, severely constraining the development process.

A major characteristic of the Kenyan economy is its openness, with the trade ratio (imports plus exports as a proportion of GDP) exceeding 40 percent since the 1960s (though the ratio has fluctuated much from period to period). This openness and the heavy reliance on a few primary products makes Kenya highly vulnerable to exogenous shocks that influence the volume and prices of these exports in international markets; hence, there is a close correlation between terms of trade and the real growth of the economy. Coffee, tea, pyrethrum, and sisal have remained the dominant commodity exports, contributing 43.0 percent of total export earnings in 1992, compared to 47.8 percent in 1964–1968 (Kenya 1993: 103). Part of this slight decline in concentration is the result of falling world prices for coffee in the early 1990s. Once Kenya's leading export and earner of foreign exchange, coffee now accounts for only 12.1 percent of export earnings, compared to 27.8 percent for tea. Petroleum exports (13.8 percent) are important, but their contribution to foreign exchange earnings is small, as Kenya mainly reexports imported petroleum products after their refining.

Individual "nontraditional" commodity exports contribute very little to Kenya's export earnings, but horticulture as a category now accounts for 12.2 percent of the total, matching the figure of coffee in 1992 (Kenya 1993: 103).[1] Kenya also hosted 663,000 visitors in 1992, making tourism the country's leading earner of foreign exchange. Tourism now accounts for approximately 28 percent of the country's foreign exchange earnings, compared to 19 percent for tea and 8 percent for coffee. Tourism declined in 1992 from 675,000 visitors in 1991 and 720,000 in 1990. These declines are largely attributed to rising political instability as a result of Kenya's return to multiparty politics. They indicate further how sensitive the Kenyan economy is to external pressures, and vice versa. Following Kenya's multiparty elections in December 1992, and the steep devaluation of the country's currency in the first half of 1993, tourism recovered as more than 800,000 visited the country.

The main merchandise imports are machinery and transport equipment, fuels, and other manufactures. Kenya's import substitution industrialization (ISI) strategy that the country pursued throughout the 1970s and 1980s drastically changed the composition of imports. Consumer goods declined from an average of 25 percent of total imports in the 1960s to about 16 percent in 1990, whereas the share of intermediate and capital goods rose from 75 percent in the 1960s to about 84 percent in 1990. This shift has made the demand for imports more inelastic, the economy more vulnerable to unexpected reductions in the supply of foreign exchange. Protection to industries was provided through import tariffs, import licensing, and quantitative restrictions. A number of studies (e.g., Hopcraft 1972) done in the early 1970s showed that the industrial sector was highly protected and that the system of protection tended to favor finishing-touch industries. This was nevertheless a period of rapid economic growth; high protection of the industrial sector was not necessary, with import licensing covering only about seventy commodities. It is only since the early 1970s that the government has actively used import licensing and other nonprice import restrictions to support the balance of payments and to protect some industries.

As noted above, Kenya did not experience a major balance-of-payments problem in the 1960s, and the country therefore did not actively seek much external finance. The country experienced its first major external payments problem in 1971, when there was a drastic rundown of reserves following an experiment in expansionary fiscal policies (King 1979). This shortfall was aggravated by the first oil crisis of 1973–1974 in which the price of oil quadrupled, pulling up the prices of other imports by about 30 percent and discouraging exports. The government reacted to these crises by imposing import and price controls, credit restrictions, and so froth; it also actively sought external capital, with general policy conditionalities spelled out in various government documents.

An IMF program was negotiated in 1975 but later abandoned when the country's balance of payments improved, thanks to a large increase in the world prices of coffee and tea in 1975–1977 (a frost in Brazil drastically reduced its coffee harvest) (Killick 1984). The proceeds of the boom were not sterilized (for example, by the creation of a stabilization fund) but were fully passed on to the farmers. The resulting expansion in aggregate demand was boosted by an increase in government expenditures and coincided with the second oil crisis of 1979–1980 and the decline in the prices of coffee and tea to normal levels, producing a serious balance-of-payments crisis beginning in 1978. Once again the government was forced to actively seek external capital, the general conditionalities of which were published in the fourth development plan (1979–1983) and in various sessional papers. These stabilization and structural adjustment policies were continued, being incorporated into the five-year development plans published in 1984 and 1989 and in other documents, particularly the 1986 sessional paper, *Economic Management for Renewed Growth* (Kenya 1986a). Even though the IMF programs negotiated in the early 1980s collapsed because Kenya exceeded the stipulated credit ceilings (Killick 1984), the government was able to successfully implement later programs and had programs with the IMF the remainder of the 1980s except in 1987.

The situation, however, has changed markedly during the early 1990s. From November 1991 to November 1993, Kenya was at an impasse with the IMF, the World Bank, and major bilateral donors. The donors suspended "quick-disbursing" program support amounting to $350 million until Kenya implemented various economic and political reforms (World Bank 1991d). The principal reason for the impasse was an increase in macroeconomic imbalances in the late 1980s and early 1990s, making it difficult for the country to satisfy IMF credit ceilings and implement trade reforms. There was also a reluctance by the authorities to aggressively implement structural adjustment policies, particularly the liberalization of grain marketing, the privatization and restructuring of parastatals, and so on. As discussed by Joel Barkan in Chapter 1 and David Gordon in Chapter 8, progress in controlling corruption, liberalizing the political system, and protecting human rights also became conditions for assistance.

The government accused the donors of imposing more stringent conditionalities than usual. In the 1980s Kenya was given a measure of leeway in meeting conditionality targets in the 1980s but not in the 1990s. Kenya's changing relationship with the international financial institutions must be seen in a broader continental context. As other countries, including Tanzania, became more aggressive in adhering to agreed-upon conditionalities, both economic and political, Kenya's relative performance came to be viewed as insufficient. Nevertheless, at a meeting of the Consultative Group of Kenya's principal bilateral donors and the World Bank held in November 1993, the donors determined that Kenya had made significant progress in satisfying several conditionalities and announced that the assistance suspended in 1991 would be resumed in 1994 as long as Kenya carried through on its remaining commitments to reform.[2]

Structural adjustment policies implemented in the late 1980s and early 1990s covered all the major sectors of the economy. Agricultural adjustment programs mainly involved raising producer prices to induce farmers to increase production, particularly of foodstuffs. Producer prices are usually reviewed every year, just before the planting season, and efforts are made to ensure timely input supplies and the provision of adequate agricultural credit. In the financial sector, the Central Bank's supervisory role over commercial banks and nonbank financial intermediaries has been enhanced, and policies to promote saving and investment (mainly by maintaining positive interest rates in real terms) have been put into place. Real deposit rates, which were negative in the 1970s and the first half of the 1980s, became positive in the late 1980s, and interest rates were fully liberalized in July 1991 (Table 4.2).

A major focus of structural adjustment was to raise the industrial sector's efficiency by increasing its outward orientation. This was to be achieved through enactment of policies such as preferential credit and insurance programs for industrial exporters (these measures are at early stages of implementation); strengthening of institutions involved with exportation, such as the Kenya External Trade Authority (KETA); establishment of a green-channel facility to expedite the handling and processing of the relevant export documents; and penetration into new markets, especially through participation in the Preferential Trade Area (PTA) for Eastern and Southern Africa, which has been in operation since 1985. Other policies included:

- Introducing manufacturing under bond, whereby production is done exclusively for the export market, simplifying the processing of export documentation and the importation of inputs. This scheme took off in 1989, and by mid-1991 eleven factories were operating in the scheme.
- Establishing export processing zones (EPZs). Sites have been identified at the Athi River near Nairobi and in Mombasa. Their development is to be funded by the World Bank and the African Development Bank, respectively. A private EPZ (Sammeer Park) was commissioned in early 1991 in Nairobi, and by midyear three firms were establishing operations there.
- Undertaking tariff reforms aimed at the gradual replacement of quantitative restrictions by tariffs.
- Shifting products to the less restrictive import license categories.
- Enhancing the effectiveness of the manufactured-exports subsidy scheme by increasing the subsidy rate and speeding up payments to exporters.
- Maintaining a "realistic" exchange rate.

The commercial policies were at least partially implemented in the 1980s. In 1980, for example, a 10 percent tariff surcharge was imposed on all imports, and there were tariff increases on over 200 items. These reforms were continued in the following year, with tariff increases ranging from 2 to 90 percent on about 1,400 items. There were also tariff *reductions* on about 20 items used mainly by export-oriented industries. The tariff reductions started in 1981 were extended in the 1980s to cover more import items, particularly in 1983–1984 and after 1987 (with the support of World Bank Industrial Sector Adjustment Credit). From 1987 to 1991 the number of tariff categories was reduced from 25 to 11, and the maximum tariff rate was reduced from 170 to 70 percent.

Although the tariff reforms implemented in the 1980s somewhat reduced the protection accorded the manufacturing sector, tariff rates increased in many industries. The average effective tariff rates on retained imports in the manufacturing sector declined from 27.4 percent in 1980 to 15.6 percent in 1988. Many industries, however, had higher average tariff rates in 1988 than they did in 1970, with only the major consumer industries—textiles and clothing, petroleum and coal products, transport equipment, and miscellaneous manufactures—having lower average effective rates (Mwega 1991). Sharpley and Lewis (1988) conclude that the average effective rate of protection increased from 31 percent in 1968 to 51 percent in 1985.

Some progress also was made toward trade liberalization. Arbitrary quantitative restrictive mechanisms such as import bans and the "no objection" certificate were eliminated in the early 1980s, and import items listed in the less restrictive categories increased. In mid-1982, for example, 317 items were moved from Schedule II to the less restrictive Schedule I, with the value of approved imports under the latter increasing from 51.6 percent of total imports in 1982 to 74.9 percent in 1983 before receding to 70.8 percent in 1985 and 68.0 percent in 1986 (Dlamini 1987). According to the World Bank (1990), the proportion of imports under quantitative restrictions declined from 12 percent in 1987 to 5.4 percent in 1991, when items were moved from Schedule IIIC to the less restrictive Schedule IIIB. Overall, the import license system was streamlined, with the average lag between license application and foreign exchange allocation reduced from six months to about three weeks, hence curtailing some of the rent-seeking behavior (World Bank 1990). In response to donor pressure as well as to demands from within, the Kenyan government eventually abolished the import licensing system in 1993.

Another export incentive was the manufactured exports subsidy introduced in 1974. By the late 1970s, however, economic observers were generally agreed that the impact of the subsidy was quite limited because the rate was quite low (at 10 percent of the f.o.b. value of goods manufactured in Kenya, with a local value-added of at least 30 percent) and because payments were subjected to much delay, in some cases of several months. There were various efforts to rectify this situation; for example, the rate was increased to 20 percent in 1980. However, because of balance-of-payments problems experienced in the early 1980s, the scheme was suspended in June 1982. The subsidy was reintroduced in December 1982 at the rate of 10 percent, with a bonus rate of 15 percent to those exporters who had increased their exports the previous year(s). This bonus rate was abolished in 1985, and the basic rate was raised to 20 percent. In 1986 the items eligible for export compensation were reduced from 2,000 to 700, then restored to 1,260. In the 1990 budget, exporters were permitted to process their claims through commercial banks to speed up payments and were given the option of claiming duty exemptions rather than export compensation on imported inputs. In early 1993 the basic rate was again reduced to 10 percent.

Finally, since 1983 Kenya has utilized a more flexible exchange rate regime. For nearly ten years the rate was adjusted on a daily basis against a composite basket of currencies of the country's main trading partners in a "crawling-peg" system. This approach was different from that employed in the first two decades of independence. Then, the country pursued a fixed exchange rate policy, with the nominal rate only adjusted occasionally (even though economic observers agree that the shilling was never grossly overvalued). Since 1983 the Kenya shilling has been depreciated significantly both in nominal and in real terms. Between 1983 and 1989 there was a 79.6 percent nominal depreciation of the Kenya shilling against the SDR and a 20.1 percent (26.5 percent) depreciation of the nominal (real) trade-weighted effective rate. The liberalization of the foreign exchange market was extended in 1992, when Foreign Exchange Bearer Certificates (which are issued against capital inflows and entitle the holder to repurchase foreign exchange at the prevailing shilling exchange rate) and exporter foreign exchange retention schemes were introduced. The market was further liberalized in early 1993, when the exchange rate was left to be determined by the interbank market, with the Central Bank only financing government imports and external debt servicing. The interbank and official exchange rates were unified later in the year, just prior to the convening of the Consultative Group in November. Finally, the Kenyan shilling was made fully convertible at market rates for transactions up to 500,000 dollars in May 1994. As a consequence of these policies, movements in the exchange rate have been largely depoliticized.

Industrial and trade liberalization therefore mainly occurred through a relaxation of the import licensing process, higher tariffs for most industries, and the depreciation of the Kenya shilling. However, stabilization and structural adjustment policies have mainly been determined by the level of the balance of payments and have only been seriously enforced when the government is implementing adjustment programs imposed and financed from outside. The balance-of-payments situation, in turn, has been significantly influenced by, among other factors, Kenya's fiscal position (which, as we saw earlier, drastically deteriorated in the late 1970s and in the early 1980s with the rise in budget deficits). The balance-of-payments position was also adversely affected by rising domestic credit, inducing the authorities to tighten import restrictions. This, in turn, adversely affected the fiscal position by reducing tax revenues, creating a vicious cycle in which import taxes made up about a fifth of total tax revenue.

A general tightening of import restrictions provided increased protection to domestic industries, which influenced the country's industrial sector in various ways. First, a predominantly monopolistic/oligopolistic industrial market structure was created; firms could earn large profits selling in the domestic markets and hence had little incentive to seek external markets. House (1981) found a significant positive correlation between industrial concentration and price-cost margins (to measure profitability) and a negative correlation between industrial concentration and exports. Utilizing data from the censuses of industrial production, he also concluded that industrial concentration increased in the 1960s but has decreased since the mid-1970s (World Bank 1987a). The industrial sector therefore relied heavily on domestic demand, clearly limiting the scope of an ISI strategy. Various studies (Sharpley and Lewis 1988, Gulhati and Sekhar 1982, World Bank 1987a) have analyzed the sources of industrial growth in Kenya and have found that the growth of the manufacturing sector was overwhelmingly driven by domestic demand followed by import substitution. Exports accounted for only a very small proportion of total manufacturing growth.

Tanzania

During the first two decades of independence, Tanzania's development strategy had three main objectives. First was to raise the absorptive capacity of the economy in order to provide a basis for the modernization of the economy. In this regard, the development of infrastructure and social services received much emphasis, taking up 52 percent of investment during 1966–1975. Second was to undertake structural transformation geared toward creating a self-sustaining economic base. This was to be achieved by enhancing the links between production and the domestic resource base, on the one hand, and between production and domestic demand, on the other. The effort was directed at raising the contribution of industrial production to the economy and significantly reducing reliance on agriculture. Until 1975, the emphasis was on simple import substitution; the Basic Industrialization Strategy implemented after 1975 was aimed at expanding import substitution. The industrial sector's investment share rose sharply from 14 percent during 1964–1974 to 33.5 percent during 1975–1982. Much of the increase came at the expense of agriculture, whose share declined by 42 percent between 1964 and 1975; real direct investment in the sector declined by 38 percent between 1976 and 1980 (Ndulu 1990: 3). The third objective, in line with adopted socialist policy, was to provide basic needs on egalitarian grounds. The Arusha Declaration (Nyerere 1967b), the cornerstone of Tanzania's socialist policy, underscored human development as a key element of the strategy. Public ownership and control of resources was the main instrument for achieving redistribution.

Tanzania's development strategy and its implementation prior to the crisis of the 1980s had four main implications for economic restructuring and recovery. First, the neglect of the mainstay agricultural sector in terms of resource allocation and incentive structure undermined the availability of overall financing, particularly foreign exchange. The decline in real growth rate of agriculture from an annual average of 3.1 percent during 1965–1973 to 0.2 percent during 1973–1980, as well as the drop in export growth rate from 4.2 percent to –5.6 percent over the same periods, largely resulted from these factors (Ndulu 1990: 345). Revamping the sector's role became a sine qua non in any efforts to reverse the crisis.

Second, an overexpansion of industrial capacity, largely financed by external resources, far outstripped the ability to utilize the capacity. This excess not only tied up scarce capital in idle or incomplete industrial plants with high resource opportunity costs but also contributed significantly to future external debt–servicing stress. This problem was partly caused by inflexibility in shifting external resources from project finance to operational maintenance need. Tariff structure, quantitative restrictions, exchange rate policy, and domestic market structures provided a high degree of protection to this sector largely at the expense of the agricultural sector and of efficiency within the industrial sector itself (Ndulu and Semboja 1991). Preferential access to low-interest finance and foreign exchange attracted domestic resources away from other sectors. Judicious consolidation of past investment to minimize the opportunity cost of tied-up capital (in idle capacity) and industrial restructuring to enhance efficiency of the sector became critical requirements for the revival of growth.

Third, growth and redistribution became fiscally unsustainable. The expansion of recurrent expenditure requirements to maintain the large and inefficient public sector and social consumption far outstripped Tanzania's sluggish revenue growth. Fiscal deficit as a proportion of GDP more than doubled, from 6.3 percent during 1966–1973 to 13 percent during 1974–1979 (Table 4.5). Decline in the tax base as a result of falling real income growth and rising tax evasion to circumvent controls were the main sources of slow revenue growth. The need to emphasize real income growth as a base for sustainable redistributive policy became clear.

Fourth, because of retrenchment in the growth of real income, the domestic savings rate steeply declined, beginning in the late 1970s (Table 4.5). As a result, investment and potential for growth were curtailed. The drying up of external resources during the first half of the 1980s further exacerbated the resource gaps, leading to the punctuation of the growth process. These resource gaps had to be closed, whether in a recessionary fashion (by reducing real activity) or via growth-oriented augmentation of resources and improved efficiency.

Table 4.5 summarizes the evolution of resource gaps in Tanzania. The resource gap pressures in both external and fiscal balances rapidly built up during 1975–1979. Current account and fiscal deficits expanded rapidly as export performance and revenue collection fell far behind the growth in imports and public expenditures. Both gaps were filled by a large increase in external resources. The commodity boom of 1975–1977 set an expansionary tempo that was not reversed with the collapse of commodity prices or the second oil shock (1978–1970). This expansionary trend exacerbated the resource gap during 1978–1982, pushing it to unsustainable levels. An attempt to maintain high levels of fiscal expenditure via monetization only led to a steep rise in inflation.

Table 4.5 Basic Indicators of Macroeconomic Resource Gaps in Tanzania[a]

	1966–1973	1974–1979	1980–1985	1986–1990
Current Account Deficit	–1.4	–7.7	–6.8	–9.5
Gross Domestic Savings	18.1	15.1	9.8	–1.4
Gross Investment	35.2	24.3	18.2	21.6
Fiscal Deficit	–6.3	–13.2	–13.4	–11.9
Recurrent Budget Balance	0.8	0.9	–4.1	–0.6
Imports as Percent of Exports	114	183	235	354

Sources: UNDP/World Bank, *Africa Development;* United Republic of Tanzania, *Economic Survey* (Dar es Salaam: Government Printer, various years); Bank of Tanzania, *Operations Report* (Dar es Salaam: Government Printer, various years).

Note: a. Average annual percent of Gross Domestic Product.

The first earnest effort toward stabilization was made under the Structural Adjustment Program (SAP), a three-year program (1982/83 to 1985/86). This program, designed by the government, turned out to be largely recessionary. To close the external deficit, further import compression via the tightening of exchange control was sought. The ratio of real imports to GDP fell from 13.2 percent in 1982 to 11.6 percent in 1983, and the current account deficit contracted by almost 37 percent over the same period. The fiscal deficit also contracted as expenditures were severely cut, particularly for development projects. Inflation rate declined slightly during 1983. That all these measures came at the expense of real growth is evident from the 2.4 percent decline in real GDP for the year. Nothing was done to redress the distorted incentive structure from 1982 to the first half of 1984 as the battle with IMF and the World Bank continued to rage. Real producer prices plummeted, the real exchange rate overvaluation reached its peak, and the real rate of interest continued to slide (Table 4.2, p. 105).

Other key policy measures were instituted in July 1984 to restructure incentives and set up a basis for a growth-oriented structural adjustment. The introduction of a liberalized "own funds" import scheme, complemented by wide-ranging price deregulation, significantly raised the profitability of redirecting proceeds of illegal exports to legal imports. Under the scheme, those with foreign exchange (no questions asked regarding source) were allowed to bring in a range of allowable imports and dispose of them at whatever price the market could bear. The increase in self-financed imports through this scheme was tremendous during the late 1980s and early 1990s, accounting for an average of 40 percent of total imports and in value terms actually exceeding official export earnings. Although originally dominated by consumer goods, these imports have over time come to be

largely capital and intermediate goods. The significantly improved availability of consumer goods contributed to the improvement of incentives for
agricultural production.

From another angle, this scheme led indirectly to a major de facto real
exchange rate depreciation. Unofficial exporters repatriated their earnings
effectively at the more depreciated exchange rate since own-funded imports
were disposed of domestically at the unofficial rate. Moreover, it set the
ground for easier accommodation of the official devaluation in 1986, as
imports were already domestically priced at much higher nominal effective
rates under the scheme.

Two other measures are notable from the July 1984 policy changes.
First, a decision was made to maintain a 5 percent annual real increase in
producer prices to redress previous erosions and sustain an attractive incentive structure for agriculture. In effect, rises in agricultural real producer
prices were highest in the period 1984/85 to 86/87. Although such increases were largely financed between 1984 and 1986 via expansion of the fiscal
deficit to accommodate the rising losses of the marketing agencies, most of
the increases after July 1986 were financed via large devaluations, which
raised prices of exportables in domestic currency. Second, the Hamad
Commission was formed to look into institutional restructuring that would
lessen the fiscal burden of the public enterprises. This restructuring was in
addition to scraping off food and agricultural inputs subsidies. Also,
improved real producer prices for agriculture, increased availability of consumer goods, and good weather contributed significantly to renewed agricultural growth in 1985 and 1986, at 3.4 percent and 8.8 percent, respectively.

The Economic Recovery Program (ERP), in force from 1986 to 1989,
was to some extent a formalization at the international level of some of the
measures instituted independently between July 1984 and July 1986 and a
rationalization of the changes in the incentive structure. The agreement,
signed with the IMF, brought increased foreign resource inflows (both pro-
gram-based and other autonomous bilateral sources). The main objective of
the program was adjustment with growth. Major new areas of adjustments
were largely oriented toward restructuring incentives in order to help generate resources and ensure their efficient utilization, thus supporting the
revival of growth on a sustainable basis.

Starting with a 135 percent devaluation of the Tanzanian shilling (TSh)
between March 1986 and July 1986, Tanzania adopted a crawling-peg
exchange rate policy. The pace of the crawl depended on how much historically accumulated overvaluation had to be redressed, as well as on new
pressures on the shilling exchange rate. Between July 1986 and July 1990
the shilling had depreciated from TShs. 40 to TShs. 145 per U.S. dollar. By
June 1991 it depreciated nominally further to TShs. 225 and by September
1993 to TShs. 448.

In April 1992 foreign exchange bureaus were opened that bought and sold foreign exchange at market rates. In effect, they constituted a legalization of the black market for foreign exchange. Foreign exchange regulations were amended to allow residents and nonresidents to hold foreign exchange locally and trade it at the bureaus. Owners of export retention funds also sold their proceeds at the bureau rates. The volume of transactions in the foreign exchange bureaus increased steadily and now covers significant volumes of imports in addition to services. Although the current spread between the "official" and the bureau exchange rates is about 15 percent, there is a deliberate effort to close the gap. Though much reduced, the black market for foreign exchange still exists, mainly for nonallowable transactions, particularly private capital flows. The spread between the bureau and black market rates is an insignificant 2 percent.

As argued earlier, the inflationary impact of the official exchange rate depreciation was negligible, as most goods were already being sold at a much more depreciated implicit parallel rate. The rise in the real growth rate and the financing of the fiscal deficit by new foreign resources rather than through monetary expansion helped bring down inflation, which declined from 33.3 percent in 1986 to 25.8 percent in 1989 and about 19 percent in 1990.

In order to mobilize domestic savings, nominal deposit interest rates were raised. They achieved a positive real magnitude of 1 percent for the first time in 1989, rising to 7 percent by 1990. Preliminary indications show that domestic financial private saving has been responsive to the rise in the real interest rate. However, worries have recently surfaced about the impact of this rise on private investment, given that it increases in real terms the cost of funds. The strategy seems to be to emphasize control of inflation as the key approach to raising real rates of interest rather than relying on nominal interest rate hikes.

Beginning in 1988, the Open General License (OGL) system was introduced, under which import licenses are offered by the Central Bank on demand. Although the scheme started with a short positive list of qualifying imports, over time this list was expanded. On the negative list are prohibited and "luxurious" imports, agreed upon jointly with donors. Imports under automatic licensing now account for about 65 percent of the total. These include goods imported through the own funds scheme, OGL, retention schemes, and foreign exchange bureau financing. In sum, from 1984 through 1992 the exchange regime went through a major liberalization. Since 1984, a rapid dismantling of price controls has also been undertaken. Product prices have by and large been freed up and are now market determined. At the height of control, 3,000 items were on the price-controlled list. By 1986, this number had fallen below 400, and by the end of 1990 only 10 products remained on the list. The 1991/92 fiscal year budget retained only petroleum products, chemical fertilizers, and essential services under price control.

Until mid-1988, Tanzania's tariff structure was relatively complex, with eighteen different rate categories ranging from 0 to 200 percent. In mid-1988 the government rationalized the tariff structure by lowering the maximum tariff to 100 percent, reducing rate categories to seven, and more or less abolishing specific rates. In June 1990 further tariff reforms were enacted—rate categories were reduced to five, with rates ranging from 0 percent to 60 percent. In July 1992 tariffs on intermediate and capital goods were abolished, and basic rates were limited to a maximum of 30 percent. The above tariff reforms reduced protective levels and made protection neutral. The earlier multiplicity of rates had provided room for negotiations between individual interests and the government, causing distortions in the protective structure.

A combination of the real exchange rate depreciation, the relaxation of import and exchange controls, and the compression of import tariff levels and categories have substantially reduced the protection accorded to local industrial enterprises. At the same time, exchange rate depreciation has reduced the extent of import cost-subsidization prevalent earlier. These reforms have put pressure on domestic firms to improve efficiency and competitiveness. Individual firms will have to restructure and reduce costs to survive. Some restructuring has occurred at the sectoral level, as the more efficient firms have expanded their output and the inefficient ones have been forced to cut back. Preliminary evidence shows such restructuring taking place as early as 1987 (Ndulu and Semboja 1991).

On the macroeconomic front, very notable impacts of the reforms are the revival of real growth and a significant reduction in the inflation rate. Real per capita incomes began to grow again after a decade and a half of decline. The dollar-denominated nominal per capita income shows a decline because of the very steep depreciation of the shilling. Real growth of production averaged 4 percent between 1986 and 1990, translating into an approximate 1 percent real growth in per capita income. A large part of the revival in growth was attributable to agriculture, although with improved import levels all other sectors, including manufacturing, recorded significant revivals in real growth. The rise in real growth and improved supplies of consumer goods also contributed to the slowing down of inflation, as did the reduction in the monetization of the fiscal deficit. Foreign resource inflows, largely in the form of import support counterpart funds, significantly helped reduce monetary growth to finance the fiscal deficit.

However, as shown in Table 4.5, both the external and the fiscal deficit rose in proportion to GDP, implying a widening of resource gaps. There are three things to note in this regard. The first is a measurement problem: With the current account deficit denominated purely in foreign currency terms and GDP in a combination that includes nontraded goods, the very steep depreciation of the shilling tends to overstate the rise in the ratio. Second, the rise in the external imbalance is attributable to a very significant rise in external debt servicing. Interest payments on the foreign debt as a proportion of GDP rose from 1.4 percent in 1985 to 7.2 percent in 1989. Third, foreign debt servicing has helped foster the rise in the fiscal deficit. Debt service as a proportion of total government expenditure more than doubled between 1983/84 and 1989/90, rising from 13 percent to 30 percent over the period. At the margin, more than 90 percent of the increase in the fiscal deficit is attributable to increased debt service (World Bank 1991).

The effectiveness of the various reforms undertaken in Tanzania will to a large extent depend on creation of an enabling institutional environment. The freeing up of the economy, effected through the reforms discussed above, has required the dismantling of various control mechanisms long institutionalized in Tanzania and reduced bureaucratic access to rental incomes associated with such controls. Pressure to change the role and the size of the public sector has ensued.

In the sphere of agricultural marketing several changes have been made. The combined monopsony and monopoly in food marketing of the National Milling Corporation (NMC) has been dismantled. Its main function now is to maintain strategic food reserves. Cooperatives and private agents currently dominate the food marketing function as well as the marketing of export crops. The role of various crop boards has been limited to external marketing, where these agencies still command a reasonable comparative advantage in terms of skill, experience, and infrastructure. However, inroads into even these functions are being made by cooperatives and private agents.

Divestiture in public enterprises has been progressing more slowly. The continued survival of efficient public enterprises in the face of much-reduced protection and budgetary subventions suggested that enterprises should be assessed for divestiture on a case-by-case basis. A World Bank study (1987b) confirmed the existence of some efficient industrial public enterprises which did as well as or better than private ones. Divestiture in public agricultural estates is now in progress, and an independent commission for parastatal reform and divestiture has been formed. In addition to identifying enterprises for liquidation and privatization, its role includes determining fair prices for sales and ensuring the appropriate restructuring and acceptable performance of remaining parastatals. The commission works closely with the Loans and Advances Realization Trust (LART), which oversees off-loading of nonperforming assets of the banking system (resulting largely from public enterprises debt overhang). The new investment code, the National Investment Act (1990), has reserved a few areas for public sector and local investors, but by and large it opens up opportunities widely, including appropriate incentives for foreign investment. The new Banking Act (1991) has opened up this sector to private investment (local and foreign), breaking a long state monopoly in this sphere. Overall, the public sector seems to be starting to work toward creating an enabling environment for economic activity by providing supportive infrastructure, security, law enforcement, and regulation. It is likely, however, that economic and social services will remain the primary concern of the public sector for the foreseeable future.

The only dialogue on reforms seems to have been between the government of Tanzania, on the one side, and external donor agencies and IFIs, on the other. Microlevel reactions to the economic crisis and the implicit internal dialogue between the government and grassroots forces is usually not part of the standard economic adjustment process. Political economists such as Goran Hyden (1983) and Robert Bates (1981, 1983) have discussed such reactions in relation to rural development in general and agricultural marketing in particular. Indeed, the process of economic adjustment in Tanzania over the last two decades can be viewed as one of a dialogue between macrolevel economic managers and microlevel interest groups. The economic crisis that began in the late 1970s sharpened the incongruence of interests at these two levels, necessitating resolutions. The assumptions of the control regime that operated effectively prior to 1977 were invalidated by severe resource gaps as the crisis deepened. Urban dwellers' desire for low-priced food supplies came into direct conflict with the interests of producers, whose real incomes fell with rapid inflation, giving rise to the growth of parallel markets. Rapid reduction in the real incomes of nonagriculturists spurred unprecedented growth in untaxed informal sector activities. Similarly, a severe scarcity of consumer goods, coupled with declining import capacity, put pressure on controlled prices and helped a parallel market for these goods become dominant at the retail level. The wide profit gap between exporting through official (at the overvalued official exchange rate) and informal (with the implicit exchange rate reflecting scarcity valuation) channels induced the growth of underground exports and imports, as well as capital flight.

The sustenance of such a multiplicity of parallel regimes alongside the formal economy made macroeconomic management impractical, inhibiting policy guidance for economic development. At the same time, the existence of the parallel regimes was driven by the needs of survival at the microlevel, with traders cashing in to earn scarcity rents at the expense of much-needed government revenue. Unless resource balance could be restored and the conflicts of interest resolved, such a situation would persist to the detriment of the process of economic development.

Policy adjustments undertaken in the early 1980s and intensified after 1984 were geared toward reestablishment of a manageable economic environment to enable continued economic and social development, which had been truncated by the severe economic crisis of the late 1970s and the

1980s. The basic thrust of the adjustments was to unify markets by allowing a more flexible trade regime; increase official producer prices in real terms to induce increased supplies in the formal markets; narrow the profitability gap between official and unofficial exports; and encourage income-supplementing activities for formal sector employees. Increased external resources solicited since 1986 are seen in this context as providing an enabling environment to catalyze the adjustment process. Conditionality pressure for access to these resources would not by itself have substituted for the internal resolution of conflicts of interest in the process of adjustment.

Ironically, the leverage of the donor community may be greater today, after the Tanzanian economy has begun to show some real improvements, than it was in the mid-1980s before the process of adjustment began. Tanzania now receives approximately $1.2 billion annually in quick-disbursing assistance, almost a third of the country's annual budget (ERB January 1991: 54). Success at macroeconomic reform has to some extent been achieved, though at the cost of increased dependence on aid. In the post–Cold War era, when donors are less hesitant to invoke conditionality and when demands for democratization and improved governance have been added to demands for macroeconomic adjustment, the recent honeymoon between Tanzania and the donor community may be nearing its end. At the annual meeting of the Consultative Group for Tanzania held in July 1993, the donors expressed serious concerns about the slow pace of privatization and especially about rising corruption on the part of senior government officials (World Bank 1993b). Though they did not invoke conditionality this time around, the implications for the future are clear.

CONCLUSIONS

The ongoing economic reforms in Kenya and Tanzania bear very close similarities. Both focus on rationalizing incentive structures to improve domestic resource mobilization and efficiency. Though economic stabilization is an important aspect of the adjustment process, the emphasis has shifted away in both cases from stability as an end in itself to stabilization for supporting growth. The underlying structural weaknesses to a large extent explain the similarities in the adjustment programs, although the IFIs' policies of conditionality have also helped bring about convergence in the programs.

The foregoing discussion has explored four main areas of similarity in the structural and managerial weaknesses in the economies of Kenya and Tanzania. Both countries have weak, dependent economies vulnerable to external shocks; resource gaps that had reached unsustainable levels before

stabilization measures were adopted; incentive structures that were seriously distorted by control systems that generated large rents to protected activities and bureaucracies, engendering inefficiencies and resource misalloca-
tion; and a large public sector that provided political patronage but drained
public resources and led to unsustainable deficits. Macroeconomic policy
reforms were mainly aimed at enhancing savings mobilization and investment efficiency; public sector reforms at controlling budget deficits; and
trade policies at liberalizing imports and promoting exports. Both countries
have significantly depreciated exchange rates in nominal and real terms,
liberalized commercial policies, and promoted exports, especially the nontraditional type. Sectoral policies have included efforts to privatize parastatals, increase real agricultural producer prices, and restructure marketing
institutions for improved efficiency.

One outcome of the adoption of stabilization and structural adjustment
policies and their vigorous implementation in the 1980s is that equity and
poverty issues appear to have taken a back seat. There is strong evidence
that growth alone will not alleviate poverty through the "trickle-down"
effect (Ravikanbur 1987). However, sustainable redistribution and poverty
eradication require a strong resource base backed by sustainable growth.
Previous experience in both countries has shown that public spending for
poverty eradication is limited by the ability of the public sector to appropriate resources from the rest of the economy. Poor growth performance
undermines the revenue base and public spending. Recent evidence (UNDP
1990) suggests that public expenditures can be restructured so that governments can simultaneously promote growth and finance programs intended
to relieve poverty.

In any case, the role of public expenditure in raising human capacity is
fundamental to longer-term growth. More attention needs to be paid to this
issue (World Bank 1991a). As Kenya and Tanzania move towards political
pluralism, there are some important unfolding perspectives relevant to the
adjustment process that we need to emphasize here. First, in situations
where distributive and patronage politics centers on access to and control of
public resources and rental incomes, the dismantling of the basis for rent-
seeking behavior is of paramount importance not only to improve economic
management but also to institute good governance. Continued adjustment
to remove rents is fundamental to a successful transition to democracy in
this context. If rent-seeking is left intact, political pluralism in the short run
may merely create cycles wherein one political beneficiary is replaced with
another. Multiparty politics in this situation becomes the politics of access
to rents, with little or no change in governance. Second, the initial stages of
political pluralism may create undue pressure on the fiscal balance as newcomers try to create and strengthen new patronage networks. An independent structure for fiscal discipline, embedded in some constitutional stipu-
lations, may be necessary to prevent fiscal deterioration. Third, as the

countries move toward a more transparent and participatory policy process, technical insulation needs to be established for balance. In this insulation, policy is set through a transparent political process. Once the choice is made, however, technocrats should be given sufficient room to implement it and to account for both the results and means. This, we feel, is fundamental to delinking patronage politics from economic management.

NOTES

1. Kenya exports a variety of highly specialized horticultural products to Europe and North America, mostly by air. These include flowers (especially carnations), green beans, mushrooms, and strawberries. Limited mainly by available air cargo capacity, horticulture has experienced a dramatic rise at a time when the rest of the economy is in the doldrums. A major reason for the rise is that, in contrast to such traditional exports as coffee and tea, horticulture is a largely unregulated industry.

2. The donors stated that progress had been made in respect to the liberalization of exchange rates and trade policy, control of the money supply, enforcement of financial sector discipline, and the liberalization of grain markets. However, much more needed to be done in respect to reducing corruption and further liberalization of the political system, particularly in ending the ethnic clashes. Kenya was also instructed to make appropriate arrangements to deal with its debt service arrears (World Bank 1993c).

5

The Politics of Agricultural Policy

Michael F. Lofchie

During the generation following independence, Kenya and Tanzania established themselves as leading examples of agricultural performance—one good, one bad. Kenya's pattern of agricultural growth was so impressive that it acquired an international reputation as one of the continent's rare economic success stories and was frequently referred to during the 1970s as one of Africa's economic "miracles." Tanzania, by contrast, stood out as an example of abysmal agricultural performance. Its agricultural decline was so extreme that by the end of the 1970s it had come to be widely regarded, alongside Ghana, as one of Africa's worst cases of economic mismanagement.

According to recent World Bank figures, Kenya's rate of agricultural growth during the period 1965–1980 was more than three times as high as Tanzania's, 5.0 percent versus 1.6 percent (World Bank 1992: 220). But even these figures understate the difference between the two countries. The World Bank calculates a country's economic performance on the basis of its official exchange rate; where a country greatly overvalues its national currency, as does Tanzania (see Figure 5.3), the Bank's figures for economic and agricultural growth will be correspondingly inflated.

A striking feature of Kenya's rate of agricultural growth was that it exceeded the country's high rate of population increase. As a result, the agricultural sector increased national wealth, helping provide material improvements in the lives of Kenya's citizens. Tanzania's rate of agricultural growth was substantially lower than its rate of population growth, so poor agricultural performance contributed to a decline in the material well-being of the Tanzanian people.

The most conspicuous and economically consequential difference in agricultural performance between the two countries had to do with the production of exportable commodities. Here Kenya's success was greatest and Tanzania's failure most severe. By the early 1980s, Kenya had emerged as one of the continent's leading exporters of coffee. Although its export volumes did not compare with those of leading Latin American exporters such as Brazil or Colombia, the quality of its product was sufficient to command a special premium on world markets. Kenya had also emerged as one of the world's leading tea exporters and was able to obtain a premium price for quality for this commodity. In addition to succeeding with coffee and tea exports, Kenya was able to take advantage of other niches of opportunity in the international marketplace, as in the production and export of horticultural products such as cut flowers, fruits, and vegetables.[1]

Tanzania's production of exportable agricultural commodities, by comparison, had utterly stagnated since independence. Although coffee production had remained at a fairly constant level, approximately 50,000 metric tons per year, even this was largely the product of massive infusions of donor assistance. Tanzania had also failed completely to develop its potential as a tea exporter. Figures 5.1 and 5.2 compare the two countries' production of coffee and tea from the mid-1960s to the late 1980s.[2]

By the late 1980s, Kenya's three most important agricultural exports—tea, coffee, and horticultural products—were generating approximately $580 million per year in foreign exchange. Tanzania's annual earnings from its three principal agricultural exports—coffee, cotton, and tea—averaged less than one-third as much, only about $180 million per year (USDA 1990: 309, 483). In marked contrast to Kenya, Tanzania had experienced severe declines in the production of exportable crops for which it had a natural potential and for which international markets existed. Undeveloped potential existed for, at the very least, cotton, sisal, cashew nuts, and tobacco. Table 5.1 illustrates the extent to which Tanzanian production of these crops had actually declined during the period under consideration. The economic cost of these declines is impossible to calculate; doing so would require an estimate of what export levels might have been attained had the agricultural economy been better managed.

Table 5.1 Tanzanian Export Crop Production and Ratio of 1980–1984 Production Average to Peak Period Production

Crop	1980–1984 Average[a]	Peak Period	Peak Average	Ratio of 1980–1984 Average to Peak Period
Cotton	47.00	1970–1972	72.67	0.65
Sisal	62.60	1964–1966	225.67	0.28
Cashews	39.00	1972–1974	131.00	0.30
Tobacco	14.40	1976–1978	18.00	0.80

Source: U.S. Department of Agriculture, Economic Research Service.

Note: a. thousands of metric tons

Figure 5.1 Coffee Production

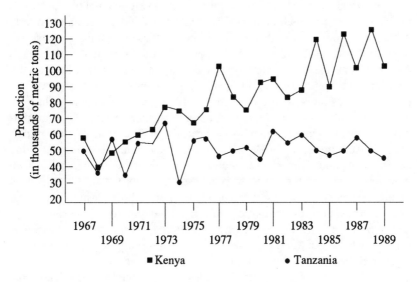

Figure 5.2 Tea Production

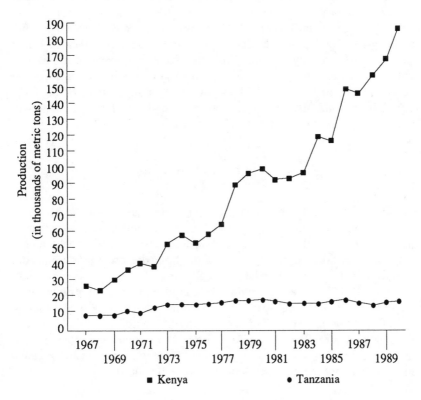

The unequal capacity to generate foreign exchange through agricultural exports had enormous bearing on the broad developmental trajectories of the two countries. Small countries such as Kenya and Tanzania are utterly dependent upon imports that are financed by these earnings. Because the industrial sectors of Kenya and Tanzania, like those of practically all African countries, have been based largely on the principle of import substitution, they generate very little foreign exchange through exports. But these countries must nevertheless meet virtually all of their industrial production requirements—including capital goods, spare parts, a large proportion of their raw materials, and often a certain amount of managerial expertise—through imports. The development and maintenance of infrastructure also depends upon imports; road- and railroad-building equipment, as well as rolling stock and fuel, must be purchased from abroad. The provision of public services is also highly dependent upon export earnings, as most medical and educational supplies must also be imported. In the same manner, agricultural success has a way of building upon itself: The earnings generated by agricultural exports help to sustain the purchase of imported inputs required for continued agricultural vitality.

The lesson is a simple one: Countries that are able to generate and sustain high levels of export earnings through agriculture are in a far better position to enjoy overall economic development than those that do not. Kenya and Tanzania illustrate this proposition perfectly. Kenya's success as an agricultural exporter helped to provide buoyancy for other important sectors of its economy, including industry and public services. Tanzania's failure to generate growth in agricultural exports was a drag on its entire economic system. The net effect was twenty or more years of falling GDP per capita in Tanzania, as against an average annual GDP per capita growth of almost 2 percent per year for Kenya (World Bank 1992: 218).

THE POLICY FRAMEWORK

Throughout the postindependence period, Kenya and Tanzania have differed profoundly in their approach to agricultural policy. Kenya's strategy has been based on the principle of comparative advantage, which emphasizes the importance of exports. Throughout the presidency of Jomo Kenyatta (1963–1978), Kenya's agricultural policymakers were strongly influenced by classical economic ideas holding that a country can best improve its economic well-being by producing the highest possible value in agricultural (or other) commodities for export. According to this doctrine, a country's choice of crops should be prompted by considerations of economic efficiency—where can a given set of inputs produce the greatest return?—and not by the composition of domestic consumption. The principle of comparative advantage is infused with optimism about the developmental benefits of trade and presupposes that a country will attain its highest level of prosperity by trading the goods it can produce efficiently for the goods its people seek to consume.

Kenya's commitment to the principle of comparative advantage was not unqualified but was partially balanced by a countervailing commitment to self-sufficiency in the production of the country's principal food staple, maize, and to having some domestic production of wheat and rice (Kenya 1981). Kenyan agricultural officials rationalized this qualification of comparative advantage by stressing that Kenyans have a strong cultural preference for white (rather than yellow) maize, which is expensive and often difficult to acquire in international markets.

Tanzanian political leaders, by contrast, declared a national goal of self-reliance, and the agricultural component of this objective was the principle of food self-sufficiency. This approach was based upon a profound pessimism about the benefits of international trade. President Julius Nyerere believed that the global marketplace is biased in favor of the rich countries. In his view, trade would not contribute to the development of poor nations that are dependent upon the export of agricultural commodities. Indeed, Tanzanian leaders, like a number of prominent development economists, are convinced that trade, far from providing economic benefits, makes their country politically vulnerable and depletes their economic resources, with the gains reaped principally by the wealthy industrial nations.[3]

The differences in underlying viewpoint between the two countries resulted in wholly different approaches to agricultural policy. To illustrate the differences, I will focus in this chapter on two policies that vitally affect agricultural performance: exchange rate policy and commodity pricing.

Exchange Rate Policy

A country's exchange rate policy is the litmus test of its government's approach to the agricultural sector. At the risk of only slight oversimplification, it can be stated that governments that overvalue their national currencies discriminate against agricultural producers and in favor of urban consumers and industrial firms.[4] Currency overvaluation imposes a tax on the income of agricultural producers, whereas a more realistic exchange rate policy does not. As a result, overvaluation has a direct and negative effect on agricultural production.

The immediate impact of overvaluation is to lower the real prices received by farmers who grow exportable commodities; they receive far fewer units of local currency per unit of production than would be the case if their nations' currencies were more realistically valued. Currency overvaluation can also create price disincentives for farmers who grow food for local consumption. The intent of currency overvaluation is typically to lower the cost of living for urban consumers by cheapening the cost of imported goods, including imported foods, especially grains. Even when imported grains do not force locally produced food staples off the market, their potential to do so has a price-suppressing effect.

Currency overvaluation also affects the productivity of the agricultural sector indirectly by increasing the cost of imported inputs. This consequence may at first appear surprising in view of the fact that the intended purpose and immediate effect of overvaluation are to lower the cost of imported goods. But because it artificially lowers the prices of traded goods, overvaluation also results in a scarcity of foreign exchange. The political question that then arises is: Whose demand for hard currency will be satisfied through the rationing system and whose will not? African governments that are motivated by a concern to maintain the political support of key strategic groups award their urban clienteles a higher priority than farming populations: These governments make foreign exchange available to urban industries for capital goods and raw materials and to urban consumers for durable goods or food items before making it available to farmers for the importation of agricultural inputs. Therefore, imported agricultural inputs become scarce. And even though their nominal price at the port of entry is lowered by overvaluation, it is virtually certain that their real price to the end user will rise because of the scarcity factor. Indeed, the middlemen who create and profit by this price differential may be among the staunchest supporters of the government in power and its commitment to the practice of overvaluation.

Overvaluation also harms agriculture by increasing the cost of labor. By subsidizing urban consumers and making life in the city relatively more attractive, overvaluation has contributed to Africa's well-documented urban influx. The result is modern Africa's supreme paradox: unemployment and underemployment in the cities where industry tends to be capital- (not labor-) intensive, and labor scarcity in the countryside, where work is available but most farmers find it difficult to compete with urban wage levels. Industries, whose costs are lowered by overvaluation, find it unattractive to increase employment levels; farmers, whose prices are lowered by overvaluation, find it practically impossible to do so.

The most revealing measurement of overvaluation is the disparity between a country's official and unofficial exchange rates. By the late 1970s, Tanzania had allowed its currency to become so grossly overvalued that purchasers in informal markets were offering many times the official exchange rate to obtain U.S., British, or other hard currencies. Kenya, by contrast, had pursued a more prudent exchange rate policy. Though there has been some overvaluation, the price levels in informal markets have rarely exceeded the official exchange rate by more than 30 percent. Figure

5.3 contrasts the patterns of overvaluation in Kenya and Tanzania. As this figure reveals, the difference in exchange rate policy between the two countries was so great that overvaluation alone adequately explains their contrasting patterns of agricultural performance. Indeed, no other single factor sheds as much light on the question of why Tanzania, which has a natural potential to produce a wide variety of tradable agricultural commodities and was once a major agricultural exporter, found itself barely able to maintain a constant level of coffee production in the early 1980s. The answer is that overvaluation, by lowering real producer prices, progressively narrowed Tanzania's comparative advantage until it could export only those items in which its comparative advantage was extreme.[5]

In addition to illustrating the broad difference in exchange rate policy between Kenya and Tanzania, Figure 5.3 also reveals the extent to which both countries began to modify their exchange rate policies during the mid-1980s. Tanzania's change was more dramatic than Kenya's. In the aftermath of its structural adjustment agreement with the IMF in 1986 Tanzania began to make major strides in the devaluation of its currency. Between 1986 and 1990, the ratio between unofficial and official rates dropped from almost 4:1 to less than 3:2. Today, even that discrepancy has been virtually eliminated. Tanzanian exchange rate policy took a dramatic step forward in 1992, when the government introduced a system of licensed private exchange bureaus that could trade currencies at market rates with few

Figure 5.3 Currency Overvaluation

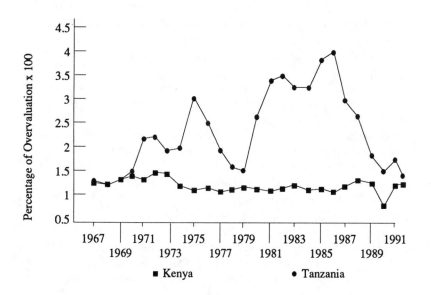

restrictions. The bureau system is politically significant because it represents a structural change in the method by which the exchange rate is determined rather than a simple devaluation administered by the Central Bank. The politically significant feature of a bureau system is that it tends to make devaluation more difficult to reverse by taking the exchange rate out of the hands of governmental authorities.[6]

Kenya, conversely, showed some evidence of weakening its long-standing commitment to a realistic exchange rate policy during the 1980s, twice allowing its currency to become more valued than at any time since independence. This occurred first during 1983 in the mood of political uncertainty and crisis following a military coup attempt in August 1982. The second occurrence came in 1986, following the coffee and tea boom of the mid-1980s, which produced a temporary abundance of foreign exchange. With the collapse of coffee and tea prices in 1987, Kenya's foreign exchange earnings fell drastically, creating a short-term scarcity of hard currency. The government was slow to devalue its currency in response to a temporary surge in demand in informal currency markets but had done so by 1989.

To prevent a recurrence of overvaluation, the government introduced a new foreign exchange system early in 1990. The new system, known as Foreign Exchange Bearer Certificates, or "Forex Cs," permitted commercial banks to offer a premium in local currency to any individual or organization exchanging $500 or more in a single transaction. The purpose of the premium was to bring the bank's effective exchange rate close to the market level. The Forex C system was a considerable improvement over the previous arrangement, which depended wholly on a fixed exchange rate set by the Central Bank. The new policy not only permitted an immediate devaluation of about 30 percent for many transactions, thereby virtually eliminating the parallel market for hard currency, but also allowed commercial banks to adjust their rates quickly to the fluctuating value of the U.S. dollar.

The Forex C system also had several important drawbacks, however. One was that it introduced a dual exchange rate system into the Kenyan economy, as the government continued to conduct its transactions at the Central Bank's official rate, which remained overvalued. A second was that it led to the emergence of a secondary market in Forex Certificates, one subject to manipulation by speculators. From the standpoint of the agricultural sector, the most important shortcoming of the new exchange rate was that it was not uniformly applied to the sale of agricultural exports: Agricultural producers continued to be paid at the older, lower exchange rate. This limitation remained in place for about two and a half years until the fall of 1992, when President Daniel arap Moi announced that producers of nontraditional agricultural exports such as horticultural products would be paid at the devalued rate and that producers of traditional exports such as coffee and tea would be able to receive the new exchange rate on half of the hard currency proceeds from the sale of their crops. This cumbersome and overly regulated system remained in effect until late 1993, when the Kenyan government agreed to allow currency transactions to occur at the interbank rate—that is, the rate at which banks lend to and borrow from one another. Because this rate is determined by the banking community, it is generally considered the freest from government control. All transactions in Kenya are presently conducted at this rate, so its benefit is being enjoyed by the producers of the country's traditional exports.

A discussion of exchange rate policy would be incomplete without some consideration of broader developmental issues. There is an argument that modest overvaluation, even though it has a negative impact on the agricultural sector, may be defensible on other economic grounds. Because overvaluation operates as a tax imposed by the government on the agricultural sector, the economic value it extracts from agriculture must be replaced elsewhere, either in the domestic economic system or, when citizens opt to send their savings abroad, in foreign banks. The developmentally relevant question has to do with which groups or economic sectors receive the benefits from this tax. As suggested above, urban consumers enjoy cheaper imported goods and lower costs for locally produced food staples. Urban industries may also benefit through cheaper imported capital goods, replacement parts, and raw materials. To the degree that domestic industry benefits from the stimulus of cheapened inputs, the overvaluation tax could be thought of as an efficient means of transferring resources from the agricultural sector to the industrial sector. This effect was typically used to justify overvaluation in Latin American countries pursuing an import substitution strategy. And those who believe that African governments ought to use their agricultural wealth to encourage industrial growth might also favor such a policy.

A theoretical case for the use of overvaluation arises out of the new institutional economics, which judges the utility of a tax partly on the basis of the cost of imposing it (Levi 1988; Nabli and Nugent 1989). According to the institutional economists, overvaluation may provide an efficient and cost-effective means of collecting tax revenue in peasant agricultural societies. The basic reason is that peasant income is all but impossible to monitor. Peasant farmers not only receive a high proportion of their income in cash but also have a variety of means of acquiring noncash income (e.g., barter or exchange of services). In addition, peasant farmers tend to acquire most of their cash income during a relatively short period, the harvest season. Because a governmental bureaucracy must by its very nature be supported on a year-round basis, its costs are likely to be high relative to the amount of tax revenue collected.

Orthodox economists, however, oppose the use of overvaluation as a form of taxation because it leads to an inefficient use of resources. In the orthodox view, industries that are provided with subsidized capital will intrinsically tend to use it less efficiently than industries that are required to pay its full cost. According to this argument, poor countries can least afford policies that permit scarce economic resources to be used below their maximum efficiency. Moreover, the capital subsidy provided by overvaluation might, by encouraging the formation of inefficient industries, stand in the way of labor-intensive enterprises that have a potential comparative advantage. In the orthodox economic perspective, neither Kenya nor Tanzania has behaved appropriately in regard to exchange rate management, and the fact that even Kenya's more successful industries have generally not moved beyond import substitution is evidence for this conclusion.

The critical issue is whether the overvaluation tax is raised to the point at which it constitutes a disincentive for agricultural production, especially production of exportable commodities. Here we find the basic difference between overvaluation in Kenya and Tanzania. Tanzania pursued the policy of overvaluation to the point where it became a fundamental disincentive on agricultural production; Kenya did not. Kenya's more limited use of the overvaluation tax has provided it with an efficient means of taxing the countryside and transferring resources to urban industries and services. That Kenya has been able to do so while sustaining high levels of agricultural exports may validate its careful and measured use of the overvaluation tax.

Commodity Pricing

The second area of agricultural policy that illustrates the contrast between Kenya and Tanzania is commodity pricing. As both Kenya and Tanzania officially determine the producer prices of their most important agricultural commodities, the most straightforward method of comparison is simply to look at the prices the two governments pay for certain key products. The only difficulty in doing so is that governmental crop-purchasing agencies pay farmers in local currency; as Figure 5.3 demonstrated, the official and unofficial values of these currencies have fluctuated considerably over time. To obtain the most meaningful comparisons, the following tables compute the annual U.S. dollar prices of agricultural commodities on the basis of *unofficial* exchange rates. These figures provide a more accurate sense of the real value of a country's agricultural prices.

Export Crops

The greatest difference in agricultural performance between Kenya and Tanzania lay in the area of export crops. Here, as Figures 5.1 and 5.2 have already revealed, Kenya vastly outperformed its southern neighbor, consistently producing greater volumes of these commodities. Not surprisingly, this gap was a direct reflection of the difference in pricing policies between the two countries. Coffee and tea prices in Kenya and Tanzania are displayed in Tables 5.2 and 5.3. These figures demonstrate why Kenya was so much more successful than Tanzania as a producer of agricultural exports. Its real producer prices for coffee at one time exceeded Tanzania's by a factor of nearly eleven; throughout the period under consideration, the price differential was consistently between five and eight. Small wonder that Tanzania's coffee production stagnated throughout the two decades from the mid-1960s to the mid-1980s.

An even greater price discrepancy exists for tea. Indeed, Tanzanian tea prices were consistently so low as to be practically inexplicable. Despite having several regions well suited for the production of this crop and despite the government's awareness of the success of smallholder tea production in Kenya, Tanzania was seemingly indifferent to the economic advantages that could be gained from greater production of this commodity.

The conclusion to be derived from Tables 5.2 and 5.3 is self-evident. The Kenyan government's policy was to pass on as high a price as possible

Table 5.2 Prices Paid to Producers for Coffee (U.S. dollars per metric ton)

	Kenya	Tanzania	Ratio, Kenya: Tanzania
1967	671.66	479.66	1.4:1
1968	776.24	535.03	1.5:1
1969	692.75	403.74	1.7:1
1970	766.97	591.10	1.3:1
1971	699.45	436.80	1.6:1
1972	752.56	502.86	1.5:1
1973	944.31	703.94	1.3:1
1974	1,143.60	520.29	2.2:1
1975	1,194.41	240.00	5.0:1
1976	2,728.65	294.12	9.3:1
1977	4,877.30	594.06	8.2:1
1978	3,479.01	680.85	5.1:1
1979	3,415.66	666.67	5.1:1
1980	3,174.70	428.57	7.4:1
1981	1,956.88	326.09	6.0:1
1982	1,944.06	364.74	5.3:1
1983	2,153.09	424.24	5.1:1
1984	2,315.66	411.56	5.6:1
1985	2,678.33	423.42	6.3:1
1986	3,443.96	315.22	10.9:1
1987	1,885.97	364.64	5.2:1
1988	2,081.43	360.00	3.8:1
1989	1,732.14	455.93	3.8:1

Table 5.3 Prices Paid to Producers for Tea (U.S. dollars per metric ton)

	Kenya	Tanzania	Ratio, Kenya: Tanzania
1967	902.07	80.91	11.1:1
1968	709.09	81.21	8.7:1
1969	680.11	70.00	9.7:1
1970	691.08	57.99	11.9:1
1971	714.84	48.67	14.7:1
1972	581.16	46.10	12.6:1
1973	607.90	55.02	11.0:1
1974	837.91	52.86	15.9:1
1975	902.57	32.00	28.2:1
1976	1,142.70	44.12	25.9:1
1977	2,636.81	99.01	26.6:1
1978	1,954.57	127.66	15.3:1
1979	1,634.58	125.00	13.1:1
1980	1,916.87	71.43	26.8:1
1981	1,627.52	54.35	29.9:1
1982	1,357.34	60.79	22.3:1
1983	1,348.15	70.71	19.1:1
1984	3,122.89	71.80	43.5:1
1985	1,934.48	74.32	26.0:1
1986	2,127.04	47.20	45.1:1
1987	1,381.22	54.70	25.3:1
1988	1,274.90	53.60	23.8:1
1989	1,196.43	50.91	23.5:1

to the individual producer and to allow decisions about the allocation of the income to be made by individual peasant households. To underpin this policy, it sought to minimize the operating costs of its coffee and tea marketing boards and to keep taxes on coffee and tea exports at a minimal level. The policy began to break down in the late 1980s, when the Moi government interfered in various ways with the established coffee marketing system. Because of its mismanagement of the principal institutions responsible for international sales of this crop, payments to farmers became subject to considerable delays, and the amount of the international sales price deducted to cover operations increased greatly. The result was increasing demoralization among coffee growers and a sharp downward trend in annual production.

The export crop pricing policy of the Tanzanian Government was exactly opposite. It treated the revenues generated by coffee and tea exports as a national economic resource. Decisions about the allocation of this resource were not to be made at the level of the individual household, but, rather, by the country's political and bureaucratic elites, especially the leading politicians in the highest councils of the ruling party—the Tanganyika African National Union (TANU) and later, CCM.

Kenya's policy of paying high producer prices meant that individual farm households had more income to expend on consumption, thereby increasing the demand for locally produced consumer goods, or on long-term investment.[7] During the 1975–1977 coffee boom, Kenya's coffee growers allotted much of their additional income to economically productive investments such as improvement of their farms. These improvements might take a variety of forms, including the acquisition of additional land or, where this was not feasible, in raising yields through the planting of new trees, the greater use of scientific inputs, or other innovations in crop husbandry. The coffee farmers also used their extra income to hire additional agricultural labor, thereby stimulating rural employment. Much private income was also invested in the development of social services, as when farmers contributed to the construction of *Harambee* (local self-help) schools.

Tanzania's policy was to maintain low peasant incomes and to treat any increased income from crop sales as a national tax. The stated objectives of this policy were to enable the government to expand the country's medical and educational services and to equalize the distribution of peasant income in the countryside. But it is doubtful that Tanzania's pricing policy satisfied either of these goals. One study concluded instead, that Tanzania's export pricing policy had mostly negative consequences (Bevan, Collier, and Gunning 1989). Most obviously, it suppressed the incomes of export crop producers and thereby minimized the possibility of secondary and tertiary benefits such as farm improvements or job creation. It therefore resulted in a lower rate of agricultural growth. Tanzanian pricing policy explains why coffee production actually began to show signs of decline during the late 1980s (Bevan et al. 1989, Chapters 7 and 8). Tanzania's coffee prices had fallen so low that many coffee farmers were abandoning the crop and turning to others whose prices were not controlled by the government.

Tanzania's pricing policy also failed to contribute to the provision of superior medical and educational services. As the agricultural base of the country's economy deteriorated, the government's capacity to maintain either the quality or the availability of these services dwindled commensurately.

Food Crops

The contrast in agricultural performance between Kenya and Tanzania is less dramatic in the food crop sector than in the export crop sector. Generally speaking, Kenya appears to have outperformed Tanzania in the production of maize and wheat, with Tanzania attaining superior output of rice. Figures 5.4, 5.5, and 5.6 display the production performance of the two countries for these crops. The graphs in these figures should be treated with great caution. Estimates of grain production necessarily require highly speculative assumptions about such matters as the proportion of the each crop that is consumed at the household level and the amount of informal interdistrict, interregional and cross-border trade. With this proviso in mind, these figures reveal the patterns of food production in the two countries.

Kenya's superior performance in maize production is of greatest importance because maize is the principal food staple of the two countries and because the production volumes involved are so much greater than for wheat or rice. (Note that the production scale for maize in Figure 5.4 is in millions of metric tons, but the production scales for wheat and rice in Figures 5.5 and 5.6 are in thousands of metric tons.) Kenya also exceeded Tanzania in the production of wheat, generally producing about three times as much (200,000 metric tons versus about 70,000 metric tons in the late 1980s) as its southern neighbor. Tanzania, however, attained higher levels of rice production than Kenya. The U.S. Department of Agriculture estimates that by the end of the 1980s Tanzania was producing between 600,000 and 700,000 tons of rice annually, compared to only 40,000 metric tons in Kenya.[8]

Figure 5.4 Maize Production

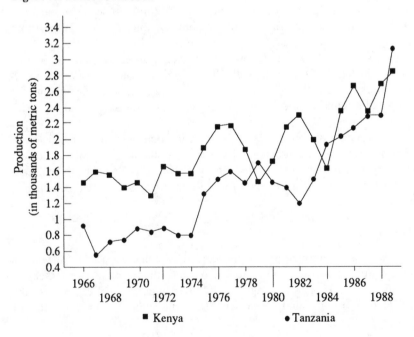

Figure 5.5 Wheat Production

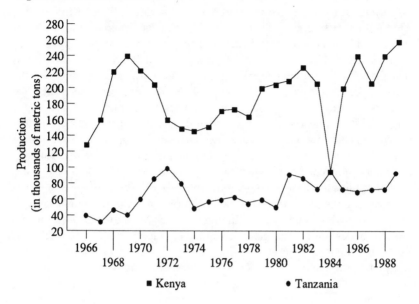

Figure 5.6 Rice Production

If the performance differences for major grain crops are narrower than the differences for the main exportable commodities, then so too are the price policy differences. Tables 5.4, 5.5, and 5.6 compare the producer prices of the two countries for maize, wheat, and rice, respectively. These tables demonstrate that although Kenya paid higher prices for food crops than Tanzania, the price disparities were not nearly as great as those for the major exports. During the 1979s and 1980s, Kenya's producer prices for food crops were generally between 1.5 and 4 times higher than those of Tanzania. By comparison with the price differentials for export crops displayed in Tables 5.2 and 5.3, these are fairly modest gaps. Moreover, were it not for the tendency of currency overvaluation to lower the real value of Tanzanian producer prices when these are given in U.S. dollars, its prices for these grains might well compare favorably with Kenya's.

The patterns of export and food crop pricing of the two countries sustain the following conclusion: Although all Kenyan agricultural producers received better prices than their Tanzanian counterparts, the difference was greater for export crop producers than food crop producers. Kenya's pattern of agricultural pricing, in other words, created a powerful incentive for

Table 5.4 Prices Paid to Producers for Maize (U.S. dollars per metric ton)

	Kenya	Tanzania	Ratio, Kenya: Tanzania
1967	40.67	29.43	1.4:1
1968	37.33	32.12	1.2:1
1969	30.33	27.47	1.1:1
1970	28.21	23.83	1.2:1
1971	36.59	16.87	2.2:1
1972	37.58	17.79	2.1:1
1973	39.90	22.97	1.7:1
1974	53.95	35.71	1.5:1
1975	78.21	30.00	2.6:1
1976	83.24	39.22	2.1:1
1977	109.20	56.11	1.9:1
1978	95.68	72.34	1.3:1
1979	107.23	83.33	1.3:1
1980	114.94	47.62	2.4:1
1981	91.74	54.35	1.7:1
1982	73.78	53.19	1.4:1
1983	95.06	55.56	1.7:1
1984	105.42	70.05	1.5:1
1985	111.72	78.83	1.4:1
1986	131.38	39.13	3.4:1
1987	115.41	45.30	2.5:1
1988	106.33	36.00	3.0:1
1989	109.64	41.79	2.6:1

Table 5.5 Prices Paid to Producers for Wheat (U.S. dollars per metric ton)

	Kenya	Tanzania	Ratio, Kenya: Tanzania
1967	65.44	64.89	1.0:1
1968	68.24	70.30	1.0:1
1969	59.89	59.56	1.0:1
1970	46.26	49.09	0.9:1
1971	55.60	37.07	1.5:1
1972	48.89	36.17	1.4:1
1973	58.67	35.17	1.7:1
1974	93.49	52.79	1.8:1
1975	117.32	40.00	2.9:1
1976	129.73	58.82	2.2:1
1977	163.19	82.51	2.0:1
1978	164.20	106.38	1.5:1
1979	173.01	112.50	1.5:1
1980	197.47	78.57	2.5:1
1981	152.94	79.71	1.9:1
1982	124.90	75.99	1.6:1
1983	137.04	75.76	1.8:1
1984	162.05	78.81	2.1:1
1985	155.75	90.09	1.7:1
1986	184.28	44.72	4.1:1
1987	162.98	49.72	3.3:1
1988	151.86	41.40	3.7:1
1989	151.79	49.39	3.1:1

Table 5.6 Prices Paid to Producers for Rice (U.S. dollars per metric ton)

	Kenya	Tanzania	Ratio, Kenya: Tanzania
1967	52.42	49.09	1.1:1
1968	55.52	57.21	1.0:1
1969	50.44	58.35	0.9:1
1970	52.00	58.09	0.9:1
1971	53.19	36.60	1.5:1
1972	49.08	38.25	1.3:1
1973	51.38	42.68	1.2:1
1974	68.14	44.21	1.5:1
1975	116.76	40.00	2.9:1
1976	148.00	49.02	3.0:1
1977	166.87	79.21	2.1:1
1978	178.77	102.13	1.8:1
1979	181.69	125.00	1.5:1
1980	181.20	83.33	2.2:1
1981	165.14	83.33	2.0:1
1982	166.99	91.19	1.8:1
1983	109.88	101.01	1.1:1
1984	107.23	105.08	1.0:1
1985	196.55	120.12	1.6:1
1986	218.87	59.63	3.7:1
1987	205.52	79.56	2.6:1
1988	184.76	69.20	2.7:1
1989	181.83	72.19	2.5:1

farmers to shift away from food crops toward export crop production. Tanzania's farmers had no such incentive. To illustrate this point, Table 5.7 compares the ratio of coffee to maize prices in Kenya and Tanzania. The table shows that Tanzania's policy from the early 1970s to the mid-1980s was to reduce the price differential between its most important export and food crops. Indeed, as coffee had high production costs, Tanzania's farmers had an incentive to shift out of this crop into the production of food crops that were less expensive to grow.

Table 5.7 Coffee-Maize Price Ratios, 1967–1989

	Kenya	Tanzania
1967	16.5	16.3
1968	20.8	16.7
1969	22.8	14.7
1970	27.2	24.8
1971	19.1	25.9
1972	20.0	28.3
1973	23.7	30.6
1974	21.2	14.6
1975	15.3	8.0
1976	32.8	7.5
1977	44.7	10.6
1978	36.4	9.4
1979	31.9	8.0
1980	27.6	9.0
1981	21.3	6.0
1982	26.4	6.9
1983	22.6	7.6
1984	22.0	5.9
1985	24.0	5.4
1986	26.2	8.1
1987	16.3	8.0
1988	19.6	10.0
1989	15.8	10.9

Note: Price ratios computed on the basis of real prices paid to farmers.

Following independence, then, Kenya created a policy environment generally favorable to agriculture, but the major objective of its pricing policy was to provide maximum incentives for export crop production. The twin epicenters of this policy were prudent management of exchange rates and consistently high producer prices for export crops. Although Kenya's policy favored the producers of exportable crops, its food crop producers also benefited from a policy environment generally favorable to the agricultural sector. In the argot of the economics profession, its food crop producers were the beneficiaries of an "externality"; that is, they gained benefits from a policy framework that was principally intended to advance the economic interest of others.

The Tanzanian policy profile is wholly different. Following independence, Tanzanian agricultural policy reflected a bias against agriculture. Despite President Nyerere's repeated insistence that agriculture was the centerpiece of a national commitment to self-reliance, Tanzania's economic system taxed agriculture in order to generate resources for the development of urban industries and governmental programs, especially medical and educational services. The price disincentives and other constraints on agriculture were so great that production of critically important exports either stagnated or plummeted, and production of food crops failed by a wide margin to satisfy local needs. Within this context, however, Tanzania's bias against the food-producing sector was not nearly as pronounced as its bias against the export sector. Throughout the 1970s and early 1980s, Tanzanian political leaders claimed that the goal of agricultural policy was food self-sufficiency, not export maximization. Although the government's efforts to attain that goal were unsuccessful, the government clearly sought to provide incentives for food crop production much more energetically than for export crop production.

Although neither country could be considered a pure case of its chosen strategy, their experiences provide an excellent illustration of the real-world consequences of these conflicting approaches. There can be little doubt that Kenya came closer than Tanzania to achieving its agricultural goals. It not only attained great success as an agricultural exporter but also, despite its primary emphasis on the production of exportable commodities, was able to produce greater volumes of two of the three major grains. As a result, Kenya was generally less dependent than Tanzania upon grain imports. Table 5.8 compares grain imports for the two countries during

Table 5.8 Grain Imports by Kenya and Tanzania (thousands of metric tons)

	1976–1980		1981–1985		1986–1990	
	Kenya	Tanzania	Kenya	Tanzania	Kenya	Tanzania
Maize	372	133	1,068	903	0	114
Rice	45	253	105	305	189	298
Wheat	270	219	578	346	882	247
Total	687	605	1,751	1,554	1,071	659
Agricultural Imports as Percent of Total Imports	7.8	9.8	9.8	10.4	8.25	6.75

three five-year periods: 1976–1980, 1981–1985, and 1986–1990. As this table also reveals, Kenya's grain imports, especially those of wheat, were increasing rapidly during the 1980s and by the end of the decade constituted a larger proportion of total imports than was true in Tanzania.

Tanzania's need to import high volumes of grains even while sacrificing agricultural exports represented a significant developmental cost and in all likelihood contributed to the decline of the country's industrial sector. During the five-year period 1981–1985, for example, Tanzania's grain imports averaged approximately 14 percent of total foreign exchange earnings, in contrast with slightly less than 10 percent for Kenya. Put differently, Tanzania's food imports had a somewhat greater tendency to "crowd out" imports of capital goods, raw materials, or other inputs that might have helped sustain a better level of industrial performance.

An important implication of the production contrasts between these two countries, however, is that they contradict a widespread myth about food self-sufficiency in modern Africa. According to this myth, food self-sufficiency is a viable alternative to an economic strategy emphasizing exports. This myth, which underlay all of Tanzanian agricultural policy, is based upon an implicit conception of African economies as consisting almost entirely of localized and largely self-sufficient farming communities. It does not deal with the continent's explosive urban growth or the emergence of large rural, nonagricultural populations. The myth of food self-sufficiency, therefore, does not take into account the increasingly intensive kinds of agricultural production necessary to provide the kinds and amounts of grain demanded by the rising proportion of nonfarming families.

Kenya's experience demonstrates that self-sufficiency in the production of food staples requires robust performance in the production of exports. Success in the latter has vital spillover benefits for other agricultural activities, including cultivation of food staples. In contemporary Africa, the production of these staples (especially maize, wheat, and rice) is as dependent upon the foreign exchange earnings generated by agricultural exports as are industrial production, the development of infrastructure, and the provision of government services. The modern cultivation of these crops has become heavily dependent upon imported inputs, including not only the fertilizers, pesticides, and herbicides used in the process of cultivation at the farm level but also the equipment and energy costs used in processing, packaging, and distribution. Indeed, because the value-to-weight ratios of these crops are low compared to those of coffee and tea, the cost of imported inputs often constitute a higher percentage of their final value than that of the exportable commodities.

EXPLAINING POLICY VARIANCE

Robert Bates's classic work, *Markets and States in Tropical Africa* (Bates 1981), seeks to present an explanation of the agricultural policies that led to agricultural stagnation in so many African countries after independence. Bates asks why the leaders of these countries pursued policies that were inappropriate for agricultural growth. The core of the answer can be briefly summarized. African political leaders, like political leaders everywhere, place a high premium on gaining and holding public office. To do so, they must create and maintain coalitions of politically loyal supporters, a process that requires economic resources. Inevitably, political leaders tend to implement policies that shift resources toward groups that help them remain in power and away from those that do not. In this process, groups that have the capacity to sustain regimes become winners; groups that do not suffer and become economic losers.

Bates's explanation of the roots of inappropriate agricultural policy rests squarely on his perception of the difference between social groupings that are politically powerful and those that are not. In his judgment, the most potent political groups are generally urban in character; to this extent, Bates's work follows the intellectual tradition of urban-bias analysis pioneered earlier by Michael Lipton (1976). He and other urban-bias theorists believe that physical proximity to the centers of political power constitutes a decisive political resource—that is, urban groups have a greater capacity to make felt their support for or opposition to a regime than do rural populations, especially small farmers. Urban groups gain political influence because of their concentration and sheer closeness to power; farmers tend to lose it because they are dispersed and difficult to organize. The end result is that urban dwellers' political influence tends to be high in proportion to their numbers, whereas farmers' tends to be lower.

The Bates/Lipton approach concludes that the problem of agricultural stagnation afflicting much of Africa is traceable to the political weakness of agricultural interests. Agricultural populations suffer because urban groups are able to obtain agricultural policies that shift economic resources away from the farming sector and toward the urban projects and services that help governments sustain themselves. Such policies make eminent sense politically but have devastating effects on agricultural performance.

When applied to agricultural policy in Kenya and Tanzania, the Bates/Lipton approach suffers from two important weaknesses. The first is an inability to explain the wide divergences in agricultural policy between the two countries. Like any highly generalized paradigm, this model is powerful in explaining similarities across countries but not well suited to explaining differences between them. This shortcoming becomes especially apparent when the theory is confronted with countries such as Kenya, whose agricultural policies have not been characterized by an urban (anti-agricultural) bias but instead have been favorable to the agricultural sector.

The second weakness is an inability to explain why governments initiate major changes in their agricultural policies, sometimes fairly abruptly. During the early to mid-1980s, both Kenya and Tanzania began such changes. Tanzania's was profound. In 1985 longtime president Julius Nyerere stepped down and was succeeded by Ali Hassan Mwinyi. Within a year, Tanzania had formally accepted a structural adjustment agreement with the International Monetary Fund and accelerated a process of policy reform that had actually begun during the final years of Nyerere's administration. Within three years, Tanzanian policy had changed from one of extreme urban bias to one that was relatively favorable to the agricultural sector. Kenya's change in approach to agricultural policy came at roughly the same time but was less dramatic. Kenyatta's successor as president, Daniel arap Moi, took agricultural policy in a substantially different direction. Although Kenyan policy remained broadly favorable to the agricultural sector as a whole, the Moi administration took a series of steps that substantially lessened Kenya's long-standing commitment to the primacy of the export sector in favor of a heightened emphasis on self-sufficiency in food crop production. Short-term changes such as these are difficult to explain using the Bates model.

In sum, the Bates model provides a compelling explanation of Tanzanian agricultural policy from independence to the 1985 presidential succession, but it is less useful in explaining Kenyan agricultural policy during the same period and not at all helpful in explaining why either country should begin to change its agricultural approach at roughly the midpoint of the last decade.

The theoretical challenge, then, is to explain Kenya's exceptionality—why it is unlike not only Tanzania but also so many other African countries that pursued inappropriate agricultural policies during the postindependence era. Kenya's experience suggests that rural political pressure, not urban bias, was the primary determinant of agricultural policy. The urban-bias approach simply does not provide an adequate portrayal of Kenya's political process; it underestimates the importance of social and institutional factors that can promote rural interests and overlooks the possibility of geopolitical variability. Joel Barkan has stated these issues in the following terms: "Any discussion of the incidence of 'urban bias' in selected Third World states must first consider the structure of political conflict and the balance of power between the countryside and the state. Questions as to why prices and the marketing structure confronting peasant producers are what they are, or why peasant access to state welfare services is rising or falling cannot be fully answered without first determining the extent and kind of influence residents of rural areas exert on the policy-making process" (Barkan 1983: 4).

The analysis that follows identifies three political factors that are more important than urban bias in explaining why Kenya and Tanzania pursued different approaches to their agricultural sectors. These are the relationship of the political elite to agricultural land; the impact of political institutions; and geopolitical differences.

Elite Ownership of Land

The urban-bias approach uncritically assumes that urban-based political elites have different economic interests than agricultural producers. This is not so in Kenya, where political elites are bound to the countryside by a powerful economic interest: ownership of agricultural land. Tanzania's elite, by contrast, is not so bound (Leonard 1984). The most important social difference between these two countries lies in the extent to which Kenya's governing elite is also a landowning elite, heavily invested in the country's farmland and deriving a considerable proportion of its income from the production and sale of agricultural commodities. Though the economic interests of Kenya's political and bureaucratic elites have become increasingly diversified in recent years and today include industry, transportation, tourist services, and banking, they remain first and foremost agricultural.

Elite land acquisition has been one of the highest priorities of Kenyan public policy since the late colonial period, when the British government first sought to enable large numbers of Africans to acquire land on a freehold basis under a program called Land Consolidation and Adjudication.[9] The idea was a simple one: convert the legal basis of landholding for African farmers from traditional tenure to freehold ownership and aggregate scattered communal plots into viable single farms. The stated purpose of this program was thus economic: Individuals who held fee simple title deeds would qualify more easily for development loans because they could offer their land as collateral. The intent of the program was also deeply political—to create a politically moderate class of landowning Africans.

The Land Consolidation and Adjudication program, which began in the early 1950s, has had an enormous effect on contemporary Kenya. It was taken up as a cornerstone of rural policy by the independent government of Kenya and, with only slight modifications, has been officially maintained to this day.[10] The program reached its height in the mid-1970s, when it successfully transferred more than 500,000 hectares per year from traditional forms of tenure to fee simple ownership.[11] Since then, the program has slowed appreciably, a trend that World Bank officials attribute to a lack of interest on the part of officials in the Moi administration. The slowing trend may also reflect the fact that the program has now covered a majority of Kenya's most arable regions. By the end of 1985, land consolidation had

covered about 6,700,000 hectares, an area about twice the size of the former European highlands (Kenya 1986c). Although the government's statistics do not indicate how many individually owned farms this represents,
unofficial estimates place the number at well over 3,000,000.[12]

The second impetus to large-scale land acquisition by the political elite
was the conversion of the former European highlands to African ownership. This region, which consisted of mixed farms, tea and coffee plantations, and cattle ranches, accounted for about one-fourth of the country's
most arable land at the time of independence. Virtually all of this land, with
the exception of the foreign-owned tea plantations, has since been converted to African ownership. The mixed-farm areas, which originally included
about 3,000 farms averaging approximately 800 acres each, today comprise
tens of thousands of small- and large-scale privately owned farms. A large
number of these mixed farms have been purchased intact by members of
Kenya's political and administrative elite.

The result of these two programs is that much of Kenya's best agricultural land, both within and outside the former European highlands, has been
acquired by government officials. The ability of this group to acquire land
has been powerfully abetted by a variety of institutional and normative factors. Among the most important of these has been the operation of market
forces. The country's private banks, for example, have always given high
preference for mortgage loans to public officials because their salaries,
which are used to guarantee the loans, are among the highest and most
secure in the country. High and secure salaries have also given government
officials a strong advantage at land auctions or foreclosure sales. In addition, government officials have enjoyed preferred access to public lending
institutions such as the Agricultural Finance Corporation.

Investment in land by members of the country's political elite has been
actively encouraged by the government, which, especially during the
Kenyatta years, applied its own version of the "stake in society" thesis to
government officials. The normative atmosphere held that individuals with
property and investments to protect would be that much more likely to
implement government policy responsibly. There was no sense that land
acquisition by the elite might raise conflicts of interest. This view was
directly articulated in an early government report on the terms and conditions of governmental service stating that "there ought in theory to be no
objection to the ownership of property or involvement in business by members of the public services to a point where their wealth is augmented perhaps substantially by such activities" (Kenya 1971).

Information about the precise amount of land owned by Kenya's highest-ranking political leaders is not publicly available. As this topic is a matter of utmost sensitivity, it has generally been considered off-limits to academic or journalistic inquiry. The exact details are not, in any case, essential
to the broad theoretical argument—namely, that the concept of urban bias

is not helpful in understanding Kenya's agricultural policy because it does not anticipate the extent of land ownership by Kenya's political elite. Kenya's agricultural policy has not been the province of leaders whose most vital interests lay in accommodating urban clienteles; rather, leaders are deeply invested in the agricultural sector (Njonjo 1977). Where the welfare of the agricultural sector is concerned, Kenya's government has been one of farmers, by farmers, and for farmers.

Tanzania has represented the opposite political situation: Urban bias has indeed been a powerful factor in the determination of agricultural policy. Even so, its postindependence experience illustrates an important and typically overlooked aspect of the urban-bias phenomenon—namely, that urban bias is as much caused *by* the actions of political elites as it is a cause *of* their actions. In Tanzania, the tendency toward urban bias was not immediately discernible at the time of independence in mid-1961. Tanzania's nationalist movement, TANU, like most others throughout Africa, was a complex mixture of urban and rural elements, combining a wide variety of regional, ethnic, and economic groups with highly diversified political outlooks. Tanzanian economic policy during the first years of independence reflected this diversity. The government's approach to the economy was largely liberal and represented an effort to balance different regional, group, and ideological interests. The transformation of the country's policy framework away from regional eclecticism and toward urban bias was not made until five years after independence. It was largely the product of a political decision to adopt a socialist strategy of development that was publicly announced in early 1967.

Tanzanian socialism decisively shifted the country's political balance against the interests of its farmers, especially those who grew exportable crops. It did so in several ways. First and foremost, socialism created a normative atmosphere in which private ownership of productive property, including agricultural land, was considered inimical to the welfare of the population as a whole. Although this atmosphere diminished the political influence of owners of all productive assets, including urban industries or commercial firms, its most decisive political impact was to reduce the influence of those who owned commercial farms, especially large-scale coffee farms.[13] The owners of industries in Tanzania were not a social group of any political significance. Tanzania was barely industrialized at the time of independence, and virtually all locally owned industries of any magnitude were owned by Asians, whose political influence was at best marginal. The few industrial enterprises not held by Asians were generally owned by foreign corporations; though many analysts hold that multinational corporations have great influence in African countries, those in Tanzania had always been outside the circles of political power. The only entrepreneurial groups of any consequence to hold positions of authority within TANU were the large-scale coffee farmers of the Arusha/Moshi and

West Lake regions. When socialism was proclaimed, these groups suddenly found themselves pariahs in their own nationalist party.[14]

The shift to socialism further marginalized the influence of the Tanzanian countryside by creating an absolute divide between landowners and the political leadership. It did so in at least two ways. First, land was legally nationalized. Although this nationalization had little practical effect on the day-to-day life of Tanzanian farmers or on their conception of individual or group rights to land tenure, it did mean that land ceased to represent an attractive target for investment. Investments in land could not be protected in the court system.

More important, socialism in Tanzania was accompanied by a leadership code that strictly forbade any government official from enjoying multiple sources of income. Whereas the Kenyan government had actively encouraged elite investment in land and had instituted several programs directly pursuant to this purpose, Tanzania took precisely the opposite course, driving an absolute wedge between political office and landownership. The Arusha Declaration stated that "every TANU and government leader should . . . in no way be associated with the practices of capitalism or feudalism" (Nyerere 1967b: 36). The legal implementation of this code meant that Tanzanians who held political office and made agricultural policy could have no economic interest in agricultural land; those with interests in agricultural land could not hold office or participate in the framing of agricultural policy.

Institutional Differences

The second shortcoming of the urban-bias approach is its tendency to underestimate the importance of a country's political institutions. Like other pressure-group approaches, it tends to view the political process as a kind of systemic "black box" that simply translates demand inputs into policy outputs. Little attention is given to the possibility that institutional differences matter greatly in determining the relative influence of different social groups. Urban-bias theorists, in other words, do not consider the possibility that political institutions may help rural populations to assert their economic interests.

Kenya's political institutions afford rural groups considerable opportunity to exercise influence at the national level; Tanzania's do not. The key institutional difference has been Kenya's system of open elections to the National Assembly. Although Kenya had a single-party political system from the mid-1960s until 1992, its system of open parliamentary elections generally gave rural voters great latitude in choosing between candidates.[15] Because local political rivals could freely stand for national office, individual campaigns were typically based on the extent to which one candidate or another could elicit favorable policies from the central government. As a result, "political careers rise and fall on the ability of elected officials to extract such services from the center."[16]

Tanzania's political institutions have operated very differently. Until Tanzania reformed its constitution and allowed multipartyism in early 1992, its system of parliamentary elections greatly limited the influence of rural electorates on public policy. The limits arose mainly from the way candidates for the Tanzanian National Assembly were chosen. Whereas in Kenya the only meaningful barrier to standing for public office was an individual's ability to mobilize and sustain a political following, prospective candidates for the Tanzanian National Assembly had to be approved by an elaborate hierarchy of party committees, including constituency-level selection committees, an Annual District Conference, and finally the party's National Executive Committee. Whereas in Kenya the requirement of party membership to stand for elected office was a mere formality and thus allowed for candidates of widely varying views, the Tanzanian system of nomination allowed practically no latitude for candidates to disagree with party policy.

The Tanzanian constitution also diminished the influence of locally elected representatives. Before the 1992 constitutional reforms, Tanzania's National Assembly was constitutionally subordinate to the governing party; its assigned political role was not to frame or to debate public policy but rather to translate the policy decisions of TANU's National Executive Committee into law. Because of this gravely weakened role, elected representatives were unable to serve as spokespersons for the policy demands or preferences of their constituents. Discussion of policy matters between the center and the countryside was instead carried out through a complex hierarchy of village, district, and regional development committees, and these have been dominated by party officials.

As a result, Tanzania's political system gave locally elected representatives little opportunity to serve their constituents by extracting policy concessions from the central government. Elected representatives to the National Assembly had great difficulty in developing even informal channels of influence. Since they were not allowed to own businesses or receive secondary incomes, they generally did not possess economic resources that would enable them to construct patron-client networks outside the country's formal institutions. The limited stature and role of the National Assembly also constrained their ability to exercise influence in other governmental institutions; for example, they appeared to lack the authority to lobby bureaucrats on behalf of their constituents, an activity heavily engaged in by their Kenyan counterparts.

The outcome of these disabilities prior to the reintroduction of multiparty politics was that Tanzania's political institutions did not provide any significant constraint on the tendency toward urban bias of the country's political leaders. As summarized at the time by Barkan: "In [Tanzania's] system, the direct influence of rural populations, and particularly rural elites, on the policy-making process is practically reduced to zero. Stated simply, there are few institutions in Tanzania through which urban based elites, government or party, are held directly accountable, even informally, to rural populations or their representatives. . . . [T]he only significant constraint on urban bias is the ideological commitment of the regime itself" (Barkan 1983: 6). As measured by the country's agricultural policy, even this constraint was of minimal importance.

Geopolitical Differences

The third weakness in the urban-bias approach is its tendency to assume that rural residence by itself poses constraints on political influence. Developing countries may vary greatly in the extent to which rural populations or their representatives have access to their capital cities. In East Africa, this variance was readily apparent as early as the colonial period. Kenya's European settler farmers had no difficulty whatsoever in making their political presence felt in Nairobi. Their influence was felt in virtually every aspect of Kenya's colonial agricultural policy—land alienation, restrictions on African cash-crop farming, compulsory labor, subsidized prices and transportation rates, and extensive governmental services for settler farmers.

Tanzania's settler farmers, conversely, had the greatest difficulty in influencing colonial agricultural policy. Their clout was limited in part because a majority were not of British descent and could not, therefore, call upon kith and kin ties to colonial administrators for leverage. Another factor was their more limited numbers—only about 3,000 settler farm families, in contrast to about 10,000 in Kenya. However, the biggest limitation was the fact that Tanzania's European settlers typically lived hundreds of miles from Dar es Salaam in the highland regions of Arusha/Moshi and around Iringa. The distance lessened their ability to seek ongoing influence in the colonial capital.

The political geography of these two countries could hardly be more dissimilar. Kenya's most productive agricultural regions, the south-facing slopes of Mount Kenya and the highlands west of the Rift Valley, are within one to two hours' drive of Nairobi. The country's richest and most productive agricultural districts are literally on the outskirts of the capital. This proximity helps facilitate the pervasive overlap of roles—farming combined with civil service employment and/or the holding of political office—that is at the heart of contemporary Kenyan politics.

The political geography of Tanzanian agriculture is altogether different, most notably in the fact that the country's most important agricultural areas not only are located three to six hundred miles from the capital city but also are great distances apart from one another. Although the region surrounding Dar es Salaam had some importance as a sisal area during the colonial period, it is today of only the most marginal agricultural significance. Coffee, for example, is grown principally in the area of Arusha/ Moshi, near the border with Kenya or in the West Lake region directly adjacent to Uganda; maize in the extreme southwestern area of the country near Mbeya, along Tanzania's borders with Zambia and Malawi; and cotton south of Lake Victoria in a region close to Zaire. The ready access to the capital city that so greatly facilitated political influence by Kenya's farmers has been unavailable to Tanzania's.

The political impact of the geographical difference is readily visible. In Kenya, rural interests, not urban ones, preoccupy the day-to-day lives of high-ranking politicians and bureaucrats. Ministers or their highest-ranking representatives are constantly called upon to meet with the representatives of agricultural organizations, to address delegations of agricultural interest groups, and to visit nearby agricultural districts. The offices of Kenya's agricultural parastatals are constantly crowded with delegations of farmers who have some issue to take up with parastatal management. Dar es Salaam creates an altogether different impression. It is a city of civil servants, mercantile enterprise, and workers in services and industries. Although Tanzania is even more economically dependent upon its agricultural sector than Kenya, the presence of agricultural lobbies or their representatives is scarcely felt. In sum, differentials in elite access to agricultural land, differences in institutional accessibility to rural interests, and striking geopolitical differences all help explain why Kenya's agricultural policies have been a conspicuous exception to the urban-bias paradigm but Tanzania's have not.

POLICY CHANGES IN THE 1980s

During the mid-1980s, however, the agricultural policies of these two countries began to change. In Kenya's case, the change in policy did not involve a fundamental shift in the government's generally proagricultural position but rather a shift in priority within the agricultural sector. In Tanzania's case, the change in policy was more comprehensive. The government began to move away from the protectionist industrial policy that had proven so harmful to the agricultural sector and to implement policies intended to restore the agricultural productivity of the preindependence period.

Kenya

The change in Kenya's agricultural policy resulted from changes in the regional, ethnic, and economic basis of the Kenyan presidency brought about by the presidential succession of 1978. The principal social basis of support for the government of President Jomo Kenyatta was the Kikuyu ethnic group, which generally inhabits the Central Province, a small but highly affluent region directly adjacent to Nairobi. The principal base of support for President Moi is the Kalenjin ethnic group, which largely inhabits the Rift Valley Province, an immense rectangular region that runs from Kenya's northern border with Ethiopia to its southern border with Tanzania.[17]

This change has produced a shift in the underlying agricultural interests of the government. Whereas the Kenyatta administration had its economic roots among export-oriented Kikuyu farmers, principally those involved with coffee production, the Moi administration has its principal economic basis among grain farmers in the Rift Valley. This change explains the figures in Table 5.5, which reveal that the present government has modified Kenya's established agricultural policy by introducing a new emphasis on attaining greater and greater volumes of wheat production. According to a study by the U.S. Department of Agriculture, the producer price index for wheat more than tripled during the decade of the 1980s, increasing from a base of 100 to nearly 350 by 1990 (Shapouri et al. 1992: 21). The new pricing policy was successful in attaining its immediate objective. Between 1975 and 1979, the final years of the Kenyatta era, Kenya's wheat production averaged about 176,000 metric tons. By the end of the 1980s (1985–1989), it had grown to about 231,000 metric tons per year, an increase of more than 30 percent.

The Moi government's increased emphasis on wheat production has had broad economic ramifications, mostly negative ones. Its principal effect has been an abrupt shift of resources away from the coffee sector. The shift also portends a diminished emphasis on long-term economic growth. As Robert Bates has suggested in his recent book on Kenya, a government based on the support of export crop producers emphasizes investment and the accumulation of economic wealth, whereas a government based on the support of food grain producers emphasizes the redistribution of wealth (Bates 1989). In a poor agrarian country such as Kenya, export farmers are society's "haves," and their principal economic interest is in policies that contribute to the long-term growth of the sector they control. Grain farmers, by comparison, are generally "have-nots" and tend as a result to favor short-term policies that redistribute wealth.[18] Because the Kenyatta administration was economically rooted in the export sector, it tended to treat that sector with special care, as an irreplaceable national endowment to be nurtured for the well-being of future generations. For the

Moi administration, Kenya's export sectors are viewed more instrumentally, as a source of economic resources to be used presently for the development of other agricultural sectors.

As discussed by Barkan and Chege in Chapters 1 and 2, respectively, the redistributive commitment that President Moi brings to his administration has its political origin in the early postindependence period. His long-standing role as a political representative of the ethnically less privileged segments of Kenyan society sheds considerable light on the change he has introduced in the goal of Kenya's agricultural policy. His administration has sought to replace the country's commitment to modified comparative advantage with an economic approach that stresses the importance of self-sufficiency in food grains.

This change involves much more than an arcane debate between competing economic theories. In contemporary Kenya, these two theories are reflections of the different and competing ethno-economic interests that supported the two presidential administrations. The principle of comparative advantage was the preferred economic strategy of the Kikuyu coffee-growing elite that dominated Kenya until 1978. This principle provided a compelling economic rationale for policies that delivered the greater share of the country's agroeconomic resources and inputs to the wealthier, export-oriented farmers of Central Province. As many of these growers actually operated mixed farms producing a combination of coffee for export and maize for domestic consumption, Kenya's particular version of comparative advantage was diluted, in that it included an emphasis on self-sufficiency in that grain.

The Moi administration, by contrast, views agricultural policy as a means to deliver economic benefits to other ethnic and regional groups in Kenya, principally those that made up the old opposition coalition, the Kenya Africa Democratic Union (KADU). Not surprisingly, grain self-sufficiency is the preferred economic strategy of the less privileged ethnic segments of Kenyan rural society, who feel they have not been able to share in the wealth generated by the country's booming exports of coffee and tea. It is paradoxical, then, that although self-sufficiency has become a kind of agricultural code language for economic leveling, the most direct beneficiaries of higher grain prices have been the Kalenjin wheat growers of the Rift Valley, who on the whole are large-scale, capital-intensive farmers. Just as the Kenyatta administration modified the principle of comparative advantage to accommodate the interests of its most influential grain-growing constituents, the Moi government has modified the principle of food self-sufficiency to foster its own clientele of export-oriented farmers. It has determinedly sought to enable ethnic groups other than the Kikuyu to share in the economic benefits of export crop production by providing increased economic incentives for the cultivation of tea in sections of Rift Valley Province, where it was not previously grown.

The list of beneficiaries of the Moi administration's agricultural policies is by no means confined to the agricultural producers of Rift Valley Province. It includes a wide range of other economic groups, such as the numerous businesses that provide services for agriculture (sales of inputs, transportation, storage, processing); those that serve the consumption interests of newly affluent, upwardly mobile farmers (housing development, retail sales); and, most noticeably, the construction firms that profit from the government's determination to improve the infrastructure of this region. In short, the new agricultural policy has created a major economic boom in the Rift Valley Province. Figures that would permit even a rough estimate of the magnitude of this boom are not yet available, but firsthand observers suggest that the Moi administration has converted the southern portions of this province from a sluggish agricultural backwater to Kenya's most rapidly growing agricultural region.[19]

But the long-term sustainability of this boom, and indeed of the country's new emphasis on food self-sufficiency, depends upon an economic theory of dubious validity. The profile of grain imports presented in Table 5.8 (page 147) suggest that Kenya may be about to repeat the Tanzanian experience of the 1970s, which demonstrated that food production is utterly dependent upon robust performance in the export crop sector. Without the latter, cereals producers quickly run up against a foreign exchange constraint that places fundamental limitations on productivity and lowers production of basic food staples. As Table 5.8 reveals, Kenya began to experience shortages of grain during the second half of the 1980s, and its cereals imports not only exceeded Tanzania's by a wide margin but for the first time also constituted a larger percentage of total imports.

Officials of the Moi administration have sought to justify their wheat strategy with an economic argument based on agricultural import substitution. They point out that by the mid-1980s Kenya's wheat imports had increased to between $20 million and $30 million per year. In the government's view, local production of this commodity would effect a considerable savings in hard currency. Government officials also claim that grain imports have few secondary benefits (e.g., employment generation), whereas funds invested in local production generate desperately needed jobs in such areas as construction and services. However, these claims wholly overlook the foreign exchange costs of grain production. As critics of the Moi administration point out, the arguments for a comparative-advantage approach to agriculture are as valid as ever. Kenya is a highly inefficient producer of wheat, a factor that may explain why, by the mid-1980s, its producer price had to be raised to about 140 percent of the world price to stimulate production. In Kenya, the foreign exchange costs alone of locally produced wheat exceed its world market price. Far from saving hard currency by growing this crop, Kenya is in fact squandering precious foreign exchange earnings to subsidize a small group of politically connected well-to-do farmers. Indeed, the policy is one illustration of why the Moi government consistently resisted the liberalization of grain markets until it was forced to do so as a condition for receiving quick-disbursing aid in late 1993 (World Bank 1993c).

Nor are the Moi government's arguments about employment generation economically convincing. There is simply no reason to believe that agricultural growth in grain-growing sections of the Rift Valley will produce more employment opportunities than further growth in the traditional export-oriented regions. The government's position is unpersuasive because it lacks any conception of opportunity cost. Though employment may have risen in the Rift Valley, the boom in that region has been purchased at enormous cost to growth elsewhere in the country. Indeed, precisely because the Rift Valley boom has involved a highly inefficient use of economic resources, it may well provide the best explanation of why Kenya's overall rate of economic growth has slumped so markedly during the Moi years.

Perhaps the most telling argument against the Moi government's approach to the agricultural sector, however, is that it has demoralized the coffee-growing area, setting the stage for the stagnation of coffee production in the late 1980s (see Figure 5.1 on page 131). To understand how this occurred and what its future impact may be, it is vitally important to be aware that the policy framework that promoted Kenya's flourishing export crop sector involved far more than exchange rate and pricing policies. It involved an economic environment in which coffee and tea producers formed a politically privileged economic stratum, one that enjoyed preferred access to whatever services and facilities the government could provide. The Kenyatta administration had allowed the country's coffee and tea producers a high degree of institutional and associational autonomy. These farmers had virtually complete freedom to organize and manage their own affairs under the broad mantle of friendly governmental supervision.

The coffee growers, for example, had been allowed to create a whole network of associations that performed vital economic functions. These included the Kenya Farmers Association (KFA), which was responsible for purchasing and distributing critical production inputs including tools, fertilizers, and pesticides not only for coffee but for maize and wheat as well; the Kenya Coffee Growers Association, principally a lobbying group that pressured the government, among other matters, for a lowered export tax on coffee and for exemption from local (county) taxes; and the Kenya Planters Cooperative Union (KPCU), which functioned as a national producer cooperative, receiving coffee from local cooperatives and arranging for the milling of coffee beans. The KPCU was especially important as the organization that made prompt cash payments to the coffee farmers, borrowing money for this purpose until it received final payment from the Coffee Board of Kenya.

Most important, these organizations were encouraged to develop comfortable and effective working relationships with one another and between themselves and the government agencies responsible to the coffee sector. Coffee farmers were also linked to the government by innumerable informal ties. The more well-to-do coffee farmers had attended the same schools, belonged to the same churches, and joined the same clubs as the government officials responsible for the well-being of this crop. They were connected with Kenya's officialdom by extended family ties and marriage connections. The end product was an atmosphere of almost palpable mutuality, a sense of shared interest between the coffee growers and the government officials. This mutuality was at the heart of high farmer morale.

As an integral part of the strategy of diverting economic resources away from Central Province and toward the Rift Valley, however, the Moi administration has sought to end the institutional autonomy of the coffee growers and to involve itself directly in the coffee economy. In 1985, for example, the government banned the KFA and replaced it with a new organization under direct governmental sponsorship, the Kenya Grain Growers Cooperative Union. The creation of this organization, which was largely staffed by members of the Kalenjin community, reversed a vitally important economic flow. Whereas coffee farmers formerly procured and distributed production inputs for themselves and for the grain-growing regions, today the reverse is true: Representatives of grain-growing areas provide production inputs for the coffee sector. Coffee farmers believe the leadership of the new organization is not sensitive to the complex requirements of coffee production.

During the late 1980s, the government also began to interfere in the organizational affairs of the KPCU by seeking to replace popular and long-standing leaders with individuals more amenable to reallocating the country's agricultural resources.[20] Although coffee has borne the brunt of the government's political interventions in export crop production, the vitality of the tea sector has also been put at risk by the new policy. As an aspect of its commitment to spread the economic benefits of tea production, the government has created new production areas called Nyayo Tea Zones that are not subject to the same stringent quality controls as the older tea-producing regions where production is supported by the Kenya Ten Development Authority. It has also sought to introduce a new means of tea pricing that rewards producers by weight rather than quality, a policy that if fully implemented would subsidize tea producers in the poorer districts of the country and impose a price penalty on higher-quality producers.

The present agricultural policy of the Moi government has been seriously criticized by the World Bank and other international donors, who believe it will produce serious difficulties in the future. Their concerns arise from the fact that Kenya's earlier track record was so impressive that it would have been difficult to sustain even under the best of circumstances.

Donor economists, however, are convinced that a future of rapid agricultural growth is even less likely given the present government's bias against the export sector.

Although the Bank's criticisms are sound, current production trends in the export sector are actually mixed. Despite the organizational changes that have demoralized the coffee farmers and resulted in falling production, the most recent production figures for tea and horticultural goods show that production of these crops has dramatically increased.[21] In addition, agricultural officials in the Moi administration defend their management of the coffee sector, claiming it would be premature to draw any firm conclusions from recent production figures. They argue that the drop in coffee production during the late 1980s has less to do with their policies than with the fact that the world market price of coffee declined precipitously following the collapse of the International Coffee Organization's quota system during the summer of 1989. The administration asserts that it had little choice but to pass on the lowered price to the coffee producers.

Despite these disclaimers, the effects of the Moi administration's interference in the coffee sector are likely to become even more apparent during the mid-1990s. As a tree crop, coffee has a long-term production cycle that is somewhat independent of short-term policy shifts. In response to falling world prices and an adverse domestic environment, however, Kenya's smallholder coffee growers slowed down in the replanting of their coffee trees during the late 1980s and began to shift from coffee production to other crops.[22] Unless coffee farmers can be induced to resume their emphasis on coffee production, the neglect of the country's coffee tree stock will be increasingly felt in the second half of the 1990s.

Kenya in mid-1994 presents a mixed agricultural picture. In suppressing the coffee sector, allegedly to pursue a strategy of self-sufficiency, the Moi administration has made a poor choice of agricultural approach, and its defense of that approach is not reassuring to those concerned about Kenya's economic future. Its efforts to implement that strategy have been politically clumsy and thus have needlessly lowered producer morale in economically vital export regions. At the same time, the government has signaled a willingness to liberalize its approach to grain marketing. In late 1993, for example, the government deregulated input prices for wheat production and announced it would proceed with a full liberalization of maize marketing.[23] The difficulty in discerning the merit of such announcements is that the Kenyan government has over the years proven singularly adept at announcing agricultural reforms in response to donor pressures for liberalization of its grain markets, then finding ways to delay or evade implementation of the promised reforms (Gordon 1992b).

The real test of the government's attitude toward the agricultural sector will be whether it is prepared to relax its rigid controls over coffee marketing. Here there is no indication of impending reform, and the reason appears to be strictly political. Coffee provides the principal economic basis of the Kikuyu ethnic community, which the government perceives as implacably opposed to the Moi regime. To allow coffee to flourish again would be to allow a growing economic base for at least two of the political parties that wish to end Moi's presidency: the Democratic Party (DP) of Mwai Kibaki and FORD-Asili of Kenneth Matiba. For the Moi regime, suppression of the coffee sector, and to a lessor extent tea, is an economic method of repressing political opposition.

Tanzania

To understand the changes in Tanzania's approach to agricultural policy during the 1980s, it is vital to appreciate the depth of the country's economic crisis. Tanzania's failure in the export crop sector had resulted in an acute foreign exchange scarcity that produced ripple effects throughout the entire economic system. Falling hard-currency earnings were the major cause of balance-of-payments deficits of staggering proportions; these, in turn, were at the heart of a skyrocketing debt crisis. By 1985 Tanzania was in arrears on most of its foreign obligations. More important, scarcities of hard currency made it impossible to procure imported industrial inputs. Most of Tanzania's industries were operating at a small fraction of installed capacity, which resulted in high rates of unemployment or hidden unemployment (as when workers were furloughed for long periods or worked only one or two days per week). Shortages of hard currency also made it all but impossible for Tanzania to maintain its physical infrastructure, a difficulty that resulted in acute deterioration of the country's road and railroad systems, creating huge transportation bottlenecks for both export and food crops.

This somewhat broad economic portrait does not begin to convey the extent to which Tanzanians had become materially poorer since their country gained independence. By the early 1980s, the lifestyles of even middle class Tanzanians such as civil servants, university lecturers, and industrial managers could best be described as threadbare. Those who had the opportunity to do so supplemented their official salaries with secondary sources of income in the informal sector. The growth of the parallel economy reduced the government's tax base, and this threatened the social services on which Tanzania had prided itself.[24] Hard-pressed to maintain educational and health services in the face of falling revenues, the government resorted to high levels of deficit budgeting. As these deficits could be financed only by massive increases in the money supply, inflation reached serious proportions, climbing to about 30 percent per year in the early 1980s (Ndulu n.d.: 2).

Tanzania's downward economic spiral set the political stage for the agricultural policy reforms of the 1980s by worsening the material circumstances of social groups that had previously benefited from the country's economic policies. By converting winners into losers, the economic crisis dissolved the political support of the groups that once comprised the government's powerful urban coalition. Not a single significant segment of that coalition was unaffected; even civil servants and parastatal employees saw the purchasing power of their salaries erode to the point where the putative benefits of overvaluation and other policies were meaningless. Day-to-day life became an excruciatingly painful matter of foraging for food in informal markets; basic necessities were often available only at unaffordably high prices. For workers in the industrial and service sectors, life had become even more difficult. Although Tanzania managed to avert widespread starvation even during the worst years of its economic decline, the poorer segments of the society suffered greatly from caloric and nutritional deficits. As economic conditions in the countryside worsened, many rural residents sought refuge or work in the capital city, creating such overcrowding that homelessness became commonplace. Individuals who were already nutritionally weakened were especially vulnerable to outbreaks of diseases such as the new strain of malaria, which became rampant in Dar es Salaam during this period. The day-to-day life of the urban poor was a constant struggle for sheer physical survival.

The political effects of economic decline also became apparent during the early 1980s. By this time, Tanzanians at all levels were aware not only of the deepening impoverishment of their society but also of the widening gap between their country and those experiencing positive economic growth, including Kenya. The worse economic conditions became, the greater was the change in the country's underlying political mood. Many who had been supporters of the regime and its leadership became first cynically indifferent, then implacably hostile to the government's policies. By alienating even those who had once benefited from urban bias, Tanzania's crisis converted support into opposition and gave rise to more and more vocal demands for economic change.

The first public divisions within the leadership took the form of the classic "reds versus experts" confrontation. The "red" faction included major sections of the governmental apparatus, including the executive committee and operational cadres of the CCM, a majority of ministries (including Labor as well as Commerce and Industry), and the employees of parastatal corporations and state industries. Even in the midst of general economic malaise, these groups believed they had more to lose than to gain if the government abandoned its statist approach to economic management. One of the most powerful voices for the old policies was the country's still-popular president, Julius Nyerere.

Opposition to the statist policy framework first began to emerge from three key ministries—Finance, Planning and Economic Affairs, and

Agriculture—and from the Central Bank. Support for economic reform was also apparent among leading members of the economics department at the University of Dar es Salaam and from the regions that had paid the highest price for economic redistribution, the coffee-growing areas of Arusha/ Moshi and West Lake. The proponents of reform reflected the new economic consensus in favoring a broadly expanded role for market forces and a timely dismantling of the statist system of economic regulation. They advocated currency devaluation, liberalization of trade and agricultural producer prices, drastic reductions in the size and scope of responsibilities of the parastatal corporations, and privatization of major industries, including banking. The reformist element also believed that Tanzania should adopt a more conciliatory approach toward the World Bank and resume a policy dialogue that had been interrupted several times during the 1970s and early 1980s.

Though initially a minority within the government, Tanzania's policy reformers had several political advantages that ultimately proved decisive. The most obvious was the blatantly inadequate performance of the old economic system, whose shortcomings could no longer be blamed on exogenous factors such as the international economy or drought. The second was the expectation that reforms would produce an immediate outpouring of financial assistance, not only from the World Bank and International Monetary Fund but also from the many bilateral donor organizations such as USAID that conditioned financial assistance on a willingness to implement the economic reforms recommended by the Bank and the Fund. The third advantage enjoyed by the reformers, one frequently overlooked in explanations of policy change, was the sheer force of intellectual ideas. During the internal debates over change versus continuity in policy, faculty associated with the Economic Research Bureau at the University of Dar es Salaam made critical contributions in building a persuasive economic case for the reformist outlook.

It is impossible to pinpoint the exact moment at which Tanzania's policy framework began to shift. Broadly speaking, it is convenient to date the beginning of the process of policy change to the second half of 1985, when Ali Hassan Mwinyi succeeded Julius Nyerere as president. Policy reform had in fact begun substantially earlier, and the change of presidents was as much the effect as the cause of changes in the country's economic framework. As early as 1982, for example, the Ministry of Planning and Economic Affairs published an economic study that stressed the need for greater economic incentives for agricultural producers, reduction of the government's large budget deficits, and greater prudence in the management of the country's money supply (Tanzania 1982a). The government began to implement some of the recommendations in this program the following year and initiated a modest program of trade liberalization that allowed Tanzanians with foreign exchange accounts far greater latitude in importing such economically vital goods as pickup trucks and plant machinery. It is nevertheless true that this incipient pattern of policy reform was given a major stimulus by the presidential succession and by the structural adjustment agreement Tanzania signed with the IMF in mid-1986.

The purpose of the IMF agreement was to launch a wholesale process of economic change to eliminate the country's system of state regulation and replace it with one allowing a much broader scope for market forces. The reform process was intended to provide greater latitude for private entrepreneurship in all sectors of the economy by changing a host of public policies, including fiscal and monetary policy, banking, and trade. Thus, reform of agricultural policy in Tanzania was not a discrete process but one embedded in the country's overall pursuit of macroeconomic reform, as discussed in the preceding chapter by Ndulu and Mwega. Certain specific reforms vital to better agricultural performance can be identified, however, including currency devaluation, price reforms, and institutional changes.

Agricultural Reforms

Currency Devaluation. The most common feature of structural adjustment programs in Africa is that changes in prices, because they can be effected by simple administrative decree, tend to precede institutional changes. This may help explain why currency devaluation is almost invariably among the earliest and most successful aspects of economic reform. Tanzania is no exception (World Bank 1991b: Vol. I). As Figure 5.3 shows, Tanzania brought about a major improvement in this area, devaluing its currency to the point where the gap between the unofficial and official exchange rates narrowed. During the early 1990s, the government has continued this process by introducing structural reforms in exchange rate policy, first initiating a Central Bank auction and then, in mid-1992, opening a system of private exchange bureaus. In early 1994 the government announced its intention to move to an interbank exchange rate.

Price Reforms. According to the structural adjustment agreement, Tanzania is committed to allowing real producer prices of agricultural commodities to rise. Initially this goal was to be accomplished through increases in the official prices paid by the parastatal crop procurement agencies. Between 1985 and 1989 the nominal producer price for maize, wheat, rice and cotton more than doubled, the price for tea nearly tripled, and the price for coffee quadrupled.[25]

Despite these nominal increases, however, Tanzania has not lived up to its promise of raising the real purchasing power of rural incomes. As Tables 5.2 through 5.6 show, the real purchasing power of the new prices for five of these commodities actually fell during the second half of the

1980s. This decrease occurred because the Tanzanian government did not increase its nominal producer prices fast enough to keep pace with the rapid currency devaluation, which reduced the dollar value of the new prices.[26]

Lagging real prices help explain why the early reform had induced only a partially favorable supply response from the agricultural sector. The most positive outcome of the price reforms was to restore self-sufficiency in maize and to bring about a doubling in cotton production.[27] Tanzania's sisal production also began to recover because of reprivatization of plantations that had been nationalized in the late 1960s and because the radical currency devaluation dramatically lowered the local wage bill relative to the world market price for this product. Coffee and tea production, however, continued to lag. The production increases that did occur, however, were sufficient to bring about an average increase in agricultural growth of about 5 percent per year between 1986 and 1991, the first period of sustained agricultural growth since the early 1960s.

The critical point here is that price changes alone are insufficient to stimulate a robust economic recovery. Institutional changes in crop marketing must accompany the price increases if the process of reform is to induce long-term behavioral changes on the part of the country's agricultural producers. In this area, Tanzania has had greater difficulty and the most important reforms have taken nearly a decade to complete.

Institutional Reforms.   The goal of agricultural reform in Tanzania is not simply to improve producer prices but to alter fundamentally the way in which prices are set. The Tanzanian government recognized as early as 1980 that its system of parastatal corporations had failed to generate production levels adequate for national needs, and President Nyerere appointed a commission of government officials and academic economists to make recommendations. This commission, which was formally known as the Task Force on National Agricultural Policy, was strongly critical of the entire system of crop procurement and marketing. Its 1982 report, *The Tanzanian National Agricultural Policy,* became something of a "Berg Report" for Tanzanian agriculture (Tanzania 1982b). Among its most important recommendations was the need to recreate private marketing channels for the country's major crops.

The overall thrust of the task force's report was to place strict limitations on the economic role of the parastatals. The National Milling Corporation (NMC), for example, was to lose its role as the country's sole legal procurement and marketing agency for grains. It was now only to create and maintain a strategic grain reserve; to purchase grain for governmental organizations such as the army, police, and hospitals; and, when necessary, to handle grain imports and food distribution. As far as pricing was concerned, the NMC might be allowed to function as a "buyer and seller of last resort"; that is, it might set a floor price at which it would purchase maize, but farmers would be free to sell to cooperatives or traders at higher price levels.

The reform of the NMC took almost a decade to implement, but by 1992 the agency had been forced to surrender its monopoly procurement status for cereals crops. Tanzania's grain producers, including maize farmers, are no longer required to sell their crops to NMC; they now can sell directly to private traders or market their crops through local primary cooperative societies. The virtual dissolution of the NMC has been of great symbolic importance. As the largest of Tanzania's crop parastatals, it had become an arch symbol of the mismanagement and excessive operating costs of the old parastatal system. Its truncated role is now widely understood as a signal that the end of the parastatal era is irreversible.

The crucial stage in parastatal reform had to do with budgeting. The long-standing practice of the Tanzanian government was to provide its parastatals with automatic government subsidies for their operating deficits. This approach introduced into the economic system a phenomenon that economists refer to as "moral hazard" by creating incentives for deficit spending. For the NMC, elimination of the budgetary entitlement did not occur until early 1992, when the government announced that, beginning with fiscal year 1993, its financial support for the NMC would be limited to a fixed annual appropriation.[28] The new budget limitation caused the NMC to become bankrupt and enabled the government to enforce its new role; funds would be appropriated only for the creation of the grain reserve. Still, the NMC's ability to resist reform efforts for nearly ten years illustrates the extent to which the parastatals have been able to avoid the reductions in staff and financial support that are inherent in Tanzania's new economic order. Each step toward modification in the parastatal structure of crop marketing has been brought about only with the greatest difficulty and then only with extreme pressure from the IMF, the World Bank, and other donors. In each major area of reform, there has been a deeply political tug of war between reformers who wish to press ahead with economic liberalization and conservatives who wish to retain as much as possible of the old statist system.

Despite delays, however, privatization of the marketing system has also been gradually extended to the principal export crops. This process began in the late 1980s when producers of less important exports including cashew nuts, oilseeds, sisal, and pyrethrum, were allowed to market their products directly rather than going through state marketing agencies. The privatization of export marketing will take another important step forward early in 1994, when the procurement of coffee, the last major crop still under state control, will be privatized. Licensed private buyers will be able to purchase and process coffee for export directly from farmers or from cooperative societies. At that point, the only remaining restriction will be a requirement that the coffee be marketed through the weekly auction of the Tanzania Coffee Board.

The 1982 agricultural task force also recommended the reestablishment of producer cooperatives. These had been banned by the government in 1976 as part of Tanzania's policy of transferring jurisdiction over all crop matters to the parastatal corporations. The task force argued that local primary producer cooperatives should be revived to act as purchasing agents at the village level; they, in turn, would market to regional cooperative unions, which would then sell to the government's various parastatal corporations (Tanzania 1982b: 167–168). Although the task force was highly critical of the government's system of crop procurement, it did not go so far as to suggest that private traders be allowed to purchase directly from the farmers. In this respect, it reflected a long-standing Tanzanian suspicion that private traders, if allowed to operate freely, would cheat highly vulnerable peasant producers.

The restoration of cooperative societies, like the elimination of the parastatal system, took over a decade to complete. Part of the problem Tanzania faced was organizational. Following the government's banning order of 1976, these cooperatives ceased to exist; their technical and managerial staffs were dispersed, and their physical and financial assets were liquidated by the government. In some cases, the government's parastatal corporations simply assumed possession of the cooperatives' facilities, including their buildings and rolling stock, and this led to still unresolved legal disputes over ownership of physical assets and compensation for seized property. In addition, the financial records and physical facilities of many cooperatives were destroyed or neglected.

Another source of difficulty was political: The government ministry responsible for assisting the revival of the cooperatives remained for a long time under the control of officials unsympathetic to the new reforms. In addition, the full rehabilitation of the cooperatives required legal changes that had to be approved by the National Assembly. And because that body was controlled, until the late 1980s, by political leaders loyal to the old economic system, it was extremely slow to pass legislation that would restore the cooperative societies' legal status. Indeed, the most important legislation, separating the cooperative movement from the direct jurisdiction of the governing party, was not passed until April 1991.

But the greatest source of difficulty has been in recreating an atmosphere of confidence. The feelings of mistrust engendered by the 1976 dissolution linger to this day. As long as former members, elected officers, and managers remain mistrustful of government intentions, it will be difficult to persuade them to return to their old positions.

CONCLUSIONS

During the 1980s, both Kenya and Tanzania initiated changes in agricultural policy that represented significant departures from the policy frameworks they had implemented following independence. For both countries, policy changes will lead to significant differences in future agricultural performance.

Kenya, departing in an economically indefensible manner from the strategy of comparative advantage that made it an African success story during the 1960s and 1970s, placed far greater emphasis in the 1980s on grain self-sufficiency and increased production of wheat. The government also took political steps that severely demoralized the nation's coffee producers, radically lowering production of this vital crop. If the government persists in this strategy, it will slow the rate of growth in foreign exchange earnings from agricultural exports and, as a result, produce serious constraints on growth elsewhere in the economy, especially import-dependent industries and services.

Tanzania, by contrast, has initiated a process of policy reform that is intended to liberalize its system of agricultural marketing. Entrenched political and bureaucratic interests have slowed the process, but by the mid-1990s the essential building blocks of a more liberal approach to the agricultural sector were all in place. It remained only to fully implement these and, more important, to do so in a manner that would give reforms a high degree of credibility. To attain a level of economic growth that will begin to make up for a generation of economic decline, it is now imperative that other areas of policy reform proceed more briskly. The issue that remains to be explored is whether this can occur under competitive party conditions.

NOTES

1. By the early 1990s, Kenya's horticultural exports had increased to approximately $150 million annually, surpassing coffee as a source of foreign exchange earnings (EIU 1992: 22).

2. Unless otherwise indicated, the agricultural data for this chapter have been generously supplied by the Developing Economies Branch and the International Trade Division of the United States Department of Agriculture. The author is grateful to Michael Kurtzig, Margaret Missiaen, and Michael Trueblood for their generous assistance. These economists join the author in issuing the by-now standard warning: African agricultural data are very imprecise, and the agricultural statistics that appear in this study should be taken only as broad approximations of agricultural performance.

3. Among the noted economists who hold this view are Rauol Prebisch, Gunnar Myrdal, and Ragnar Nurske. For one example, see Singer and Ansari (1977).

4. The concept of currency overvaluation is often misstated. For the sake of terminological clarity, a currency is overvalued when the exchange rate is too low—that is, when *too few* units of local currency are offered per unit of hard convertible currency such as the U.S. dollar. Devaluing a currency therefore consists of *increasing* the number of units offered of the local currency for each unit of the convertible currency.

5. The author is indebted to Professor J. Clark Leith of the Department of Economics, University of Western Ontario, for this observation.

6. In March 1994, the currency bureaus were offering TShs. 500 per $1 U.S. There was said to be a modest parallel market at the rate of approximately $1 = TShs. 540, the rate at which Tanzanian citizens were allowed to buy hard currency for travel abroad.

7. This material draws heavily on the outstanding study by David Bevan, Paul Collier, and Jan Willem Gunning (1989).

8. The USDA figure for Tanzanian rice production should be treated with particular skepticism. Until the early 1980s, the Economic Research Service (ERS) of USDA offered estimates of Tanzanian rice production that were only about half as high as those provided by the Food and Agriculture Organization (FAO) of the United Nations, about 200,000 metric tons versus about 400,000 metric tons annually. Because budget reductions then made it increasingly difficult to generate independent annual estimates of this and other crops, officials in the ERS made a policy decision to adopt the FAO figures, and the ERS estimates were revised accordingly.

9. This program is commonly referred to as the "Swynnerton Plan" after the colonial official, R. J. M. Swynnerton, who devised it in the early 1950s (Swynnerton 1954).

10. The major difference between the present program and that of the colonial government is that the Kenya government no longer seeks to consolidate scattered holdings into a single plot. Instead, it relies upon the forces of the marketplace to do so.

11. A hectare is approximately 2.2 acres. Thus, during this period the land registration program averaged over 1 million acres per year, or more than 1,500 square miles.

12. This is probably a cautious estimate, based on an average farm size of just over 2 hectares, or about 5 acres.

13. Tanzania's most important agricultural export at the time was sisal, but the sisal estates were, like Kenya's tea plantations, principally owned by foreign individuals or firms.

14. The dilemma of Tanzania's liberal, nonsocialist nationalists quickly became a crisis when a number of important party figures were arrested and accused of treason. Their trial, which occupied most of 1969, constitutes an episode of Tanzanian political history that has never been adequately documented.

15. The one exception to this pattern was the 1988 parliamentary election, which was openly "rigged" by the Moi government to insure its reelection.

16. This analysis is much influenced by Barkan (1983: 5ff).

17. The term Kalenjin does not denote a single ethnic group but rather a number of ethnic groups loosely clustered under the generic term "nilohamitic." These include, for example, the Nandi, Kipsigis, and Elgeyo-Marakwet. President Moi is a member of the Tugen subgroup of the Kalenjin.

18. Bates's theory squares perfectly with the economic figures reported by the World Bank. From 1965–1980, Kenya's rate of overall economic growth was 6.8 percent. From 1980–1990, it averaged only 4.2 percent. During the earlier period, its rate of agricultural growth was 5.0 percent; during the latter, 3.3 percent (World Bank 1992: 220).

19. The author is grateful to Kenyan informants who have requested that their names not be cited.

20. These events were regularly reported in the *Financial Review,* a popular economic journal that was banned in April 1989.

21. To understand why this is the case, it would be necessary to deal separate-

ly with the institutional structure of the tea economy and why it has proven more resistant to governmental intervention (Lamb and Muller 1982).

22. Early estimates of marketed coffee production for 1994 anticipate marketed production of approximately 65,000 metric tons, about half the level of the late 1980s.

23. The government announced that the role of the National Cereals and Produce Board (NCPB) would be to create a strategic maize reserve. But because the size of the reserve was estimated at one year's total maize production, this would still leave the NCPB in a position to exercise great control over the maize market.

24. For a full account of this sector see Maliyamkono and Bagachwa (1990).

25. The use of the unofficial exchange rate is especially important because it helps remove the inflation effect from real producer prices.

26. Although Tanzania's prices increases may seem large, they are in fact not nearly as high as in African countries that have had greater success with economic reform, such as Ghana. Between 1985 and 1989, the Ghanaian price for cocoa, the country's major agricultural export, increased five and one-half times, from 30,000 Ghanaian cedis per metric ton to 165,000 cedis per metric ton.

27. It is entirely plausible that both these increases reflect a decrease in cross-border trade rather than real improvements in domestic production levels.

28. Tanzania's fiscal year 1993 began on July 1, 1992, and extends through June 30, 1993.

6

Coping with
Urbanization and Urban Policy

Richard Stren, Mohamed Halfani, Joyce Malombe

As Kenya and Tanzania entered the third decade after independence, a
number of important changes in urban life began to assert themselves. At
first these changes were almost imperceptible, but by the end of the 1980s
their cumulative effect had produced a substantial shift in the nature of
urban life and in the policies and politics that both acted upon and were
generated by the urban sector. At the root of these changes were two major
trends: a relentless population growth in urban centers combined with a
failure to expand public services and infrastructure at a corresponding
level; and the progressive centralization of political power with respect to
the cities, limiting local authorities' ability to deal with urban problems on
their own terms. The result, in both Kenya and Tanzania, was an increasing
demand for more associational and political autonomy at the urban level—a
demand that began to be expressed in the electoral politics of the 1990s.

All over sub-Saharan Africa, cities grew very rapidly during the 1960s
and 1970s. From 1948 to 1962, the urban population of Kenya grew at an
annual average compound rate of 6.6 percent, or about twice the rate of the
population as a whole; from 1962 to 1969 the rate was 7.1 percent; and
from 1969 through 1979 the rate was 7.9 percent,[1] with growth rates for the
ten largest towns ranging from 3.3 percent in Mombasa through 31.7 percent in Meru (Table 6.1). These rates moderated during the 1980s, when
almost all towns showed a decline in growth rates, only Nairobi remaining
at the previous level.

Tanzania's urban-growth profile resembles that of Kenya. From 1957
to 1967, the urban population of mainland Tanzania grew at an annual
average rate of 6.0 percent; from 1967 through 1978 the growth rate
reached 8.9 percent per annum.[2] As in Kenya, the overall rate of urban
growth moderated during the late 1970s and 1980s, although by 1992 the
Tanzanian Bureau of Statistics had still not calculated the exact figure.[3]
However, as Table 6.2 shows, the average annual growth rate of eight of
the ten largest towns in Tanzania fell over the 1978–1988 period as compared with the 1967–1978 period.

Table 6.1 Population Growth of Selected Urban Centers in Kenya, 1969–1989

Urban Center	Province	Population 1969	1979	1989	Annual Growth Rate (%) 1969–1979	1979–1989
Nairobi	Nairobi	509,286	827,775	1,346,000	5.0	5.0
Mombasa	Coast	247,073	341,148	465,000	3.3	3.2
Kisumu[a]	Nyanza	32,431	152,643	185,100	16.8	2.0
Nakuru	Rift Valley	47,151	92,851	162,800	7.0	5.8
Machakos	Eastern	6,312	84,320	116,100	30.0	3.3
Eldoret[a]	Rift Valley	18,196	50,503	104,900	10.8	7.6
Nyeri[a]	Central	10,004	35,753	88,600	14.0	9.5
Meru	Eastern	4,475	70,439	78,100	31.7	1.0
Thika	Central	18,387	41,324	57,100	8.4	3.3
Kitale	Rift Valley	11,573	28,327	53,000	9.4	6.5

Sources: Kenya Population Census 1969, Vol. II (Nairobi: Statistics Division, Ministry of Finance and Economic Planning, 1971), p. 1; *Economic Survey 1991* (Nairobi: Government Printer, 1991), p. 34.

Note: a. Centers whose boundaries were extended between 1979 and 1989.

Table 6.2 Population Growth of Selected Urban Centers in Tanzania, 1957–1988

Urban Center	Region	Population 1957	1967	1978	1988[a]	Annual Growth Rate (%) 1957–1967	1967–1978	1978–1988
Dar es Salaam	Dar es Salaam	128,742	272,821	757,346	1,234,754	7.8	9.7	5.0
Mwanza	Mwanza	19,877	34,861	110,611	182,899	5.8	11.1	5.2
Tanga	Tanga	38,053	61,058	103,409	138,274	4.0	4.9	3.0
Mbeya	Mbeya	6,932	12,479	76,606	135,614	6.0	17.9	5.9
Morogoro	Morogoro	14,502	25,262	61,890	117,760	5.7	8.5	6.6
Arusha	Arusha	10,038	32,452	55,281	117,622	12.5	5.0	7.8
Moshi	Kilimanjaro	13,726	26,864	52,223	96,838	7.0	6.2	6.4
Tabora	Tabora	15,361	21,012	67,392	93,506	3.2	11.2	3.3
Iringa	Iringa	9,587	21,746	57,182	84,860	8.5	9.2	4.0
Kigoma	Kigoma	16,255	21,369	50,044	77,055	2.8	8.1	4.4

Sources: Saitiel M. Kulaba, "Local Government and the Management of Urban Services in Tanzania," in Richard E. Stren and Rodney R. White, eds., *African Cities in Crisis: Managing Rapid Urban Growth* (Boulder: Westview Press, 1989), p. 210, Table 8.1; *Tanzania Sensa 1988* (Population Census), National Profile, Summary (Dar es Salaam: Bureau of Statistics, n.d.); *National Data—Reform, Finance, Services and Housing in Tanzania* (Dar es Salaam: Ardhi Institute, 1986), p. 13, Table 2.1; and A. C. Mascarenhas, *Urban Growth in Mainland Tanzania* (Dar es Salaam: Unpublished paper, n.d.).

Note: a. In calculating the figures in this column, wards designated as "mixed" in the 1988 census are treated as urban.

Although rates of urban growth moderated during the 1980s, they remained high in comparison to the overall rate of population growth, which in Kenya was 3.4 percent and in Tanzania 2.8 percent. During the 1980s, both countries witnessed an important deterioration in the quality of life in urban centers. This deterioration—which was evident with respect to housing, urban services, and opportunities for remunerative employment— probably had an effect on rates of urban growth, as the relative attractiveness of urban versus rural opportunities was reduced. Nevertheless, as urban centers continued to grow, the result was a serious "service squeeze"; larger and larger urban populations received less of the services they needed per capita. For Dar es Salaam, for example, Saitiel Kulaba shows an overall decline of 8.5 percent from 1978/79 through 1986/87, in terms of expenditures on services and infrastructure (measured in constant currency units). When the effects of increased population are added, the decline reached 11 percent per year on a compound basis. Overall, whereas urban development budgets fell by 25 percent in real terms during this period, the total Tanzanian development budget rose by 108 percent (Kulaba 1989b: 143). Considering that a city such as Dar es Salaam was unable to spend more than the equivalent of U.S. $5.80 per capita on urban services in the early 1980s, this decline was sharply felt at the local level.

Dar es Salaam's neighbor to the north, Nairobi, has been able to maintain a significantly higher level of services and infrastructure, spending roughly ten times more per capita than Dar es Salaam during the same period. Nevertheless, Nairobi's services dramatically deteriorated during the 1980s along with its revenue base. The capital expenditures of the Nairobi City Commission (in real U.S. dollars per capita) for water and sewerage fell from $27.78 in 1981 to $2.47 in 1987, and maintenance expenditures fell from $7.29 to $2.30 over the same period (Mazingira n.d.). Over a six-year period, this represents an average annual decrease of approximately 28 percent, compounded, when both capital and maintenance expenditures are added together. Similar calculations for expenditures on public works over the same period show an annual decrease of 19.5 percent, compounded; and for social services an annual decrease of 20 percent, compounded. Such figures suggest an alarming erosion in the ability of modern African cities to service the needs of their populations. The decline in services placed increasing stress on the poorest segments of the urban population in their continuing struggle for survival.

It is worth noting that this finding directly contradicts one of the more commonly held assumptions of the "urban bias" argument reviewed by Michael Lofchie in the preceding chapter. According to this argument, cities gain infrastructural investment at the expense of the rest of the country. But as this evidence shows, not only did cities lose infrastructural investment in relation to the country as a whole, but individuals who were forced to move to the cities because of the failures of rural development— the new urban poor—bore the brunt of urban decline during the 1980s. The crisis in urban services and the response patterns of the two governments to urban needs can be seen as the two most important themes in the complex story of urban politics and policies over the last decade. To unravel the key elements of this story, we shall look at each of the countries in turn.

KENYA

The growth of Kenya's towns has produced a number of adverse consequences. As we have suggested, these include shortages and deterioration of urban services, but they also include the inadequate provision of remunerative modern sector employment. During the 1980s and early 1990s, a number of governmental efforts were made to respond to these problems. Thus, in an important initiative in 1983, the Kenya government launched the District Focus for Rural Development (Kenya 1983a), an undertaking intended to decentralize the decisionmaking process and strengthen institutional capacity at the local level. This initiative—which in the end amounted to deconcentration rather than effective decentralization—was extended to the urban areas and complemented by a "rural-urban balance" strategy, whereby urban infrastructure would be developed in order to stimulate the economic development of both urban centers and their agricultural hinterlands (Kenya 1986a). In the larger cities, on the initiative of President Daniel arap Moi, a *jua kali* (Kiswahili for "hot sun") program was established to support small-scale, informal-sector artisans through credit, training, and physical facilities for work. The success of these programs was compromised by many factors, among them the slowing down of the economy, the inability of local authorities to manage the larger cities, and the introduction of structural adjustment policies in the 1980s. By the end of the period under review, urban planning policies were largely quiescent and inoperative in the face of institutional and resource deficiencies; slums and squatter settlements were more pronounced than ever; and poverty and squalor were increasingly visible indicators of a decaying urban environment.

Housing and Urban Services

At the time of independence, Kenya's urban centers displayed extreme inequalities in the level of services provided (Lee-Smith 1989: 279). The government's immediate response to the expanding and underserviced population was to address the housing issue. A parastatal, the National Housing Corporation (NHC), was established in 1967 with a mandate to build public housing estates throughout the country. The government also placed increased emphasis on rural development so as to reduce rural-to-urban migration. There was a call for the unemployed to go back to the land. This policy was accompanied by massive demolition of squatter settlements, particularly in Nairobi, from the 1960s through the early 1970s (Stren 1975: 272–273). Although the National Housing Corporation and local authorities combined to construct a great deal of housing by the late 1970s, it was impossible—especially given the high cost of the dwellings relative to the incomes of the majority of urban dwellers—to meet more than a small proportion of the total demand. For example, the combined efforts of the formal public and private housing sector only managed to provide a total of about 58,820 units between 1977 and 1987, compared to an estimated annual household formation of 380,000 (Kiamba, Malombe, and Muchene 1992: 12). The end result of this mismatch in demand and supply has been continued expansion of squatter settlements and increased densities in existing low-income areas.

By 1970 the Nairobi City Council (predecessor of the City Commission) began to realize that construction of urban infrastructure and other facilities to match the growth of a largely low-income population was needed. This move was supported by donor agencies such as the World Bank and USAID, who provided funds for development of sites and services and (somewhat later) squatter upgrading projects.[4] By 1980 these two strategies constituted 60 percent of the government's entire urban housing program in Kenya (Macoloo 1988: 163), representing a major shift from provision of complete housing units to provision of infrastructure. These projects were implemented in most urban centers in Kenya by the NHC, whose activities began to expand tremendously. From 1967 to 1970 the NHC completed 722 housing units in Nairobi; between 1971 and 1974, 5,518 were constructed. Similarly, between 1975 and 1979, 5,260 housing units and service sites were completed. By the early 1980s, however, this production began to fall dramatically. Over the seven years from 1980 through 1986, 2,041 units were completed, including 385 mortgage housing units, 600 tenant purchase units, and 1,056 sites and services plots (Malombe n.d.). An important reason for the fall in NHC's production—at least with respect to formal housing units—was that its housing was high-cost and could not be afforded by the poor. The same applied to housing constructed by other public agencies. Although more sites and services projects were developed in the late 1970s and early 1980s, they, too, tended both to be highly subsidized by the state and too expensive for the poor. As international agencies began withdrawing their support from these kinds of urban projects, Kenyan agencies could no longer continue to promote this approach to urban development.

These problems became more severe in the 1980s, when formal housing development decreased despite increased demand. The situation was complicated by the slowing down of the economy and the inability of both central and local government to provide basic services. As a major government report indicated, public investment in urban infrastructure declined as a share of gross fixed capital formation from 14.3 percent during the period 1971–1977 to 12.1 percent between 1978 and 1984. Public housing was sharply affected by this trend, with per capita expenditure (in constant 1984 prices) for each new urban resident declining from 2,560 Kenyan shillings (KShs) for 1971–1977 to KShs 1,350 in 1978–1984, a decrease of almost 50 percent (Kenya 1986a: 49).

Because of the shortage of housing for low-income families, squatter and informal settlements grew apace. According to a government housing survey published in 1983, between 1976 and 1982 the recorded output of housing units in the formal sector represented only 20.5 percent of the increase in new urban households. This suggests that over the same period the informal sector provided 79.5 percent of new urban housing (Kenya 1983b: 12). Indeed, the proportion of all housing in Kenya's thirty-two urban centers that the government itself classified as "semipermanent/temporary" in 1983 was 41.5 percent.[5] In Mombasa, the country's second largest city, the figure was as high as 69.1 percent, while in Kisumu, the third largest city, the comparable figure was 64.1 percent. Although the proportion was relatively low for Nairobi at 33.3 percent, the percentage undoubtedly increased (as in most of the other towns as well) throughout the 1980s; one writer has argued that between 1979 and 1989 the informal sector in Nairobi accounted for 60 to 80 percent of all the housing constructed (Hoek-Smit 1989: 9). Indeed, one has only to look at published statistics for residential building plans approved by the Nairobi City Commission to understand the magnitude of the problem. From 1982 through 1990, when (based on census figures) the equivalent of approximately 100,000 households were added to Nairobi's population, only 8,554 private residential plans were approved by the commission (Kenya 1991: 138). Because most of these plans involved single-household residences, close to 90 percent of the new housing required was either not being built (resulting in increased overcrowding) or was being built illegally in the informal sector. The capacity of the informal sector to provide necessary housing was not enhanced when, in two massive operations in May and November 1990, the Nairobi City Commission demolished the homes of some 40,000 Nairobi slum dwellers.[6] Other, smaller demolitions followed in November of the same year, displacing thousands more.

The primary source of development activity in informal settlements has become people's own initiative as individuals or groups. Indeed, one study comparing two formal and two informal low-income settlements in Nairobi and Bungoma showed that the latter (with the help of outside agencies and their own community organization) had more effective refuse collection and community facilities than the formal settlements receiving direct government assistance (Mazingira 1982). Over time, the lower-income groups have built a structure of specialized associations to deal with specific needs. These have been assisted by many other groups, including religious and charity organizations and a variety of nongovernmental organizations (NGOs) (Kiamba, Malombe and Muchene 1992: 15). More generally, as the central government has been able to fund fewer and fewer activities at the local level (either directly or through the local government system), the work of NGOs in providing services has become more important. A 1989 study of 80 NGOs in Nairobi showed that NGOs provide a wide range of basic services—from child care and nutritional counseling through population and family planning, health, primary education, and secondary education. Most of the major hospitals in Nairobi are run by NGOs, which also provide for 9 percent of all primary education and 27 percent of all secondary education. The study observes that the majority of the NGOs surveyed "have their projects located in low-income residential areas, and especially the informal settlements" and that "the main target group for most NGOs is poor children" (Bubba and Lamba 1989: 9).

Other problems related to housing include the lack of services and poor maintenance of those that exist. For example, the urban housing survey of 1983 revealed that 65 percent of the households in Kenya's towns were inadequately serviced by garbage collection, with pickups occurring three times per month or less. For Nairobi, fully 80 percent of the households surveyed responded in this category (Kenya 1983b: 53). Public criticism of the garbage service in Nairobi reached a peak in 1985, when *The Weekly Review* featured a large cover photograph of a pile of uncollected garbage, entitling its collection of lead articles "City in a Mess"—a sad parody on Nairobi's official slogan, "City in the Sun." As the magazine put it: "It has always been proudly referred to as the Green City in the Sun. But today, Nairobi presents a picture of a city rotting from the inside. Over the past 18 months, the main city news in the local press has been about mounting piles of stinking refuse, dry water taps, gaping pot-holes and unlit streets" (*Weekly Review,* January 25, 1985: 3). In 1986, as garbage continued to pile up on the streets, the president appointed a "special director of civic operations"—a retired brigadier—to take charge of garbage collection in Nairobi. However, by mid-1989 a combination of lack of local finance and administrative difficulties had so hamstrung the efforts of the special director that his post was abolished. Municipal officials estimated that the city needed one hundred refuse-removal vehicles to effectively serve a city of more than one million inhabitants; in reality, only ten vehicles were in working order (out of a total fleet of only forty) in August 1989. At the end of 1990, wrote the *Weekly Review,* "piles of stinking refuse . . . have continued to be a fact of life" (*Weekly Review,* November 9, 1990: 14).

Employment and the Informal Sector

At the same time the level of public support for urban services and infrastructure was declining, formal employment stagnated in the towns, and the informal economy burgeoned. Nairobi, whose population was growing at a compound rate of 5.0 percent during the 1980s, showed an increase in formal wage employment of 3.0 percent in the period 1982–1990. Mombasa, with a population growth of 3.2 percent during the 1980s, was barely able to keep pace, increasing formal wage employment 3.2 percent annually in the same period (Kenya 1991: 235). But in most towns, the urban labor force expanded more rapidly than modern sector employment. In addition, jobs created in the modern sector catered mainly to skilled labor, largely ignoring untrained workers, who made up a majority of the low-income population. This group has increasingly been forced to fend for itself. By the late 1980s, one knowledgeable estimate put informal employment at 40 percent of total urban employment, considerably higher than the 30 percent generally suggested in official projections (Ondiege and Aleke-Dondo n.d.). A comprehensive analysis of Kenyan statistics shows that from 1985 to 1988, nonagricultural "small-scale enterprises" (the official Kenyan designation for the informal sector) grew at an annual rate of 11.1 percent, whereas "self-employed and family workers" (another informal sector category) grew at an annual rate of 9.6 percent. By contrast, nonagricultural wage employment during the same period grew annually by only 3.6 percent (Livingstone 1991: 653).

The increasing informalization of the urban economy in Kenya over the last two decades reflects a number of major changes in employment patterns. One important trend is the increased importance of women in many low-capital sectors of urban economic life. For example, in his study of informal activities in the late 1980s, Ian Livingstone noted that women were dominant in small-scale urban trade, both wholesale and retail (Livingstone 1991: 653–657). A detailed case study of food hawkers in Nairobi indicated that 68 percent were women. Many of these hawkers were unlicensed and (when they traded in downtown areas of the city) constantly harassed, so that informal social support mechanisms had become very important. Winnie Mitullah claimed that some 25,000 hawkers in Nairobi "are always at war with the city authorities" (Mitullah 1991: 16).

Extending the purview of the informal sector, particularly with respect to food provision, a number of studies have begun to look at informal agriculture. An important study of urban households in six towns in Kenya showed the importance of local self-help crop production for food consumption. According to the Mazingira Institute's data, 56 percent of those who work on urban crop production were women (the figure is as high as 62 percent in Nairobi); 29 percent of all households grew food within urban areas; and 17 percent kept livestock. Extrapolating from this six-town study for the whole of urban Kenya, Mazingira estimated that, at the time of the survey, 25.2 million kilograms of crops worth about $4 million were being produced in urban areas in Kenya per season. Most of the urban crop and livestock production was consumed as subsistence by the households themselves.

The results of this study were confirmed by another researcher several years later, working only in Nairobi. In the second study, 64 percent of those working in urban agriculture were found to be women, and most did not sell their produce. Both studies excoriated the Nairobi City Commission for harassing small agricultural producers, arguing that the urban authorities should support this growing and vital urban activity. As Donald Freeman wrote:

> [T]he shambas of Nairobi and other urban centers, which for too long have been ignored by researchers and harassed by administrators, may be viewed as symbols of a group of vigorous, energetic and determined workers who, despite poverty and misfortune, have the drive to succeed and to better their existence. Their plots of cropland are gardens of hope, not wastelands of despair. Acceptance of seasonal cultivation by the urban community and by its current and future administrators as a legitimate part of the city environment does not imply the abandonment of orderly urban planning or good city government. For Nairobi . . . the benefits of incorporating urban agriculture into the economic structure must surely outweigh the disadvantages (Freeman 1991: 121–122).

Another important area of informal economic activity that became more prominent during the 1980s was urban transport. The issue was of considerable political importance in Nairobi, although—along with concerns for all urban services—it was also a central problem in many of the larger towns elsewhere in Kenya. During the 1960s and 1970s public transport was the functional responsibility of the Kenya Bus Service (KBS), an overseas subsidiary of United Transport Overseas, which operated in several countries. The Nairobi City Council (or City Commission during the period 1983–1992) has had a 25 percent share in KBS. Since 1934 KBS has held the official monopoly of transport in Nairobi, although this status has become increasingly meaningless with subsequent legislation. But because of population growth in outlying areas of the city, which are not effectively served by KBS routes, and because KBS could not effectively generate enough income to increase the quantity and quality of its service, "pirate" competitors began seriously to take passengers away from KBS in the early 1970s. These pirate vehicles (as they were originally called) came to be known as *matatus*, based on the Kikuyu words for "three ten-cent pieces," the fare originally charged. Although matatus were exempted in 1973 by President Kenyatta from Transport License Board requirements for public service vehicles, they were harassed by the police because of traffic violations and unsafe operation until 1984, when they were formally legalized.

By this time, the matatus had managed to gain over 42 percent of the daily passenger market in Nairobi. Following their legalization, they grew in number and sophistication (Lee-Smith 1989). In 1988 the Nairobi City Commission reported that the approximately 800 25-seater and 800 14-seater matatus carried a quantity of passengers equivalent to 650 large buses. In that same year, KBS maintained a fleet of only 300 buses, and the government-established Nyayo Bus Services operated a further 75 buses (Nairobi 1988: 41–42). In sum, by the late 1980s the once-informal matatus had considerably surpassed the public transport system in carrying capacity throughout Nairobi. Although the matatus perform an important function by providing transport services for (largely) poorer Nairobi residents inadequately served by the public system, they are still expensive, overcrowded, and frequently dangerous. The police regularly fine these vehicles for violations; however one study carried out in the early 1980s showed that the average matatu generated three times as much revenue for the police in bribes as it did in fines payable to the government (Lee-Smith 1989: 287–288). Although matatus are now legal, many Kenyans believe they are not effectively regulated.

The Institutional Response: Constraints on Local Authorities

For some time, local authorities in Kenya have not been providing satisfactory services to urban dwellers. During the last decade, local government performance has been adversely affected by a number of problems. One of the major problems has been through the addition of district development committees, under the aegis of the district commissioners, which has resulted in a further shift of decisionmaking power from local to central government. To increase the revenue base for local authorities, the central government provided an additional revenue source in the form of a new "service charge" in late 1989. Though the intake from this new source of revenue has been considerable, improvement in services have not been immediately visible. Other major problems experienced by local authorities are an inflexible revenue base; lack of access to productive, reliable, and collectable financial resources; poor financial management; lack of employee incentives; and inadequate training. These problems and constraints have left many local authorities struggling to make ends meet; many cities consistently run on deficits, and a significant number are heavily in debt. Access to capital is insufficient, investment in infrastructure is generally inadequate, and maintenance is poor (Smoke 1992: 73).

The most heralded failure in local government in Kenya is Nairobi. Early in March 1983, the minister for local government, Moses Mudavadi, called a press conference in Nairobi and announced that the central government had decided to suspend "all meetings of the [Nairobi City] council and all committees thereof, and to exclude indefinitely with immediate effect the mayor, the deputy mayor and all councilors from council premises" (*Weekly Review,* March 11, 1983: 4). The City Council, which since 1920 (when it was only a Municipal Committee) had always had at least some elected members, was for the first time in sixty-three years put under the complete control of nominated officials. Several weeks later, citing "gross mismanagement of council funds and poor services to the residents," the minister placed Nairobit's approximately 17,000 municipal employees and all buildings and services under the direct control of a commission, which he himself appointed. Although the original intention of the commission had been to "clean up" the council and reestablish elected local government, the government passed various motions through the National Assembly extending the life of the commission until both national and local elections were held in December 1992. Over this ten-year period, various ministers of local government confirmed the selection of five different chairmen of the Nairobi City Commission. None of these high-profile appointees was closely associated with the region around Nairobi; with only one exception,[7] all were either professionals or former politicians from provinces other than Central Province, the home base of the Kikuyus, who make up 35 percent of Nairobi's population. Part of the motivation for dismantling the Nairobi City Council was to take the control of a substantial political base away from Central Province leaders. By 1982, just before the new Nairobi City Commission was created, the council had an annual level of recurrent and capital expenditure of K£41,380,791 ($65,424,175 at the December 1982 exchange rate) with 15,899 employees (Nairobi City Commission 1982: 53). Outside the central government and perhaps the railways, the council was the largest public organization in Kenya.

The hypothesis that taking administrative control over Nairobi was part of a more general strategy by the Moi regime to undermine the national power base of the Kikuyu is reinforced by three other related facts and events during the 1980s and early 1990s. First, there was the removal from office and discrediting of Charles Njonjo, the Kiambu-based attorney general, in 1984. Second, it is perhaps more than a coincidence that none of the ministers of local government during the 1980s and 1990s was a Kikuyu politician. Finally, it was argued in some circles that the brutal destruction of the squatter villages of Muoroto, Kibagare, and Kangemi—whose low-income residents came largely from the northern Kikuyu district of Murang'a—was intended to reduce the influence of this district in Nairobi (Macharia 1992).

Whatever the validity of this hypothesis, there is little evidence that, even before it took control of the City Council, the government ever made any serious effort to improve municipal services in Nairobi. For example, commenting on the financial position of the council in 1983, Nairobi's town clerk observed in his annual report:

The financial position of the then City Council when the Commission took over was at its worst. By the beginning of 1983, the debts owed to the Council stood at KShs. 323 million. Although effort was made to collect debts, it was possible to collect only KShs. 16 million by the end of the year under review. It is worth noting that government parastatal bodies who are some of our biggest debtors have not responded positively to our efforts and approaches. For instance Kenya Railways owed the Commission over KShs. 77 million in rates by the end of 1982. To effectively collect all our debts, it is paramount that the Government comes to our aid. . . . The assistance becomes all the more important since the Government has intimated that no further grants will be extended to local authorities (Nairobi City Commission 1983: 1–2).

At the end of 1983, by which time the City Commission had been in operation for nine months, the rate arrears owing to it were 30 percent higher than the figure for the previous year. Though 61 percent of these rate arrears were owed by private individuals (many of them powerful politicians and senior bureaucrats), the remaining 39 percent were owed by agencies of the Kenya government, most notably Kenya Railways (22 percent) and the commissioner of lands (17 percent). By the end of 1986, the amount owed to the commission in arrears was considerably in excess of the yearly annual expenditure figure (exact details were not available because an extensive fire in the commission's offices destroyed many important records).[8] Not only were government departments continually among the largest debtors of the Nairobi City Commission during the 1980s and early 1990s, but the general consensus was that the quality of services steadily declined during this period. By 1991 a lengthy article in *The Weekly Review* entitled "Filthy, Ailing City in the Sun" concluded:

Since central government took over the running of the city through appointed officials in 1983, services in Nairobi have grown unspeakably bad, with desperate changes from one administration to the next only making the situation worse. The inevitable conclusion is that the underlying problems of the city have never ever been tackled, while a bloated and insensitive bureaucracy with around 19,000 employees consuming more than KShs. 70 million a month in wages [about $2.9 million] sits comfortably in place. Drastic action is clearly required before the corruption, incompetence and irresponsibility that have slowly eaten up City Hall lead to the final disintegration of the city (*Weekly Review*, July 12, 1991: 18).

The multiparty elections of December 1992 ushered in a new chapter in the turbulent history of Nairobi—and of urban local government politics in Kenya. One of the major new parties, FORD-Kenya, specifically called in its election manifesto for the granting of increased autonomy to local government. In a major rally in Mombasa, for example, party chairman Jaramogi Oginga Odinga declared that, unlike the ruling Kenya Africa National Union (KANU), which had undermined the local council "through

giving power to corrupt, incompetent and unpopular leaders, while perse-
cuting strong and popular councilors, Ford would let the people choose
their own civic leaders to run local authorities" (*Weekly Review*, January
31, 1992: 12). As has always been the case in Kenya, local and national
elections were held at the same time. But whereas KANU had always cap-
tured both levels of seats in the urban wards and constituencies in the past,
in this election the opposition parties won most of the parliamentary seats
in the major urban areas and took control of twenty-three of the twenty-six
municipal councils, including Nairobi. In Nairobi, KANU won only one of
eight parliamentary seats and seven of the fifty-five elected seats on the
City Council. Very soon after the election of Stephen Mwangi (FORD-
Asili) as the new mayor of Nairobi in February 1993, a power struggle
between the local councils and the central government of Daniel arap Moi
began to take shape. Aside from using his power under the Local Government Act to nominate only KANU members to fill up to 25 percent of the
seats in every council, the minister of local government, William ole
Ntimama, issued a series of directives that curtailed the powers of the may-
ors. For the Moi regime, the newly elected urban councils were a political
force to be reckoned with. For its opponents, especially the members of the
urban middle class, the councils were a vehicle by which to achieve a measure of autonomy from the regime.

An interesting example of the new importance of urban politics for the
Kenyan middle class was the successful organization by Mayor Mwangi
and key members of the business and professional communities of a large
convention in July 1993 entitled "The Nairobi We Want." The conference,
which ran for three days in the auditorium of City Hall, attracted 1,000 par-
ticipants. Funded and sponsored by the World Bank and the German-based
Friedrich Naumann Foundation, the conference was jointly opened by
Mwangi and ole Ntimama in a public display of mutual respect. Blessed by
the resident director of the World Bank, who gave the keynote address, the
conference reviewed the problems of public service management in seventeen areas of urban life, including transportation, housing, markets, the
informal sector, environment, water and sewage, governance, and finance.
A similar conference was held in Kisumu in December, and others were
being planned for Kenya's other major municipalities. By the end of 1993,
Kenya's urban elites had begun to mobilize themselves to reverse the decay
in urban life, notwithstanding the fact that the minister of local government
continued to frustrate their initiatives.

TANZANIA

By 1980, the end of the third five-year plan, it had become quite evident
that the strategy adopted for socialist development in Tanzania was hinder-

ing urban development. Thirteen years after the Arusha Declaration, anticipated outcomes of imparting education for self-reliance, promoting collec-
tivist rural production, improving productivity, and transforming agriculture into the main base of the economy were not forthcoming. As Michael
Lofchie has shown in the preceding chapter, peasant farmers were given
few incentives, so agricultural production fell. With this fall, primary
school leavers did not have the skills or motivation to remain in the rural
areas. Neither villagization nor collectivization improved peasants' welfare, and rural services and infrastructure had not improved significantly.
As a result, rural conditions were not attractive enough to arrest the rapid
migration toward the urban centers. Thus, between 1967 and 1978 the population in urban centers doubled, mostly because of migration. These new
arrivals had to be provided with shelter, services, and jobs.

The urban centers' ability to absorb the influx of rural migrants was
limited by the administrative framework within which the policy of socialist development was to be implemented. One of the main effects of the so-
called decentralization policy (in operation from 1972 through 1978) was
to dismantle urban councils throughout the country. Like Kenya's subsequent experience with District Focus, this exercise merely extended the
bureaucracy to lower administrative levels while retaining all effective
power and authority at the center. The district development committees
established in the towns had a rural production orientation and therefore did
not accord any importance to the maintenance of urban social and economic infrastructure. More attention was given to improving production in the
villages around the urban centers. Furthermore, the authority over revenue
mobilization remained with the central government. All taxes and fees were
collected by the central government treasury and then remitted to the districts as subventions upon approval of the suggested plans. Besides reinforcing a dependence on the state, this system also discouraged any financial requests for urban-related activities, which in the mind-set of the time
were considered to be consumption rather than production oriented and
thus unnecessary. Urban centers had neither the political space nor the
resources to cope with the new situation.

The socialist development strategy in Tanzania also involved the
deconcentration of economic activities away from Dar es Salaam. The second five-year development plan identified nine towns that were to act as
"growth poles" for future development. All planned industries were to be
distributed to these nine towns, a move that was expected to change the
direction of migration and to initiate a multiplier effect that would lead to a
more balanced spatial impress of development. The third five-year plan,
which was adopted in 1975, reinforced this approach by outlining a "basic
industrial program" that fostered a system of industrial integration with
coherent vertical and horizontal linkages.

These strategies proved unworkable. By 1985 more than 60 percent of total industrial establishments were still concentrated in Dar es Salaam. The rest were mostly in established urban areas such as Arusha, Moshi, Tanga, and Mwanza. Morogoro was the only town that had become a new industrial center during the post-Arusha period. At the same time, the basic industrial strategy was preempted by the difficulties caused by the 1978–1979 war with Uganda, the oil crisis, the breakup of the East African Community, and a severe drought. All these factors, plus the low rate of return to Tanzanian farmers, combined to intensify urban migration, particularly to Dar es Salaam. The urban policy process in Tanzania during the 1980s was a product of an attempt to cope with the interplay of the above three dynamics—a high rate of urbanization, a virtual breakdown of the system of urban management, and an acute economic crisis. How this complex dynamic manifested itself in physical form, the measures taken by the state, and the response of urban civil society will now be discussed.

Housing and Urban Services

Between the pronouncement of the Arusha Declaration in 1967 and the third population census in the postindependence period (in 1988), the urban population in mainland Tanzania more than quadrupled. During the same period the registered housing stock grew slowly. Between 1964 and 1969 it was estimated that the annual demand for new urban housing was 37,000 units. By 1981 the demand had reached 250,000 units, and in 1991 it was over 600,000 units (Tanzania 1992a: 197). One consequence of this precipitous increase in demand was significant overcrowding. In fact, by 1988 34 percent of urban households (with an average population of more than four people) lived in one-room accommodations (Tanzania 1992b: 125). Whereas in 1978 about 45 percent of the urban population consisted of households with more than two persons living in a room (Kulaba 1989b: 225), by 1988 the number had declined only to 39 percent (Tanzania 1992b: 98). As Saitiel Kulaba observes, such conditions create health hazards, social problems, and distress among the families so housed (Kulaba 1989b: 225).

Another significant by-product of increasing urbanization and limited growth in the formal housing stock in Tanzania has been the proliferation of squatter settlements. A survey conducted by the government in 1980 found that 65 percent of residential houses (available and under construction) were in squatter areas. Toward the end of the decade the situation had not significantly changed. In 1986 70.4 percent of Mbeya's residential units were in unsurveyed areas; in 1987 82.1 percent of Tabora's residential units were in squatter areas; in 1987 58.0 percent of the residential housing in Arusha was located in squatter areas; and in 1988 half of the housing in Morogoro was located in unsurveyed or squatter areas (Tanzania 1992a:

197). Within the Tanzanian context, "squatter settlement" described the legal status of the housing units within the settlement rather than the physical condition of the units. In fact, close to 95 percent of "squatter" houses were constructed of permanent or semipermanent materials such as wood, cement, and iron sheets. In recent years, a high proportion of squatter houses were built by middle- and high-income earners. The major problem, however, was the absence of basic services. Most of these houses did not have access to clean water, electricity, solid-waste disposal facilities, drainage systems, or proper roads.

A less visible effect of the housing crisis in Tanzanian urban centers was the consolidation of a housing submarket that fostered rent-seeking and speculative behavior. Besides the rental costs, a prospective tenant had to meet the costs of getting information about a likely vacancy, had to pay an acceptable referee to vouch for his or her character, had to offer generous "thank you" money to the landlord (to protect the agreement before moving into the room), and had to pay, in advance, an annual rent. In most cases the tenant had to repair a door, a window, or a leaking roof, with the costs deducted over a long time. As a result of the multiple payments, there evolved a lucrative speculative (informal) business of "rental locators," adding to the already high cost of housing, another layer of costs that fell most heavily on low-income earners.

Aside from overcrowding and the greater incidence of squatting on unsurveyed and unserviced land, another effect of the housing shortage was the increase in rents. The average rent in Dar es Salaam for a room in a house without an indoor water system and electricity was between 25 and 40 Tanzanian shillings (TShs.) in the 1960s, when the urban minimum wage was around TShs. 180; the average monthly rent for an equivalent room in 1993 was between TShs. 1,000 and 1,500, depending upon location and building condition. With the current minimum wage at TShs. 4,500, the share of housing costs in the monthly income of a minimum wage earner has increased from a range of 14–22 percent to a range of 22–33 percent. As the proportion of income spent on housing increased from the 1960s through the 1990s for low-income wage earners, the proportion of income spent on food also increased. Whereas low-income households in Dar es Salaam spent approximately 56 percent of their average total expenditures on food in 1965, the figure had risen to 85 percent in 1980, according to one study (Bryceson 1985: 513).

One consequence of the increase in the real cost of food and the decrease in purchasing power of wages was an almost visible escalation in the incidence of various agricultural practices in Tanzanian towns. Despite some disagreement over whether raising animals and crops in an urban setting should be discouraged or supported by the authorities, these practices became very common among all income groups. One scholar pointed out, for example, that between 1984 and 1988 2.3 percent of all reported traffic accidents in Dar es Salaam were caused by roaming cows, sheep, or goats (R. Shauri, cited in Kironde 1992a: 1284). Another noted the enormous increase in banana, orange, and pineapple seedlings sold in Dar es Salaam from 1987 to 1989 and an overall 40 percent increase, from 1985 through 1988, in the number of agricultural animals kept in the city (as registered by the City Council livestock office). Altogether, J. M. Lusugga Kironde observed, a total of 5,741 dairy cattle, 5,764 goats, 13,383 pigs, 785,341 chickens, and 8,100 ducks were recorded by the City Council livestock office in 1988 (Kironde 1992a: 1285). Senior government ministers, including (reportedly) the prime minister, kept large herds of dairy cattle in the capital. In the 1980s and 1990s, most of the eggs, milk, and spinach consumed in the urban areas was produced within urban boundaries.

Exacerbating the severe scarcity of good housing and increasingly high cost of food, other urban services were in short supply. In the area of water supply, for example, the "service squeeze" became much more serious during the 1980s. As Kulaba pointed out:

> Most urban water supply schemes were built more than 30 years ago when towns had small populations. For example, the water supply system in Moshi town was built in 1956 when the population of the town was only about 13,000 people. Since then, the scheme has undergone expansion . . . but the present piped water supply meets less than 50 percent of the demand for water in Moshi.
>
> The water supply is serious in Dar es Salaam where the scheme is very old. Although the water scheme has undergone a number of rehabilitation exercises and expansion programs, the demand of 264,000 cubic meters a day still exceeds the present supply of 182,000 cubic meters—notwithstanding the fact that the installed capacity is . . . 270,000 cubic meters per day. Shortage of water has become a common phenomenon, with many users and areas of the city doing without water for several hours a day or even for days in a week or month. Water shortages in turn force many big users like textile factories, soft drink factories and beer factories to close their operations or to operate below their installed production capacity (Kulaba 1989b: 156–158).

In most Tanzanian towns, only half the demand for water service was provided for. The small amount available had to be shared among industries, institutions, and domestic users. The tendency was for low income areas to go without water for extended periods.

Another disturbing aspect of the crisis in service delivery was garbage accumulation. In 1986 it was estimated that the total daily production of garbage in Tanzania's nineteen regional capitals amounted to 3,000 tons. However, the actual amount of refuse collected daily was only 728 tons, or 24.27 percent. A total of 2,282 tons were left uncollected each day. In Dar es Salaam alone, 928 tons of garbage—or 88 percent of the estimated production of solid waste—was left undisposed of every day (Kulaba 1989a: 236–237). Again, the neighborhoods where the majority of the people resided had neither roads for collecting vehicles to pass through nor their own disposal facilities. In those areas all the garbage was left to pile up.

The most conspicuous feature of urban Tanzania during the 1980s was the condition of its roads. Almost 90 percent of the existing road system needed major rehabilitation, not simply repairs. The roads were full of craterlike potholes. In some towns the solution was to scrape off the surface entirely to level the roads to the depth of the potholes. The consequence was to create urban valleys during the rainy season, causing even further damage to the roads. Compounding this situation was the absence of feeder roads running into squatter settlements; the topography within which they were located made access roads difficult to construct. In most cases these areas depended upon footpaths. The condition of urban roads, which was aggravated by poor or even absent drainage systems, had a damaging effect on vehicles. It increased wear and tear and hence created a high demand for foreign exchange for importing spare parts. It also increased accidents and reduced efficiency and mobility.

Another service that was under stress, particularly by the early 1980s, was commuter transportation. The exaggerated horizontal sprawling of urban centers because of population growth compounded the problem of mobility. Whereas urban areas expanded, basic services and employment opportunities remained concentrated at the center. This created a heavy demand for transportation facilities because it was no longer feasible to walk around the city. The transportation problem was most acute in the city of Dar es Salaam, where the capacity of the company that had the monopoly of providing transport services within the city continued to dwindle from a peak of 119,686 average passengers per day in 1982 to 15,847 average passengers per day in 1991 (Tanzania 1992a: 212). By 1991 it was reported that the city needed a total of 713 serviceable buses, as compared to the available 32 buses operated by the public corporation (Usafiri Dar es Salaam or UDA) and the 355 registered private buses, on a daily basis. No wonder, in a survey conducted during the same period, it was found that 245 private buses operated without proper registration and licenses (Tanzania 1992a: 203). Most of these privately owned vehicles—called *daladalas* (after the five-shilling coin, or *dala*, originally charged as fare) in Dar es Salaam—did not meet established safety standards; they drove recklessly in the rush for passengers, overloaded, and, in the opinion of many, overcharged.

The Institutional Response

Hardly five years after the abolition of urban local authorities in 1972, the government began to receive complaints about the service situation in the urban centers. Prolonged water shortages, uncollected waste, poorly or nonmaintained roads, and lack of malaria controls made the cities virtual health hazards. By the early 1980s a severe cholera outbreak was caused by this situation. But as early as October 1976, the prime minister was compelled to appoint a high-powered committee to suggest ways of rectifying the situation. The committee was chaired by a minister of state in the prime minister's office and included a number of members of the National Assembly and senior civil servants. On the basis of its deliberations, the committee recommended that:

- The prevailing overemphasis on rural development at the expense of urban areas should be done away with. Instead, development of both rural and urban areas should be seen as complementary.
- Urban centers should be graded, and those with higher growth rates should be allocated adequate numbers of competent personnel.
- Urban laws and by-laws should be enforced as before the decentralization exercise.
- Funds should be allocated to the councils for basic services.
- Urban recreation areas should be maintained (Kulaba 1989b: 82–83).

As a result of these recommendations in 1977, the president announced the establishment of urban councils, and on April 15, 1978, the Urban Council (Interim Provisions) Act was passed by the National Assembly, coming into effect on July 1 of the same year. The main objective of this act was "to provide for the establishment of Urban councils, to provide for their functions and for matters incidental thereto."

Besides the stipulation that the new authorities were to receive funds for their estimated expenditure from parliamentary allocation and required to deposit all the money they collected in a consolidated fund, the system was to operate under the statutes formulated during the colonial period such as the Municipal Ordinance of 1946 and the Local Government Ordinance of 1953. In 1980 the government issued a more coherent policy on urban development that addressed the issues of "regulating the running, servicing and development of urban centers, and giving the inhabitants power to plan their development affairs and share in their execution" (Bukurura 1988). This policy formed the basis for the Local Government (Urban Authorities) Act of 1982, which made major modifications in the colonial statutes to take into account the contemporary situation.

The reestablishment of the urban authorities elevated the status of a number of urban centers. Towns such as Morogoro, Mwanza, Mbeya, and Dodoma were assigned municipal status. Similarly, smaller towns such as Kibaha and Korogwe were designated as townships. Their new status gave these urban centers more power and authority, but they were now expected to be less dependent on grants from the central government. However, the powers vested in the reestablished urban authorities were insufficient to let them manage effectively. The urban councils lacked sufficient manpower, equipment, and finance, and the central government retained all the important sources of revenue, as well as final approval over development plans. Urban councils functioned more or less as subsidiary departments of the central government (Bukurura 1988 and Halfani 1989). Though this pattern was consistent with the overcentralized character of the entire Tanzanian political system during this period, central government control severely curtailed the capacity of local urban councils to manage rapid urban growth.

One state response to the urban crisis which created havoc in Tanzania's urban centers during the early 1980s was Oparesheni Nguvu Kazi (Operation Labor Force). Backed by the Human Resource Deployment Act of 1983, the government embarked on what it described as an operation to deploy into productive activity every able-bodied person in the country. The operation had two main components. The first was the rounding up and repatriation to their home villages of all urban dwellers who were considered "unemployed"—essentially, most of the people working in the informal sector. Those who were designated under the act were given travel allowances and, upon reporting to the party and government representatives at their destination, were to be resettled on assigned pieces of land for farming.[9] A second component of Oparesheni Nguvu Kazi involved the easing of licensing conditions for small-scale enterprises in urban centers. The licenses were made much chaper, had less stringent conditions attached, and did not require income tax payment. The purpose of these licenses was to enable informal sector operators such as hawkers, vendors, and artisans to engage in legally recognized productive activities.

The arrests and repatriation of those defined as "unemployed" created chaos in many urban areas. Many women who worked in the home and who normally did not carry any means of identification were picked up on the street and detained until their husbands could release them. Moreover, the Nguvu Kazi operation coincided with the "anti-economic saboteurs' campaign," which involved arrests of anybody with goods suspected of having been illegally obtained. Given the prevailing acute shortages of the time, "illegal goods" could range from a single tube of Colgate toothpaste or a kilogram of sugar to expensive electronic equipment. Another weakness of Nguvu Kazi was that many of those who were actually repatriated to their home villages simply reboarded the same train or bus and found their way back to the city. After less than four months the campaign lost all semblance of public support and was allowed to dissipate.

The licensing component of Nguvu Kazi, however, has been maintained by the government. Despite periodic confrontations between informal sector operators and urban authorities (who, in the name of enforcing health regulations, undertake mass confiscation and destruction of trading barns, equipment, and products), there has been considerable political pressure (from as high as the president's office) to protect the vendors. In a few cases, licenses have been abused by high-income earners to operate sophisticated hair salons (with imported equipment), butcheries, and retail shops. But on the whole, informal-sector activities have been subject to fewer harassments since the mid-1980s than was the case in the 1970s.

A more popular state response during the 1980s pertained to the transportation problem. In 1983 the government removed import restrictions and lowered taxes and duties for pickup vehicles. It also recommended that all buses owned by government ministries and parastatal institutions should provide services on a commercial basis during off-peak hours. Besides generating revenue for their corporations, this move went some distance toward easing the public transport problem, especially in Dar es Salaam. Another initiative was taken in 1986, whereby private transporters were permitted to operate legally in the urban centers after going through motor vehicle safety inspection and entering into a subagent contract with the public transit authority. Pickup trucks were allowed to carry passengers after putting in a back cover and suitable seats. The fares were to be regulated by the government. Partly as a result of these initiatives, the problem of transport in the urban centers has improved remarkably, though the government has not been able successfully to regulate roadworthiness of the vehicles or strict adherence to the routes to which they have been allocated. In Dar es Salaam, for example, transporters have been avoiding some routes because bad road conditions make it unprofitable to operate.

There was also some intervention in the sphere of urban law and order. The declining capacity of the government to provide basic services during the 1980s put the police force under increasing pressure in both rural and urban areas. The force suffered from poor roads, a shortage of motor vehicles, poor telephone systems, and inadequate housing and offices. These constraints reduced the capacity of the force to combat an increasing wave of crime, especially in urban centers. In 1989 a newly appointed minister of home affairs introduced the *sungusungu* system of volunteer neighborhood patrols in the urban areas to assist the police. Essentially, this was an extension of a traditional security system among pastoral communities aimed at protecting themselves against cattle rustlers (Campbell 1987). This move has been very popular in low-income neighborhoods and has led to a significant reduction in the level of crime.

There were also some major projects initiated by the state during the 1980s with the support of the World Bank and the United Nations Center for Human Settlements. These included the Urban Sector Engineering project; the Strengthening of Local Government project; and the Dar es Salaam Sustainable Cities project. The first project addressed what were considered to be high-priority needs in nine urban centers: developing an institutional framework for effective local government; improving financial performance plans; undertaking infrastructure rehabilitation and expansion; undertaking research on urban household demand in four towns, including Dar es Salaam; and more effectively mapping all nine major urban areas. The Strengthening of Local Government project involved the identification of priority issues through a national workshop; a survey of local government structures and performance; and the identification of training needs. Sustainable Cities focused on the strengthening of local capacity to plan, coordinate, and manage environment/development interactions. It also aimed to prepare a long-term, integrated development plan and investment strategy. During the 1980s, the World Bank funded a forestry project whose objective was to address the issues of land titles and markets; the final goal was to produce the first computer-based geographic information system in the country. As most of these projects are still in various stages of implementation at the time of writing, it is not possible to judge their impact.

In 1982 a National Housing Development Policy was announced, with six major objectives: 1) to improve the quantity and quality of low-income housing; 2) to mobilize and facilitate the easy acquisition of building land, finance, and materials; 3) to encourage and assist individuals to build or buy their own houses; 4) to encourage the production and use of local building materials; 5) to encourage better house maintenance by owners and occupiers; and 6) to support squatter upgrading operations. The policy anticipated that employers would use part of their profits to invest in housing and that local authorities, as well as the ailing National Housing Corporation (NHC) and the Registrar of Buildings, would help the self-employed in housing construction. By 1994, however, the role of the government in housing provision remained minimal. None of its institutions made any significant contribution in implementing the multiple objectives of the 1982 National Housing Development Policy. Indeed, whereas the NHC had built an average of 1,163 units per year during the period 1962/63 to 1971/72, and 410 units per year during the period 1972/73 to 1981/82, its production fell to an average of only 30 units per year in the period 1982/83 to 1989/90. Not only did its financial base deteriorate, as (after 1973) it had to borrow money at commercial rates, but it was beset with management problems and severe resistance from tenants when it attempted to raise rents from purely nominal levels during the 1980s (Kironde 1992b). In this weakened state, the NHC was in no position to carry out any elements of the government's policy that did not involve construction.

The major initiative in this field came early in 1990, when, as part of institutional restructuring in the Economic Recovery Program, the National Housing Corporation was merged with the Registrar of Buildings. By this time, public sector provision of housing was at an all-time low. After the completion of phase two of the sites and services and squatter upgrading projects during the early 1980s, the World Bank had shifted away from its earlier "housing" approach, and the Tanzanian government was not in a position to replicate the projects on its own.

All the above interventions had some bearing on the alleviation of the urban crisis of the 1980s, but they did not constitute a coherent policy toward urban development. They were merely ad hoc responses to a crisis situation. In fact, the exigencies of urban development were not given any attention in the development strategies pursued at this juncture. Neither the short-term Structural Adjustment Program nor the long-term Economic Recovery Program paid any regard to the urban sector as such. The macro-economic approach to the economy that undergirded these programs allowed for disaggregation by sectors but was insensitive to subnational spatial patterns. As a result, what was "local" or "urban" received little attention (Stren et al. 1992: Chapter 2).

Emerging Patterns of Pluralism and Civil Society

The tendency toward a state monopoly of politics that began in the mid-1960s culminated in the proclamation of the supremacy of the Tanganyika African National Union (TANU) in 1971, and the establishment of Chama cha Mapinduzi (CCM) in 1977. In fact, by the end of the 1970s the fusion of the party and the bureaucracy had been completed, leaving the space for autonomous political action heavily circumscribed. At the same time, the nationalization of buildings in 1971 and the restrictions imposed by the Leadership Code of the Arusha Declaration prevented private investment in urban growth, particularly in real estate. Although the post-Arusha period gave some support to urban dwellers through the maintenance of overvalued exchange rates and low prices paid to peasant farmers, it was also characterized by a repressed urban civil society and muted social and economic differentiation.

By 1986, as we have seen in other chapters in this book, the Tanzanian state could no longer resist IMF loan conditionalities. Already in 1985, the ruling party had adopted a new program that recognized the prevalence of capitalist elements during a period it considered a transition toward socialism. The following year the government signed an agreement with the IMF accepting the adoption of a liberal market-oriented development strategy. Among the consequences of this major policy change was the unleashing of private capital in the real estate sector. There was a sudden mushrooming of luxurious houses in the urban centers. The most visible reflection of this new dynamic was the changing skyline of Kariakoo in downtown Dar es Salaam, where old, ramshackle houses were rapidly replaced with expensive high-rise buildings; at the same time, new "villas" were being constructed along the beach. The same pattern was emerging in other urban centers, as prime land on hillslopes and waterfronts was developed with capital that had been previously invested outside the country.

Import liberalization permitted conspicuous consumption, marked by the appearance of expensive automobiles, television sets with satellite dishes, and fancy boutiques. These gave a new form to Tanzanian urbanization; besides bringing a renewed vibrancy to city life, they emphasized the element of differentiation. The former closet "dollar millionaires" (as they are referred to in Tanzania, to distinguish them from "shilling millionaires") appeared to flaunt their wealth in the cities, where street beggars, shacks, and slums contrasted with beachfront bungalows and where vendors competed for space in front of new upscale boutiques.

The crystallization of inequality manifested itself in changes in the urban form, a worsening economic crisis, and a state that was forced to withdraw from the provision of many functions. These conditions allowed for the emergence of new forms of associational life. Collective associations were formed by butchery owners, taxi drivers, daladala operators, market vendors, cart pullers (*mikokoteni*), and even squatter communities. In the case of Dar es Salaam, for example, residents of the Tabata squatter area developed a strong association that successfully fought for the removal of the garbage dump that had been used by the city for over twenty years. Similarly, residents of Makongo and Changanyikeni were able to fight off an eviction order by the military, which claimed ownership of the land.

New forms of social networks began to emerge in the 1980s and 1990s. Difficulties in obtaining credit from the banking institutions led to the formation of rotating credit networks (*upatu*). Women took turns providing each other with interest-free capital for starting businesses or solving social problems (Tripp 1992). A modified version of ethnic associations of the 1940s and 1950s was reestablished in the 1980s. Urban residents from other districts formed "development associations" with the aim of promoting development in their home districts while fostering a closer network in the town of residence. Such associations have been able to mobilize resources to build schools, roads, and dispensaries in their respective districts. Ministers and members of parliament have participated in such endeavors without being seen as promoting ethnicity in national development. In general, the forces promoting multipartyism in Tanzania appear to have much stronger roots in the urban than in the rural areas of the country. The urban areas have also emerged as centers of other activities associated with political and economic liberalization, including the establishment of an independent press, the emergence of a host of nongovernmental organizations, and the growth of professional and business associations such as the Law Society of Tanzania and the Chamber of Commerce.

CONCLUSIONS

By the early 1990s urban centers in Kenya and Tanzania had followed a similar trajectory for over a decade. In both countries, stagnant and even declining economies severely reduced the public resources available for urban public infrastructure and services. Though Kenya's urban system began from a much higher economic plateau than Tanzania's, both showed declining investment in urban infrastructure per capita, with an increasing tendency for small-scale private enterprise (particularly in housing and transport) to cater to popular needs. Whereas muscular and highly capitalized national housing programs had built thousands of units in both countries for low- and middle-income families during the 1960s and 1970s, these programs came to a virtual standstill by the late 1980s. And in the face of a burgeoning informal sector in both countries, formal urban land-use planning structures had very little effect on the continued growth of the large towns. Tanzania reinstituted democratic local government beginning in the late 1970s and continued to support democratic local government through the 1980s and 1990s; the Kenyan government took administrative control of its largest urban government in 1983, not permitting free elections until the country's first multiparty balloting in December 1992.

If the 1960s and 1970s were a period of high-profile, ideologically charged initiatives in the realm of urban public policy, the 1980s and early 1990s have been a period in which both countries have merely tried to cope. Failing to define a coherent urban policy, both governments were reacting to a severe decline in resources and the growth of an informal economy that undermined most of the planning structures previously put in place so arduously in the late colonial and early postindependence periods. Squatter areas grew in size, public health conditions deteriorated, public services—water supply, garbage collection, public transport, education— declined, and the taxable resources available to local institutions to respond to these challenges dried up. The Kenyan state intermittently attempted to clean up its capital city with massive slum-clearance operations, and the Tanzanians attacked their urban informal sector with the euphemistic Human Resources Deployment Act, but by the end of the period under review neither approach had shown any positive results; in fact, the political unpopularity these measures had generated had (at least for a time) reduced the legitimacy of both governments. By contrast, when either government decided to support rather than to confront the informal sector—as in the case of the legalization of matatus in Kenya and daladalas in Tanzania or support for the jua kali sector in Kenya—the political climate improved. But as both governments progressively disengaged from providing urban services, collective efforts at the community and voluntary group level took on more importance, and urban dwellers began systematically to question and to criticize local (and national) governments for their failures to sustain necessary functions. The movement to political pluralism in both countries gained much of its energy from these sources.

NOTES

1. For urban population growth figures, see Ondiege and Obudho (1988: 121).

2. Saitiel Kulaba (1989a: 209) gives the 1967–1978 figures as 11.1 percent, whereas the Tanzanian census (Tanzania: 1991) gives the figure as 8.9 percent. Some of the difference results from the classification by different analysts of periurban areas as either urban or rural.

3. The Tanzania census states: "Current figures from the 1988 census indicate a lower growth rate of the urban population when compared to the urban growth experienced from the 1978 census. Details will be given in future publications" (Tanzania 1991: 5).

4. Sites and services projects, which were popularized by the World Bank in the 1970s, involved the allocation of fully serviced plots to individual households, who would then be given some level of support to construct their own housing on site. Squatter upgrading, which began to take the place of the sites and services approach by the early 1980s, was a less expensive approach to low-cost housing, consisting of the construction of limited infrastructure (such as a few access roads, water, electricity, connections, and some community facilities) in an existing slum or squatter area, with a minimum of support for individuals to improve their own dwellings. Though sites and services projects began from a cleared (or uninhabited) area, the upgrading projects were implemented in an existing settlement.

5. According to the *Urban Housing Survey* (Kenya 1983b: 38–39): "A structure is defined as permanent if its outer-walls [sic] are constructed of such materials as stones, blocks, concrete or bricks. This group includes houses, maisonettes and block [sic] of flats. The semi-permanent/temporary comprise non-durable groups, e.g. swahili, shanty and 'other' temporary materials." Later on the same page, the *Survey* opines concerning the high proportion of semipermanent/temporary residential structures in Mombasa and Kisumu: "Both towns have the problem of prevalence of semi-permanent/temporary structures which require quick corrective measures in favour of more permanent, low cost housing to cater for the poor sector of the urban population who cannot afford expensive housing."

6. For different interpretations of these demolitions, see Macharia (1992) and Ndolo (1990).

7. The exception was Daniel Gathumbi Kongo, chosen by the forty-seven other commissioners as the chairman of the Nairobi City Commission in January 1992. Kongo, who was born in Nairobi, was a prominent businessman who had been elected as a councillor in 1979.

8. Personal communication to Richard Stren, June 1987.

9. For accounts of this legislation and its effects, see Shaidi (1984), Miti (1985), Armstrong (n.d.), and Lugalla (1989).

7

Education for Self-Reliance and Harambee

Brian Cooksey, David Court, Ben Makau

For Tanzania and Kenya, as for most African countries, the education system was the great gain of the independence movement. Amid the widespread belief that colonial authorities had deliberately limited African access to education, the significance of its acquisition lay in two major factors, one economic and one political. First, education was generally perceived to be the means to economic and social development at the national level and the route to employment and improved social status for individuals. Leaders of the new nations, themselves graduates of modern universities, propagated the belief that education would be crucial in their country's overall development. The view was echoed among the citizenry. In most communities the presence of even one educated individual fueled the conviction that education was the gateway to improved economic and social status.

Second, education offered for the new governments a means of forging national unity and reducing inequalities that were part of the colonial legacy and a threat to fragile inherited nationhood. One of the major inequalities in both countries was in the distribution of education itself. The historical origins of disparity lay in the economic mode of colonial development, the uneven spread of missionary activity, and the variable intensity of local self-help activity. The seriousness of these disparities as threats to nationhood and social cohesion derived from the fact that they tended to coincide with ethnic, linguistic, religious, and economic cleavages. These, in turn, tended to find expression in particularistic loyalties and associated demands for a greater share of national resources. Because of education's perceived economic importance, the demand for regional equality became the demand for more schooling. From the standpoint of the new elites the challenge was to maintain national unity and social cohesion by ameliorating inequalities in the distribution of educational facilities and opportunities (Court 1976).

The sheer economic and political importance of education, as well as the instrumental view of it held by the new regimes, made it one of the primary components of the centralization process that began shortly after independence. The nature of educational development has been reflected in the political economy of both societies. Throughout the postindependence period, the rise of the one-party state and the bureaucratic governing class, its systematic expansion of control over other institutions, and its concentration of resources have been the most fundamental determinants of developments in the education sectors of both Kenya and Tanzania.

In Tanzania the process of centralizing the education sector began with the nationalization of private (mainly church) schools, the introduction of political education and the replacement of British by local examinations. It accelerated after 1967 when, under the banner of *ujamaa* socialism, emphasis was placed upon primary education and adult literacy, with expansion of other types of instruction strictly curtailed. In Kenya, where school creation was allowed to grow virtually unchecked, control was exercised through school registration and inspection systems, a single national examination and accreditation system, and judicious dispensations of central funding. In both countries educational policy was handed down from above. In Tanzania, "Education and Self Reliance" (Nyerere 1967) was never enthusiastically embraced as a policy by either parents, teachers, or administrators. In Kenya, educational policy increasingly became a topic that was closed to public debate, and was formally declared to be so in 1983. In that year, the government introduced the controversial 8:4:4 system of education whose primary purpose was to prepare primary and secondary school leavers for self-employment, but which also reorganized the educational system to consist of eight years of primary education, four years of secondary school and four years of university for those able to pursue higher education.[1] In Tanzania the impact of centralization was more total and pervasive than in Kenya, first because the intellectual content of policy was more radical and compelling, and second because the party machinery was more efficient in enforcing central policy.

In the immediate postindependence period, education policy in both countries reflected the urgent need to fill the manpower gap caused by the rapid departure of expatriate civil servants. The expansion of primary education was given low priority, and manpower self-sufficiency was rapidly achieved through staff development schemes and the promotion of junior cadres. In the late 1960s, a sharp divergence in educational policy began that continued for twenty years. Although educational policy in both countries remained highly centralized, the ideological justification for the use of education differed sharply and did so in respect to social equity and national integration (Court and Kinyanjui 1980). In Tanzania the publication of "Education for Self Reliance" (ESR) inaugurated a policy aimed at removing divisive elitist tendencies, whose emergence was symbolized by resistance to the introduction of compulsory national service by students of the University of Dar es Salaam in 1966. Under the new policy, resources were channeled toward primary education and adult literacy in a concerted effort to create a mass base for participatory socialist construction. Postprimary educational expansion was strictly limited and planned in accordance with projected medium and higher level national manpower requirements.

Accompanying this new structure of resource allocation were a series of measures relating to the curriculum and educational experience itself and having a specifically socializing intent. The Kiswahili language was given greater emphasis as a measure of social integration; examinations were downgraded and supplemented by a system of continuous assessment; political education was sharpened by the inclusion of practical military discipline; and schools were required to develop self-reliance activities, typically a school farm. The fundamental objective of these steps was to submerge any sense of separateness arising from a student's regional origin, social background, or educational experience within the deeper national identity of the socialist Tanzanian (Court 1973).

Kenya, with its relatively open market economy, adopted a very different approach to the inherited problems of social inequity and regional disparities of access to education. Rather than restrict entry to postprimary education, Kenya allowed social demand to run its course. As documented later, the result was a massive increase in secondary school enrollment in the years 1968–1983. The equity argument for this policy was that permitting expansion would give greater access to those from previously underrepresented parts of the country; the economic rationale was that a more educated populace could only be good for economic development. The underlying ideology was that of merit-based equality of opportunity, with performance measured by standard national examinations. In this period Kenya, unlike Tanzania, made little attempt to use the curriculum as an explicit socialization device for purposes of national integration.

Neither country was ever a pure representation of a socialist or capitalist model. Kenya never fully refined its meritocratic ideal, and in Tanzania there was always tension between the rhetoric of mass socialization and the reality of elite selection. From the beginning of the 1980s both countries moved toward characteristics of the other in the face of internal and external demands upon their educational systems. For example, Tanzania removed the ceiling on public secondary education, endorsed the expansion of private secondary schools, opened a second university, and lost momentum on literacy campaigns and universal primary education. In contrast, Kenya moved in the direction of ESR-type policies with its 8:4:4 system, stressing "relevance," vocational practicality, and a broad range of examinable subjects. Kenya also removed the A-level and introduced district quotas for secondary and university access. Meanwhile, in both countries educational quality began to fall rapidly.

Whatever the philosophical and policy differences between Tanzania and Kenya in the early years of independence, as the century draws to a close both countries are subject to common structural constraints, including indebtedness, poverty, corruption, and increasingly limited resources for social services. These ensure a degree of convergence in education as in other policy domains. As a result of the deep economic crisis of the 1980s and the impact of state policies, basic education has stagnated quantitatively in Tanzania and declined dramatically in qualitative terms in both countries. A combination of policy inadequacies and resource constraints have made the educational crisis in Tanzania exceptionally severe. Despite Tanzania's relatively high international profile over the years, Kenya has consistently committed a much higher proportion of government spending to education than Tanzania and has been substantially more successful in sustaining high primary enrollment ratios and, until recently, academic standards.

In the following sections we attempt to trace the divergent and convergent trends in Kenyan and Tanzanian education, particularly in the recent period of political and economic reform. What new local circumstances are likely to determine educational policy and performance into the next century? What are the main ingredients required to reverse the present downward spiral in quality? It should be noted from the start that independent Kenya started off with advantages over Tanzania in terms of educational facilities and enrollments. In 1961 Kenya had roughly ten primary and middle school pupils for every six in Tanzania and about ten secondary students for every nine (Fisher 1966).

By 1991 when both countries had populations of about 25 million primary enrollment differentials remained similar, but Kenya had over ten

Table 7.1 Comparative Education Statistics 1991

	Kenya	Tanzania	Ratio, Tanzania: Kenya
Primary Pupils	5,456,000	3,507,384	0.64
Teachers	173,370	98,174	0.57
Teacher/Pupil Ratio	1:31.5	1:35.7	
Enrollment ratio	76.3[a]	54.5[b]	0.71
Secondary Students	614,161	166,812	0.27
Teachers	30,120	8,649	0.29
Teacher Student Ratio	1:20.4	1:19.3	
University Students	41,000	3,146[c]	0.08

Sources: World Bank World Development Report 1992, Table 1; 1988 population census for Kenya and Tanzania; *Tanzania Economic Trends*, Vol. 5, No. 1 (1992).

Notes: a. six- to fourteen-year-olds
b. six- to thirteen-year-olds
c. 1990 figures

secondary students for every three in Tanzania and no less than thirteen university students for every one. Although the exact figures are contested, Kenya is spending a much larger proportion of a much larger total budget on education than Tanzania. These figures point to a huge quantitative and qualitative gap between the two countries' education systems, particularly at the postprimary level. Egalitarian policies in postcolonial Tanzania added a further downward pressure on quality over and above that resulting from absolute resource constraints. But Kenya has also adopted some leveling policies over the second half of the postindependence period that have seriously undermined quality.

KENYA: FROM *HARAMBEE* TO *NYAYO* AND BEYOND

By 1963, when Kenya became an independent nation, modern formal education had become a central issue in the country's political agenda. Second only to the alienation of land to European settlers, the denial of education to the indigenous people was regarded by the nationalist leadership as the worst raw deal of colonial rule. Thus, the expansion of educational opportunities was seen as an important responsibility of government in independent Kenya. Leaders of the new nation, themselves products of modern education, propagated the belief that education would be crucial in the country's overall development, and the population was hungry for rapid progress in education. However, the successful development of education in the postcolonial period was by no means assured. By 1963, four features that would dominate the future dynamics of growth (often in undesirable directions) were already apparent.

First was a general belief that the state should play the central role in planning and managing development (including education), as it had in colonial Kenya. Second was a widespread perception that the role of education was to prepare its beneficiaries for white-collar jobs (Court and Ghai 1974); this attitude translated into disdain for learning that sought to link school with the workplace. Third was a clear duality in financing policies; although the colonial state in Kenya controlled policy, it never took full responsibility for financing education, so religious bodies, communities, and parents played a major role in meeting the capital and recurrent expenses of institutions. Fourth, reflecting the uneven regional development of the colonial era, was a system of education replete with inequity. Some geographical regions and communities were grossly underrepresented, as were females (Kinyanjui 1974).

Since 1963, the four features above have remained central in the generation of the dynamics of educational policy. The current status of education reflects not only these four influences but also a rapidly growing population, continuing demand for education, a downturn in the economy, and growing donor assistance to development. Currently Kenya's education system is characterized by 1) quantitative growth but deteriorating quality; 2) unemployment of educated youth despite a lack of skilled manpower for certain positions in the economy; 3) constraints in financing despite substantial donor assistance; and 4) inequalities of access and achievement between social classes and geographical areas and between males and females.

Politics and Educational Development

Since 1963 education has continued to feature prominently in the rhetoric of leaders, a theme around which they sought to mobilize and hopefully unite the people. The case of *Harambee* provides an excellent illustration.

The call to Harambee was first sounded by Jomo Kenyatta in 1963. He and Daniel arap Moi, his successor as president, presented Harambee as an important part of African traditional culture that should assist modern development. Many communities took the cue and mobilized resources to set up educational institutions, particularly secondary schools. By the mid-1970s communities were setting up more new secondary schools than the government. In this way, Harambee made it possible for many more children to go to school. But rapid growth had a number of untoward effects. Politicians used Harambee to solicit support at election time. The patron-client relationships, which Barkan (1984) suggests replaced political activity through political parties, was oiled by Harambee donations from rich and powerful patrons. In reality the leadership used Harambee to divert political energies that could have been spent in questioning a centralized and authoritarian state.

In the new Kenya, education was seen as part of the politically sensitive core of national life. Thus, a number of institutions were set up to control education policy and management at the national level. The 1966 Teachers Service Commission (TSC) Act made all teachers state employees. The 1969 Education Act streamlined central administration and professional management, reducing the legal powers of the minister and director of education, school inspectorate, curriculum supervisors, and local school managers. A 1980 law established the Kenya National Examinations Council (KNEC) as the sole body for conducting examinations outside the university. The 1985 Kenya Commission for Higher Education Act set up an agency to coordinate the development of all postsecondary education in the country.

Ideally, the Ministry of Education, with the other institutions described above, would have provided a sound division of labor in managing education. In practice the TSC, the KNEC, and the universities have not always been able to exercise the autonomy stated in the laws which set them up. Major policy decisions have been made at the political center without adequate involvement on the part of the relevant educational authorities. Single-party and populist rule have shaped the education sector in often unfortunate ways. The government, through the Ministry of Education, emasculated the other institutions charged with special responsibilities in education. Policymaking was increasingly separated from planners and professionals and often negated their advice, instead following the dictates of the political leadership (Friedrich-Naumann-Stiftung 1992).

This approach to policymaking was illustrated by the decision, announced by presidential decrees in 1974 and 1979, to abolish formal fees in primary schools. Planners and professionals were caught unaware. The resulting higher enrollments necessitated the employment of a large number of untrained teachers, and unbudgeted funds had to be found to meet the higher teacher salary bill. Required to construct and provide facilities for the greatly expanded system, parents soon realized that primary education was not free (Nkinyangi 1980).

In the 1980s the making of educational policy by political fiat increased, as demonstrated by the introduction of the primary school milk scheme (1979), changes in the procedure for selecting students for entry into secondary schools (1983), the introduction of the 8:4:4 system (1983), and the decision to more than double university intake (1987–1990). In addition to ignoring the advice of planners and professionals in the government, the leadership was unwilling to allow public debate before sanctioning new policies (Nyong'o 1992, Oruka 1992). The *Daily Nation* noted that "little honest and critical evaluation of [8.4.4] has occurred since its inception. Criticism or suggestions for improvement, prior to the multiparty politics, were shunned as they were likely to be misconstrued as anti-Nyayo or anti-progress. The fad . . . was to praise the program unreservedly or shut up."

Educational Expansion and Employment

During the first decade of independence education had a high premium as a source of middle- and high-level manpower. The urgent need to fill positions previously held by expatriates contributed to the rapid expansion of education. By the early 1970s most positions in the public service had been Kenyanized. However, this success exacerbated the perception that ever more education was the route to high status (Kenya 1976). Because most of the positions taken over by Kenyans were administrative jobs in the public service, certificated skilled training beyond general education was not deemed as necessary. Thus, general courses, particularly in the relatively cheaper arts, were legitimized as all that was needed for a high-status position in the economy. This attitude was bolstered by a severe countrywide shortage of science and mathematics teachers, and the inability of both the government and the Harambee movement to provide all secondary schools with the resources for effective teaching of science.

With regard to the private sector, Kenya lacked comprehensive policies linking the processes of formal education to the workplace, particularly in relation to medium- and large-scale private ventures requiring scientific and technical knowledge. In line with its policy of encouraging economic development through private capital, the government was content to leave the specialized education and training of personnel to employers. Some individuals with scientific and technical education were able to find relevant jobs in either the public or private sector. Moreover, it was increasingly recognized that curricular development and implementation should take into account the skills needed in the economy (Kenya 1984, 1988, 1989). However, for the majority general education continued to be regarded as the gateway to high economic and social status.

In addition to preparing its recipients for salaried employment, education enhances social development, providing a sound foundation for better approaches to agriculture, entrepreneurship, health, and civic awareness (World Bank 1989c). Thus, one of Kenya's success stories is the rapid growth of basic education since independence. Between 1963 and 1991 the number of primary schools increased from 6,052 to 15,196. During the same period secondary schools grew from 151 to 2,647 (Kenya 1988, 1992a). The corresponding enrollments are shown in Table 7.2. In 1989 the proportion of females in primary school rose to 49 percent, and by 1991 44 percent of secondary school students were female (Kenya 1992a). However, at the secondary levels girls were concentrated in the relatively poor-quality Harambee and private schools. Overall, female enrollment at the secondary level as a percentage of total secondary enrollment is impressive when compared to stagnating or declining enrollment ratios in Tanzania and elsewhere in sub-Saharan Africa (World Bank 1988).

Despite the increase in total enrollment, Kenya's primary schools were characterized by high rates of waste. Only six out of ten students in the 1976 cohort took the primary leaving examination in 1982, and only five out of ten in the 1985 cohort sat for the exam in 1992 (Economic Survey 1977–1986; Kenya National Examinations Council). Between 1982 and 1992 dropout rates between Standards 1–4 averaged 29 percent for boys and 26 percent for girls. At Standards 4–8 the figures were 35 percent for boys and 44 percent for girls (*Economic Survey* 1984–1987; Kenya National Examinations Council).

As the number of graduates increased rapidly, the economy was not able to provide all of them with salaried employment. By the mid-1970s most school leavers were unable to find jobs in the modern sector of the economy (ILO 1972, Makau 1985a); during the 1980s the situation

Table 7.2 School Enrollments in Kenya 1963–1991 (in thousands)

Year	Primary	Secondary
1963	892	31
1968	1,210	101
1973	1,816	175
1978	2,995	362
1983	4,324	494
1988	5,124	540
1989	5,389	641
1990	5,392	619
1991	5,456	614

Sources: Annual Reports of the Ministry of Education and Economic Survey (various issues).

worsened, as ever more university graduates joined the ranks of the unemployed (Hughes 1985, Kenya 1989). In January 1991 a local periodical observed that "six months after completing their studies, an estimated 3,500 of the 6,700 [graduates] of the four public universities are still without jobs and are likely to remain so well into mid-1991, when another 6,000 will be dispatched to the labor market." In addition to the fact that the educational system was producing job aspirants faster than the modern sector of the economy was creating jobs, unemployment reflected the mismatch between what was being learned in school and the skills required in the workplace (Bennell 1981, Hughes 1985, Kenya 1989).

Unemployment of graduates consequently became a matter of public concern. Aware of the political implications of unemployment, the government took two major steps to stem the tide: It created additional jobs in the public service and adapted school curricula to encourage self-reliance (read "self-employment"). Because the government had heavily promoted education as the key to development, it could hardly reverse its stance once available jobs in the modern sector had been filled, so it created an increasing number of jobs in the public service as an expedient (Kenya 1982, Loubser 1982, Hughes 1985, Kenya 1989, Friedrich-Naumann-Stiftung 1992). Thus, total civil service employment rose from 133,000 in 1978 to 272,000 by 1991. In addition, there were about 200,000 teachers, 110,000 employees of parastatals, and 43,000 employees of local government authorities (Directorate of Personnel Management). But the rapid expansion of tertiary education soon outstripped the state's ability to absorb graduates, with a consequent reemergence of the unemployment issue and demands that the state do something about it (*The Standard,* January 25, 1993).

In 1983 the government launched the 8:4:4 program, adding to prevocational subjects to the core curriculum of schools to help prepare primary and secondary school leavers for self-employment. Starting with the cohort entering Standard 8 in January 1985, the basic primary school curriculum was expanded to include arts and crafts, home science, business education, Kiswahili, music, and religious education. With effect from 1986, the secondary curriculum was expanded to include at least two prevocational subjects (Kenya 1984, Makau 1985a). In political terms, the 8:4:4 initiative attempted to shift responsibility for creating employment away from the state. The rationale was that pressure on already constrained public resources would be reduced if the majority of school leavers could generate their own economic opportunities. However, the policy proved to be far too ambitious and was unable to forge the desired cause-and-effect relationship between education and the economy (Court and Kinyanjui 1985). Moreover, it put additional financial pressure on parents and communities. Because many (particularly secondary) schools could not afford the additional facilities, students could not adequately prepare for public examinations (*The Standard,* March 1, 1990). Many teachers trained for the former curricula were unable to handle the new prevocational subjects adequately, and the new subjects meant reduction of the time previously devoted to mastery of basic literacy, numeracy, and natural and social sciences (Makau, 1985a).

Costs and Financing of Education

The 1989–1993 Development Plan identified relevance and cost as the major educational issues to be addressed (Kenya 1989). These two issues were closely related. The economic crisis of the 1980s discussed elsewhere in this volume exerted steady downward pressure on national budgets and private educational outlays. This funding squeeze and the poorly planned expansionary populist policies described above largely account for the current educational crisis in Kenya, although the proportion of the national budget spent on education and training rose to about 40 percent in 1989. As cautioned by the 1989–1993 Development Plan, the increasing claim of the education system on national resources seriously threatened to reduce development resources for other sectors of the economy.

The abolition of the two-year preuniversity A-level course in the 8:4:4 system caused university enrollments to grown rapidly. In 1988 the universities planned to admit about 3,000 students, but the government insisted on their admitting 7,201, with a similar number being admitted in 1989. Enrollment was doubled again in 1990, when the last Form 6 leavers were admitted together with the first 8:4:4 Form 4 leavers. Thus, total enrollment in the four public universities rose to about 40,000 in the academic year 1990–1991.

This expansion in matriculation caused university expenditure to rise faster than the total allocation for education. From 1985 to 1990 total recurrent educational expenditure increased by 10 to 20 percent per annum, whereas university expenditure increased by 19 to 43 percent. Consequently, higher education's slice of total recurrent expenditure rose from 11 percent in 1985–1986 to 22 percent in 1990–1991. In order to construct the physical facilities for the enlarged university sector, development allocations to other sectors were drastically reduced, and budgeted recurrent grants to nonuniversity institutions were diverted. This trend had serious repercussions in schools and the community. School resources (particularly at the secondary level), already in a sorry state (Makau 1985b), were further constrained. By 1992 little in the way of government grants, including salaries for nonteaching staff, was being received in schools. In order to cover the shortfall, schools were forced to resort to higher user charges, so that families who could not afford to pay had their children forced out of the education system.

The funneling of an increasing proportion of the education allocation to the university level did not prevent a steep falloff in quality. Budgets for learning resources, research, staff development, and maintenance of existing facilities were slashed. Large classes in many departments rendered the delivery and evaluation systems inefficient and ineffective. The resulting lowered quality of education, combined with the curbing of academic freedom by the political system and the prospect of the eventual unemployment of the majority of students, led to increasing frustration among both staff and students. Student strikes and confrontation with the government became the norm, and the universities were closed for long periods with depressing regularity.

Inequality of Educational Opportunities

As pointed out earlier, the Kenyan leadership adopted a laissez-faire development approach that was not concerned with alleviating regional disparities in development, including education. Implicitly, Harambee and other development activities meant that some communities would develop (and therefore claim extra support from the state) at a greater rate than others. Harambee entailed parental and community responsibility for capital development of schools, provision of learning materials, and payment of formal fees in secondary schools. But over time, declining government support has shifted more and more of the educational burden onto parents and local communities. Reacting to media reports that many families could no longer afford the increasingly high fees charged by secondary schools, in early 1993 the minister of education stated clearly that payment of such fees was the responsibility of parents. "Parents' associations and boards of governors [are] empowered to levy extra charges. . . . [T]he ministry itself could not dictate what each school should charge as that [is] the prerogative of parents and [depends] on each institution's projects" (*Daily Nation,* February 12, 1993).

Ironically, shifting the burden onto parents means that education is increasingly only available to the rich. Thus, wealthy districts move ahead—which is the opposite of what was intended. Nevertheless, some attempts were made to reduce the serious regional disparities that Harambee led to in practice. With assistance from donor funding, a number of boarding primary schools were built in the country's semiarid and arid districts. These facilities benefited a considerable number of children who would otherwise not have been in school.

From 1963 on, selection into secondary school was controlled through district-based quotas. In 1983 the quota system was strengthened to give the more backward districts greater opportunities for secondary schooling. Although no formal quotas were used in selecting for higher education, the rapid increase in university admissions in the 1980s could to some extent be explained through similar reasoning. With expanded admissions (i.e., lowered entry qualifications), formerly poorly served districts could expect more of their youth to enter university. The quota system worked toward equalizing opportunities but devalued academic merit as the basis of advancement. Further, because these measures were not part of a well-articulated overall development policy, they exacerbated the unemployment of graduates and the constraints in financing education.

By the early 1990s the comparatively low enrollments in the arid and semiarid districts and the disadvantaged position of females, particularly in postprimary education, still needed attention. However, the major issue was that poorer families were being priced out of education. By early 1993 the combined effects of nonpayment of government grants to schools and a depressed economy had left a substantial number of parents unable to pay fees. One report claimed that 80,000 students had been unable to take their Form 1 places for this reason. Other reports indicated that growing numbers of selected students faced the same problem at provincial and national schools (*The Standard,* January 12 and February 20, 1993). The government's policy of empowering parent-teacher associations to administer user charges meant that the better schools became the exclusive province of parents who could afford to pay high fees. Parents who could not afford to pay the fees in these schools were forced to seek places in lower-quality institutions.

Donor Aid to Education

After 1963 external loans and grants played a significant role in the development of education in Kenya. Donor funding was particularly beneficial in four major areas. First, external funds constituted a large proportion of capital investments in education, particularly the construction of physical facilities and provision of equipment. Second, organizations such as the Anglo-American Teachers for East Africa program in the 1960s, the U.S. Peace Corps, and the British Overseas Volunteers Service, as well as expatriate staff on loan to universities and other institutions, provided expertise at a time when little or none was available locally. Third, external funding was crucial in building capacity in the educational system. A large number of Kenyans benefited from scholarships for study overseas. Capacity building also took the form of assisting research and development in education. Donor aid was crucial in providing facilities and materials (e.g., textbooks and journals) and funding educational research and development at institutions such as the Institute for Development Studies (University of Nairobi), the Bureau of Educational Research (Kenyatta University), the Kenya National Examinations Council, the Kenya Institute of Education, and the Kenya Education Staff Institute. Fourth, donor aid addressed the needs of educationally disadvantaged areas and groups. Through a multiplicity of nongovernmental organizations (NGOs), aid was channeled to such diverse projects as school lunch schemes in famine-prone areas, the informal education of school dropouts, education for the disabled, and the provision of nearly all the educational requirements of semiarid and arid areas.

However, donor aid has not been an unmitigated blessing. The World Bank's concern with making education in Kenya more equitable and tailoring university enrollments to available resources and quality considerations could have had a beneficial influence on policy. However, this part of the package was not followed, and the Bank's emphasis on raising user charges in social services has tended to exacerbate inequality.

Also, over the years Kenya has been saddled with a number of aided educational projects that did not address the issues of relevance and long-term financial sustainability. For example, new approaches to teaching and learning science and mathematics, popularized in the West in the early 1960s and associated with advances in space technology, were introduced into Kenya's primary and secondary schools. A lot of donor funds were devoted to curriculum development (technical assistance, training, and provision of materials). However, the endeavor paid scant attention to the relevance of the new science and mathematics in a predominantly agricultural society. Also not fully addressed were the complexity of orienting learning to less didactic pedagogical approaches or the constraints involved in providing science facilities and materials to a rapidly growing number of schools. It is no wonder that at the end of the 1970s, when the West began to question the new science and mathematics, Kenya backtracked to more traditional forms of these subjects.

Somewhat similar to the foregoing were projects that attempted to establish linkages between education and the economy. Three of these, all aimed at diversifying the secondary school curriculum, stand out: Agriculture: Principles and Practices (funded by USAID, 1964–early 1970s), Industrial Education (funded by Sweden through SIDA, 1961–1982), and the use of computers in the curriculum (funded by the Aga Khan Foundation, 1982–1989). These projects were characterized by two major drawbacks (Narman 1985, Hawkridge et al. 1990, Makau 1990). First, they were based on capital-intensive technology that very few Kenyan schools could afford. In each school, the industrial project required construction of a large workshop equipped with expensive machinery and tools, including electric saws and drills, welding equipment, wood and metal lathes, and the agricultural project involved a tractor with a plough, a harrow, and a grain planter. This expensive approach was out of touch with the reality of the Kenyan environment and ruled out widespread replication. Second, in relation to relevance, the donors failed to convince the Kenya system that the new subjects should be integrated fully into the mainstream curriculum. Up to 1993 computer studies (or a similar subject) was not included in the final secondary school examination. Although agriculture and industrial education were examined, success in them was not a requirement for selection into related courses in higher education. As a consequence, teachers and students continued to treat the new subjects as peripheral.

Several features of the Kenyan political economy give grounds for concern about the future of education: a politically centralized system, high popular demand for education despite growing unemployment, increasing inequity, and the inability to provide quality education despite continued external assistance. Nevertheless, the future is not altogether bleak. First, the problems and possibilities of education are now better understood than they were thirty years ago. Similarly, Kenya stands to gain in the future from the considerable development of human resources that has taken place through formal education. Second, a national educational infrastructure—which, with suitable modifications, could manage and guide change for the better—has been created. Third, there are signs that the political system is not impervious to the need for reform. The Ministry of Education has initiated moves to make the 8:4:4 curricula more manageable. After the 1990–1991 peak in university enrollments, the government, with World Bank prodding, agreed to slow down the intake and to orient it more toward science and technology courses. Fourth, the tradition of parental and communal involvement in the financing and management of public institutions, coupled with the growth of a private sector in education, constitute a sound base for development of well-organized participation at the local level.

Fifth, there are signs of donor recognition of the importance of active indigenous involvement (World Bank 1988), and thus the possibility exists that donor aid could be integrated into locally developed and internalized programs. Sixth, the Kenyan economy is receptive to the technological changes taking place elsewhere. New technologies have taken root in agriculture, manufacturing, business, research, and public management. This guarantees continuation of a lively debate on how education and training could help prepare beneficiaries for the emerging modern economy. Last and most important, with the reintroduction of multiparty politics in 1992, Kenya is witnessing the beginnings of a system of governance that could foster transparency and accountability in the management of public affairs. The new approach to governance could meaningfully devolve the management of public affairs, including education, to local government and thus enhance wider participation. Above all, political transparency and accountability should mean increased awareness of the dangers of continued inequity in educational opportunities.

TANZANIA: EDUCATION FOR SELF-RELIANCE

Education policy and development in postindependence Tanzania can be divided into three phases, which we may call the national consolidation phase (1961–1966), the socialist phase (1967–1982), and the "crisis and adjustment" phase, which continues to date.

The initial postindependence phase saw the nationalist takeover of the colonial schools, which were racially segregated, unevenly distributed throughout the country, in part fee-paying, largely run by Europeans and Christian churches, and externally oriented in ideology, quality, and certification procedures. The first African government of Tanganyika therefore took the usual postindependence measures to consolidate national, i.e. African, control of the education system. These included the abolition of racial and religious segregation, the nationalization of curricula and examinations, some attempts to reduce inequalities in school coverage, changes in curriculum, and the partial abolition of fees (Morrison 1976).

During this period the main preoccupation of the government was to train personnel to take over administrative responsibilities from the departing European and Indian bureaucrats and managers. The speed of this transition put severe limits on the ability of the state to implement ambitious and radically new policies in the education and other sectors. As in Kenya, this first period was characterized by mass popular enthusiasm for education and, in the few areas where primary school enrollments were already high, for more secondary schooling. Official policy favored "closing the manpower gap"; consequently, spending on primary education fell relative to other sectors during this first phase. Equity issues were limited to desegregating the few racially exclusive schools.

The second phase corresponded to the adoption of a socialist political orientation and the publication of *Education for Self-Reliance,* which became an integral part of the Tanzanian socialist development strategy. Equity—which placed basic education for all citizens before secondary and higher education for the few—was one of the central concerns of ESR policy. Nyerere built up a considerable constituency for his egalitarian reforms both at home and abroad. The less developed regions and ethnic groups came to benefit from a geographical quota allocation of the limited number of secondary school places. The quota system and other initiatives also helped Nyerere subordinate the more educationally and socially advanced areas, especially Kilimanjaro and Kagera, to central state power. Commentary by local and foreign observers was generally highly supportive of ESR. But few politicians, middle-class parents, cash crop farmers, or bureaucrats had any prior warning of or subsequent sympathy with a policy that directly challenged their own and their children's educational ambitions.

ESR was without doubt one of the most systematic attempts in the Third World to mold a cooperative, nonelitist, adaptive (to local economy and culture), and socially leveling education structure. With the benefit of hindsight, it is relatively easy to identify the theoretical and practical weaknesses of ESR. The economic crisis of the 1980s, the rise of World Bank/IMF structural adjustment policies stressing cost-effectiveness and sustainability, and the evident shortcomings of ESR all served to undermine the policy. A presidential commission appointed in 1980 recommended a more technically oriented and less ideological education policy. The commission's report cleared the way for the expansion of secondary, including private, education. But the move away from ESR has only been partial, and a number of major equity features of the system still remain, including the district/gender selection quota for Form 1 entry.

The 1980s witnessed a deepening financial and managerial crisis in the state sector, which led to both internal and external pressures to loosen central control of the education system. These pressures revealed the central authorities' weakness in formulating policy, establishing priorities, and planning effectively. The vested interests, lack of accountability, and low functional capacity of the national education bureaucracy posed major obstacles to progress. Inefficiency and corruption increasingly undermined popular confidence in the state's ability to deliver services, including education.

There has been a defensive reaction on the part of the national bureaucracy to retain its hegemony and dwindling legitimacy. However, the nongovernment pressure groups needed to bring about effective decentralization and quality control in educational finance and management have not yet crystallized. For the moment, the national bureaucracy still exercises relatively unchallenged formal control over the administration of the school system, despite the reintroduction of local councils, the mushrooming of private secondary schooling, and other signs of liberalization. It is somewhat premature, therefore, to characterize the present "post-ESR" phase of policy adjustment as successful liberalization or the reassertion of a more "bourgeois" or technocratic ideology. To do so would be to exaggerate the degree to which ESR was "socialist" (rather than nationalist, populist, and statist) in the first place, as well as the degree to which the "post-ESR" phase represents a really fundamental break with the past. The central government continues to monopolize educational functions that could be better performed by local governments, community-based organizations, and the private sector.

Implementing Education for Self-Reliance: 1967–1982

The first significant feature of the ESR period (1967–1982) was the strong orientation toward expanding basic education. This period saw attempts to make primary education terminal, as well as curriculum reforms and the introduction of nonexamination assessment of performance. It was also the period of important campaigns to achieve universal primary education (UPE) and eradicate illiteracy, neither of which proved sustainable.

The second feature was the restriction of expansion in the postprimary sector and the introduction of nonacademic recruitment criteria. The limited number of Form 1 places in government boarding schools were allocated on a district/sex quota basis, a system that spread opportunities to educationally more backward parts of the country and drastically diluted the quality of Form I entrants. After 1974, recruitment to the University of Dar es Salaam was dependent on the completion of two years of postschool employment, mandatory national service, official sponsorship, and party vetting. The number of mature entrants rose rapidly as a result, and the ability of students fell. Secondary and postsecondary educational opportunities were increased at a rate thought to be commensurate with the national need for appropriately qualified manpower.

Fundamental influences on educational quality can be traced to the redistributive aspects of ESR and the progressively debilitating effects of the economic crisis on educational budgets. The proportion of the recurrent budget going to education grew from 20 to 24 percent during the 1970s (Carr-Hill 1984: 13) but fell back to only 10 percent during the 1980s (World Bank 1991c: 3). Resource constraints became so severe during the 1980s that stagnation in official enrollments and continuing qualitative decline went hand in hand. By 1987, real per capita expenditure on education was only two-thirds the level of 1975 (World Bank 1991: 4).

The implementation of ESR led to a rapid growth of primary enrollments during the late 1970s but sluggish growth at secondary and postsecondary levels. Total primary enrollments increased from under half a million in 1961 to three-quarters of a million in 1967, then doubled to a million and a half in 1975. Standard 1 enrollments increased by nearly 75 percent between 1976 and 1978 (to 878,000) but have stagnated at between 500,000 and 600,000 ever since. Between 1978 and 1988 the proportion of seven- to thirteen-year-olds attending school fell by over 20 percent. In 1988 district-level enrollments of this age group varied between 30 and 70 percent (TADREG 1992), indicating large and growing inequalities. The leveling effects of UPE have been steadily eroded.

The surge in primary enrollments contrasts with a mere 54 percent increase in secondary enrollments between 1967 and 1975. By the time the report of the presidential commission was published (1984), secondary enrollments were just under 70,000. Following UPE, only 3 percent of primary school leavers went on to secondary school, surely one of the lowest rates in the world. The policy of terminality was successful in this respect. Moreover, the reform of university entrance regulations in (1974), caused the number of female and science undergraduates to fall significantly. Enrollments at the University of Dar es Salaam rose from 1,894 in 1974 to 2,980 in 1982. In 1990, total university enrollments in the country were still only 3,210—less than in 1984. The overall decline in the quality of secondary education has meant that adequately qualified school leavers for higher education are falling in number, especially in science and applied science subjects. In spite of the relaxation of entry requirements, the proportion of girls at the University of Dar es Salaam fell from 21.3 percent in 1980 to 18.8 percent in 1990 (Malekela, Ndabi, and Cooksey 1990). Total teacher college enrollments also fell, from 17,500 in 1980 to 16,300 in 1991. In 1991, one-third of the nation's forty-two training colleges had enrollments less than 80 percent of capacity (World Bank 1991c: 29). Three-quarters of public secondary teachers hold only diplomas, and forty percent of private secondary teachers are only trained as primary school teachers.

Adult literacy was a major component of the ESR policy and a focus of considerable government and donor investment over the years. Officially, by the late 1980s over 90 percent of adults had acquired basic literacy, but there is strong evidence that these figures were not far from the realm of fantasy. The last national literacy examination results were canceled after complaints of irregularities. In many parts of the country, the official literacy program has effectively ceased (TADREG 1993). In 1993, the Minister of Education admitted for the first time that literacy levels had started to fall.

ESR has given all districts an equal chance of obtaining secondary school places. An analysis of examination results in 1985 showed that in Kinondoni District of Dar es Salaam, a male candidate had to score 63 percent to gain admission to a government secondary school, whereas a girl from Dar es Salaam Rural District ònly needed to score 40 percent. Less than 1 percent of girls in Mtwara Region's rural districts managed to score 50 percent in the examination, compared to about 20 percent of boys in Dar es Salaam. Currently the "quota system is under review to determine if it can fulfill its objectives without unduly penalizing high achieving students" (Tanzania 1992d: 5). The pressure for expanded private secondary schooling in educationally advanced areas during the 1980s probably reflected in large part the frustration of above-average students blocked by the quota system. But the extremely poor quality of most private schools may prevent many capable students from realizing their full potential.

Partly because of the quota system's impact on quality, three-quarters of Form 4 students did not proceed to Form 5—and this in a highly selective system where, until recently, only a minute percentage of primary leavers could obtain secondary school places. For a population of 25 million, Tanzania had only 10,500 upper secondary (Form 5 and 6) students. The most regrettable aspect of ESR is that it managed to combine extremely high-cost boarding school education with extremely mediocre academic achievements. Transport and catering costs accounted for a disproportionate share of the secondary education budget. As part of current cost-sharing policies, parents with children in boarding schools are now expected to cover these nonacademic costs. The government is under pressure to abandon the boarding school system in favor of lower-cost day schools.

ESR was designed to make primary schooling terminal, agriculture-based, and relevant to the needs of the village community. In practice, however, the only lasting (and generally unpopular) innovation has been the school farm. Former President Nyerere has admitted the failure of ESR: "There are very few, if any, primary or secondary schools where this policy has been applied to the full." As regards parents, "too many of them believe that their children are simply being used as laborers for the benefit of the teachers" (*Daily News* 1983). A recent village-level study of attitudes toward primary education (TADREG 1993) found generalized disillusionment among parents. The majority thought that standards were falling; that children did not learn very much in school; that teachers were incompetent, underqualified, and undisciplined; and that secondary school places were increasingly monopolized by the children of the rich.

The promotion of Kiswahili has been rightly praised as one of the nation-building achievements of the Nyerere years. However, the abrupt transition from Kiswahili to English at entry to Form 1 created serious learning problems for most students, for whom English was an increasingly unfamiliar foreign language. As fewer and fewer secondary school teachers (and almost no primary school teachers) speak English easily, the de facto secondary school language of instruction is Kiswahili.

Hailed as a breakthrough in educational theory and practice, *Education for Self-Reliance* had one fundamental flaw: It did not correspond to the way in which the population at large—rich and poor, urban and rural, young and old—perceived the utility of formal education. The needs of the population were defined for them, without consultation. Parents who withheld their children from school or allowed them to drop out prematurely were said by head teachers, regional commissioners, and ministers alike to be ignorant of the value of education.

State Responses to the Educational Crisis in the 1980s

The economic downturn documented in Chapters 4 and 5 of this volume was a major cause of deterioration in the education sector. But even without the crisis, overall educational quality and efficiency would have seriously declined as a result of ESR. In this section we deal with the official response to the crisis in relation to educational finance, the introduction of cost sharing, and the opening of secondary schooling to more private initiatives.

Until recently, official per capita resources allocated to education were falling steadily for a decade or more. Inflation and falling tax income meant large shrinkages in recurrent and capital budgets across the board, the major cause of declining per capita spending on education. Expenditure per primary pupil is said to have fallen by more than a third between 1980 and 1987 (Wagao in Cornia et al. 1992: 34). Moreover, relative spending on education seems to have gradually declined throughout the postindependence period. Whereas many countries, including Kenya, continue to invest up to a quarter of recurrent budgets in the education sector, Tanzania managed less than 10 percent in 1988/89, down from 15 percent in 1983/84 (Andersson and Rosengart 1988, quoted by World Bank 1991c: 3). In recent years, the downward trend seems to have been reversed in both absolute and relative terms, as the government has made a concerted effort to channel more recurrent finance into the social sectors. The 1990/91 budget allocated 13 percent of recurrent expenditure to education. The goal is to raise the education budget to 20 percent of current expenditure and to "allocate an appreciable proportion to basic education" (Tanzania 1992d: 4).

Apart from increasing spending on primary education, the Tanzanian government responded to the educational crisis in a number of ways. Understandably, it underplayed the depth and seriousness of the crisis itself. Until recently, the party-state leadership continued to cite UPE and adult literacy as enduring development gains and to treat the crisis as a largely exogenous financial problem. The education authorities tended to concentrate on second-order priorities, continuing to expand rather than to reform the system. Its areas of focus included promoting community secondary schools at the district level (when such schools are already supported), introducing an open university (when many present university places are unfilled), and opening schools for especially gifted children (when schools for ordinary children are generally below minimum standards). Recent policy statements have emphasized achievement of UPE and universal literacy by the year 2000, but there has been little or no discussion of where the resources are to come from or how resource utilization is to be improved to realize these laudable but overambitious objectives. Currently, less than 10 percent of seven-year-olds are enrolled in Standard 1 (TADREG 1992).

The policy of cost sharing took on special importance in the late 1980s and early 1990s as a way of reducing financial shortfalls in the education sector. Donor agencies had been advocating this policy for some time, although parents had been paying fees and other charges for a number of years. UPE was partly financed out of a flat-rate contribution, which parents continued to pay. More important, parents were now expected to cover most of the cost of primary school construction and maintenance, desks and school materials, examinations, and numerous other items. Parental contributions to primary schooling may have been as large as government expenditure on the sector (TADREG 1993). Secondary school fees were reintroduced in 1984. By 1991 boarders were required to pay a high proportion of the cost of their transport and accommodation, one of a number of sources of conflict between the state and students at the University of Dar es Salaam in the last two years.

The issue of cost sharing was ideologically and emotionally charged in Tanzania, where the children of the poor are not supposed to be excluded from education. The rural study cited above (TADREG 1993) found that parents were not against the idea of paying for education, but they complained bitterly that they were not getting value for money. Their contributions tended to disappear into school and local government coffers with no impact on the quality of services.

Cost sharing, though a visible and controversial issue, was nevertheless only one of a number of fundamental unresolved issues facing Tanzanian education. The government responded to the financial crisis by increasing educational spending and encouraging more parental and community contributions. But the major structural constraints on educational efficiency and quality—lack of official accountability, divided administrative responsibilities, overcentralization of decisionmaking—remained largely unresolved.

For many, the only solution was withdrawal. Wealthy or influential families opted out of the national education system; the rest adapted to declining standards as best they could. Increasing numbers of rural and poor urban parents gave up on the school system, as suggested by declining enrollment ratios over the last decade. In some cases rising costs may have been the crucial factor; in many others, the apparent futility of sending children to school (in terms of learning useful skills or competing for secondary school places) led parents to seek other options. Rural communities with the financial and organizational means took steps to prevent declining quality; those with neither money nor organization watched as the village school literally collapsed before their eyes.

While primary enrollments stagnated, secondary enrollments have more than doubled. Most of the increase was concentrated in private schools, which now account for 57 percent of all secondary enrollments compared to 42 percent ten years ago. The combination of rapidly falling primary enrollment and rapidly rising secondary enrollment suggests that a very significant process of social differentiation has been taking place.

The expansion of secondary enrollments, especially rapid after 1984, has been explained in terms of a pent-up social demand for secondary schooling resulting from increased primary enrollments under UPE (Samoff 1987). A cursory perusal of enrollment trends is sufficient to disprove this assessment. There *was* a growing demand for more secondary schooling, but this demand was and is highly concentrated among certain social classes, certain regions, and certain ethnic groups. Poor rural parents turned away from primary eduction just as the better-off urban parents began pressuring for new secondary schools for their sons and daughters. To date, this hugely significant class phenomenon has not been systematically analyzed.

In recent years, official education policy moved from an emphasis on comprehensive state controls and relatively "free" education toward greater reliance on private/community schooling initiatives. Reforms during the last decade included greater freedom for church, NGO, community, cooperative, and other non-state educational initiatives; the introduction of substantial fees and other official charges, especially in higher education ("cost sharing"); and (proposed) devolution of power from the center to lower levels within the official system (Tanzania 1992d). These policies were partly a response to popular pressures for liberalization in the face of the evident inability of the state to finance and run the school system effectively. They also reflected pressure from donor agencies, especially the World Bank.

These recent changes raise the question of whether a process of privatization might help reverse the long-term decline of Tanzanian education but limit education to those who can pay. Most institutions in the country reflect the ideology of state-party hegemony, so it is difficult to distinguish strictly between "public" and "private" domains. Many key actors increasingly "straddle" the two sectors. For example, a number of national and district trust funds have prominent national and local politicians as patrons, whereas their boards of trustees may include district and village councils, cooperative societies, party and government dignitaries, and donor organizations. None of these can be termed "private." Donors (including churches, NGOs, and volunteer organizations) often channel monies and personnel directly through trust funds, thus bypassing the central government. Those best placed to solicit donor support include national-level politicians and civil servants in the forefront of the NGO movement, which has grown rapidly in the last few years. The recently established National Education Trust Fund, which gives grants for the expansion of private secondary schools, was established and is funded by donors under the current World Bank/IDA education loan to Tanzania.

This private/public ambiguity does not mean there are no authentic community or other private (mainly nonprofit) initiatives setting up and running schools, nor does it suggest that civil servants and politicians cannot in certain circumstances represent interests other than those of the central state apparatus. Many districts or wards in the country have education trusts organized by their local elites, with those in Dar es Salaam playing a critical role in mobilizing finance, official recognition, and even donor assistance (e.g., volunteer teachers). The personal commitment of these elites decreases the likelihood of misuse of educational funds, which is a danger when these are managed by cooperatives or the ruling party. Nevertheless, finding good teachers, managers, and accountants poses formidable problems to nongovernment secondary schools. Parallels with the Harambee practiced in Kenya during the 1970s are worth noting.

Certain collective attempts to maintain quality can be briefly cited. Organized pressure can be applied to protect certain state schools against invasion by the masses, but there is little elite parents can do collectively to prevent the invasion of the few quality schools by other members of the elite. Conscientious and determined parents' associations can contribute to the upkeep of classrooms and book supply, keep local education officers on their toes, and find ways to appoint the best teachers and heads to "their" schools. Though not well documented, there appears to be a creeping privatization of primary education in some areas, and elite parents can use influence to get their children places in the high-fee private schools, where demand for places outstrips supply.

Individually, parents can take certain measures to improve the chances that their children will obtain Form 1 places in a government secondary school. One is to transfer a child to a school in the local regional or district headquarters, where there are more day-school opportunities outside the quota system and where standards are higher than in the village school. Another is to repeat Standard 7 and take the leaving examination a second time, an illegal but widespread practice. Less legitimate, but apparently increasingly common, is the manipulation of the selection process itself. The nontransparency of the examination system (individual and school-level results are never published) has led to widespread accusations of systematic cheating, particularly in the early 1990s, involving senior politicians and all rungs of the education bureaucracy. Illicit practices include selling examination papers, giving answers to selected pupils, and changing names and papers between successful and unsuccessful candidates.

Declining standards have pushed some wealthier parents to send their children to better schools elsewhere, Kenya being a popular choice. But very few parents can afford to do so. In general, middle-class parents have not been able to guarantee their children as good an education as they enjoyed themselves. The leveling forces of ESR have been so powerful that many English-speaking parents have Kiswahili-speaking children (although there are also ideological explanations for this phenomenon—middle-class Tanzanians are much more "indigenized" than their Kenyan counterparts when it comes to language). Educated but poor parents look on resignedly as their children receive an increasingly substandard education in over-crowded and underequipped classrooms with underqualified and poorly motivated teachers.

Not surprisingly, the best schools and teachers are to be found in urban centers, especially Dar es Salaam. Competition is high for places in public day schools. Although the poorest of the poor are marginal to the school system, the children of the working masses aspire to obtain secondary school places. In urban areas it is normal for primary and secondary teachers to offer tuition classes after school hours. They use the same classrooms and often teach the same students—albeit to those who can pay the additional fees. Tuition is against official policy, but it is one way in which some teachers supplement their meager salaries.

Church-owned secondary schools were nationalized in 1974. Once elite, high-quality establishments, they have succumbed to the downward pressure on educational quality and are now suffering from the same crisis as the rest of the system. Only seminaries—which have traditionally provided high-quality academic education—have kept up some semblance of quality; almost all of the top ten schools in terms of examination performance are junior seminaries. The most sought-after private schools for girls are run by the Catholic church. A few private schools are considered worth the extra fees even for children who are successful in the national examination.

In recent years, steps have been taken by the Christian churches, both Protestant and Catholic, to take back ownership of some of the schools and colleges nationalized earlier. Government policy seemed to support the move. In 1992 President Mwinyi announced that the government was prepared to return church schools to their former owners. Within a week he retracted the announcement, supposedly because a local Muslim cultural organization (known by its Kiswahili acronym of BALUKTA) had protested that such a move would lead to the exclusion of Muslim students from church schools. Religion has become a source of political cleavage in Tanzania in recent years, and the need to redress educational inequalities between Muslims and Christians has become a sensitive issue.

Trends in Educational Inequality

From independence to the present, the Tanzanian state has attempted to use educational policy to reduce the potential for social conflict which educational and class inequalities related to ethnicity and religion may incur. In practice, state control has always been only partial, and inequalities between rich and poor families, regions, and religions have grown steadily. By 1991 well over half of all secondary students (56 percent) were attending private schools (Tanzania 1992e). In 1990 five of the twenty mainland regions accounted for 59 percent of all private schools, the bottom twelve regions only 24 percent. Thus, although government schools were more or less evenly distributed throughout the country, private school expansion was extremely uneven. Moreover, by 1992 46 percent of private secondary schools were run by Christian churches, whereas less than 6 percent were run by the official Muslim organization, BAKWATA (Malekela, personal communication).

A recent survey of students in six southern and central regions found that half the private school students had fathers with secondary education or above, compared to only a third of public school students (Cooksey 1991). A rough indication of social selection trends among students attending government schools can be obtained by comparing the 1991 survey results with an earlier study of Form 4 students (Malekela 1983). Table 7.3 shows a clear trend favoring the children of more educated urban parents in gaining access to government secondary schools. The selection process among boys and girls reflected the inequalities described above. With the help of the quota system, girls represented 42 percent of Form 1–4 students in government schools in1992, whereas in private schools girls took up nearly half (47 percent) of all Form 1–4 places (Tanzania 1992e). Few parents would send their daughters to secondary school before their sons, so many of the girls attending private schools likely had brothers who are also in school. Only educated and/or monied families were in a position to send all or most of their children to secondary school.

Table 7.3 Parental Characteristics of Form 4 Students Attending Government Schools, 1980 and 1990

	Students' fathers			Students' mothers		
	1980	1990	Change (%)	1980	1990	Change (%)
Primary education or less	83	64	–23	94	75	–20
Farmers	57	36	–37	80	45	–44
Employees	13	33	+154	–	–	–
Businessman	10	17	+70	3	8	+167

Sources: Malekela (1982), Cooksey (1991).

From the available evidence, it appears that inequalities in access to the country's primary and secondary schools are growing dramatically. Whereas ESR strove to minimize the importance of social origins in determining educational opportunities, latent inegalitarian tendencies have been reinforced by more recent cost-sharing, private schooling, and community participation policies. The repeated claim that the rising demand for private secondary schooling is a general phenomenon cutting across class boundaries is difficult to defend empirically (Samoff 1987, 1990).

Educational Reform in the 1990s

Donor assistance now plays an increasingly crucial role in the Tanzanian education system. In the last decade, donors have pushed for major policy reforms as conditions for further assistance. As in other sectors, this shift toward conditionality reflects the evident failure of past policies—and of donor support. Although the financial muscle of the donor agencies is considerable—they spent an estimated U.S. $46 million in the education sector in 1992—it has yet to be demonstrated that their policy options can be implemented successfully (DANIDA 1993). Donors have made further aid dependent on major policy reforms in educational finance, division of responsibilities between central and local government, and changes in the private and NGO sectors. But with the partial exception of increased user charges, no major reforms have been implemented to date. The national authorities are more concerned with keeping the besieged education system afloat than with initiating major policy changes. Moreover, such changes affect their own vested interests, offend populist principles, and might encounter resistance from teachers, parents, or students. Despite the lack of progress, donors continue to start new projects and finance a substantial share of recurrent expenditure.

The growing policy influence of donors—particularly but not exclusively the World Bank—stems from the fact that they are much more aggressively reform-oriented and better equipped with staff and money to undertake basic policy research and analysis than the Tanzanian authorities. Indeed, the latter have major problems in undertaking critical policy analysis and coming up with a realistic reform policy. This vacuum has been filled in the short run by donor assistance, but because the proposed reforms are not locally "owned," they are more likely to fail.

Throughout the postindependence period, donors have helped erect physical structures but have failed completely to build institutions. Throughout the late 1970s and early 1980s, donors became increasingly aware of the serious institutional and policy limitations to project implementation, but these were ignored for many years. Poor or negative performance and the misuse of aid were not sanctioned for extended periods. The

World Bank is the only donor to date to reflect frankly on its past failures in the Tanzanian education sector. "Within a two year period [after independence] most of the optimistic judgments about absorptive capacity made in the first country review were thrown into doubt. . . . In sector after sector and report after report, the capacity to identify, plan and implement projects and to manage and operate completed projects was described as being extremely poor" (World Bank 1990). Other major criticisms of the World Bank's review of its education sector projects in Tanzania include: lack of a well-conceived and consistent strategy for selecting project components; overabundance of donor funds, which led to a "scrambling for bits and pieces to support in different programs"; a disastrous secondary diversification program, which was foisted on a reluctant government and failed in part as a result of "Bank pressure to move faster"; technical assistance personnel, who typically arrived late and were not fully utilized by the government; late completion of projects; inadequate supervision during implementation; and lack of meaningful dialogue with local actors on policy issues.

The donor-backed package for education in the 1990s includes the following: establishing a sustainable financial base for the education system via increased user charges and other community or individual contributions; raising teachers' salaries and offering other incentives; improving teacher training and the supply of teaching materials to schools; building capacity for central planning, policymaking, research, and management; enlarging the role of private schools; removing state monopolies in book writing, production, and distribution; and decentralizing educational management. The donors intend to mount a large joint program of support to basic education, including the financing of recurrent expenditure. This is not as radical a departure as it may seem. Donor support, though generally underreported in government budgets, already accounts for the lion's share of both recurrent and development expenditure (Daun and Fagerlind 1991). A number of donors, including the Dutch and the Danish, are beginning to channel education support directly to districts, thus avoiding the central authorities. It is not obvious that the "absorptive capacity" of local governments is superior to that of the central authorities, however, and pumping relatively large amounts of money into selected districts raises the tricky question of equity. The World Bank continues to launch ever larger and more ambitious projects despite its own recognition of Tanzania's poor implementing capacity.

With or without donor pressures, it is not clear how a nonaccountable and overcentralized education bureaucracy can be expected to initiate radical reforms, whatever their scope or ideological content. Such questions are bound up with the nature of the political economy and the effectiveness of the still embryonic democratic challenge to the present power structure. It is probable that major educational reforms will only occur when there are radical changes in the balance of political forces. Donor interests and pressures can affect the process but cannot determine outcomes. For the amount of aid they contribute to education, the donors have remarkably little influence over what goes on. Rather, they continue to heavily subsidize the non-performing central authorities and monopoly parastatals. The World Bank—concerned to move ever larger amounts of project money—is the worst offender.

In recent years, "donor fatigue" has set in, the result of providing long-term support for essentially nonviable institutions. Some bilateral agencies have already announced their intended total or partial withdrawal from Tanzania. Such a trend would further increase the strategic importance of the multilateral agencies, in particular the World Bank. But unless the Bank undertakes major reforms of its own, it is highly improbable that such a development would yield positive results.

LESSONS AND DIRECTIONS

In both Tanzania and Kenya, the central tenets that governed education policy in the last twenty years have been steadily discarded. Kenya, having gone through the rapid expansion of secondary education on which Tanzania is now embarking, faced an irresistible demand for wider access to higher education, which resulted in the creation of four new universities and a doubling of student enrollment in the space of five years. At the same time, the continuing pressure on secondary school places from a growing primary school–age population, arrival at the extreme limits of available public financial resources, and expanding unemployment led the Kenya government to introduce its 8:4:4 policy, ostensibly designed to foster self-employment.

The theory, particularly at the primary level, had much to commend it. However, it was introduced too hastily, without adequate planning or public discussion and with a woeful shortfall of resources necessary to sustain it. The main result has been a comprehensive decline in the quality of education and massive public disaffection with the educational system as a whole. With ever-increasing momentum, the Kenyan elite are opting for private education at ever lower levels of the system—private schools that do not follow the Kenyan curriculum at all and that lead inexorably to further education in Europe, North America, or South Africa. At the primary level, poor parents in Kenya's rural areas are, as in Tanzania, beginning to lose faith in the value of education, and enrollment ratios are beginning to fall. At the upper levels, a class-based system of public and private education is steadily becoming entrenched.

In Tanzania, pressures to scrap the ESR policy built up early among elite and middle-class parents, and the policy was gradually abandoned, especially after 1982, although its legacy is still in evidence. The rapid expansion of mostly private, low-quality secondary schools reflects the nature of contemporary class formation in Tanzania: a relatively small group of mainly urban, middle-class parents highly committed to extending educational opportunities to their children, and a much larger group of mainly rural and poor urban parents opting or being forced out of the educational system. Poverty (especially in the less developed rural areas), user charges (including school fees), and a decline in the perceived utility of formal education help account for this mass rejection of public education, which has yet to be officially acknowledged. The seriousness of Tanzania's educational crisis can be gauged from the depressing fact that today only about half the school-age population is going to school. Attempts to eliminate illiteracy have also been largely unsuccessful.

In Tanzania the most successful educational policies since independence have been in the field of political socialization. Curriculum changes, the use of Kiswahili in primary school, the district quota for secondary school entrance, the opening of universities to adult students, and the national boarding school system have probably had a considerable long-term integrating effect. But the price paid in terms of falling educational quality has been enormous. Also, increasing class-related educational selection may erode these gains in the present era of relative decontrol. The high degree of overlap between class, religious, ethnic, regional, and gender inequalities makes education a potential minefield for future politicians and policymakers.

For Kenya the broad measures of success lie in the management of rapid growth and the quality of school provision of the early years of independence, the breadth and depth of later forms of expansion, and the extension of opportunity to previously unserved areas. The lack of educational attention to the idea of nationhood in a context of increasingly charged ethnic division, the creeping departure from merit criteria, and the academic mediocratization of the system that has followed unplanned expansion with inadequate resources are prominent on the debit side of the educational ledger.

Although girls' enrollments have improved relative to boys' up to Form 4, their position has actually declined in absolute and relative terms in both countries from Form 5 to the university level. Girls are overconcentrated in private, generally poor quality, secondary schools. Improving educational quality is of paramount importance if investment in education is to pay off, particularly in regard to the developmental benefits derived from educating girls. Likewise, improvement in science, technology, and math instruction must be high on the agenda for both Kenya and Tanzania if they are to improve the national pool of employable talent.

Though we acknowledge some of the impressive achievements of educational development in both Kenya and Tanzania, we have found it hard to avoid rather bleak characterizations of the educational scene in both countries after the early, heroic period of ESR and Harambee. Tanzania has one of the most inefficient and low-quality educational systems imaginable. Yet lessons have been learned, and the situation is not static. It is again possible to find grounds for optimism in some of the changing forces and new issues that are beginning to arise.

The emergence of pluralistic politics is certain to release creative energies in education, as in other spheres. However, the achievement of a more diversified politics will take more time than was suggested by the euphoria of its first manifestations. The extent to which communities can meaningfully influence what goes on in their schools will depend upon the extent to which interest groups of different types organize to represent particular educational interests and priorities alongside those of the state.

The erosion of civil service salaries and the flight of competent people to the private sector have reduced the ability of government ministries to implement policies. Likewise, economic liberalization and pluralistic politics are likely to accentuate the decline in the state-run education system as students, teachers, and parents seek new options. At the same time, innovative new educational forms and improved quality are likely to emerge from the variety of new alliances and groupings—churches, mosques, NGOs, private trusts, local communities—that are taking up the challenge of educational provision.

The economies of both Kenya and Tanzania have to improve dramatically on their performance in the last few years if education is to revive. However, much can be achieved through the more efficient use of existing resources. The discipline of the World Bank has been criticized in both countries, but it comes as a necessary counterbalance to the sloppy use of resources that has bedeviled both Kenya and Tanzania. If there was a stronger local constituency for realism, efficiency, and accountability in resource utilization, the World Bank/donor approach to educational reform would not be dismissed as unjustified interference in national affairs, and more productive use of resources might be attained.

In the current state of poverty and indebtedness, donor agencies have become increasingly influential and tend to dominate the policy debate. The trend is toward donor corsortia supporting programs rather than fragmented projects and therefore wielding greater potential influence through the lever of conditionality. The specter of a permanent donor presence and the further erosion of autonomy looms over the education system; the notion of a dialogue between equals is meaningless in a context of dependence. Donors can only play a useful role where their support is ideologically acceptable, where it can be absorbed productively into programs and projects, and where its application is accompanied by a sense of accountability on both sides. Recent educational history in both Kenya and

Tanzania is replete with situations where money was thrown irresponsibly at projects. Fortunately, the seriousness of the situation is beginning to provoke donors to pay more systematic attention to building capacity and developing cadres of responsible policymakers, without which donor funds can have little beneficial effect.

Education achieves developmental goals best by providing general skills to the mass of the population. This is why UPE was a heroic and intelligent goal in Tanzania and should remain a major long-term objective in both countries. Kenya's past investments in education have resulted in a credible 76 percent primary school enrollment ratio, compared to Tanzania's 55 percent. In Tanzania, the lowering of educational standards has left instruction in useful skills, including basic literacy and numeracy, desperately inadequate. In terms of both quality and quantity, Kenya is still a generation ahead of Tanzania with respect to the general educational standard of the population. In this respect, encouraging rather than trying to constrain social demand for education has been a success on its own terms, whereas the opposite approach, adopted in Tanzania, has proven a failure. To be fair, Kenya's more developed economy gave it advantages over Tanzania. But the officially sponsored overexpansion of higher education in Kenya is unsustainable and arguably wrongheaded. Putting a cap on further expansion, however, may lead to popular protest.

New forces are beginning to emerge that will shape the response to the current situation and offer some hope for arresting further decline. Pluralistic politics and market economics are the two most important factors because they will accentuate the breakup of the state-run monopoly that in recent years has so constrained thinking about relevant educational policies in both countries. Better-conceived and -coordinated donor support could also be a force for positive change. For better or for worse, aid to education is going to be a major factor in years to come.

CONCLUSIONS

Kenya and Tanzania now have thirty years of experience with national systems of education designed not simply to create an educated populace but also to provide means of social control, national coherence, and economic growth. In the 1990s, with both countries having committed themselves to political pluralism, education remains at the forefront of the agenda.

The contradiction between quality and equality has been a central tension of educational politics in the two countries and will remain so in the era of pluralism. None of the new political parties in either country has come up with a compelling alternative education policy that attempts to address this contradiction. In a situation where the state remains weak, leaders of whatever political stripe will be tempted to use educational expansion as a populist solution for national problems. Yet there is little hope for sustainable educational expansion in either country without rapid economic growth and an expanding tax base. In Kenya in particular, expansion as a way of incoporating previously undereducated groups would appear to have reached its economic limit. In Tanzania, general expansion would not in itself appear to be an effective means of addressing historical disparities of educational opportunity between Christians and Muslims, and more direct means of affirmative action would be fraught with political risk. The alternative—placing more of the burden for running schools upon parents and communities—runs the risk of worsening inequalities, helping to fuel ethnic conflict in Kenya and potential religious conflict in Tanzania.

Creating an education system that promotes rather than restrains economic development remains a challenge for both Kenya and Tanzania. It makes little sense to expand educational enrollment at all levels if the economy is declining. In both countries the relationship between education and the economy is characterized by too many aspirants for the majority of wage-paying jobs, a curriculum that bears limited relationship to the functional requisites of the employment structure, and a declining capacity to provide high-quality professional expertise for the specialized positions that *are* available. The political implications of these asymmetrical relationships are unemployment, delinquency, crime, reduced security, the rapid growth in street children (which is evident in the urban centers of both countries), and the ultimate specter of urban anarchy. The economic implications of the inevitable conflict between quality and equity are bound up with the political ones. They necessitate some hard choices in the allocation of resources, both within the education sector and between it and other productive sectors.

There can be little doubt that Education for Self Reliance and those sections of the 8:4:4 system related to primary education had a fundamental relevance for both countries, which remain predominantly rural. Though the intention was sound, implementation proved difficult. In neither case was a broad-based consensus on the two ideals achieved, and the incentives were less promotive of terminality and self-employment than they were of the benefits of continuation and accumulated certification.

The leaders of Tanzania and Kenya know that the attainment of an educational system geared to the reinvigoration of rural life requires the revival and meaningful implementation of earlier ideals. However, the realization of these goals will depend upon the degree to which the leaderships of the two countries are willing to pursue serious decentralization and effective systems of local government, which in turn seem more likely to occur under political pluralism than under the aegis of a long-entrenched one-party state. The greater the degree of effective decentralization, the more likely is the achievement of education systems that are diversified rather than monolithic, relevant rather than abstruse, accountable rather than inscrutable, responsive rather than prescriptive, autonomous rather than dependent, and, above all, supportive of rather than threatening to economic development and social cohesion. As they contemplate the twenty-first century, the peoples of Kenya and Tanzania deserve no less from their education systems.

NOTE

1. The new system replaced that inherited from the British which consisted of six years of primary school, four years of ordinary secondary school ("O levels"), two years of advanced secondary school ("A levels"), and three years of university.

8

International Economic Relations, Regional Cooperation, and Foreign Policy

David F. Gordon

The late 1980s and early 1990s witnessed dramatic changes in the external environments facing both Kenya and Tanzania. At the broad level of the international system, the end of the U.S.-USSR confrontation and the subsequent demise of the Soviet Union removed both a major actor in and an entire dimension of the international relations of Africa. In addition, the end of the Cold War interacted with Africa's continuing economic crisis to lead to the increasing marginalization of the continent in global affairs, with ramifications for both Kenya and Tanzania in terms of economic relations and foreign policy (Callaghy 1991).

At the same time, the regional issues that had been the dominant focus of Kenyan and Tanzanian energies were also fundamentally changing, albeit in very different ways. Growing anarchy in much of the Horn of Africa, the emergence of a relatively stable regime in Uganda under Yoweri Museveni's National Resistance Movement, and the gradual resolution of the international conflicts in Southern Africa provided a much less fertile ground for what had been major regional involvements for Kenya (in the Horn) and Tanzania (in Southern Africa).

Finally, their continuing economic crises and growing reliance on international donors limited the will and the capacity of both Kenya and Tanzania to sustain an active role in foreign affairs. It also brought relations with the donors—on issues of both economic reform and (especially in the case of Kenya) political liberalization—to a dominant position in the foreign policy agenda of each country.

The late 1980s and early 1990s mark what can be thought of as the third phase in the evolution of the foreign relations of Kenya and Tanzania. In this phase, international relations are playing a relatively less significant role in both countries than they played during the second period, as the foreign policy agendas of both countries have become more narrow and focused. Especially in Tanzania, which had a proactive approach to international relations in an earlier era, foreign policy has become predominantly reactive.

During the first phase, which lasted roughly from independence until the mid-1970s, there was remarkable continuity in both the issues Kenya and Tanzania faced and in how each country responded. The legacies of colonial rule and narrowly defined regional issues dominated their agendas. Each country, despite some important differences in policy content, undertook an essentially low-key approach to foreign affairs.[1] Much energy was focused on influencing the operations of the East African Community the regional organization created in 1967 to promote regional cooperation (though in practice it became a focal point for regional tension). As regards the broader international system, Tanzania, as part of its overall turn to the left after 1967, attempted to shift away from its close ties to the United Kingdom and the other Western powers. China became a major partner, especially during the building of the Tanzania-Zambia railway. Kenya, by contrast, sought to diversify its linkages among the Western powers and resisted the temptation to seek a "self-reliant" path while attempting to improve its overall position in the international order.

The latter 1970s saw the shift to the second phase in the foreign relations of Kenya and Tanzania. During this period, both countries became much more actively involved in foreign affairs, and the issues on their respective foreign policy agendas broadened and were transformed. In particular, issues relating to the colonial legacy gave way to broader regional and international issues and to relations with the IMF and the World Bank. The global context of this change was marked by the heightened importance of Africa in the geostrategic considerations of the world's superpowers; the rise of militant Third Worldism following the emergence of the Organization of Petroleum Exporting Countries (OPEC) as a powerful global force; and the growing involvement of the IMF and the World Bank in promoting economic adjustment in developing countries. The regional context for the shift to the second stage was the breakup of the EAC, superpower involvement in the growing conflicts in the Horn of Africa and Southern Africa, and the growing personal enmity between Tanzania's president, Julius Nyerere, and the Ugandan dictator, Idi Amin.

During the second phase, Tanzanian foreign policy was proactive on a number of dimensions. Tanzania became an important player in international North-South politics as a major protagonist for the New International Economic Order. In particular, President Nyerere became a spokesman for the newly emboldened South. At the same time, Tanzania played a very active role in the international politics of Southern Africa, becoming a leading force in the Front Line States (FLS) and in the emergence of the Southern African Development Coordination Conference (SADCC) (Tostensen 1982). Tanzania also developed much closer relations with the USSR, whereas its relationship with China, though still very warm, became less substantive. Closer to home, Tanzania embarked on one of the boldest and most controversial initiatives in the brief history of African international relations—the January 1979 invasion of Uganda, which led to the toppling of Idi Amin in April of that year.

Kenya, though less proactive than Tanzania, also expanded its foreign policy horizons during the second phase. If Kenya eschewed an active role in the Third World movement, it did become a more prominent player in the regional conflicts in the Horn and developed a much deeper strategic relationship with the United States. In the 1977–1978 Ogaden War, Kenya gave active support to Ethiopia against Kenya's traditional antagonist, Somalia, despite the presence on the Ethiopian side of Soviet advisers and thousands of Cuban troops. At the same time, partially in an effort to protect itself against Somali irredentism, Kenya substantially increased its ties to the United States and began a much more open identification with the West on Cold War issues. In 1979 Kenya signed an agreement providing the United States access to Kenyan military facilities; in return, Kenya became a major recipient of U.S. military assistance in the 1980s.

THE MARGINALIZATION OF AFRICA

Both Kenya and Tanzania are heavily affected by a general trend in sub-Saharan Africa: the continent's marginalization, both economic and political, in the broader global system, and the increased dependence of African states upon external resources, especially quick-disbursing "nonproject" foreign assistance that eases balance-of-payments pressures and provides budgetary revenues. A range of evidence and data lead to the conclusion that Africa is of decreasing importance to the major actors in the international system, be they the leading Western countries, the newly industrialized states, multinational corporations, or large international banks.

A main part of the reason is economic: Africa produces a declining share of world output, specifically of internationally traded goods. Africa's share of world trade declined from nearly 4 percent in the mid-1960s to only 1 percent in 1990 (IMF 1990). Economic growth in Africa during the past twenty years has been the slowest for any part of the globe. When the continent's population explosion is taken into account, there has been virtually no real income growth in most African countries during this period. Africa's economic sluggishness must be contrasted with phenomenal growth in the newly industrialized countries (NICs) of Southeast Asia, respectable growth in the rest of Asia, the emergence from the debt crisis of much of Latin America, and the opening of new markets in the former communist world. Given these comparisons, Africa's economic performance appears even worse than it actually has been.

In the mid-1970s, during the rise of OPEC, developing countries began to get increased attention from the leading industrial powers, including the United States, by calling for the creation of a New International Economic Order (NIEO). It was widely perceived that OPEC's ability to dramatically push up the price of petroleum presaged the more general rise of "commodity power"—the capacity of primary producer countries to leverage their market influence into international political clout. The institutional mainfestations of the NIEO were the Group of 77 within the UN, the Non-Aligned Movement (NAM), and the UN Conference on Trade and Development (UNCTAD). No sub-Saharan African country played a larger role in the movement for the NIEO than Tanzania, and President Nyerere emerged as one of the most visible international spokesmen for the cause.

As it turned out, though, the rise of OPEC proved to be an exception to actual trends in the global economy and the international division of labor. In fact, commodity-producing countries have been negatively affected by the evolution of the global economy, and African countries have been the most vulnerable and have adjusted the least successfully to these changes. The evolution of the international division of labor has hurt Africa in two ways. First, Africa's traditional commodities—including minerals and other natural resources, tropical beverages, and various agricultural products—are of decreasing importance to an international economy whose leading edge emphasizes postindustrial high-tech commodities and services. Second, other developing countries, especially in Asia, have greatly expanded their production of commodities (e.g., coffee, palm oil, tea) that were once largely produced in Africa. This competition has driven down the value of these commodities and caused African countries to lose market share. The value of this loss in traditional exports since the late 1970s roughly parallels the cumulative value of African debt and is equal to nearly $10 billion per year (Greene 1989). Nor has Africa succeeded in diversifying its export base. Unlike other developing regions, the range of products exported from Africa today is not very different from that of a generation ago.

Lagging export production is both the result of a poor investment climate and the cause of further deterioration in the investment climate. At the time of independence, the productivity of investment in Africa was broadly parallel to that of the rest of the developing world and generally higher than that of the industrialized countries. However, the productivity of investment in Africa now lags well behind all other regions of the developing world; the rate of return on investment has dropped from over 25 percent in the 1960s to an estimated 2.5 percent in the early 1980s (World Bank 1989a).

When the international recession led to a contraction of global lending around 1980, it was not surprising that Africa was the region hardest hit, in relative terms. At that point Africa's economic crisis emerged fully blown.

By the mid-1980s, nonconcessional capital flows to Africa, which had been nearly $10 billion per year in the late 1970s, had dropped to less than $1 billion annually (World Bank/UNDP 1992). Commercial lending and foreign investment in Africa simply ground to a halt. By the late 1980s, with the remarkable transformations in Eastern Europe, radical reforms in several Latin American countries, and significant changes in both of the Asian giants (China and India), Africa was the only area of the world that was neither an existing nor an "emerging" market. For the international private sector (i.e., commercial banks, investment houses, and multinational firms), Africa had quite simply ceased to be part of the picture.

Kenya (and to a lesser extent Tanzania) has been negatively affected by the growing belief in international business circles that Africa is simply a sinkhole that swallows money with little or no long-run return. From the late 1950s through the 1970s, one of the engines of Kenyan growth was its status as a regional center for investment and finance. The strategy of both the colonial regime in the final period of British rule and the Kenyatta government after independence had been to aggressively promote Kenya as the nucleus of a regional economy that stretched north into the Horn, West into Zaire, and as far south as Zambia (Leys 1974). This strategy was quite successful, playing a major role in Kenya's achieving more than 5 percent per annum economic growth between the late 1950s and 1980. But in the 1980s international banks dramatically lowered their presence in Kenya, and a large number of international firms either sold their assets or stopped investing new capital to keep their operations competitive. Although these moves were largely made in response to both domestic Kenyan factors and the weakened regional market in East Africa, the speed and extent of disinvestment was substantially influenced by the "bad neighborhood effect"—the general belief that Africa was simply not a place to make money—and by the strength of alternative geographical markets.

Tanzania, in the aftermath of President Nyerere's 1967 Arusha Declaration, took an essentially hostile attitude to foreign investment and forbade foreign banks from operating in the country. Even before then, the country had a much smaller international investment base than did Kenya. Disinvestment from Tanzania was most rapid in the 1970s and thus preceded the general marginalization of Africa from international capital markets. Tanzania would suffer from these trends again in the late 1980s, when it changed its approach to one of encouraging foreign investment but had virtually no success in wooing new flows from outside East Africa.

If trends in the global economy are one source of Africa's marginalization, the end of the Cold War is another. Especially in the period following the collapse of Portuguese colonialism in the mid-1970s, Africa became caught in the global competition between the United States and the Soviet Union. At the time, most observers of African affairs, as well as a number of African leaders (the most articulate among them President Nyerere), decried the greater entanglement of Africa in the East-West conflict. The most commonly heard analogy was the East African proverb that "when two elephants quarrel it is the grass that suffers." However, it is now clear that there was an upside to the Cold War confrontation as far as Africa was concerned. Although it fueled a number of regional conflicts, especially in Angola and in the Horn of Africa, the very existence of a superpower rivalry kept Africa "on the map" of international relations, fueled interest in the continent within the policy circles of the great powers, and provided a certain degree of influence for a number of African countries. In addition, during the Cold War the great powers abhorred a vacuum and thus tended to act as a force against the spread of major instability, precluding some of the nascent instabilities within African states from developing into major crises of political regimes. Since the end of the Cold War, political vacuums have rapidly developed in a number of regions and countries within Africa—Liberia, the Horn, Zaire and most recently and tragically, Rwanda—without eliciting the "system maintenance" type of response that would have been forthcoming from the Great Powers (and France) during an earlier era (Michaels 1993). Finally, great power interest provided a constraint against lesser powers' ability to "stir the pot" of unrest. Especially significant here are efforts by hard-line countries of the Middle East to exert influence. Ironically, the withdrawal of great power interest may have made individual African countries *more* vulnerable to manipulation by outsiders, particularly other African states and Muslim fundamentalists. As a result, the threat of civil unrest and political decay looms over the entire continent.

Both Kenya and Tanzania were able to operate relatively successfully and profitably in the Cold War setting. In the early and middle 1980s, Kenya was able to establish a strategic relationship with the United States that brought a large volume of military and economic assistance and established a degree of interdependence between the two countries. If the United States was useful to Kenya because of arms and money, Kenya was useful to the United States for access to the Indian Ocean and the Horn of Africa and for the port and airfield facilities at Mombasa and other military bases (Makinda 1983). This interdependence was important, providing Kenya with substantial leverage in relations with the United States, other Western donor nations, and international agencies such as the World Bank.

Tanzania played the Cold War card very differently but with at least equal success. Tanzania viewed the increased intrusions of the superpowers as an even greater reason for strict nonalignment and was critical of the United States and Soviet Union for viewing all events in the world through the East-West lens. But at the same time, Tanzania's position of influence within the Third World and the Non-Aligned Movement, plus its role in the Front Line States and SADCC, gave both superpowers incentives to maintain significant ties. Especially after the fall of Idi Amin, Tanzania became the focal point of Soviet and East Bloc interest in East Africa. In addition,

Tanzania's strong stands on nonalignment and apartheid constituted a major rationale for a very large aid program provided by Scandinavian donors. Thus, as in Kenya, the existence of the Cold War facilitated a degree of interdependence in Tanzania's ties to influential external actors (Gordon 1988).

With the end of the Cold War in the late 1980s, Africa became much less important to the major players in the global system. The main impact in both Kenya and Tanzania has been to remove the degree of interdependence the Cold War brought to their relations with outside powers. Kenya became vulnerable to pressure from the donors to limit corruption, improve its human rights performance, and move to a multiparty system. Tanzania lost influence because of the end of the Cold War, the rapid political changes in South Africa, and the demise of militant Third Worldism in the context of the changing international division of labor. As a result, Tanzania also lost leverage with various international actors and became vulnerable to pressures similar to those that faced Kenya. Each country's response to this new situation will be addressed in detail later in this chapter.

Though Africa is becoming increasingly marginal in the post–Cold War era, it is also increasingly dependent upon international donors. In particular, African countries need foreign exchange to purchase inputs, to maintain even a modicum of debt repayment, and to provide the counterpart funds that finance the operations of governments and enable them to avoid inflationary deficit financing. Between 1980 and 1990, foreign aid as a proportion of GDP for Africa as a whole more than doubled. If Nigeria is excluded, the total amount of foreign aid Africa receives yearly is approaching 10 percent of the continent's GDP (GCA 1993).

Thus, Africa is rapidly emerging as the welfare region of the international economy. The continent's international economic relations are increasingly focused not on issues of trade and investment, as in other global regions, but on issues of foreign aid. Though Africa's share of new global private investment has plummeted, its share of worldwide development assistance has dramatically increased. Nearly one-third of all development assistance now goes to Africa, more than double the proportion Africa received in 1970 (World Bank 1989a). Perhaps the major issue facing Africa in the near future is whether it will be able to sustain this very high level of international resource transfers in the absence of the Cold War setting, with powerful imperatives for shifting aid flows to Eastern Europe and the countries of the former Soviet Union and/or for diminishing the overall level of aid.

Kenya and Tanzania, though not even near the worst cases in Africa, are both increasingly dependent upon foreign public (and highly concessional) resource flows. Of roughly $3 billion in annual foreign exchange income in Kenya, roughly one-fourth is foreign assistance or other public international flows.[2] For Tanzania, of less than $2 billion in total foreign exchange income, approximately half is from foreign public sources.[3] In recent years, Tanzania's foreign aid has been substantially higher than the total net investment, public and private, in the entire economy. Later in this chapter I will examine the international politics of foreign aid for both Kenya and Tanzania.

REGIONAL RELATIONS AND DIPLOMACY

The regional context facing Kenya and Tanzania has also dramatically changed in recent years. The period between the mid-1970s and the mid-1980s saw both countries playing increasingly active roles in regional relations, with Kenya becoming heavily involved in the conflicts in the Horn of Africa while Tanzania became a major player in the international relations of Southern Africa. This period also witnessed growing bilateral conflict between the two countries, followed by a slow and often painful process of rapprochement. In the period since the mid-1980s, in contrast, Kenya and Tanzania have taken lower regional profiles, whereas relations between the two, though not as close as in the early postindependence period, have normalized. The reduced regional activity is the result of three factors: changing regional circumstances; the costs and limitations of regional activism; and the economic crisis and growing dependence upon external resources, which has forced both countries to focus their attention on relations with their major international creditors.

In Kenya's relations with neighboring countries, traditional concerns of territorial security and economic development have predominated. Kenya has generally attempted to maintain friendly and stable relations with its neighbors but has not always been able to do so. It is difficult to have stable relations with unstable neighbors, especially when those nations' leaders (e.g., Somalia's Barre, Sudan's al-Bashir, Uganda's Museveni) have sometimes had hostile aims toward Kenya. But the problem Kenya has faced in its regional diplomacy is partly the result of a degree of Kenyan arrogance stemming both from its colonial legacy as a regional center and from the fact that Kenya until the 1990s has been better able to promote economic development and sustain domestic stability than any of its neighbors. Kenya has sometimes overestimated its own capacities and underestimated the difficulties its neighbors could pose. If the quiet diplomacy of the first period of Kenyan foreign policy had difficulty sustaining a regional context conducive to Kenyan interests, so did the more active approach of the second period.

In contrast, Tanzania's regional diplomacy has gone well beyond the themes of national security and economic development. The goals of meaningful national and continental independence in a more equitable global community have motivated Tanzania's approach to international affairs and led the country to become a key player in the struggle against colonialism and apartheid in Southern Africa. The international stature of former President Julius Nyerere gave Tanzania a role far beyond what its resources and location warranted. In the latter 1970s, Tanzania's consuming involvement in Southern Africa heavily influenced its own behavior in East Africa, in particular the conflict with Ugandan dictator Idi Amin. Nyerere concluded that African states weakened their claim for international support in Southern Africa by their unwillingness to criticize oppressive regimes in black Africa. This conviction led to the Tanzanian army's invasion of Uganda to overthrow Amin in 1979. Though the campaign was a short-term success, its cost and Tanzania's inability to easily extricate itself from Uganda were important factors behind the later retrenchment in Tanzanian regional policy.

Kenya-Tanzania Relations

Relations between Kenya and Tanzania have been marked by a combination of cooperation and suspicion that go back to the days of colonial rule. In the early 1950s, the British created fiscal and monetary arrangements and infrastructure services common to all of East Africa (Newlyn and Rowan 1954). Even then, senior officials of the Tanganyikan colonial government distrusted white settler–dominated Kenya and argued that these interterritorial arrangements did not equally distribute the benefits of cooperation. At independence, the leaders of Tanzania (along with those of Uganda) sought a new basis of regional cooperation; the Kenyan leadership was preoccupied with domestic political conflict and gave little attention to regional issues. All of the new East African leaders (accustomed to working together in the anticolonial struggle) took regional cooperation for granted. They failed to realize that independence would make further regional integration more, rather than less, difficult once separately defined national interests came to the fore.

The Kampala Agreement of 1964 was intended to provide the basis for more balanced cooperation among the three East African states. It sought to limit trade imbalances and to reallocate investment so as to enhance industrialization opportunities for Uganda and Tanzania. The new arrangements were never effectively implemented, and in the following years pressure for a new regional structure grew. In 1967 the East African Community (EAC) was established to "strengthen and regulate industrial, commercial and other relations of the partner states in order that there be accelerated and sustained expansion of economic benefits within East Africa, the benefits of which shall be equally distributed." The three countries agreed to a scheme to equalize trade through the allocation of industries. Four autonomous corporations were set up to manage the railways, harbors, airways, postal services, and telecommunications. The EAC headquarters was established in Arusha, Tanzania.

Although cooperation in the EAC was encouraging in the initial years, relations between the member countries began to deteriorate by 1970. Part of the problem was ideological. Nyerere's 1967 Arusha Declaration led Tanzania to socialism and a self-reliant strategy of development. Two years later, Uganda embarked on a similar policy shift set forth in the Common Man's Charter. These ideological trends reinforced existing divisions within the EAC, where Tanzania (and Uganda) had long felt that Kenya was benefiting disproportionately. Tanzania and Uganda diminished their commitment to the market-expanding elements of the EAC, supporting only the components that were directly preferential.

But despite elements of the EAC Treaty designed to equalize trade and industrialization among the partner states, Kenya continued to dominate interterritorial commerce. As a consequence, the other two partners took protectionist steps. In 1972 exchange controls and import restrictions were reimposed, thus dissolving the common monetary area and weakening the common market arrangements. Financial and personnel restrictions were also placed on the four service corporations, limiting their efficiency. Essentially, nationals of each country became confined to working in their own country. Divergent domestic economic policies put further strain on the cooperative mechanisms: Kenya emphasized growth and continued foreign investment, whereas Tanzania (and Uganda) emphasized redistribution and restricted the role of foreign interests (Ravenhill 1979).

Idi Amin's coup against Ugandan President Milton Obote in 1971 further impaired EAC cooperation. President Nyerere detested Amin from the beginning and refused to meet with him. As a result, the EAC's highest body, the East African Authority (comprising the presidents of the three member countries), did not meet after 1971, precluding any high-level negotiations to rectify problems in the EAC. Uganda's economic collapse under Amin added to the difficulties facing the regional arrangements.

The EAC limped on for several more years, but its weakening performance further eroded the commitment to it among each of the partner states. In 1977, growing ideological conflict and failed brinksmanship by both Kenya and Tanzania led to the actual breakup of the community. By 1976, the four common service corporations faced overwhelming difficulties caused by the cumulative impact of interstate financial restrictions and ongoing political conflicts. By the end of that year, only East African Airways (EAA) remained operational as a community venture, and it was grounded early in 1977. Kenya, believing that Tanzania was in no position to retaliate, set out to form its own national carrier, using equipment from EAA as its core. Tanzania retaliated by closing its five-hundred-mile border with Kenya. In June 1977, the EAC officially died (Potholm and Fredlund 1980).

Both Kenya and Tanzania paid dearly for the collapse of regional cooperation. In absolute and direct terms, Kenya was probably hurt more. Exports to Tanzania dried up, and the border closure shut off the land route to Zambia, which had become a significant importer of Kenyan goods. The demise of regional cooperation was also a significant factor in weakening the investment climate in Kenya, especially in the manufacturing sector, as a large part of Kenya's appeal to investors had been the prospect of a substantial (and expanding) regional market. On the Tanzanian side of the border, the most important immediate impact was the loss of tourism; its most spectacular attractions (e.g., Ngorongoro Crater and the Serengeti) are adjacent to the Kenya border, and Tanzanian tourism had historically depended upon Kenya-based tour operators for the bulk of their clientele. Tanzanian consumers were also hurt when they lost access to many commodities for which there were no consistently supplied alternatives. Over the longer run, the border closure and the demise of the community were important factors contributing to the rise of smuggling and the informal economy in Tanzania, which highlighted the limitations of that country's socialist experiment.

The closure of their common border and the collapse of the EAC led both Kenya and Tanzania to reorient their regional relations. Kenya improved political ties and economic links to Ethiopia and the Sudan, sought new markets in the Middle East, and weakened ties with Israel. Although Kenya had earlier followed the lead of other African states in breaking formal diplomatic relations with Israel, solid commercial and intelligence ties had remained. In the late 1970s, as its trade with the Middle East expanded, Kenya became much more pro-Arab in political orientation. For Tanzania, the collapse of the EAC and Nyerere's extreme dislike of Idi Amin led it to focus its attention on the African regional issue that was most germane to the larger international community—the conflicts in Southern Africa. Later in this chapter I will examine both Kenya's role in the Horn and Tanzania's in Southern Africa.

Just as Idi Amin's successful coup was a key event in the collapse of East African regional cooperation, his removal created the basis for the reemergence of normal relations between Kenya and Tanzania. Until Amin's fall, Tanzania felt that Kenya's continuing trade with Uganda, especially the supply of oil, was propping up Amin. Kenya, for its part, was wary of Nyerere's intentions in moving militarily against Amin, fearing either political instability or possible military encirclement. In October 1978 Amin's forces invaded and occupied the Kagera salient in northwest Tanzania, declaring it to be part of Uganda. Nyerere, infuriated, vowed to drive the Ugandan troops out of his country and get the Organization of African Unity (OAU) to condemn Uganda's aggression. The OAU attempted to mediate the conflict rather than condemning Amin. Now even more enraged, Nyerere decided that unilateral action to remove the strongman was justified. In January 1979 Tanzanian troops, supported by several anti-Amin Ugandan exile groups, began to march on Kampala. Tanzania, expecting Amin's foreign support to erode, hoped to play a limited role in his ouster. The Soviets finally withdrew their military support from Uganda, but Amin successfully sought Libyan military assistance. Tanzania then decided to throw all of its weight into the struggle and sent in a 40,000-man expeditionary force. Amin fled in April 1979, and his regime collapsed (Umozurike 1982).

Over the next six years, Tanzania found it extremely difficult to extricate itself from Uganda. The Tanzanian army couldn't help but become the de facto authority, and Tanzania became caught up in the extremely complicated maneuvering of various anti-Amin forces. It was most closely linked to former president Milton Obote, whom Nyerere felt shared his socialist vision of development. Unfortunately for Tanzania, Milton Obote's second Ugandan government (1981–1984) proved nearly as bloody as Amin's. Whereas Kenya feared that Tanzania was attempting to set up a socialist puppet state in Uganda, Tanzania was in fact going bankrupt because of the Ugandan quagmire. Estimates of the cost of the Ugandan adventure range from $500 million up; there is little question that the affair was one of the primary factors behind the country's financial crisis of the 1980s.

Amin's removal eventually led to efforts by both Kenya and Tanzania to patch up their own conflict. The former recognized that Tanzania's actions in Uganda did not have anti-Kenyan motivations, and its enmity toward Tanzania was also diminished by the death in 1978 of Kenya's founding president, Jomo Kenyatta, and the removal from power of a number of the Kenyan politicians who had been most hostile to Tanzania. For its part, Tanzania, reeling from the financial burden of the Uganda affair, was no longer willing to sustain the costs of the border closure. In addition, Dar es Salaam was seeking to present international donors, especially the World Bank and the IMF, with a more pragmatic image to facilitate its access to much-needed resources. In November 1983, an agreement was reached among Kenya, Tanzania, and Uganda on the distribution of the assets and liabilities of the old EAC, and the border between Kenya and Tanzania was reopened. In 1985 President Nyerere visited Kenya, where he was praised by President Moi; shortly thereafter Nyerere stepped down from the presidency and was succeeded by Ali Hassan Mwinyi. Mwinyi accelerated the normalization process, refusing in 1986 to give asylum to several Kenyan dissidents. In the late 1980s Mwinyi and Moi visited each other's capitals, and the border between the two countries again became wide open (Gordon 1987).

Although it was quite possible to reestablish normal relations, it has been more difficult to recreate institutions of economic cooperation and integration, despite the stated interests of all parties in doing so. In May 1987, the three former EAC partners agreed to set up a permanent commission on regional cooperation and sought to promote cooperation in transport and communications, scientific research, and commerce and trade. But setting up a commission is one thing; actually reestablishing real linkages of cooperation is quite another. In the period since 1987, there have been literally dozens of meetings at both the political and technical levels among representatives of the three states. But it has been quite difficult to move beyond intent to concrete actions.

In December 1993, the three East African presidents signed a Tripartite Agreement expressing their intentions to speedily reestablish the East African Community. In particular, they committed themselves to freeing up the movements of goods, services, and people across national borders and to coordinating foreign policies. But there are still reasons to be skeptical about the recreation of the EAC. Part of the problem is the unresolved question of what is to be the geographical scope of cooperative efforts. Since the demise of the EAC, other (and broader) regional institutions have moved into the economic cooperation arena. Both Kenya and Tanzania are members of the Preferential Trade Area for Eastern and Southern Africa (PTA), a UN-sponsored group seeking to create a common market stretching from the Horn to Southern Africa. Tanzania is also a member of SADC, the Southern Africa Development Community (formerly SADCC, the Southern African Development Coordination Conference), which promotes economic cooperation among the majority-ruled states in Southern Africa. Is there still a role for a specifically East African form of cooperation? It is not certain that the Tripartite Agreement of December 1993 provides a definitive answer to this question.

Kenya and the Horn of Africa

If the demise of the EAC damaged Kenya's national interests, a more fundamental threat was perceived to the country's north. The northeastern part of Kenya is populated by ethnic Somali and was claimed by Somalia at the close of the colonial era. During the first few years of independence, the Kenyan army fought a low-level counterinsurgency against rebels supported by Somalia. In 1967 a detente was reached between the two countries, but relations again worsened after Siad Barre came to power in Somalia in 1969 and established a nationalist regime with close ties toward the Soviet Union. Somalia renewed its claims to both northeast Kenya and to the Ogaden region of Ethiopia. Joint enmity to Somalia and hostility to Soviet involvement in the region led to very close ties between Kenya and the Ethiopian emperor, Haile Selassie.

In the mid-1970s, a creeping military coup overthrew the imperial feudal oligarchy in Ethiopia and set up a revolutionary regime. The USSR attempted to create a "Pax Sovieticus" between Somalia and Ethiopia but failed; Soviet strategists soon began to tilt toward Ethiopia. In reply, Barre expelled the Soviets and adopted a pro-Western stance. His appeals fell on receptive ears in Washington, and the United States quickly enhanced Somali military strength as a counter to heavy Soviet support for the revolutionary regime in Addis Ababa. In 1977 war broke out between Somalia and Ethiopia in the Ogaden, and nationalist fervor ran high in Somalia. There were several incidents on the Kenya-Somalia border. In Nairobi, geopolitical logic outweighed ideological considerations, and Kenya strengthened ties with the revolutionary government, the Dergue, in Addis. At the same time, Kenya began a military buildup of its own and sought much closer ties with the United States, culminating in the U.S.-Kenya Base Rights Agreement of 1979. Kenya's decision to seek these ties was driven by the expectation that they would both reassure Washington, which was concerned about Kenya's friendliness with the new regime in Addis, and provide a deterrent against Somali efforts to threaten Kenya more directly.

By the early 1980s, Barre's expansionist aims had been effectively rebuffed, and Kenya's relations in the Horn again began to shift. The United States effectively mediated the discord between Nairobi and Mogadishu, and although relations remained cool, Kenya's sense of threat was removed. Kenya had high hopes that an overall easing of tensions in the Horn might provide an opportunity to establish broader, more stable relations with all of its northern neighbors (Bennett 1986). In the second half of 1985, it took the lead in efforts to mediate civil conflict in Uganda, which had never achieved political stability after the fall of Amin. At the same time, Nairobi was actively involved in diplomatic efforts with Addis, Mogadishu, and the government of the Sudan to establish an overall zone of stability in northeast Africa. But Kenya's good intentions and active efforts were to no avail.

By the mid-1980s, all of the existing regimes in the Horn—Ethiopia, Somalia, and the Sudan—were beginning to decay from within. In 1983 the Sudanese president, General Numeiry, imposed the main elements of Sharia law in an effort to preempt Islamic opposition. In April 1985 Numeiry was overthrown, and a period of political instability ensued in the Sudan. The new regime, unlike its predecessor, tried to maintain good relations both with the Sudan's traditional allies, the United States and Egypt, and with Muammar Qaddafi of Libya. However, as time wore on, Libyan influence in Khartoum increased, much to Kenya's chagrin, and by 1989 the Sudan had become fully allied with Libya in opposition to Egypt and the United States. The political evolution in Khartoum inflamed the conflict in the southern Sudan, where the largely Christian population strongly opposed living under an Islamic state. Kenya responded by offering succor to the rebels of the Southern Peoples Liberation Army (SPLA). Relations between Nairobi and Khartoum dramatically deteriorated, as the two governments exchanged accusations about supporting armed insurgents. At the same time, there were increasing signs that Libya was interested in undermining President Moi's regime in Kenya, partially because of Moi's growing ties to Washington and partially because of Kenya's position as the strongest state in the region.

Libya's objective were facilitated by the accord it was able to establish with the new government of Yoweri Museveni in Uganda and by the emerging hostility between Uganda and Kenya. Relations between Kenya and Museveni became strained when the latter's National Resistance Army (NRA) took control of Kampala in December 1985, only weeks after President Moi had succeeded in brokering a peace accord between the still-reigning Okello regime and the NRA. In 1987 tension between Kenya and Uganda rose when reports emerged that Uganda was facilitating Libya's training of Kenyan dissidents. Museveni's motivation in courting Libyan ties is not very clear but may be connected to his early years as a radical nationalist at the University of Dar es Salaam. Over the next several years there were a number of diplomatic and border incidents. In late 1987 Kenya closed the Libyan embassy in Nairobi and expelled the Ugandan high commissioner. Though tensions didn't escalate into armed conflict, relations between Nairobi and Kampala remained chilly. In 1989 tensions again flared up when an unidentified plane dropped two bombs in northern Kenya. Kenyan intelligence believed the plane was Libyan and that it took off from a base in either Uganda or the Sudan. Again tensions eased, only to reemerge in 1991, when the two countries exchanged accusations of impending invasion. In 1992 and 1993, Uganda moved to distance itself from Libya, and the bilateral relationship between Kenya and Uganda substantially improved.

At the same time, Kenya took the lead in regional efforts to mediate the conflict between Khartoum and the rebels in the south. The Khartoum government had become more aggressive in its efforts to Arabize and Islamicize this Christian and animist territory. Regional governments, led by Kenya, attempted to bring all sides together in an effort to end a conflict that had claimed 500,000 lives in the past decade.

In regard to Ethiopia and Somalia, by 1989 Kenya had managed to establish very close relations with each regime. Unfortunately, both were in a state of advanced decay. In Ethiopia, the Dergue faced the dilemma of weakening support from the Soviet Union at a time when the regionally based opposition movements within Ethiopia—in Eritrea and Tigray—were increasingly taking the military initiative. In Somalia, escalating conflict between rival clans reduced the authority of President Barre to the point that he became known as the "mayor of Mogadishu." In 1990 Kenya sought to mediate each of these conflicts but with little result. In early 1991, Barre was forced out of Mogadishu, and Somalia quickly deteriorated into anarchy. In Ethiopia, the Dergue proved incapable of containing the liberation movements and was eventually defeated by them in May 1991. A fragile peace ensued, but fissiparous pressures remain immense, with Eritrea obtaining its independence from Ethiopia in May 1993.

The collapse of Ethiopia and Somalia has led to an influx of approximately 800,000 refugees into Kenya, at the same time creating a vast stock of free-floating weaponry that pays no attention to the formalities of national borders. Though Kenya played very little role in generating the political decay in the Horn of Africa, it has been very vulnerable to it. The deployment of U.S. and UN peacekeeping forces in Somalia in 1993 actually increased the influx of refugees into Kenya and weakened security in Kenya's Northeast Province. When the deaths of U.S. peacekeepers in October 1993 led Western forces to retreat out of Somalia, Kenya became the focal point for negotiations among the warring factions. The Somali warlords reached an agreement in Nairobi in March 1994 to establish a new government in Mogadishu. Whether this will lead to a restoration of order in Somalia is unclear. If it does not, Kenya will remain vulnerable to an influx of both refugees and weapons across its northern border.

Tanzania and Southern Africa

If Kenya redirected its regional involvement into the Horn of Africa following the collapse of the EAC, Tanzania reoriented its involvement toward the conflicts in Southern Africa. From the early days of its independence, Tanzania has played a major role in supporting the liberation struggles in Southern Africa. Since the 1960s, Dar es Salaam has been the headquarters for the Liberation Committee of the OAU and has provided both a diplomatic base and a point of refuge for many of the Southern African liberation groups. Over time, there evolved a close bond between the Tanzanian political leadership and the leadership of the Southern African movements. When the Rhodesian crisis began in 1965, Tanzania helped Zambia overcome its dependence on transportation routes through Southern Africa. In the early 1970s it provided the main rear base for the Front for the Liberation of Mozambique (FRELIMO). Later, Tanzania did the same for the Zimbabwe African National Union (ZANU) and for the African National Congress (ANC) of South Africa. The collapse of Portuguese colonialism in 1975 put the whole future of the region into question and led both the United States and the USSR into a more active role in the subcontinent. This presence, in turn, led the African states to perceive the need for a higher profile. It was this changing context, along with the problems in regional cooperation in East Africa, that encouraged Tanzania to build on its already substantial linkages with Southern Africa to become a leading force in the international diplomacy of that region.

Tanzania became the most important spokesman for the Front Line States (FLS) and a leader in the regional integration activities of the majority-ruled nations in Southern Africa. In the late 1970s, Tanzania played a significant role in bringing about the peaceful settlement of the Rhodesian conflict and the creation of the new state of Zimbabwe in 1980. President Nyerere was the chief designer of the FLS strategy, which combined assistance to and support for the guerrilla struggles with diplomatic pressure on Western powers to play an active role in seeking a negotiated settlement leading to majority rule. Guerrilla warfare was the lever with which to push the United States and the United Kingdom into the negotiation process (Jaster 1983).

At two points during 1979, Nyerere made forceful interventions that kept the protracted Zimbabwe negotiations on track. Early in the year, he warned the United States and the United Kingdom of the dangers of recognizing the "internal settlement" regime of Bishop Muzorewa, at a time when political pressure in both countries was building for such an approach. Later in the year he urged ZANU guerrilla leader Robert Mugabe not to quit the negotiations and resume the armed struggle. Nyerere's role in the FLS, along with his two specific interventions, earned him recognition as one of the architects of Zimbabwe's independence.

Tanzania built upon its role in the FLS to participate heavily in the regional cooperation initiatives in Southern Africa. Tanzania hosted, in Arusha, the first meeting of the SADCC in 1979. SADCC brought together the nine majority-ruled states in Southern Africa with four main objectives: 1) reduce economic dependence upon South Africa; 2) forge links to establish equitable regional integration; 3) mobilize resources to promote implementation of national and regional policies; and 4) secure international support for SADCC's strategy of economic liberation. Though these goals were extensive, SADCC's achievements have been limited. The conference has served two important political purposes: first, structuring a large proportion (some $2.6 billion per year) of the huge flow of foreign assistance to the region; second, providing a forum for exchange of views on economic development among member countries (Gordon 1989). But SADCC has not been successful in generating regional economic cooperation or development in Southern Africa. In the period since 1979, there has been regional economic stagnation, a contraction in trade among member countries, virtually no new private investment, and little change in the dependence of member countries on South Africa. The limited results are in many ways not surprising, as SADCC's primary objective was political: to block the formation of a South African–led "Constellation of States" and to take advantage of the Western donors' willingness to substitute assistance to majority-ruled Southern African states in place of economic sanctions against South Africa. With the astounding domestic changes in South Africa, SADCC faces major challenges concerning its future structure and role.

As the 1980s wore on, Tanzania's ability to play a major diplomatic role in Southern Africa diminished. The Reagan administration in the United States was less willing than its predecessors to accepting Tanzania's leadership role in African diplomacy, especially given Tanzania's opposition to the U.S. regional policy of "constructive engagement" with South Africa. In addition, by the latter years of the decade, Pretoria's approach to regional policy had become much more nuanced, providing incentives for behind-the-scenes dealmaking rather than high-profile international diplomacy, which was Tanzania's strong suit. Tanzania played only a peripheral part in the negotiations leading up to Namibia's independence in 1990, a far cry from its central role in the Zimbabwe negotiations a decade earlier. Relations also became more complicated with Tanzania's closest ally in the region, Mozambique. Tanzania initially criticized Mozambique for entering into the Nkomati Accords, which were intended to normalize relations between Mozambique and South Africa, in 1984. Over time, however, Tanzania came to realize how limited its neighbor's options were. Between 1986 and 1988, Tanzania provided Mozambique with 3,000 troops to bolster FRELIMO's efforts against the South African–supported MNR rebels. The deployment became a logistical and political nightmare and drained the Tanzanian treasury in the absence of an international patron willing to pick up the tab. The difficulties with the Mozambican military engagement were symptomatic of the changes that forced Tanzania's foreign affairs retrenchment in the late 1980s. Finally, in late 1988, under pressure from the IMF and the World Bank, the troops were brought home.

Tanzania's leadership transition from Nyerere to Mwinyi signified a lowering in the priority given to international affairs, despite Dar es Salaam's constant insistence to the contrary. The settlement of the Namibia conflict in 1990, along with the legalization of the ANC and subsequent return to South Africa of ANC exiles during the same year, marked the probable end to Tanzania's major role in the Southern African subcontinent. Symbolically, the ANC's training camps in southern Tanzania were returned to the Tanzanian government in 1992. In late 1993, Tanzania helped push the radical Pan Africanist Congress (PAC) into the South African elections when they closed down the PAC's military base. To the extent that Tanzania does play a regional role in the future, it will probably again be in East Africa.

THE INTERNATIONAL RELATIONS
OF ECONOMIC RESTRUCTURING

By the late 1980s, the predominant foreign affairs issue for both Tanzania and Kenya had become relations with the international donor community concerning financial support for economic restructuring. In both countries, the international financial institutions (IFIs) and other donors have been at the forefront of a decade-long effort to promote economic reform and bring about sustainable economic growth. This process has led to periods of severe conflict with the donors. In neither case has the outcome of reform been full economic recovery nor the transformation to a vibrant, market-based economy. Rather, the results of donor efforts have been partial reforms. Both the Kenyan and Tanzanian governments have initiated adjustment measures, but neither has followed through with the basic institutional and attitudinal changes needed to carry through a transformation to market-oriented and private sector–led growth. As discussed by Benno Ndulu and Francis Mwega in Chapter 4, adjustment efforts have had some success in eliminating the worst distortions and in restoring low-level economic growth, but they have not transformed either policymaking or the overall economic environment (Gordon 1993).

Economic reform was put on the agenda in Tanzania in 1980 in response to 1) the increasingly obvious limitations to the state-centered and socialist strategy that had been followed since 1967 and 2) the immediate adverse impact in 1979 of the rise in the international price of oil, the Ugandan war, and the international recession that lowered the demand (and hence the price) for many of the country's exports. On the domestic scene, there was growing anarchy in the state-run marketing system, price management had become less and less effective (with an ever growing portion of the productive economy withdrawing to the informal market), cross-border smuggling was rife, and effective budgetary management had completely disappeared (Bierman and Wagao 1984).

To meet this crisis, Tanzania sought short-term financing from the international community. Between 1980 and 1986, Tanzania was locked in a struggle with the IMF over access to much-needed IMF resources, and to the resources of the World Bank and other donors that would follow the signing of an IMF agreement. A number of agreements were initiated, but implementation was never carried very far. President Nyerere was particularly hostile to the IMF. In 1980 he publicly castigated the Fund for "attempting to exploit" the country's difficulties. At the time, Nyerere was a leading radical voice in the Non-Aligned Movement, which shaped his inability to compromise with the IMF. Until 1986 Tanzania was unwilling to devalue its currency, seeing the issue as one of national sovereignty; the IMF insisted that without such a move, donor resources would be wasted. Throughout the first half of the 1980s, the economy continued to deteriorate, starved of external resources and lacking a coherent economic reform program.

In 1986, under the new presidency of Ali Hassan Mwinyi and ever less able to defend the existing rate of the shilling, Tanzania agreed to a substantial, if phased, devaluation. Since then Tanzania's relations with the IMF and the World Bank have become much stronger, and Tanzania has once again become one of the largest recipients of concessional aid. Amounts rose to one-quarter of GDP in 1989 and one-third of GDP in 1990. Under the impetus of these resource flows, economic growth has been restarted and a degree of confidence restored. Despite these successes, however, economic reform efforts have been sporadic, and Mwinyi has faced strong opposition, especially within the party hierarchy, to his cooperation with the IFIs. The country still needs to undertake further and even more difficult structural reforms in the areas of financial market liberalization and parastatal restructuring and privatization. Details of the economic reform program in Tanzania are given in Chapters 4 and 5.

Although Kenya's conservative and relatively market-oriented government might have been expected to have smooth relations with the IFIs, this has not been the case. By the end of the 1970s, despite continuing economic growth, four disturbing domestic economic trends were becoming visible and exacerbated the impact of external shocks on Kenya: The first was a decline in the productivity of investment; the second was a slowing down of formal private sector job creation, which in the context of Kenya's very high population growth was leading to increasing unemployment and underemployment; the third was a growing public finance problem; and the fourth was a growing imbalance between exports and imports in the balance of payments. In addition to these structural weaknesses, Kenya in the late 1970s was increasingly dominated by "crony statism," a syndrome marked by the extraction and distribution of rents to support clientele networks, expansion of the state, and the purchase of public support via welfare services and subsidies. The effects of external shocks, growing domestic economic problems, and "crony statism" were made worse by the breakup of the East African Community and economic and/or political crisis in virtually all of Kenya's neighbors, which largely erased what had been a significant market for exports and an important draw for foreign investors. Thus, when the second oil shock struck in 1979, the stage was set for the IFIs and other donor agencies to place economic restructuring on the policy agenda in Kenya (Gordon 1992).

Economic reform efforts in Kenya can be divided into three periods. The first, beginning in 1979 and lasting until 1985, was characterized by weak initial efforts to stabilize the economy, followed by more successful ones. On the strength of this performance, government's relationship with the IMF dramatically improved during this period. On structural reform, however, the period was marked by aborted efforts and growing conflict between the government, on the one hand, and the World Bank and USAID, on the other. The second period, beginning in late 1985 and lasting until the late 1980s, saw weakened stabilization efforts but the initiation of a wide range of structural reforms—e.g., trade liberalization, agricultural marketing reform, and financial market liberalization. This period was marked by much more cordial relations between Kenya and the donor community. In 1986 the government issued a sessional paper which articulated a very ambitious reform program and won renewed donor support (Kenya 1986a). In fact, during this period Kenya became touted by the World Bank as a model of successful structural adjustment (Corbo, Fischer, and Webb 1990). In 1989 the third period of the reform effort began. This phase has involved very difficult political decisions concerning the status of the parastatal sector and efforts to generate a more sustainable fiscal balance. In addition, by 1989 the donors had again become disappointed by the slow pace of reform implementation. These concerns were reinforced by growing corruption at the top of the Kenyan political system and emerging pressure from donors to seek not only economic change but more open political systems as well.

Controversy about the role of external actors in economic reform has focused on their use of conditionality to leverage policy change. It is not easy to precisely define conditionality. In general, it refers to agreements wherein donors make financial transfers (either grants or loans) to recipients in exchange for policy changes by the latter. However, the nature of the relationship between resource transfers and policy changes is a source of disagreement among observers of conditionality. Donors themselves tend to portray this relationship as *reinforcement*—i.e., that the resource transfer provides an added incentive for the recipient government to implement policy changes to which it is already committed.[4] Critics of the IFIs have viewed the relationship as *imposition*—i.e., that the donors utilize financial transfers to enforce inappropriate policy changes on otherwise unwilling governments.[5] Academic analysts have tended to conceptualize the relationship as one of *purchase*—i.e., that the donors "buy" reforms that governments, for one reason or another, would otherwise hesitate to make (Mosley 1987).

Beginning in 1990, conditionality took on an added political dimension. There was a growing consensus in the international community that economic development was in part dependent upon improved governance and accountability. Many of the key donors (including the World Bank, USAID, Germany, and the Scandinavian countries) began to condition balance-of-payment support on political, as well as economic policy, reforms. Kenya was one of the first countries where this "new" conditionality was applied.[6]

Although the donors took the leading role in setting the agenda for change in Kenya and Tanzania, other factors have also motivated economic reform. Agreement about the need for reform has been promoted as well by the general reorienting of global strategies for growth—a new belief in the efficiency of markets, a more open stance toward the international economy, a larger role for entrepreneurship. These tenets have taken hold in other areas of the developing world and Eastern Europe as well as Africa. The remarkable changes transpiring in the former communist world and the rise of the "four tigers" of Southeast Asia have inspired a growing number of Kenyan and Tanzanian intellectuals to rethink the essence of development policy. A young generation of technocrats imbued with faith in economic reform is emerging in both countries. Thus, the role of donor financial leverage in promoting reform has been a substantial factor but hardly the only one.

It is useful to make a distinction between the financial leverage of "pure" conditionality and the broader instruments of influence that, in practice, have accompanied IFI and other donor policy-based operations. Financial leverage, while the most visible element of conditionality, is part of a much broader pattern of donor influence on economic reform. Intellectual and political influence have also been particularly important. The IFIs have been the main conduit for the diffusion of liberal economic thought in Kenya and Tanzania. The IFIs conduct extensive training programs that are attended by both middle- and senior-level government technocrats. In addition, several policymakers from both countries have actually worked for international donor agencies. The IFIs and other donors involved in policy reform have provided extensive technical support, especially to core economic units such as central banks, ministries of finance, and ministries of planning. Taken together, these activities constitute a tremendous intellectual impact on the way in which economic policy is perceived in East Africa, especially by technocrats (Kahler 1989).

This influence has been particularly important in Tanzania. Given that country's poor economic performance, government technocrats have been forced to consider alternative models and strategies. The financial dependence of the Tanzanian government on the IFIs gave these agencies unusual access to economic policymakers. Over time, their interaction helped substantially to change the terms of the policy debate in Tanzania. A decade ago, the economic discourse was conducted in Marxist-socialist terms far different from the neoclassical theory that dominates in the IFIs. Today, the terms of the economic debates, both domestically and between the Tanzanian government and the IFIs, has evolved dramatically in the direction of the categories propounded by the IFIs. These changes would not have come about without the ongoing interactions with the IFIs.

Another, more sensitive form of input from the IFIs and donors is political influence. According to their charters, the IFIs are supposed to be strictly apolitical. However, they have never really been apolitical, and the rise of conditionality forced them inexorably into a more overtly political stance. Increasingly, as the 1980s wore on, the donors most directly engaged in policy reform coordinated closely with individuals at the highest technical levels of the bureaucracy. In both Kenya and Tanzania, a key political role was played by "credible technocrats," individuals having the ear of senior government officials and the respect of the donor agencies. In Kenya (and to a lesser extent in Tanzania), World Bank representatives have played an important role in coordinating and enhancing the political influence of these technocrats. Thus, although conditionality theoretically entails the exertion of financial leverage, in practice it has involved varying mixes of financial, intellectual, and political influence.

By the late 1980s, there was a broad consensus within both Kenya and Tanzania on the necessity for economic reform. Beyond this consensus, however, economic reform has been a bitterly contested terrain of public policy and a major source of conflict between each country and its international creditors. Conditionality, and the external resources that go with it, tended to turn economic reform efforts into a game whereby donors attempted to "buy" as much reform as they could with a given amount of money and each government tried to get as much money as they could for as little reform as possible. Reforms were enacted to increase donor resources rather than to improve economic performance. Decisions concerning economic reform too often become responses to external pressures and attempts to maximize external resource flows rather than efforts to grapple with imperative domestic problems.

Nor were the donors as powerful in this relationship as they might have appeared. The IMF has generally been able to generate policy reform on narrow stabilization measures, including devaluation, but the conditionality used by the World Bank and the bilateral donors has proven too blunt an instrument for promoting broader economic reform. Though it has been effective in placing economic reform on the policy agenda and getting the ball rolling, it has played a far less positive role in sustaining the process. The financial leverage of conditionality was more apparent than real when donors moved beyond the general goal of promoting economic change. Kenya was able to use its strategic relationship with the United States to limit the pressure for economic reform. Moreover, once promoters of reform develop large stakes as creditors in a situation in which repayment is problematic, as is the case in both Kenya and Tanzania, their goals for policy transformation may become subordinated to their creditor interests. Similarly, because the IFIs and the donor agencies have assumed the task of providing a financial cushion for both countries in the context of an unsustainable balance-of-payments situation, the conditionality attached to their financial transfers have lost some of its credibility. The evidence suggests that external finance cannot easily be both an instrument for softening the effects of external shocks and recession and a lever for promoting economic restructuring. Thus, it is perhaps not surprising that the IFIs' impact on the process of economic restructuring in both Kenya and Tanzania has been less than overwhelming.

CONCLUSION: RESPONDING TO GLOBAL REALITIES

Earlier in this chapter, I examined the changing international context brought about by the end of the Cold War and Africa's increasing marginalization in the global system. In this concluding section, I will look at how these new global realities quickly led to new pressures for both Kenya and Tanzania. Of the two, the Kenyan case is the more dramatic and significant. As was discussed earlier, in the 1980s Kenya enhanced its political and military ties to the United States. These ties helped Kenya become the darling of the Western donors and a major recipient of quick-disbursing foreign aid despite its rather mixed record in actually implementing economic reform programs.

In the 1980s, supported by large volumes of foreign aid, President Moi became increasingly dictatorial, centralizing political power into his own office, rewarding ethnic compatriots, and repressing dissent. Details of these changes are discussed by Joel Barkan in Chapter 1. Leading Western diplomats, though unhappy about the turn in Kenyan affairs, nonetheless were loath to criticize Kenya too strongly or publicly. In 1987, U.S. Representative Howard Wolpe caused a ruckus by holding a press conference at the end of a visit to Kenya in which he criticized the human rights record of the Moi regime. Although Wolpe's views were weakly supported by the U.S. State Department, his intervention was viewed in diplomatic circles as "unconstructive." Official policy was still not to rock the boat.

In late 1989, the communist governments of Eastern Europe began to collapse. In his New Year's sermon for 1990, one of Kenya's leading pastors openly compared the communist regimes in Europe to Africa's one-party states and suggested that the latter should meet a similar fate. Though the government ridiculed the analogy, the floodgates of pent-up political opposition began to swell. Also in late 1989, a new U.S. ambassador, Smith Hempstone, arrived in Nairobi. A conservative Republican, Hempstone was expected by many to coddle the anticommunist Moi regime. But Hempstone was quickly disgusted by the growing authoritarianism, sycophancy, and corruption of the Moi government and expressed his disapproval from the beginning. In addition, Hempstone, a former journalist, refused to be constrained by the traditional boundaries of diplomatic style. If, during the Cold War, a U.S. ambassador had expressed such views in this way, he would have raised the ire of the Defense Department and the CIA, who would have weighed in as a counterbalance. But in the context of

1990, Hempstone had unusual leeway to shape a new U.S. approach to Kenya, and he took it.

At the same time, conflict was brewing between Kenya and its creditors over the terms of their relationship. At the November 1989 meeting of the Consultative Group of donors in Paris, concern was expressed over the slow implementation of economic reform and growing corruption in the use of foreign aid. In early 1990 USAID included a section on poor governance in its assessment of the constraints on development in Kenya. Later in the year, Moi expelled several Norwegian diplomats, which led to a suspension of the generous Norwegian aid program. Meanwhile, there was severe discomfort among the donors when the ruling party announced that it was going to build a sixty-story building to serve as its headquarters in one of Nairobi's few remaining urban green zones. Donor pressure thwarted the international financing for the headquarters, and the affair further weakened the donor confidence in the Moi regime.

The signal event in 1990, however, was Ambassador Hempstone's speech in May to the Nairobi Rotary Club, in which he stated that the U.S. Congress was likely to enact guidelines directing U.S. assistance to nations that nourish democratic institutions, promote human rights, and practice multiparty politics. Unlike some Hempstone speeches, this one was delivered in diplomatic language. The reaction of the Kenyan government and Moi supporters was swift and virulent. Hempstone was denounced for infringing upon Kenya's sovereignty, and president Moi reiterated his belief that multiparty politics was inappropriate for Africa. The very phrases Moi used were reminiscent of those used by colonial administrators a generation earlier in their opposition to African nationalism. If Hempstone's speech raised the ire of the government, it also inspired the opposition. Kenyans opposed to the regime felt, rightly or wrongly, that they had the support of the United States.

By the end of 1990, Moi had positioned Kenya at the forefront of those African countries resisting both popular democratic pressure and international appeals for political liberalization. This was in many ways an amazing turnaround for a country that had only a few years before been the darling of the Western donors. For his part, Smith Hempstone was at the forefront of those trying to reshape U.S. Africa policy to a more forceful prodemocracy stance. At the November 1990 Consultative Group meeting, criticism of Kenya was openly expressed. Even the Japanese, whom Kenya had been wooing, expressed public dismay at corruption and poor governance. Clearly, a confrontation was brewing.

In 1991 public demands for a multiparty system within Kenya grew ever more intense. At the same time, there was a growing donor consensus that unless there was a significant reduction in corruption, substantial improvements in human rights, and more open political participation and accountable government, then Kenya should not continue to receive such high levels of foreign assistance. This consensus was facilitated by the extraordinary success of the Kikuyu and Luo intelligentsia in shaping the views of Nairobi's international community against the Moi government. Western donors were fully comfortable with the "liberal" attitudes of the educated Kenyan middle class but uncomfortable with the authoritarian and patrimonial approach of Moi and his cronies. The United States took the lead in putting pressure on the regime, making ever more direct threats about the withdrawal of foreign aid. Moi himself appeared not really to understand the changes that had been brought about by the end of the Cold War, and his few pragmatic advisers were either unwilling or unable to reach him. At the November 1991 donor's Consultative Group meeting, twelve nations, along with the World Bank, suspended new quick-disbursing assistance until fundamental political and economic changes were instituted. The U.S. development assistance program dropped from $60 million in 1991 to $19 million in 1992 and $17 million in 1993 and 1994. Moi's intransigence made Kenya a precedent-setting case for political conditionality in Africa.

Moi finally got the message. Political parties were legalized within a matter of weeks, in December 1991, and Kenya began to improve its economic management, especially in the area of macroeconomic policy, which remained the primary concern of the IMF and the World Bank. But Moi still hoped international interest would wane and that Hempstone would be recalled before Kenya was forced to hold elections. Moi continued to resist a full political opening, even after he announced in October 1992 that national elections would be held in December. The United States and other donors monitored the run-up to the Kenyan election, and Hempstone continued to be critical of the Kenyan authorities (World Bank 1993c).

Despite severe electoral irregularities, nearly two-thirds of Kenyan voters cast presidential ballots against Moi. But because of the fragmentation of the opposition, Moi achieved a plurality victory. Still, a return to the status quo ante in Moi's relationship with the United States and the donor community is highly unlikely. Kenya will continue to be under strict scrutiny. After the November 1993 meeting of the Consultative Group, the World Bank began to restore balance-of-payments support, but most bilateral donors have not followed suit. It will take a consistent implementation of an ambitious reform program for the Kenyan government to regain the full confidence of the donor community (World Bank 1993c).

If Kenya felt abandoned by its Western friends, who insisted on exerting unwanted political pressure, Tanzania was literally abandoned by its East Bloc friends, whose regimes ceased to exist. As discussed earlier, Tanzania's international standing had been bolstered by its position as a leader of the Non-Aligned Movement. In the early 1990s, the country suddenly found itself without an international conflict to be nonaligned toward. Tanzania had been one of the most successful African countries in maneuvering through the Cold War thicket, gaining both external resources and a good degree of international political stature. The end of the Cold War has put both of these achievements at risk. Whereas Kenya was threatened by more active involvement from its traditional allies, Tanzania is threatened by a simple lack of interest from external actors.

The 1980s had seen a steady growth in communist bloc presence in Tanzania, as Moscow decided to utilize Dar es Salaam as one of its regional centers in Africa. This decision was driven by the international status of President Nyerere and by the presence in Dar of representatives of many of the Southern African liberation movements. Tanzania became one of the largest recipients of Soviet military assistance in Africa, ranking just behind Angola and Ethiopia for much of the decade. By the late 1980s, there was also increasing economic assistance both from the USSR and from other East Bloc countries.

Despite its strong ties to the East Bloc, Tanzania always avoided any real alignment with it. The Western powers thus had a strong incentive to maintain a strong presence in Dar so as to compete with the USSR for influence. The West's role was reinforced by the long-standing Scandinavian support for Tanzania, driven by ideological support for Nyerere's version of non-Marxist socialism and self-reliance. The West was also motivated by an interest in monitoring East Bloc activities.

In 1990, after the collapse of the communist states of Eastern Europe and with the growing crisis in the USSR, there began a rapid exodus from Tanzania of former East Bloc nationals, whose new regimes could not afford an expensive international presence and lacked any real interests in the country. Unfortunately for Tanzania, this decampment coincided with the rapid downsizing of the ANC, which had been legalized in South Africa. The departure of the East Bloc and of the ANC diminished the West's interest in maintaining such a large presence in Tanzania, and so Western countries also began to downsize their embassies. So far, the loss of Western personnel has not been matched by a substantial lowering of Western aid. But Tanzania's loss of international status as a result of the end of the Cold War has diminished its ability to maneuver among different sets of international actors.

Unlike Kenya, Tanzania has not faced intense donor pressure for political reform, for several reasons. First, Tanzania's human rights record, though not perfect, has been far superior to Kenya's. Second, the degree of high-level corruption, especially with regard to donor funds, has been substantially lower in Tanzania than in Kenya, though corruption is now on the rise. Third, there hasn't been a highly vocal and articulate group of expatriate Tanzanians in Western capitals urging punitive action against their government; there *has* been such a group of Kenyans. Finally, the Tanzanian government has managed to stay "ahead of the wave" on the democratization issue. In early 1990 former president Nyerere, whose earlier writings had been among the most important justifications of the single-party state in Africa, publicly stated that it might be time for Africa to rethink its political options (Nyerere 1990). Since then, Tanzania has set out on a home-grown process of political liberalization. Nonetheless, Tanzania's ability to maintain high levels of external resources in the 1990s will fully depend upon continued progress on economic reform and effective management of the process of political liberalization.

As both Kenya and Tanzania look forward to the international challenges of the coming years, the foreign policy issues and dilemmas they face have substantially converged. A decade ago, a comparison of Kenyan and Tanzanian foreign relations would have emphasized the differences between the two countries. Between the mid-1970s and mid-1980s, the two countries adopted very different approaches to the East-West conflict and became heavily involved at opposite ends of a vast continent. In contrast, in the past several years both countries have sought appropriate mechanisms for regional integration and have tried to maintain good relations with external creditors in a context marked by growing dependence.

One thing is clear: The old norm of comparing Kenya and Tanzania through the lens of capitalism versus socialism is no longer very useful, especially in the area of foreign relations. Ironically, formally socialist and nonaligned Tanzania now enjoys stronger relations with the Western powers than does traditionally capitalist and pro-West Kenya. More important, both countries face the very daunting challenge of maintaining political stability and restoring economic dynamism in a region marked by political decay and flagging investor confidence. And both countries face the dilemma of relating to a global environment in which Africa has become simultaneously marginalized and dependent.

NOTES

1. For the first phase of foreign policy in Kenya see Okumu (1977); for the first phase in Tanzania see Noli (1977).
2. Government of Kenya and Central Bank of Kenya publications.
3. Government of Tanzania and Bank of Tanzania publications.
4. For a statement of the "reinforcement" position by senior World Bank staff, see Corbo and Fischer (1990).
5. For an example of the "imposition" perspective, see Browne (1984).
6. For the donors' statement on the imposition of conditionality at the November 1991 meeting of the Consultative Group on Kenya see (World Bank 1991c).

Bibliography

Africa Analysis
Var.   *African Analysis*. London.
Africa Confidential
Var.   *Africa Confidential*. London.
Africa Events
Var.   *African Events*. London.
Africa Watch
1993   *Divide and Rule: State-Sponsored Ethnic Violence in Kenya*. New York and Washington: Africa Watch, A Division of Human Rights Watch.
African Development
Var.   *African Development*. London.
Anderson, G., and G. Rosengart
1988   *Education in Tanzania Government Expenditure 1983–87* (mimeo). Stockholm: Swedish International Development Agency.
Armstrong, A.
n.d.   "Urban Control Campaigns in the Third World: The Case of Tanzania." Occasional Paper Series No. 19, Department of Geography, University of Glasgow.
Banks, Arthur S.
1970   "Modernization and Political Change: The Latin American and Amer-European Nations," *Comparative Political Studies* 2, 4: 405–418.
Baregu, Mwesiga
1992   "The Economic Origins of Political Liberalization and Future Prospects." Paper presented at the 8th National Economic Policy Workshop, November 30–December 2, 1992, Economic Research Bureau, University of Dar es Salaam.
1993   "The Rise and Fall of the One-Party State in Tanzania," in Widner 1993.
Barkan, Joel D.
1976   "Further Reassessment of the 'Conventional Wisdom': Political Knowledge and Voting Behavior in Rural Kenya," *American Political Science Review* 70, 2: 452–455.
1978   "Bringing Home the Pork: Legislator Behavior, Rural Development and Political Change in East Africa," in Lloyd Musolf and Joel Smith, eds., *Legislators and Development*. Durham: Duke University Press.
1983   "'Urban Bias,' Peasants and Rural Politics in Kenya and Tanzania." Report #1, Department of Political Science, University of Iowa.
1984a   *Politics and Public Policy in Kenya and Tanzania*. New York: Praeger Publishers.
1984b   "Comparing Politics and Public Policy in Kenya and Tanzania," in Barkan 1984a: 3–42.

1992   "The Rise and Fall of a Governance Realm in Kenya," in Hyden and Bratton 1992: 167–192.

1993   "Kenya: Lessons from a Flawed Election." *Journal of Democracy* 4, 3: 85–99.

Barkan, Joel D., and Michael Chege

1989   "Decentralising the State: District Focus and the Politics of Reallocation in Kenya," *Journal of Modern African Studies* 27, 3: 431–454.

Barkan, Joel D., and Frank Holmquist

1989   "Peasant-State Relations and the Social Base of Self-Help in Kenya," *World Politics* 41, 3: 359–380.

Barker, Ernest

1961   *Principles of Social and Political Theory.* New York: Oxford University Press.

Bates, Robert H.

1981   *Markets and States in Tropical Africa.* Berkeley: University of California Press.

1983   *Essays on the Political Economy of Rural Africa.* Cambridge: Cambridge University Press.

1989   *Beyond the Miracle of the Market: The Political Economy of Agrarian Development in Kenya.* New York: Cambridge University Press.

Bendix, Reinhard

1978   *Kings or People: Power and the Mandate to Rule.* Berkeley: University of California Press.

Bennell, P.

1981   "A Quantitative Assessment of the Utilization of Engineering Manpower in Kenya." IDS Working Paper No. 381, University of Nairobi.

Bennett, Pramilla

1986   "The Horn: Burying the Hatchet," *Africa* 175: 36–37.

Berg, Robert J., and Jennifer S. Whitaker, eds.

1986   *Strategies for African Development.* Berkeley: University of California Press.

Berger, Peter

1992   "The Uncertain Triumph of Democratic Capitalism," *Journal of Democracy* 3, 3: 7–16.

Bevan, David, Paul Collier, and Jan Willem Gunning

1989   *Peasants and Government: An Economic Analysis.* Oxford: The Clarendon Press.

Beyond

1988   *Beyond.* Nairobi: National Council of Churches of Kenya.

Bienen, Henry

1970   *Tanzania: Party Transformation and Economic Development,* revised edition. Princeton: Princeton University Press.

1974   *Kenya: The Politics of Participation and Control.* Princeton: Princeton University Press.

Bierman, Werner, and Jumanne H. Wagao

1984   *Response to Crisis: The IMF and Tanzania.* Dar es Salaam: Economic Research Bureau.

1987   "The IMF and Economic Policy in Tanzania: 1980–84," *Journal of African Studies* 14, 3: 118–126.

Boesen, Jannik, et al.

1977   *Ujamaa: Socialism from Above.* Uppsala: Scandinavian Institute of African Studies.

1986   *Tanzania: Crisis and Struggle for Survival.* Uppsala: Scandinavian Institute of African Studies.

Bollen, Kenneth A., and Robert W. Jackman
1985   "Economic and Non-Economic Determinants of Political Democracy in the 1960s," *Research in Political Sociology* 1.

Browne, Robert
1984   "Conditionality: A New Form of Colonialism," *Africa Report* (September).

Bryceson, Deborah Fahy
1985   "Food and Urban Purchasing Power in Tanzania," *African Affairs* 84, 337.

Bubba, Ndinda, and Davinder Lamba
1989   "Urban Management Country Case Study: Kenya." Unpublished paper presented to African Urban Management Seminar, Harare, Zimbabwe.

Bukurura, Sufian Hemed Bukurura
1988   "Law and Practice of Urban Authorities in Tanzania." Unpublished paper, University of Warwick.

Business Times
Var.   *The Business Times.* Dar es Salaam.

Callaghy, Thomas M.
1990   "Lost Between State and Market: The Politics of Economic Adjustment in Ghana, Zambia and Nigeria," in Nelson 1990.
1991   "Africa and the World Economy: Caught Between a Rock and a Hard Place," in Harbeson and Rothchild 1991.
1993   "Political Passions and Economic Interests: Economic Reform and Political Structure in Africa," in Callaghy and Ravenhill 1993.

Callaghy, Thomas, and J. Ravenhill, eds.
1993   *Hemmed In: Responses to Africa's Economic Decline.* New York: Columbia University Press.

Campbell, Horace
1987   "Popular Resistance in Tanzania: Lessons from the Sungu Sungu." Unpublished seminar paper presented in the Department of History, University of Dar es Salaam, September 3, 1987.

Campbell, Horace, and Howard Stein, eds.
1992   *Tanzania and the IMF: The Dynamics of Liberalization.* Boulder: Westview Press.

Carr-Hill, R.
1984   *Primary Education in Tanzania: A Review of the Research.* Stockholm: SIDA Education Division Documents.

Chege, Michael
1992   "Remembering Africa," *Foreign Affairs* 71, 1: 146–163.

Cliffe, Lionel
1967   *One-Party Democracy: The 1965 Tanzania General Elections.* Nairobi: East African Publishing House.

Cliffe, Lionel, and John Saul, eds.
1972   *Socialism in Tanzania: Politics.* Nairobi: East African Publishing House.
1973   *Socialism in Tanzania: Policies.* Nairobi: East African Publishing House.

Cohen, John M.
1993   "The Importance of Public Service Reform: The Case of Kenya," *Journal of Modern African Studies* 31, 3: 449–476.

Collier, Ruth B., and David Collier
  1991   *Shaping the Political Arena.* Princeton: Princeton University Press.
Cooksey, Brian, A. Ishumi, G. Malekela, and J. Galabawa
  1991   "A Survey of Living and Working Conditions of Primary and Secondary School Teachers on Mainland Tanzania." Mimeograph, Swedish International Development Authority, Dar es Salaam.
Corbo, Vittorio, and Stanley Fischer
  1990   "Adjustment Programs and Bank Support: Rationale and Main Results," Unpublished manuscript, World Bank, Washington.
Corbo, Vittorio, Stanley Fischer, and Steven Webb
  1990   "Adjustment Lending and the Restoration of Sustainable Growth." Washington: The World Bank.
Cornia, Giovanni, R. van der Hoeven, and T. Mkandawire, eds.
  1992   *Africa's Recovery in the 1990s.* New York: St. Martin's Press.
Coulson, Andrew
  1982   *Tanzania: A Political Economy.* Oxford: The Clarendon Press.
Court, David
  1973   "The Social Function of Formal Schooling in Tanzania," *Africa Review* 3–4: 578–593.
  1976   "The Education System as a Response to Inequality in Kenya and Tanzania," *Journal of Modern Africa Studies* 14, 4.
Court, David, and Durham Ghai, eds.
  1974   *Education, Society and Development: New Perspectives from Kenya.* Nairobi: Oxford University Press.
Court, David, and Kabiru Kinyanjui
  1980   "Development Policy and Educational Opportunity: The Experience of Kenya and Tanzania," in Gabriel Carron and Ta Ngoc Chau, eds., *Regional Disparities in Educational Development.* Paris: IIEP, 325–409.
  1985   "Education and Development in Sub-Saharan Africa: The Operation and Impact and Education Systems," in Berg and Whitaker 1986.
Dahl, Robert A.
  1971   *Polyarchy: Participation and Opposition.* New Haven: Yale University Press.
Daily Nation
  Var.   *The Daily Nation.* Nairobi: The Nation Group Ltd.
Daily News
  1983   "Nyerere Questions Education Policy," *Daily News,* July 7, 1983.
Danish International Development Agency (DANIDA)
  1993   "Donor Assistance to the Education Sector in Tanzania." Mimeograph, Danish International Development Agency, Dar es Salaam.
Daun, H., and I. Fagerlind
  1991   "Policy and Basic Education in Tanzania." Mimeograph, University of Stockholm.
Diamond, Larry J.
  1992   "International and Domestic Factors in Africa's Trend Toward Democracy." Working Papers in International Studies, I-92-14, The Hoover Institution, Stanford University.
  1993   "Ex Africa . . . A New Democratic Spirit Has Loosened the Grip of African Dictatorial Rule," *Times Literary Supplement,* July 2, 1993, 3–4.
Dlamini, A. T.
  1987   "Management of Foreign Exchange Reserves Through Quantitative

Controls: The Kenyan Experience." MBA Research Paper, University of Nairobi.

Economic Intelligence Unit (EIU)
1992 *EIU Country Report No. 1 1992: Kenya.* London: Economic Intelligence Unit.

Economic Review
Var. *The Economic Review.* Nairobi: The Economic Review Ltd.

Ekeh, Peter
1975 "Colonialism and the Two Publics in Africa: A Theoretical Statement," *Comparative Studies in Society and History* 17, 1: 91–112.

Elderkin, Sarah
1993 "Goldenberg: The Monumental Rip-Off," *Daily Nation,* July 30–August 6, 1993.

Economic Research Bureau (ERB)
Var. *Tanzanian Economic Trends: A Quarterly Review of the Economy.* Dar es Salaam: Economic Research Bureau of the University of Dar es Salaam.

Ergus, Zaki
1980 "Why Did the Ujamaa Village Policy Fail?" *Journal of Modern African Studies* 18: 451–478.

Family Mirror
1993 "Time for President Mwyini to Resign." Editorial, *Family Mirror* 109 (September).

Fanon, Frantz
1967 *The Wretched of the Earth.* Harmondsworth: Penguin Books.

Fisher, C.
1966 "Education," in S. Diamond and Fred Burke, eds., *The Transformation of East Africa.* New York: Basic Books.

Fransman, Martin, ed.
1982 *Industry and Accumulation in Africa.* London: Heinemann.

Freeman, Donald
1991 *A City of Farmers. Informal Urban Agriculture in the Open Spaces of Nairobi, Kenya.* Montreal and Kingston: McGill–Queen's University Press, 1991.

Friedrich Naumann Stiftung (FNS)
1992 *A Blue Print for a New Kenya: Post Election Action Programme.* Nairobi: Friedrich Naumann Stiftung.

Furnivall, J. S.
1939 *Netherlands India.* Cambridge: Cambridge University Press.

GCA (Global Coalition for Africa)
1993 *1992 Annual Report.* Washington: Global Coalition for Africa.

Gertzel, Cherry
1970 *The Politics of Independent Kenya.* Evanston: Northwestern University Press.

Gordon, David F.
1987 "Anglophonic Variants: Kenya Versus Tanzania," *The Annals.* Philadelphia: American Academy of Political and Social Science.
1988 "The Bear Restrained: Soviet Activities in East Africa," in Dennis Bark, ed., *The Red Orchestra: The Case of Africa.* Stanford: Hoover Institution Press.
1989 "Heterodox Thoughts on SADCC." A paper prepared for the USAID Mission to Mozambique (December 1989).

1992a "Reform and Politics: Guidelines for AID Practitioners," in Lancaster 1992.

1992b "The Political Economy of Economic Reform in Kenya," in Lancaster 1992.

1993 "Debt, Conditionality and Reform: The International Relations of Economic Restructuring in Africa," in Callaghy and Ravenhill 1993.

Greene, Joshua
1989 "The External Debt Problem of Sub-Saharan Africa," *IMF Staff Papers* (December 1989).

Gulhati, R., and U. Sekhar
1982 "Industrial Strategy for Late Starters: The Experience of Kenya, Tanzania, and Zambia," *World Development* 10, 11 (949–972).

Halfani, Mohamed
1989 "Towards the Enhancement of Local Government Capacities in Tanzania." Dar es Salaam: Institute of Development Studies.

Harbeson, John, and Donald Rothchild, eds.
1991 *Africa in World Politics.* Boulder: Westview Press.

Hawkridge, D., J. Jaworski, and H. McMahon
1990 *Computers in Third-World Schools: Examples, Experiences and Issues.* London: Macmillan.

Helleiner, G. K.
1990 "Structural Adjustment and Long-Term Development in Sub-Saharan Africa." Paper presented at the workshop on Alternative Development Strategies in Africa, Oxford University.

The Herald
Var. *The Herald.* Harare.

Himbara, David
1993 "Myths and Realities of Kenyan Capitalism," *Journal of Modern African Studies* 31, 1: 93–107.

Hirschman, Albert O.
1991 *The Rhetoric of Reaction.* Cambridge: Harvard University Press.

Hoek-Smit, Marja C.
1989 *Evaluation of Umoja 11; An Experimental Housing Project in Nairobi.* Nairobi: United States Agency for International Development.

Holmquist, Frank
1984 "Self-Help, the State and Peasant Leverage in Kenya," *Africa* 54, 3: 72–91.

Hopcraft, P.
1972 "Outward-looking Industrialization: The Promotion of Manufactured Exports from Kenya." Discussion Paper No. 141, Institute for Development Studies, University of Nairobi.

Hornsby, Charles P. W.
1989 "The Social Structure of the National Assembly in Kenya, 1963–83," *Journal of Modern African Studies* 27, 2: 275–296.

Hornsby, Charles P.W., and David W. Throup
1992 "Elections and Politics Change in Kenya," *Journal of Commonwealth and Comparative Politics* 30, 2: 172–199.

1995 *The Triumph of the System: The Rise and Fall of Multiparty Politics in Kenya.* London: James Curry.

House, W.
1981 "Industrial Performance and Market Structure," in Tony Killick, ed., *Papers on the Kenya Economy.* Nairobi: Heinemann Educational Books, 339–345.

Hughes, R.
  1985   "Higher Education and Employment in Kenya: A Liberal Interpretation of the Literature," IDS Working Paper No. 426, University of Nairobi.
Huntington, Samuel P.
  1968   *Political Order in Changing Societies.* New Haven: Yale University Press.
  1984   "Will More Countries Become Democratic?" *Political Studies Quarterly* 99: 198–222.
Hyden, Goran
  1980   *Beyond Ujamaa in Tanzania: Underdevelopment and an Uncaptured Peasantry.* Berkeley: University of California Press.
  1983   *No Shortcuts to Progress: African Development Management in Perspective.* Berkeley, University of California Press.
  1987   "Capital Accumulation, Resource Distribution, and Governance in Kenya," in Schatzberg 1987.
  1995   *The Political Factor in Development: Tanzania in Comparative Perspective.* Charlottesville: University Press of Virginia.
Hyden, Goran, and Michael Bratton, eds.
  1992   *Governance and Politics in Africa.* Boulder: Lynne Rienner Publishers.
International Labour Organisation (ILO)
  1972   *Employment, Incomes and Equality: A Strategy for Increasing Productive Employment in Kenya.* ILO: Geneva.
International Monetary Fund (IMF)
  1990   *IMF Survey* 19, 14 (July 1990).
Jackson, Robert
  1977   *Plural Societies and New States: A Conceptual Analysis.* Berkeley: Institute of International Studies, University of California.
Jaster, Robert
  1983   "A Regional Security Role for Africa's Front-line States," *Adelphi Paper* 180.
Johnson, K., and P. Kelly
  1986   "Political Democracy in Latin America 1985: Partial Results of the Image-Index Survey," *LASA Forum* 17, 1.
Johnson, Paul
  1993   "Colonialism's Back—and Not a Moment Too Soon," *New York Times Sunday Magazine,* April 18, 1993: 22, 43–44.
Johnston, Bruce F.
  1989   "The Political Economy of Agricultural Development in Kenya and Tanzania," *Food Research Institute Studies* 21, 3: 205–264.
Kahler, Miles
  1989   "International Financial Institutions and the Politics of Adjustment," in Joan Nelson, ed., *Fragile Coalitions: The Politics of Economic Adjustment.* New Brunswick: Transaction Books.
Kenya (Republic of Kenya)
  1965   *African Socialism and Its Application to Planning in Kenya.* Sessional Paper No. 10. Nairobi: Government Printer.
  1971   *Report of the Commission of Inquiry on Public Service Structure and Remuneration.* Nairobi: Government Printer.
  1976   *Report of the National Committee on Educational Objectives and Policies* (NCEOP). Nairobi: Government Printer.
  1981   *National Food Policy.* Sessional Paper No. 4. Nairobi: Government Printer.

1982   *Report and Recommendation of the Working Party on Government Expenditures.* Nairobi: Government Printer.

1983a *District Focus for Rural Development.* Nairobi: Office of the President.

1983b *Urban Housing Survey 1983. Basic Report.* Nairobi: Ministry of Works, Housing and Physical Planning and Ministry of Planning and National Development, 1986.

1984   *The 8-4-4 System of Education.* Nairobi: Ministry of Education.

1986a *Economic Management for Renewed Growth.* Sessional Paper No. 1. Nairobi: Government Printer.

1986b *Budget Rationalisation Programme.* Treasury Circular No. 3. Nairobi: Ministry of Finance.

1986c *Statistical Abstract of 1986.* Nairobi: Government Printer.

1988   *Report of the Presidential Working Party on Education and Manpower Training for the Next Decade and Beyond* (WPEMT). Nairobi: Government Printer.

1989   *Development Plan 1989–1993.* Nairobi: Government Printer.

1991   *Statistical Abstract 1991.* Nairobi: Central Bureau of Statistics.

1992a *Economic Survey.* Nairobi: Government Printer.

1992b *Report of the Parliamentary Select Committee to Investigate Ethnic Clashes in Western and Other Parts of Kenya.* Nairobi: Government Printer. (This report is now unavailable from the Government Printer but was substantially republished by the *Daily Nation* in October 1992.)

1993   *Economic Survey.* Nairobi: Government Printer.

1994   *Economic Survey.* Nairobi: Government Printer.

Kiamba, M., J. Malombe, and R. Muchene.

1992   *Urban Management Instruments for Neighbourhood Development in Selected African Cities: The Case of Kenya.* Nairobi: University of Nairobi, Department of Land Development.

Killick, R.

1990   "Structure, Development and Adaptation." AERC Special Paper No. 2, African Economic Research Consortium, Nairobi.

Killick, T.

1984   "Kenya, 1975–81," in T. Killick, ed., *The IMF and Stabilization: Developing Country Experiences.* London: Heinemann Educational Books, 166–216.

King, J. R.

1979   *Stabilization Policy in an African Setting: Kenya 1963–73.* London: Heinneman Educational Books.

Kinyanjui, Kabiru

1974   "Distribution of Educational Resources and Opportunities in Kenya," IDS Discussion Paper No. 28, University of Nairobi.

Kironde, J. M. Lusugga

1992a "Received Concepts and Theories in African Urbanisation and Management Strategies: The Struggle Continues," *Urban Studies* 29, 8: 1277–1291.

1992b "Rent Control Legislation and the National Housing Corporation in Tanzania," *Canadian Journal of African Studies* 26, 2: 306–327.

Kitching, Gavin

1980   *Class and Economic Change in Kenya: The Making of an African Petite Bourgeoisie, 1905–70.* New Haven: Yale University Press.

1978   "Politics, Method and Evidence in the Kenya Debate," in Henry

Bernstein and Bonnie K. Campbell, eds., *Contradictions of Accumulation in Africa.* Beverly Hills: Sage Publications.

Kulaba, Saitiel
1989a "Local Government and the Management of Urban Services in Tanzania," in Stren and White 1989.
1989b *Urban Management and the Delivery of Urban Services in Tanzania.* Dar es Salaam: Centre for Housing Studies, Ardhi Institute.

Kuper, Leo, and M. G. Smith eds.
1971 *Pluralism in Africa.* Berkeley: University of California Press.

Lamb, Geoffrey, and Linda Muller
1982 "Control, Accountability and Incentives in Successful Development Institutions." World Bank Staff Working Paper No. 550.

Lancaster, Carol, ed.
1992 *The Politics of Economic Reform in Africa.* Washington: Center for Strategic and International Studies.

Lee-Smith, Diana
1989 "Urban Management in Nairobi: A Case Study of the Matatu Mode of Public Transport," in Stren and White 1989, 276–304.

Lele, Uma, ed.
1992 *Aid to African Agriculture: Lessons from Two Decades of Donors' Experience.* Baltimore: John Hopkins University Press.

Lele, Uma, and Richard L. Meyers
1987 "Growth and Structural Change in East Africa: Domestic Policies, Agricultural Performance, and World Bank Assistance, 1963–1987." MADIA Background Paper, Part 1, World Bank, Washington, D.C.

Lemarchand, René
1972 "Political Clientelism and Ethnicity in Tropical Africa: Competing Solidarities in Nation-Building," *American Political Science Review* 66, 1: 68–90.

Lenin, V. I.
1917 *State and Revolution.* New York: International Publishers House, 1932 and 1943.

Leonard, David K.
1984 "Class Formation and Agricultural Development," in Barkan 1984a.
1991 *African Successes: Four Public Managers of Kenyan Rural Development.* Berkeley: University of California Press.

Levi, Margaret
1988 *Of Rule and Revenue.* Berkeley: University of California Press.

Leys, Colin
1974 *Underdevelopment in Kenya: The Political Economy of Neo-Colonialism 1964–71.* Berkeley: University of California Press.
1978 "Capital Accumulation, Class Formation and Dependency: The Significance of the Kenya Case," *Socialist Register 1978.*

Lipset, Seymour Martin
1960 *Political Man.* Garden City, N.Y.: Doubleday.

Lipset, Seymour Martin, K. R. Seong, and J. C. Torres
1990 "A Comparative Analysis of the Social Requisites of Democracy." Paper presented at the Annual Convention of the American Political Science Association, San Francisco, August 30–September 3.

Lipumba, N. H., N. E. Osoro, and B. Nyngetera
1990 "AERC Workshop Paper." Mimeograph. Nairobi: African Economic Research Consortium.

Livingstone, Ian
   1991   "A Reassessment of Kenya's Rural and Urban Informal Sector," *World Development* 19, 6: 651–670.
Lofchie, Michael
   1965   *Zanzibar: Background to Revolution.* Princeton: Princeton University Press.
   1989   *The Policy Factor: Agricultural Performance in Kenya and Tanzania.* Boulder: Lynne Rienner Publishers.
Lonsdale, John
   1981   "States and Social Progress in Africa: A Historigraphical Survey," *African Studies Review* 24, 2–3: 139–225.
Loubser, J. J.
   1983   *Human Resource Development in Kenya: An Overview.* Ottawa: Canadian International Development Agency.
Lugalla, J.P.
   1989   "The State, Law and Urban Poverty in Tanzania," *Law and Politics in Africa, Asia and Latin America* 2, 131–157.
Macharia, Kinuthia
   1992   "Slum Clearance and the Informal Economy in Nairobi," *Journal of Modern African Studies* 30, 2: 221–236.
Macoloo, Chris
   1988   "Housing the Urban Poor: A Case Study of Kisumu Town, Kenya," *Third World Planning Review* 10, 2: 159–174.
Makau, B.M.
   1985a "Education Planning and Development in Kenya: The 8-4-4 School Curriculum and Its Implications for Self-employment," IDS Working Paper No. 433, University of Nairobi.
   1985b "Equity and Efficiency in Financing Secondary Education in Kenya: Key Issues in State-Community Partnership," IDS Working Paper No. 429, University of Nairobi.
   1990   *Computers in Kenya's Secondary Schools: Case Study of an Innovation in Education.* Ottawa: IDRC.
Makinda, Samuel
   1983   "From Quiet Diplomacy to Cold War Politics: Kenya's Policy," *Third World Quarterly* 5, 2:30–319.
Malekela, G.
   1983   "Access to Secondary Education in Sub-Saharan Africa: The Tanzanian Experiment." Ph.D. thesis, University of Chicago.
Malekela, G., D. Ndabi, and B. Cooksey
   1990   "Girls' Educational Opportunities and Performance in Tanzania," TADREG Research Report No. 2, Dar es Salaam.
Maliyamkono, T. L., and M.S.D. Bagachwa
   1990   *The Second Economy in Tanzania.* Athens: Ohio University Press.
Malombe, Joyce M.
   n.d.   "The Impact of Site and Service Projects on the Urban Housing Market: The Case of Dandora, Nairobi." Unpublished Ph.D. thesis, University of Western Ontario.
Martin, Denis
   1978   "Zizanie en Tanzanie? Les elections tanzaniennes de 1975, ou les petits nons du Mwalimu," in Guy Hermet and Alain Rouquie, eds., *Aux Urnes l'Afrique.* Paris: Pedone, 79–117.
   1988   *Tanzanie: l'invention d'une culture politique.* Paris: Fondation National des Sciences Politiques.

1990 "L'invention des Cultures Politiques: Esquisse d'une approche compara-tiste a partir des experiences africaines." Paper prepared for the Conference on The Relationship Between the State and Civil Society in Eastern Europe and Africa, Bellagio, Italy, February 5–11.

1992 "'Demokrasia ni Nini?' Fragments swahili du debat politique en Tanzanie," *Politique Africaine* 47, 109–134.

Mazingira Institute
1982 "Community Participation in Low-Income Urban Settlements in Kenya." Unpublished study for UNCHS (Habitat), Mazingira Institute, Nairobi.

n.d. *Nairobi: The Urban Growth Challenge.*

Mbithi, Philip M., and Rasmus Rasmusson
1977 *Self-Reliance in Kenya: The Case of Harambee.* Uppsala: Scandinavian Institute of African Studies.

McHenry, Jr., Dean
1981 *Tanzania's Ujamaa Villages: The Implementation of a Rural Develop-ment Strategy.* Berkeley: Institute of International Studies.

1992 "Democracy and the Party System: The Impact of Multi-partyism on Tanzanian Politics." Paper presented at the Annual Meeting of the African Studies Association, November 20–23, 1992. Atlanta: African Studies Association, 1993.

Michaels, Marguerite
1993 "Retreat from Africa," *Foreign Affairs* 72, 1: 93–108.

Migdal, Joel
1988 *Strong Societies and Weak States.* Princeton: Princeton University Press.

Miller, Norman N.
1970 "The Rural African Party: Political Participation in Tanzania," *American Political Science Review* 64, 2: 548–571.

Miller, Norman N., and Rodger Yeager
1994 *Kenya: The Quest for Prosperity,* second edition. Boulder: Westview Press.

Miti, Katabaro
1980 "Party and Politics in Tanzania," *Utafiti* 5, 2: 180–202.

1985 "L'operation *Nguvu Kazi* a Dar es Salaam. Ardeur au travail et controle de l'espace urbain," *Politique Africaine* 17: 88–104.

Mitullah, Winnie
1991 "Hawking as a Survival Strategy for the Urban Poor in Nairobi: The Case of Women," *Environment and Urbanization* 3, 2 (October 1991).

Moore, Jr., Barrington
1966 *Social Origins of Dictatorship and Democracy.* Boston: Beacon Press.

1978 *Injustice: The Social Basis of Obedience and Revolt.* London: Macmillan.

Morrison, D. R.
1976 *Education and Politics in Africa: The Tanzanian Case.* Nairobi: Heinemann.

Mosley, Paul
1987 *Conditionality as Bargaining Process: Structural Adjustment Lending 1980–1986.* Princeton: International Finance Section, Princeton University.

Msekwa, Pius
1974 "Party Supremacy." M.A. thesis, University of Dar es Salaam.

Msemakweli, John
1993 "Helping Those Who Help Themselves," *Express,* September 2–8.

Mueller, Suzanne
    1980   "Retarded Capitalism in Tanzania," *The Socialist Register.*
Mukandala, Rwekaza
    1990   "Post 1990 Election Politics in Tanzania." Unpublished paper,
            Department of Political Science, University of Dar es Salaam.
    1993   "State Power and Political Institutions in Tanzania in the Eighties," in
            Widner 1993.
Mwega, F. M.
    1990   "An Econometric Study of Selected Monetary Policy Issues in Kenya."
            ODI Working Paper No. 42.
    1991   "An Overview of Trade/Macro Policies and the Industrialization
            Experience in Kenya in the 1970s and 1980s." Mimeograph, University
            of Nairobi.
Nabli, Mustapha K., and Jeffrey B. Nugent
    1989   *The New Institutional Economics and Development.* North-Holland:
            Elsevier Science Publishers.
Nairobi City Commission or City Council
    1982   *Abstract of Accounts for the Year Ended 31st December 1982.* Nairobi:
            Nairobi City Hall, 1983.
    1983   *Annual Report 1983.* Nairobi: Nairobi City Hall, 1984.
    1988   *Nairobi—The Capital City of the Republic of Kenya.* Nairobi: Nairobi
            City Hall.
Nairobi Law Monthly
    Var.   *Nairobi Law Monthly.* Nairobi.
Narman, A.
    1985   *Practical Subjects in Kenyan Academic Secondary Schools: A Tracer
            Study.* Stockholm: Swedish International Development Authority,
            Education Division.
National Council of Churches of Kenya (NCCK)
    1992   *The Cursed Arrow: Contemporary Report on the Politicised Land
            Clashes in Rift Valley, Nyanza and Western Provinces.* Nairobi: National
            Council of Churches of Kenya.
National Election Monitoring Unit (NEMU)
    1993a   *The Multi-Party General Elections in Kenya: 29 December 1992.*
            Nairobi: National Election Monitoring Unit.
    1993b   *Courting Disaster: A Report on the Ethnic Clashes.* Nairobi: National
            Election Monitoring Unit.
Ndolo, Chris
    1990   "The Poor Too, Have Rights: We Created the Shanties, We Must Let
            Them Be," *Nairobi Law Monthly* 28: 16–118.
Ndulu, Benno J.
    n.d.   "The Current Economic Stagnation in Tanzania," African Studies Center,
            Boston University.
    1986   "Governance and Economic Management," in Berg and Whitaker 1986:
            81–107.
    1987   "Stabilization and Adjustment Policies and Programmes: Tanzania,"
            WIDER country study no. 17.
    1990   "Constraints and Prospects for Medium Term Growth in Tanzania" in
            Taylor 1990.
Ndulu Benno, and J. Semboja
    1991   "Trade and Industrialization in Tanzania." Paper for the WIDER project
            on Trade and Industrialization.

Needler, Martin C.
1968 "Political Development and Socioeconomic Development: The Case of Latin America," *American Political Science Review* 62, 3: 889–897.

Nelson, Joan M.
1984 "The Political Economy of Stabilization: Commitment, Capacity, and Public Response," *World Development* 12, 10: 983–1006.
1990 *Economic Crisis and Policy Choice: The Politics of Adjustment in the Third World.* Princeton: Princeton University Press.

Newlyn, W. T., and D. C. Rowan
1954 *Money and Banking in British Colonial Africa.* Oxford: Clarendon Press.

Njonjo, Apollo
1977 "The Africanisation of the White Highlands: A Study of Agrarian Class Struggles in Kenya." Ph.D. dissertation, Department of Political Science, Princeton University.

Nkinyangi, J. A.
1980 "Education for Nomadic Pastoralists: Development Planning by Trial and Error," in J. G. Galaty, D. Aronson, and P. C. Salzman, eds., *The Future of Pastoral Peoples.* Ottawa: International Development Research Corporation.

Nnoli, O.
1977 *Self-Reliance and Foreign Policy in Tanzania.* New York: NOK Publishers.

Nyerere, Julius K.
1962 "Ujamaa: The Basis of African Socialism" in Nyerere 1967a: 162–171.
1963 "Democracy and the Party System," in Nyerere 1967a: 195–203.
1965 "Guide to the One-Party State Commission," in Nyerere 1967a: 261–265.
1967a *Freedom and Unity: A Selection from Writings and Speeches, 1952–65.* New York: Oxford University Press.
1967b "The Arusha Declaration and TANU's Policy on Socialism and Self-Reliance," in Nyerere 1967a: 231–250.
1967c "Education and Self-Reliance," in Nyerere 1968: 267–290.
1967d "Socialism and Rural Development," in Nyerere 1968: 337–366.
1968 *Freedom and Socialism: A Selection from Writings and Speeches, 1965–67.* New York: Oxford University Press.
1973 *Freedom and Development: A Selection from Writings and Speeches, 1968–72.* New York: Oxford University Press.
1990 Report of a press conference, *Daily News* (Dar es Salaam, February 21, 1990).
1992 Speech to National Conference of CCM, February 18, 1992.

Nyong'o, Peter Anyang
1992 "The One-Party State and Its Apologists," in P. A. Nyong'o, ed., *Thirty Years of Independence in Africa: The Lost Decades?* Nairobi: African Academy Science Publishers.

O'Donnell, Guillermo, and Philippe C. Schmitter
1986 "Tentative Conclusions About Uncertain Democracies," in O'Donnell, Schmitter, and Whitehead 1986.

O'Donnell, Guillermo, Philippe C. Schmitter, and L. Whitehead, eds.
1986 *Transitions from Authoritarian Rule: Prospects for Democracy.* Baltimore: Johns Hopkins University Press.

Okumu, John
1977 "Kenya's Foreign Policy," in O. Aluko, ed., *The Foreign Policies of African States.* London: Hodder and Stoughton.

Okumu, John J., with Frank Holmquist
   1984   "Party and Party-State Relations," in Barkan 1984: 45–69.
Ominde, S. H., ed.
   1988   *Kenya's Population Growth and Development to the Year 2000 AD.*
          Nairobi: Heinemann Educational Books.
Ondiege, P. O., and C. Aleke-Dondo
   n.d.   "Informal Sector Assistance Policies in Kenya." Unpublished
          paper, University of Nairobi, Department of Urban and Regional
          Planning.
Ondiege, P. O., and R. A. Obudho
   1988   "Population Growth and Demand for Rural and Urban Housing," in
          Ominde 1988.
Oruka, H. O.
   1992   *Oginga Odinga: His Philosophy and Beliefs.* Nairobi: Initiatives
          Publishers.
Phelps, M. G., and B. Wasow
   1972   "Measuring Protection and Its Effects in Kenya." Institute of
          Development Studies Working Paper, University of Nairobi.
Potholm, C. P., and R. A. Fredlund, eds.
   1980   *Integration and Disintegration in East Africa.* Washington: University
          Press of America.
Pratt, Cranford
   1976   *The Critical Phase in Tanzania 1945–68.* Cambridge: Cambridge
          University Press.
Przeworski, Adam
   1986   "Some Problems in the Study of Transition to Democracy." O'Donnell,
          Schmitter, and Whitehead, 1986.
Ravenhill, John
   1979   "Regional Integration and Development in Africa: Lessons from the East
          African Community," *Journal of Commonwealth and Comparative
          Politics* 17, 3: 227–246.
Ravikanbur, R.
   1987   "Structural Adjustment, Macroeconomic Adjustment and Poverty: A
          Methodology for Analysis," *World Development* 15, 2: 1515–1526.
Reimer, R.
   1970   "Effective Rates of Protection in East Africa," Institute of Development
          Studies Staff Paper No. 78, University of Nairobi.
Riddell, Roger
   1988   *Foreign Aid Reconsidered.* Baltimore: Johns Hopkins University Press.
Riker, William H.
   1962   *The Theory of Political Coalitions.* New Haven: Yale University
          Press.
Rosberg, Carl G., and John Nottingham
   1966   *The Myth of Mau Mau.* New York: Praeger.
Rosberg, Carl G., and Robert H. Jackson
   1982   *Personal Rule in Black Africa: Prince, Autocrat, Prophet, Tyrant.*
          Berkeley: University of California Press.
Rueschmeyer, Dietrich, Evelyne Huber Stephen, and John D. Stephen
   1992   *Capitalist Development and Democracy.* Chicago: University of Chicago
          Press.
Samoff, Joel
   1987   "School Expansion in Tanzania: Private Initiatives and Public Policy,"
          Comparative Education Review 31, 3: 333–362.

1990   "The Politics of Privatization in Tanzania," *International Journal of Education Development* 10, 1.

1991   "The Facade of Precision in Education Data and Statistics: A Troubling Example from Tanzania," *Journal of Modern African Studies* 29, 4: 669–689.

Sandbrook, R.
1982   *The Politics of Basic Needs: Urban Aspects of Assaulting Poverty in Africa.* London: Heinemann.

Schatzberg, Michael, ed.
1987   *The Political Economy of Kenya.* New York: Praeger.

Shaidi, L.
1984   "Tanzania: The Human Resources Deployment Act of 1993: A Desperate Measure to Contain a Desperate Situation," *Review of African Political Economy* 31: 82–86.

Shapouri, Shala, Margaret Missiaen, and Stacey Rosen
1992   *Food Strategies and Market Liberalization in Africa: Case Studies of Kenya, Tanzania, and Zimbabwe.* Washington: United States Department of Agriculture, Economic Research Service.

Sharpley, J., and S. R. Lewis
1988   "Kenya's Industrialization, 1964–84," IDS Discussion Paper No. 242, Institute for Development Studies, Sussex.

Singer, Hans, and Javed Ansari
1977   *Rich and Poor Countries.* London: George Allen and Unwin.

Sklar, Richard L.
1988   "Beyond Capitalism and Socialism in Africa," *Journal of Modern African Studies* 26, 1: 1–21.

Smith, A.
1969   "Socio-Economic Development and Political Democracy: A Causal Analysis," *Midwest Journal of Political Science* 13, 1: 95–125.

Smith, William Edgett
1971   *We Must Run While Others Walk.* New York: Random House.

Smoke, Paul
1992   "Small Town Local Government Finance in Kenya: The Case of Karatina Town Council," *Public Administration and Development* 12, 1 (February 1992).

Society
Var.   *Society Magazine.* Nairobi.

Sorokin, Boyce
1992   "End of an Affair," *Africa Events* (January 1992): 22–23.

Standard
Var.   *The Standard Newspaper.* Nairobi.

Stren, Richard
1975   "Urban Policy and Performance in Kenya and Tanzania," *Journal of Modern African Studies* 13, 2: 272–273.

Stren, Richard, and Rodney White, eds.
1989   *African Cities in Crisis: Managing Rapid Urban Growth.* Boulder: Westview Press.

Stren, Richard, et al.
1992   *An Urban Problematique: The Challenge of Urbanization for Development Assistance.* Toronto: Centre for Urban and Community Studies.

Swynnerton, R. T. M.
1954   *A Plan to Intensify the Development of African Agriculture in Kenya.* Nairobi: Government Printer.

Tamarkin, M.
  1978   "The Roots of Political Stability in Kenya," *African Affairs* 77, 308:
          297–320.
Tanganyika African National Union (TANU)
  1971   *TANU Party Guidelines (Mwongozo).* Dar es Salaam: Printpak.
Tanzania (United Republic of Tanzania)
  1965   Presidential Commission Report, *The Establishment of a Democratic
          One-Party State.* Dar es Salaam: Government Printer.
  1982a   *Structural Adjustment Programme for Tanzania.* Dar es Salaam: Ministry
          of Planning and Economic Affairs.
  1982b   *The Tanzania National Agricultural Policy.* Dar es Salaam: Task Force
          on National Agricultural Policy.
  1991   *1988 Population Census: Preliminary Report.* Dar es Salaam: Bureau of
          Statistics.
  1992a   *Economic Survey 1991.* Dar es Salaam: Government Printer.
  1992b   *1988 Population Census: National Profile.* Dar es Salaam: Bureau of
          Statistics.
  1992c   *Tume ya Rais ya Mfumo wa Chama Kimoja au Vingi vya Siasa Tanzania*
          (Presidential Commission on Multiparty Policy in Tanzania, Francis
          Nyalali, chair). Mimeograph, 3 volumes. Dar es Salaam.
  1992d   *Status Report on Education in Tanzania.* Dar es Salaam: Ministry of
          Education and Culture.
  Var.   *Basic Education Statistics in Tanzania.* Dar es Salaam: Ministry of
          Education.
Tanzania Development Research Group (TADRGE)
  1992   "Poverty-focused Primary Education Project: A Description and Analysis
          of Key Data and Documentation." Mimeograph. Dar es Salaam.
  1993   "Parents' Attitudes and Strategies Towards Education in Rural
          Tanzania." Mimeograph. Dar es Salaam.
Taylor, Lance
  1987   "Macro Policy in the Tropics: How Sensible People Stand," *World
          Development* 15, 12: 1407–1436.
  1993   *The Rocky Road to Reform: Adjustment, Income Distribution, and
          Growth in the Developing World.* Cambridge: M.I.T. Press.
Thomas, Barbara P.
  1985   *Politics, Participation and Poverty: Development Through Self-Help.*
          Boulder: Westview Press.
Throup, David W.
  1987a   *Economic and Social Origins of Mau Mau, 1945–53.* Athens: Ohio
          University Press.
  1987b   "The Construction and Destruction of the Kenyatta State," in Schatzberg
          1987: 48–53.
Tignor, Robert L.
  1976   *The Colonial Transformation of Kenya.* Princeton: Princeton University
          Press.
Tordoff, William
  1967   *Government and Politics in Tanzania.* Nairobi: East African Publishing
          House.
Tostensen, Arne
  1982   *Dependence and Collective Self-Reliance in Southern Africa.* Uppsala:
          Scandinavian Institute of African Studies.

Tripp, Aili Mari
    1989   "Women and the Changing Urban Household in Tanzania," *Journal of Modern African Studies* 27, 4: 601–624.
    1990   "The Informal Economy and the State in Tanzania." Ph.D. dissertation, Northwestern University.
    1992   "Local Organizations, Participation, and the State in Urban Tanzania," in Hyden and Bratton 1992: 221–242.

Umozurike, U.O.
    1982   "Tanzania's Intervention in Uganda," *Archiv des Volkerrechts* 20, 1.

Union of Multiparty Democracy (UMD)
    1991   "UMD Policy Statement," *Family Mirror* (Dar es Salaam), October 1991.

United Nations Development Programme (UNDP)
    1990   *Human Development Report.* New York: Oxford University Press.
    1993a   *The Internally Displaced Population in Kenya, Western and Rift Valley Provinces: A Need Assessment and a Program Proposal for Rehabilitation.* By John Rogge, consultant. Nairobi: United Nations Development Programme.
    1993b   *Programme for Displaced Persons.* Nairobi: United Nations Development Programme.

United States Department of Agriculture (USDA)
    1983   *Agriculture Situations Report: Tanzania.* Nairobi: United States Department of Agriculture, February 14, 1983.
    1990   *World Agriculture: Trends and Indicators, 1970–89,* Statistical Bulletin No. 815. Washington: United States Department of Agriculture (Economic Research Service).

van Donge, Jan Kees, and Athumani J. Liviga
    1986   "Tanzanian Political Culture and the Cabinet," *Journal of Modern African Studies* 24, 4: 619–639.

von Freyhold, Michaela
    1979   *Ujamaa Villages in Tanzania: Analysis of a Social Experiment.* New York: Monthly Review Press.

Wasserman, Gary
    1976   *Politics of Decolonization: Kenya Europeans and the Land Issue, 1960–1965.* London: Cambridge University Press.

Waters, Tony
    1992   "Cultural Analysis of the Economy of Affection in Tanzania," *Journal of Modern African Studies* 30, 1: 163–175.

Weekly Review
    Var.   *The Weekly Review.* Nairobi: Weekly Review Ltd.

Widner, Jennifer A.
    1992   *The Rise of a Party State in Kenya: From Harambee to Nyayo.* Berkeley: University of California Press.
    1993   *The Economics of Political Liberalization in Africa.* Baltimore: Johns Hopkins University Press.
    1994   "Single Party States and Agriculture Policies: The Cases of the Ivory Coast and Kenya," *Comparative Politics* 21 (January), 127–147.

World Bank
    1979   *Accelerated Development in Sub-Saharan Africa.* Washington: The World Bank.

1987a *Kenya: Industrial Sector Policies for Investment and Export Growth.*
       Washington: The World Bank.
1987b *Tanzania: An Agenda for Industrial Recovery,* Vols. I and II.
       Washington: The World Bank.
1988   *Education in Sub-Saharan Africa: Policies for Adjustment,
       Revitalization, and Expansion.* Washington: The World Bank.
1989a *Sub-Saharan Africa: From Crisis to Sustainable Growth.* Washington:
       The World Bank.
1989b *World Development Report 1989.* New York: Oxford University Press.
1989c "University Education in Kenya: Trends and Their Implications for
       Costs, Financing and Occupation." Mimeograph, World Bank and Kenya
       Ministry of Education, Nairobi.
1990   *Kenya, Stabilization and Adjustment: Toward Accelerated Growth.*
       Washington: The World Bank.
1991a *World Development Report 1991.* New York: Oxford University Press.
1991b *Tanzania Economic Report: Towards Sustainable Development in the
       1990s,* Vols. I and II. Washington: The World Bank (Country Operations
       Division, Southern Africa Department).
1991c "Teachers and the Financing of Education," Southern African Depart-
       ment, Report No. 9863TA. Washington: The World Bank.
1991d "Press Release, Meeting of the Consultative Group for Kenya." Paris:
       The World Bank, November 26, 1991.
1992   *World Development Report 1992.* New York: Oxford University Press.
1993a *Social Indicators and Development.* Washington: The World Bank.
1993b "Press Release, Meeting of the Consultative Group for Tanzania." Paris:
       The World Bank, July 1993.
1993c "Press Release, Meeting of the Consultative Group for Kenya." Paris:
       The World Bank, November 23, 1993.
1994   *Adjustment in Africa: Reforms, Results, and the Road Ahead.* New York:
       Oxford University Press.
World Bank/UNDP
1992   *African Development Indicators.* New York: United Nations.
Yeager, Roger
1989   *Tanzania: An African Experiment,* second edition. Boulder: Westview
       Press.
1994   *Adjustment in Africa: Reforms, Results, and the Road Ahead.* New York:
       Oxford University Press.

Index

Accountability, 2, 4, 19; internal, 51; lack of, 51, 55; need for, 97; political, 20, 31, 85

African Development Bank, 114

Africanization: of civil service, 9, 12; of economy, 85, 107; institutional, 13–14

African National Congress, 250

Africa Watch, 36, 70

Afro-Shirazi Party, 9, 21, 51

Agriculture: bias against, 102; comparative advantage in, 132–133, 135, 159; credit in, 113; exports, 5, 13, 22; farmer's cooperatives, 6; growth rates, 22*tab;* incentives, 120, 134, 146, 166, 188; informal, 182; markets, 39, 107; neglect of, 117, 118; output in, 110; peasant, 188; policy, 105–106, 129–171; political weakness of, 149; production, 20, 88, 102, 134; recovery of, 29; reforms in, 167–170; reliance on, 117; stagnation in, 149; state intervention in, 23, 26; Tanzania national policy, 168; urban, 88, 182–183, 190–191

Aid, financial, xiv, 6, 87, 253; African dependence on, 3, 125, 237; conditions on, 28, 37, 40, 42, 49, 61, 96, 113, 166, 197, 253; in Economic Recovery Program, 29, 31; to education, 212–215; international community pressure in, xiv, 28; postponement of, 52; quick-disbursing, 29, 31, 35, 37, 38, 40, 44*n28,* 113, 125, 160, 237; and structural adjustment, xiv, 30, 47; suspension of, 29, 42*n2,* 55, 113

Amin, Idi, 236, 237, 240, 243, 244, 245, 246

Amnesty International, 36

Anglo-American Teachers for East Africa, 213

Anyona, George, 59, 60

Apartheid, 1, 2

Arusha Declaration, 5, 15, 47, 83, 87, 93, 117, 154, 188, 189, 197, 244

Asian community, 30, 31, 34, 73, 86, 153

ASP. *See* Afro-Shirazi Party

Associations: agricultural, 72; autonomy of, 18–19; business, 19, 34; civic, 48; collective, 198; community-based, 19; dependence on external funding, 19; development, 198; ethnic, 18, 20, 26, 198; farmer's cooperatives, 6, 10; Harambee, 19, 72, 141; law and order, 44*n21;* nationalist, 80; nongovernmental, 19, 89, 181; party control of, 13; political, 90; professional, xiv, 19, 34, 48, 51, 72; and provision of basic services, 19, 44*n21;* rural, 18, 19, 21, 34; self-help, xiv, 19, 21, 26, 72, 141; student, 51; sungusungu, 44n21; tribal, 80; urban, 181; voluntary, 78, 89; women's, 13, 18, 20, 26, 51, 72

Authoritarianism, 2, 3, 4, 36, 57, 60, 67, 72, 77

Authority: challenges to, 22; consolidation of, 8, 9; "parental, " 94, 95; political, 9

Balance-of-payments, 35, 37, 43*n14,* 44*n28,* 109, 112, 115, 116, 164, 237

Bank of Tanzania, 29

Barkan, Joel, 1–42, 86, 113, 150, 156

Barongo, Edward, 62

Barter, 21

Basic Industrialization Strategy (Tanzania), 117

Bates, Robert, 124, 149, 172*n18*

Bendix, Reinhard, 49

Benin, 72

Berg Report, 42*n1,* 168

British Overseas Volunteers Service, 213

Budget: balance, 119*tab;* deficits, 1, 21, 29, 35, 37, 40, 108*tab,* 109, 110, 166; for education, 211

Budget Rationalization Programme (Kenya), 110
Bukoba Native Cooperative Union, 20

Canada: economic assistance from, 49, 52; opposition to abuses in Kenya, 61
Capital: access to, 184; external, 112; flight, 110, 124; flows, 109, 116, 239; goods, 111, 122, 137; imports, 120; private, 121, 197; tied-up, 118
Capitalism, 13, 88; and democracy, 50; industrial, 49, 50; managed, 107; patron-client, xiii, 4, 7, 14, 15
CCM. *See* Chama cha Mapinduzi
Central Bank of Kenya, 27, 39, 44*n25*, 44*n27*, 59, 113, 116, 136, 166
Central Organisation of Trades Unions, 19, 26, 51
CHADEMA. *See* Chama cha Democrasia na Maendeleo
Chama cha Democrasia na Maendeleo, 33, 62, 63, 64, 67, 70, 71, 73, 74, 93, 95, 141, 197
Chama cha Mapinduzi, 21, 28, 31, 32, 47, 51, 53, 54, 55
Chege, Michael, 21, 47–74
China, 3, 6, 236, 239
Churches: autonomy of, 19; fundamentalist, 57; in Kenya, 19, 20, 26; political attitude of, 57; relations with state, 57–58; in Tanzania, 20
Church of the Province of Kenya, 57
Civic Rights Movement, 63
Civic United Front, 33, 62, 64, 66
Civil service, 2, 5, 7, 13–14, 209. *See also* Sector, public; Africanization of, 9, 12; autonomy of, 17; bloated, 21; income erosion in, 165; political control of, 18, 24; political opposition in, 59; professionalism of, 17
Clergy, xiv; demands for reform from, 2, 36; in opposition, 26, 57
Coffee: exports, 20, 110, 111, 127*n1*, 129, 137; markets, 140; prices, 106*tab*, 111, 112, 136, 139, 139*tab*; production, 25, 130*tab*, 135, 158, 160, 163, 168, 173*n22*
Coffee Board of Kenya, 26, 160
Cold War, end of, 1, 240, 241; effect on Africa, 3; and strategic value of Africa, 36, 44*n32*
Colonialism, 7, 11, 12, 13, 16, 43*n10*, 236; preservation of institutions of, 5, 16

Committee for Free Political Parties, 66
Conditionality. *See* Aid, conditions on
Conflict: ethnic, 10, 34, 52, 69, 76; party, 90; policy, 64; political, 34; religious, 10; social, 224; tribal, 26, 37, 38, 69
Consultative Group for Kenya, 37, 38, 40, 42*n2*, 45*n36*, 52, 61, 113, 116
Consultative Group for Tanzania, 31, 125
Convergence, xiii
Cooksey, Brian, 201–233
Cooperative Union of Tanzania, 20
Corporations: foreign, 172*n13*; multinational, 5, 153
Corruption, xiii, 7, 21, 24, 27, 30, 31, 34, 37, 40, 48, 51, 53, 54, 63, 64, 72, 85–87, 113, 125, 204, 241
COTU. *See* Central Organisation of Trades Unions
Court, David, 201–233
CUF. *See* Civic United Front
Currency: bureaus, 172*n6*; crash, 27; depreciation, 109, 116, 122, 123; devaluation, 28, 29, 39, 111, 120, 135, 136, 166, 167, 253, 254; domestic, 120; foreign, 122; hard, 136, 137, 160, 164, 172*n6*; markets, 136; overvaluation, 106, 129, 133–138, 137, 138, 171*n4*; single, 7; speculation, 136; trade, 135–36
Current account deficits, 108*tab*, 109, 118, 119*tab*, 122
CUT. *See* Cooperative Union of Tanzania

Daladalas, 199
Debt: crises, 164; external, 36, 111, 118, 123; service, 103*tab*, 111, 116, 118, 123, 127*n1*, 241
Democracy: bourgeois, 49, 50; and capitalism, 50; demands for, 1, 31, 125; and economic growth, 50, 75–99; and economic reform, 41; establishment of, 41; evolution of, 78; jeopardy thesis, 54, 70; liberal, 4; multiparty, xiv, 2, 31, 32; and poverty, 77, 98; prospects for, 41; resistance to, 50; transition to, 39, 41, 95, 98
Democratic Party, 38, 53, 61, 62, 68, 164
Development: associations, 198; and capacity to import, 102; capitalist, xiii; community, 21, 86; constraints on, 9, 97; and democracy, 50; divergent, 8, 14–21; economic, 4, 109; educational, 206–207; housing, 179; human, 117; infrastructure, 117, 132, 148; market-oriented, 85; pat-

terns, 9; regional, 12; rhetoric of, 87;
rural, 108, 124, 177, 193; social, 208;
strategy, 8; trickle-down process, 107,
108, 126
Diamond, Larry, 1
Drought, 110, 189

East African Airways, 244
East African Authority, 244
East African Community, 47, 110, 189, 236,
243, 244, 245, 254
Economic: adjustment, 1, 2, 101–127; competition, 13; decay, 8, 21–28; dependence, 77, 101, 102, 125; deregulation,
87; development, 4, 109; differentiation,
95; diversification, 101; growth, 75–99;
liberalization, 1, 30, 64; management, 9,
48; mismanagement, 101–102; modernization, 117; policy, 86; reform, xiii, 1, 8,
28–40, 101, 104, 106–125, 166, 254; regulation, 166; stabilization, 125; stagnation, xiii
Economic Recovery Program (Tanzania), 29,
31, 120, 196, 197
Economy: of affection, 78; Africanization of,
85, 107; control of, 87, 88; market, 1, 7,
43*n16,* 86, 96; mismanagement of,
21–22, 28; mixed, 107; political,
106–125; and politics, 84–89; regional,
15; second, 88; state intervention in, 23;
structural features, 101–127
Education, 5; access to, 201, 203, 205,
211–212, 224–226; curriculum, 203, 208;
decline in provision of, 27; distribution
of, 201; donor assistance for, 212–215,
226–228; and employment, 207–210;
ethnic favoritism in, 60; expansion of,
207–210; expenditures for, 24; financing,
210–211; inequality in, 224–226; infrastructure, 213; nationalization of schools,
202; policy, 222; political, 203; and politics, 206–207; primary, 19, 181, 202,
203, 207, 208, 215, 217, 218, 220; private, 203, 213, 218, 222, 225; provision
of, 30; quality of, 211, 223; rural, 6; secondary, 17, 19, 25, 181, 203, 211, 212,
215, 218; for self-reliance, 201–233; state
intervention in, 65; universal, 217; university, 17, 25, 209, 212
Elections, 17; competitive, 5, 49; democratic,
96; direct, 16; and ethnicity, 56, 68; fragmentation in, 82; fraud, 28, 36, 57, 61,

68, 82, 91, 172*n15;* multiparty, 52–53,
186; open, 5; parliamentary, 155; party
requirements, 32; primary, 91; queue voting in, 37, 57, 58, 91, 92; voter turnout,
28
Embu peoples, 11
Employment: and education, 207–210; ethnic
favoritism in, 60; formal sector, 125;
informal sector, 181–184; lack of access
to, 11; public sector, 36; urban, 134, 177;
wage, 182
Equity, 5, 27, 107, 117; and growth, 87
ERP. *See* Economic Recovery Program
(Tanzania)
Ethiopia, 30, 84, 96, 237, 245, 248, 249, 250
Ethnic issues, 9, 15, 45*n34,* 52, 76; accommodation, 79–84; associations, 18; in
elections, 68; factionalism, 48; hostility
to Asians, 30; inequalities, 73; redistribution of resources, 24; role in politics,
10
Europe, Eastern, 6, 36, 54, 58, 72, 77, 96, 98,
239, 241
European Community, economic assistance
from, 49, 52
Exchange: bureaus, 167; control, 119;
decline in, 23; foreign, 23, 27, 29, 39, 88,
104, 109, 111, 112, 116, 117, 121, 132,
134, 136, 166, 171*n1,* 241, 242; rates, 29,
104, 105*tab,* 106*tab,* 114, 115, 118, 120,
122, 127*n1,* 129, 133–138, 167, 173*n25,*
197; regimes, 121; regulations, 27
Export(s), 39, 103*tab;* agricultural, 5, 13, 22,
23, 129–132; coffee, 110, 111, 127*n1,*
129, 137; commodity, 20, 111, 138–148;
controls, 122; crop, 130*tab,* 138–141;
discrimination, 23; diversification, 110;
documentation, 114; earnings, 111, 132;
growth rates, 117; horticultural, 111,
127*n1,* 130, 163, 171*n1;* illegal, 119;
incentives, 146; informal, 124, 125; manufactured, 110, 115; nontraditional, 136;
performance, 102; primary, 102; processing zones, 114; production, 5, 30, 39,
106; retention funds, 121; subsidies, 114;
tea, 111, 127*n1,* 130, 137, 163

Fabianism, 87
Family planning, 44*n22,* 181
Fanon, Frantz, 56
Farmer's cooperatives, 10
FLS. *See* Front Line States

FORD. *See* Forum for the Restoration of
   Democracy
FORD-Asili, 38, 61, 68, 164, 187
FORD-Kenya, 38, 61, 68, 186, 187
Foreign Exchange Bearer Certificates, 116,
   136
Foreign relations, 6, 9
Forex C system. *See* Foreign Exchange
   Bearer Certificates
Forum for the Restoration of Democracy, 37,
   52, 53, 60, 61, 73
France, 240; economic assistance from,
   49
Front Line States, 236, 240, 251
Fundikira, Chief Said Abdallah, 32, 53, 55,
   62, 63, 70, 71

Gatabaki, Njehu, 60
Gecaga, Udi, 85, 86
Germany: economic assistance from, 2, 36,
   49; protest against repressions, 52, 61
Ghana, 30, 129
Gitari, Bishop David, 57
Gordon, David, 29, 35, 113, 235–262
Government: conditions of, 75–99; urban,
   184–187, 192–197; Westminster model,
   89, 92
Great Britain, 5; economic assistance from,
   2, 49; opposition to abuses in Kenya, 61
Gross domestic product, 108, 110, 118, 119,
   122, 123, 132, 241; Kenya, 22*tab;*
   Tanzania, 22*tab,* 29
Gross national product, 77, 108

Halfani, Mohamed, 175–200
Hamad, Seif Shariff, 62, 66
Hamad Commission, 120
Harambee, 19, 26, 72, 141, 201–233,
   206
Health care, 6, 19, 24, 181
Hempstone, Smith, 36, 45*n33,* 60, 258–
   260
Hirschman, Albert, 50, 54, 70
Holmquist, Frank, 51
Homelessness, 38
Horticulture, 111, 127*n1,* 130, 163, 171*n1*
Housing, 178–181, 189–192
Human Resources Deployment Act, 199
Human Resources Deployment Act (1983),
   194
Huntington, Samuel, 75, 76, 77
Hyden, Goran, 21, 75–99, 124

ICDC. *See* Industrial and Commercial
   Development Corporation Imanyara,
   Gitobu, 60
Import(s), 103*tab;* capacity, 124; cereal, 160;
   composition of, 111; compression, 110;
   consumer goods, 119–120; controls, 112,
   122; demand for, 112; dependence, 102;
   and development, 102; grain, 147*tab,*
   148; and infrastructure, 132; irregular,
   59; liberalization, 198; licensing, 112,
   114, 115, 121; luxury, 121; own funds
   scheme, 119, 120; prices, 109; restrictions, 112, 115, 116; self-financed, 119;
   subsidization, 122; substitution, 5, 23,
   109, 111, 117, 132, 138; support counterpart funds, 122; tariffs, 112; volume of,
   110
Income: allocation, 140; declines in, 22, 65;
   distribution, 5, 104, 109; equalization,
   23; foreign exchange, 242; housing, 190;
   inequities, 107; peasant, 137, 140; per
   capita, 22, 29, 88, 122; producer, 105,
   106; reduction, 124; rental, 123, 126;
   rural, 23, 167; secondary, 164; tax, 194;
   transfer, 107; urban, 179
India, 239
Industrial: capacity, 118; concentrations,
   116; investment, 117; liberalization, 116;
   privatization, 166; production, 116; pro-
   tectionism, 157
Industrial and Commercial Development
   Corporation, 85
Industrialization: early, 49; import substitution, 5, 109, 111, 117, 132
Inflation, 21, 24, 40, 60, 105, 105tab, 106,
   108, 109, 118, 119, 121, 122, 164
Infrastructure: common, 7; development,
   117, 132, 148; education, 213; investment, 177, 184, 199; maintenance, 132;
   neglect of, 164; physical, 88, 164; public,
   88; rehabilitation, 196; social, 102;
   urban, 179, 180
Institutions: administrative, 13–14;
   Africanization of, 13–14; decay of, 72;
   inherited from colonial period, 7, 16;
   political, 154–156; reform of, 168–170;
   restructuring of, 15, 120
Insurgencies, 36; Mau Mau, 12, 43*n10,* 80;
   Saba Saba, 52, 59
Interest rates, 103*tab,* 105, 105*tab,* 113, 121
International Monetary Fund, xiv, 2, 29, 39,
   44*n27,* 47, 87, 101, 108, 109, 112, 113,

119, 135, 150, 166, 167, 197, 236, 246, 252, 254
Investment: direct, 117; domestic, 60, 109; efficiency, 126; foreign, 5, 13, 60, 75, 104, 123, 124, 239; gross, 108*tab,* 119*tab;* industrial, 117; infrastructural, 177, 184, 199; local, 123, 124; long-term, 141; managed, 13; policy, 113; private, 5, 13, 104, 121, 124, 197; public, 123, 180
Islam in Africa Organization, 66
Israel, 245

Japan, 2, 3, 52
Johnston, Bruce, 75
Judicial Services Commission (Kenya), 17, 26

KADU. *See* Kenya African Democratic Union
Kalenjin peoples, 11, 24, 38, 69, 82, 86, 158, 159, 162, 172*n17*
KAMAHURU. *See* Committee for Free Political Parties
Kamana, C. Stanley, 63
Kambona, Oscar, 55, 62
Kampala Agreement, 243
KANU. *See* Kenya African National Union
Kaoneka, Lucas Mahindo, 62
Kariuki, G.B.M., 58
Kariuki, J.M., 81, 86
Kariuki, Ngotho, 59
Kathangu, J., 59
Kawawa, Rashidi, 92
Kenya, 11, 12; agricultural policy, 129–171; attempted coup in, 25, 48, 57, 81–82, 110, 136; Budget Rationalization Programme, 110; churches in, 20; civil society in, 18–20, 56; constitutional amendments in, 25, 26, 52, 53, 67, 80, 81, 90; development strategy, 107–117; economic performance, 5, 6, 13, 22–28, 103*tab;* education in, 202, 203, 204, 204*tab,* 205–215; elections in, 5; ethnic groups in, 10, 80–82; European community in, 11; external influences, 95–98; foreign policy, 6, 235–259; gross domestic product, 103*tab,* 110, 132; gross national product, 108; housing, 178–181; income, per capita, 22; National Assembly, 5, 26; opposition in, 56–61; patron-client capitalism in, 4, 7, 14, 15; political parties in, 16, 89–92; population

growth, 175, 176*tab;* reform in, 35–40; relations with Tanzania, 243–248; relations with West, 5, 6; state-society relations, 89–92; urbanization, 178–187
Kenya African Democratic Union, 10, 11, 13, 39, 53, 80, 89, 90, 159
Kenya African National Union, 10, 11, 13, 16, 25, 38, 47, 48, 52, 57, 58, 61, 67, 68, 70–71, 72, 80, 81, 82, 89, 90, 91
Kenya African Union, 74*n1*
Kenya Bus Service, 183
Kenya Coffee Growers Association, 160
Kenya Coffee Planter Cooperative Union, 59
Kenya Commission for Higher Education Act, 206
Kenya Debate, 59
Kenya Education Staff Institute, 213
Kenya External Trade Authority, 113
Kenya Farmers Association, 18, 23, 26, 160, 162
Kenya Grain Growers Cooperative Union, 26, 162
Kenya Institute of Education, 213
Kenya National Examinations Council, 206, 213
Kenya National Trading Corporation, 85
Kenya People's Party, 25
Kenya People's Union, 13, 51, 80, 90
Kenya Planters Cooperative Union, 23, 26, 160
Kenya Power and Lighting, 59
Kenya Railways, 186
Kenya Tea Development Authority, 44*n27,* 59, 162
Kenyatta, Jomo, 8, 10, 15, 16, 19, 35, 51, 80, 81, 82, 85, 86, 87, 90, 132, 158, 159, 206, 246
KETA. *See* Kenya External Trade Authority
KFA. *See* Kenya Farmers Association
Khaminwa, John
Kibaki, Mwai, 53, 82, 164
Kikuyu Embu Meru Association, 18
Kikuyu peoples, 10–11, 12, 15, 17, 24, 25, 37, 38, 39, 44*n20,* 53, 69, 72, 73, 80, 81, 82, 84, 85, 86, 91, 158, 185
Kiliku, Kennedy, 70
Kilimanjaro Native Cooperative Union, 20
Kisii peoples, 69
Kiswahili, 7, 10, 47, 64, 83, 203, 210
KNTC. *See* Kenya National Trading Corporation
KPCU. *See* Kenya Coffee Planter

Cooperative Union; Kenya Planters Cooperative Union
KPU. *See* Kenya People's Union
KTDA. *See* Kenya Tea Development Authority
Kuria, Gibson Kamau, 58

Labor: agricultural, 141; collective bargaining for, 65; costs of, 134; division of, 49, 241; movement, 20; skilled, 182; strikes, 74n1; unions, 6, 13, 56, 65; urban, 181–184
Land: acquisition, 151; agricultural, 194; auctions, 152; availability of, 88; consolidation, 151–152; dispossession from, 11; elite ownership of, 151–154; fee simple deeds, 151; illicit sale of, 59; nationalization of, 154; planning, 59; redistribution of, 85; reform, 109; resettlement, 12; state ownership, 104; tenure, 154; use, 59
Land Consolidation and Adjudication, 151
Land Freedom Army, 12
Latin America, 36, 77, 95, 98, 137, 237, 239
Law Society of Kenya, 26, 36, 58, 72
Law Society of Tanzania, 198
Leadership Code (Tanzania), 104, 197
Liberalization: economic, 1, 30, 64; foreign exchange, 116; import, 198; industrial, 116; of interest rates, 113; market, 113, 127n1, 160, 163, 254; political, xiv, 4, 33, 35, 41, 52, 61, 113, 235; trade, 1, 115, 116, 166
Liberia, 84, 240
Libya, 249
Lipset, Seymour, 4, 50, 75, 76, 77
Lipton, Michael, 149
Literacy, 202, 203, 217, 218, 220. *See also* Education
Little General Election, 13
Loans and Advances Realization Trust, 123
Lofchie, Michael, 20, 23, 29, 75, 105, 129–171, 177, 188
Lonhro East Africa, 85, 86
Luhya peoples, 11, 53, 69
Luo peoples, 11, 17, 37, 53, 69, 73, 84
Luo Union, 18

Maasai peoples, 12
Maendeleo wa Wanawake, 19, 51, 73
Makau, Ben, 201–233
Malacela, John, 70

Malombe, Joyce, 175–200
Mandela, Nelson, 3
Manufacturing: under bond, 114; exports, 110; growth rates, 22tab; protection, 114–115; state intervention in, 23
Mapalala, James, 32, 33, 55, 62, 64, 66
Marando, Maberere, 33, 62, 63
Market(s): agricultural, 20, 23, 107, 124; black, 104, 121; coffee, 140; common, 7; currency, 136; deregulation, 28–29, 39; distorted, 101; domestic, 118; economy, 7, 43n16, 86, 96; financial, 254; food, 123; industrial, 116; informal, 165; international, 102, 111, 130, 133; liberalization, 113, 127n1, 160, 163, 254; open, 75, 111; parallel, 124, 136; penetration, 114; prices, 105; protection, 118; regulation of, 1; state intervention in, 21, 23, 29, 41; tea, 140
Marx, Karl, 49
Matatus, 199
Matiba, Kenneth, 36, 37, 52, 53, 59, 61, 82, 91, 164
Mau Mau insurgency, 12, 43n10, 80
Mazrui, Ali, 73
Mboya, Tom, 81
Meru peoples, 11
Middle East, 245
Migration, urban, 19, 134, 178–179, 188
Mijikenda peoples, 11
Mjoya, Reverend Timothy, 58
MMD. *See* Movement for Multiparty Democracy
Moi, Daniel arap, 11, 24, 25, 26, 35, 37, 38, 48, 51, 52, 61, 67, 68, 69, 72, 81, 82, 84, 86, 87, 90, 91, 96, 97, 136, 150, 158, 159, 187, 206, 246, 249
Moore, Barrington, 4, 50, 74
Movement for Multiparty Democracy, 70
Mozambique, 250, 252
Mtei, Edwin, 33, 62
Mtikila, Charles, 62
Mudavadi, Moses, 184
Muge, Bishop Alexander, 57
Muite, Paul, 58, 73
Muliro, Masinde, 60
Multipartyism, 47–74
Mwakenya movement, 57
Mwangi, Moses, 187
Mwangi, Stephen, 187
Mwega, Francis, 23, 29, 101–127, 167

Mwinyi, Ali Hassan, 29, 30, 31, 32, 33, 43*n8,* 44*n31,* 48, 54, 63, 65, 66, 84, 88, 94, 97, 150, 166, 224, 246, 252, 254

Namibia, 252
National Assembly (Kenya), 5, 16, 17, 26, 67, 68, 90, 91, 154
National Assembly (Tanzania), 5, 18, 32, 83, 92, 155
National Cereals and Produce Board, 59, 173*n23*
National Coffee Board, 20
National Convention for Construction and Reform-Maguezi, 33, 62
National Council of Churches of Kenya, 19, 26, 36
National Democratic Party, 37, 58
National Executive Committee, 16, 18, 55, 92, 93, 155
National Housing Corporation, 178, 179, 196
National Investment Act, 123
Nationalism, 11, 62, 66, 80
Nationalization, 87–89
National Milling Corporation, 20, 123, 168, 169
National United Front, 66
NCCK. *See* National Council of Churches of Kenya
NCCR. *See* National Convention for Construction and Reform Party
Ndulu, Benno, 23, 29, 101–127, 167
NEC. *See* National Executive Committee (Tanzania)
Neocolonialism, 4
New International Economic Order, 236
Nigeria, xiii, 7, 95
Njonjo, Charles, 81, 82, 185
Nkomati Accords, 252
Non-Aligned Movement, 6, 97, 240, 253
Ntimama, William ole, 187
Nyalali, Chief Justice Francis, 32, 54, 55, 94
Nyamora, Pius, 60
Nyayo, 24
Nyayo Bus Services, 184
Nyayo Tea Zones, 162
Nyerere, Julius, 8, 9, 11, 15, 21, 29, 31, 32, 43*n8,* 44*n31,* 48, 51, 53, 54, 63, 66, 73, 83, 87, 88, 92, 93–94, 96, 97, 133, 147, 150, 165, 166, 168, 216, 236, 243, 244, 245, 246, 251, 252
Nyong'o, Anyang, 60

Obote, Milton, 244, 246
Odinga, Jaramogi Oginga, 37, 53, 58, 59, 60, 61, 81, 186
Odinga, Raila, 52
Ogaden War, 237
OIC. *See* Organization of Islamic Countries
Okullu, Biship Henry, 57, 58
Okumu, John, 51
Oparesheni Nguvu Kazi, 194
Open General License, 121
Operation Labor Force, 194
Opposition, 97, 165; ban on, 38; by clergy, 26, 57; divisions in, 68–69; emergence of, 21; ethnic tensions in, 38; and foreign journalists, 60; government fear of, 25; growth of, 37; intimidation of, 51, 94; legalization of, 37; parties, 51, 52, 53; political, 13, 47–48, 59, 60, 63; power struggles in, 71; press, 47, 54, 60; professional, 60; resistance to, 67; social forces in, 56–67; socioeconomic attributes of, 48; state response to, 67–71; student, 64–65, 81; weakness of, 33
Organization of African Unity, 97, 245–246; Liberation Committee, 250
Organization of Islamic Countries 33, 44*n31,* 66
Organization of Petroleum Exporting Countries, 236
Organization of Tanzania Trade Unions, 65
Organizations. *See* Associations
OTTU. *See* Organization of Tanzania Trade Unions
Ouko, Robert, 52, 53, 91
Oyugi, Edward, 59

Pan-Africanism, 9
Pan Africanist Congress, 252
Parastatals, 23, 85; economic role of, 168; excessive costs of, 169; income erosion in, 165; political opposition in, 59; privatization of, 29, 36, 40, 44*n29,* 113, 123, 126, 254; production levels, 168; reform of, 123, 169; and resource allocation, 85, 103, 104; responsiveness of, 2; restructuring of, 113
Party of Democracy and Development. *See* Chama cha Democrasia na Maendeleo
Party of the Revolution. *See* Chama cha Mapinduzi
Paternalism, 67

Patronage, 4, 14, 16, 25, 26, 27, 48, 59, 79, 81, 84, 85, 86, 88, 91, 126, 206
Peace Corps, 213
Peasant: agriculture, 188; coping strategies, xiv; income, 137, 140
Pemba, 65
Pluralism: coercion in, 84; consensus in, 84, 88–89; patterns of, 197–198; theories of, 78; Western model, 84
Policy: agricultural, 25, 105–106, 129–171; anticorruption, 48; bias against agriculture, 102; debate, 5; developmental, 14; economic, xiv, 86, 94, 101–127; educational, 202, 206, 207, 222; exchange rate, 118, 133–138; fiscal, 109, 110, 112, 167; investment, 113; macroeconomic, 28, 126; objectives, 84; public, 5, 25, 87, 90, 155, 167; redistributive, 21, 24, 41, 79, 117; reform, 126, 150, 165, 166; savings, 113; structural adjustment, 40, 63, 101, 108, 111, 112, 113, 116; trade, 127n1; urban, 175–200; variances, 149–157
Policymaking, 17; extraparliamentary, 89; party role in, 16; private, 79; process, 14, 16; removal from public arena, 93; rural influence, 150, 156
Political: accountability, 20, 31, 85; activism, 50; adjustment, 2; autonomy, 80; culture, 10; decay, 8, 21–28; economy, 106–125; education, 203; freedoms, 2; instability, 2, 111; institutions, 5, 154–156; interventionism, 87; liberalization, xiv, 4, 33, 35, 41, 52, 61, 113, 235; marginalization, 82; opposition, 59, 60, 63; parties, 16, 50, 81, 89. *See also* individual parties; persecution, 58; prisoners, 27, 36, 68; process, 77; reform, xiii, 1, 8, 10, 21, 28–40; representation, 16; repression, 2; resources, 149; rivalries, 84; theory, 15
Political Parties Act (Tanzania), 32
Politics: of agricultural policy, 129–171; communitarian model, 84, 88; conditions of, 78–99; constitutionalizing, 95; deep, 78, 79; and economy, 84–89; and education, 206–207; and external factors, 77; high, 78, 79; multiparty, 47–74, 82; pork barrel, 79
Population: government access to, 90; growth, xiii, 22tab, 41, 44n22, 129, 175, 237; rural, 5; urban, 75, 175, 177
Posts and Telecommunications, 59
Poverty, 107, 108, 126, 204; urban, 177

Preferential Trade Areas, 114
Presbyterian Church of East Africa, 57, 58
Press: control of, 51, 68, 70; freedom of, 2, 34, 49, 68; harassment, 39; independent, 36–37, 64; opposition, 47, 54, 60; party control of, 6, 13; political coverage of, 18; state-controlled, 54
Price(s): coffee, 112, 136, 139, 139tab, 146tab; commodity, 138–148; consumer, 27; controls, 112, 121; cost margin, 116; deregulation, 119, 163; distortions, 104; domestic, 108, 110; "getting right, " 1–2; imports, 109; international, 106tab; maize, 144fig, 146tab; market, 105; pressure on, 109; production, 106tab, 119, 120, 140, 141; reforms, 167–168; rice, 145fig; tea, 112, 136, 139, 140tab; wheat, 145fig, 163
Privatization, 1, 29, 36, 40, 44n29, 113, 123, 125, 126, 166, 169, 254
Production: agricultural, 20, 36, 88, 102, 134; cereal, 22, 23; coffee, 25, 131fig, 135, 158, 160, 163, 168, 173n22; export, 30, 39, 106, 114; food, 160; incentives, 105, 146; income, 105; industrial, 116, 117; maize, 142, 142fig, 148; prices, 119, 120; rice, 142, 143fig, 148, 172n8; rural, 188; smallholder, 23; socialist, 20; of state-owned industry, 22; subsidized, 107; tea, 130tab, 160, 168; voluntary cutbacks, 21; wheat, 143fig, 148, 158
Provincial Administration (Kenya), 17
Public Services Commission (Kenya), 17, 26

Recession, 35
Reform: adjusted, 29; agricultural, 167–170; commitment to, 113; constitutional, 93; dangers to, 3; demands for, 49; economic, xiii, 1, 8, 28–40, 101, 104, 106–125, 166, 254; education, 226–228; fundamental, 1; institutional, 168–170; land, 109; leveraging, 3; parastatal, 123, 169; partial, 29, 35–36; policy, 126, 150, 165, 166; political, xiii, 1, 8, 10, 21, 28–40; pressure for, xiv, 1–42, 36, 39; price, 167–168; resistance to, 2, 3, 33, 35, 37, 169, 253; tariff, 114, 122
Regime, authoritarian, 2, 3, 4, 36, 57, 60, 67, 72
Religious issues, 9, 48, 71, 240; conflict, 10; Islamic movements, 66
Rent-seeking, 21, 59, 104, 115, 126, 190

Repression, xiii, 2, 25, 26–27, 36, 45*n35,* 52, 60, 67–68, 70, 96

Resistance, passive, xiv

Resource(s); access to, 104; allocation, 84, 85, 87, 103, 104, 203; balance, 124; control of, 117; external, 118; foreign, 120, 122; gaps, 101, 102, 108*tab,* 118, 119*tab,* 122, 125–126; inefficient use of, 137; inflow, 120, 122; mobilization, 105, 125; political, 149; public ownership of, 117; redistribution, 24, 117; state control of, 104; transfer of, 138; waste of, 88

Rights: civil, 48, 55, 62; human, xiv, 2, 36, 37, 40, 48, 49, 53, 58, 60, 63, 66, 72, 113, 241; individual, 53, 58, 64; political participation, 91

Rubia, Charles, 36, 37, 52, 59, 91

Rural: associations, 18, 21, 34; cooperative societies, 34; development, 108, 124, 177, 193; education, 6; growth rates, 36; income, 23, 167; inequality, 41; origins, 71; political pressure, 150; population, 5; poverty, 40; production, 188; repatriation, 194; self-help, 19; villagization, 5, 29; voting, 154

Rwanda, 240

"Saba Saba, " 52, 59

SADCC. *See* Southern African Development Coordination Conference

Scandinavia: economic assistance from, 2, 36, 49, 52, 55, 241; protest against repressions, 52, 61

Sector, business, xiv

Sector, formal, 180

Sector, industrial: decline in, 148; efficiency in, 113; reliance on domestic demand, 116–117

Sector, informal, xiv, 124, 164, 165, 199; employment in, 181–184, 194; and government repression, 36; harassment in, 194–195; housing in, 180

Sector, manufacturing: and domestic demand, 117; parastatals in, 23

Sector, nongovernmental, 92

Sector, private, 5, 109; credit to, 110; ethnic dominations in, 86; growth of, 30; reduction of, 30; regulation of, 5; state relations with, 104

Sector, public, 104, 123; credit to, 111; efficiency in, 123; employment, 36; inefficiency of, 118; maintenance of, 118;

patronage in, 86; privatization in, 1, 29; and resources, 126

Shikuku, Martin, 60

Sklar, Richard, xiv

Smuggling, xiv, 21

Social: cohesion, 201; conflict, 224; consumption, 118; degeneracy, 48; development, 208; differentiation, 95; disruption, 76; equity, 202; expectations, 76; infrastructure, 102; interests, 47; justice, 107; needs, 87; networks, 198; orders, 78; services, 117, 177, 204, 213; tension, 76; welfare, 21, 24, 27, 29, 30, 35, 40, 107

Socialism, xiii, 4, 5, 6, 14, 15, 23, 30, 31, 43*n5,* 43*n16,* 48, 50, 72, 73, 75, 83, 88, 93, 153–154; failure of, 3, 7, 54, 63, 94

Somalia, 2, 4, 84, 237, 242, 248, 250

South Africa, 2, 7, 72, 96, 241, 250, 252

Southern African Development Coordination Conference, Southern African Development Community, 236, 240, 247, 251, 252

Southern Peoples Liberation Army, 249

Soviet Union, 3, 6, 77, 236, 239, 241

Squatter settlements, 179, 180, 185, 189, 190, 192, 200*n4*

Standard of living, 2, 22

State: intervention, 5, 21, 23, 26, 29, 41, 65, 87, 140; legitimacy of, 17, 18, 20, 94; mismanagement, 21–22, 28; ownership of land, 104; political subordination of, 6; postcolonial, 17; redistributive policies of, 21; regulation, 167; relations wieth churches, 57–58; in resource allocation, 103, 104; response to Harambee, 19; response to opposition, 67–71; society relations, 28, 78, 89–95

Steering Committee for a Multiparty System, 32, 53, 54

Stren, Richard, 27, 175–200

Structural adjustment, 1, 40, 63, 101, 108, 111, 112, 113, 116, 119, 135, 150, 167; and financial aid, xiv, 30, 47; Tanzanian, 29

Subsidization: of agriculture, 23; export, 114; housing, 179; import, 122; manufacured exports, 115; of production, 107; of social welfare, 24; urban, 134

Sudan, 84, 242, 245, 248, 249

Sungusungu, 44*n21,* 195

Sweden. *See* Scandinavia

Switzerland, 52
Swynnerton Plan, 172n9

Tanganyika African National Union, 5, 9, 16,
18, 20, 21, 51, 62, 74, 80, 92, 93, 141,
197
Tanganyika Federation of Labor, 62, 65
TANU. *See* Tanganyika African National
Union
Tanzania: agricultural policy, 20, 129–171;
associations in, 13; Basic
Industrialization Strategy, 117; churches
in, 20; civil society in, 20–21, 51,
197–198; constitutional amendments in,
9, 32, 92; detribalization in, 83–84;
development strategy, 117–125; economic performance, 6, 13, 22–28, 103tab;
Economic Recovery Program, 31, 120,
196, 197; education in, 202, 203, 204tab,
215–228; ethnic groups in, 10, 83–84;
external influences, 95–98; foreign relations, 6; gross domestic product, 103tab,
118, 119, 122, 132; housing in, 189–192;
income, per capita, 22, 29, 88, 122;
Leadership Code, 104; merger with
Zanzibar, 9, 65–6, 83; National
Assembly, 5, 32; nationalization in,
87–89; new constitution in, 21; in Non-
Aligned Movement, 6; Open General
License, 121; opposition in, 62–67; party
control in, 6; political parties in, 16,
92–95; population growth, 175, 176tab;
reform in, 28–35; relations with Kenya,
243–248; resistance to reform, 3; self-
reliance policy, 5, 133, 147; socialism in,
4, 5, 6, 14, 15, 23, 30, 31, 48, 72, 73, 75,
83, 88, 93, 153–154; state-society relations, 92–95; structural adjustment in, 29,
119, 135, 167; tensions with islands, 9;
urbanization in, 187–198; villagization
in, 20, 23
Tanzania Coffee Board, 169
Tanzanian Association of Non-Governmental
Organizations, 44n21
Tanzanian People's Party, 62
Tanzania Parents Association, 18, 20
Tanzania-Zambia Railway, 236
Tariff(s): import, 112; reductions, 114;
reform, 114, 122; structure, 118,
122
Task Force on National Agricultural Policy,
168

Tax(es): agricultural, 147; and currency
overvaluation, 133, 137; evasion, 118;
export, 24; on foreign exchange, 106; and
Harambee, 19; income, 194; revenue
reduction, 116, 118; to subsidize farmers,
23
Tea: exports, 111, 127n1, 130, 137, 163;
markets, 140; prices, 106tab, 112, 136,
139, 140tab; production, 25, 130tab, 160,
168
Teachers Service Commission Act, 206
Too, Mark arap, 86
Tourism, 43n9, 92, 111, 151, 245
Trade, 47; cross-border, 142, 173n27; currency, 135–136; deficits, 12; development benefits of, 133; growth of, 103tab;
international, 43n9, 133; liberalization, 1,
115, 116, 166; managed, 13; merchandise, 109; patterns of, 13; policy, 127n1;
regional, 9, 12; terms of, 110, 111;
unions, 51, 93
Transportation, 183–184, 192, 195
Trusteeship, 4, 43n7
Tugen peoples, 82
Tumbo, Kasanga, 62, 63

Uganda, 12, 30, 235, 236, 237, 242, 243,
244, 249
Uhuru, 64, 80
UMD. *See* Union for Multiparty
Democracy
Unemployment, 56, 107, 108, 134, 164, 179,
209, 211
Union for Multiparty Democracy, 33, 62, 63,
64, 73, 74
Union of Tanzania Workers, 65
United Nations: Center for Human
Settlements, 195; peacekeeping forces,
250
United States: Agency for International
Development, 42n3, 166, 179, 214; economic assistance from, 2, 36, 42n3, 49,
52; interests in Africa, 3; protest against
repressions, 52; relations with Kenya, 5,
237, 240
United Transport Overseas, 183
Urban: agriculture, 88, 182–183, 190–191;
civil organization, 44n21; commercial
class, 50; deterioration, 27; employment,
134, 177, 181–184; food supply, 124,
148; government, 184–187; income, 179;
industry, 137, 147; inequality, 41; infra-

structure, 179, 180; migration, 19, 134, 188; policy, 175–200; politics, 175; population, 75, 175, 177; poverty, 177; professionals, 62; services, 177; subsidization, 134; transport, 183–184; umemployment, 56; workers, 56

Urbanization, 175–200

Villagization, 5, 20, 23, 29, 188

Water supply, 19, 191
Widner, Jennifer, 51, 96
Women: associations of, 18, 19, 20, 26, 51, 72; credit networks of, 198; in informal sector, 182; school enrollment, 208, 218; in urban agriculture, 182–183

World Bank, 2, 29, 39, 42*n1,* 42*n2,* 44*n29,* 47, 49, 52, 87, 97, 101, 108, 109, 113, 114, 115, 119, 123, 129, 166, 179, 213, 236, 240, 246, 252, 254

Zaire, 2, 240
Zambia, 70, 72, 250
Zanzibar, 33, 44*n31,* 54; foreign relations of, 43*n9;* merger with Tanganyika, 9, 65–66, 83; move toward secession, 66, 71; tensions with mainland, 9
Zanzibar United Front Party, 66
Zimbabwe, 250, 251

About the Book
and the Editor

For nearly twenty years, Kenya and Tanzania were regarded as paradigms, respectively, of patron-client capitalism and one-party socialism and were compared frequently to determine which system was more appropriate for Africa. Since the late 1980s, however, the two have faced a series of similar challenges, and each has been forced to embark on a dual process of structural adjustment and political liberalization—a process hastened by rising demands for reform from within coupled with increased pressures from the international community. The authors of this book consider comparatively how Kenya and Tanzania have pursued this dual process, as well as the likely outcomes.

The book begins with an analysis of the common problems confronting the two countries during the 1980s and the internal and external pressures for reform in each. An overview of their approaches to political and economic adjustment follows. The discussion then shifts to an in-depth consideration of the return to multiparty politics in both countries, and policy revisions in the areas of macroeconomics, agriculture, urban development, education, and foreign policy.

Joel D. Barkan is professor of political science at the University of Iowa. In 1992 and 1993 he served as the first regional governance adviser for East and Southern Africa for the United States Agency for International Development. Prior to that he taught or was a visiting research fellow at the University of Dar es Salaam and the University of Nairobi. He is the author of *University Students, Politics and Development in Ghana, Tanzania, and Uganda* (1975); the coauthor of *The Legislative Connection: The Politics of Representation in Kenya, Korea and Turkey* (1984); and the editor of *Politics and Public Policy in Kenya and Tanzania* (1984). A frequent contributor to journals and anthologies on African politics, his most recent articles have appeared in *World Politics,* the *Journal of Democracy,* and the *Journal of Modern African Studies.*

293